PAUL KNITTER
TOWARDS A PROTESTANT THEOLOGY OF RELIGIONS

MARBURGER THEOLOGISCHE STUDIEN

11

herausgegeben von

Hans Graß und Werner Georg Kümmel

N.G. ELWERT VERLAG MARBURG

1974

PAUL KNITTER

TOWARDS A PROTESTANT THEOLOGY OF RELIGIONS

A CASE STUDY OF PAUL ALTHAUS AND CONTEMPORARY ATTITUDES

(Mit deutscher Zusammenfassung)

N. G. ELWERT VERLAG MARBURG

1974

© by N. G. Elwert Verlag Marburg 1974
Printed in Germany
Druck: Anton Hain KG, Meisenheim am Glan
ISBN 3 7708 0485 6

To
Bernd and Renate Jaspert
whose friendship and support stand behind these pages

Table of Contents

X

Foreword

In a variety of ways, this study is the product of our ecumenical age. We live in a "planetized world" in which men impinge upon the lives of each other not only technologically, economically, culturally − but also religiously. Hindus, Buddhists, Muslims and Christians have become neighbors both intellectually, because of the ease with which ideas today are disseminated, and existentially, because of what we might term the modern world's "migration of nations". For Christians of the West, this means that Christianity, whether it likes it or not, *is* encountering the World Religions.

This study was born of the desire to clarify and promote this encounter and dialogue between Christianity and the religions of the world. A first step, however, in going about this encounter requires that Christians try to clarify what are the possibilities, the "openings", the foundations in Christian theology itself for such a dialogue with men of other faiths. We need a Christian theology of the religions.

In order to elaborate such a theology − which today is still sadly lacking in clarity and conviction − Christian theologians of all denominations must come together and dialogue with each other. By drawing on the particular richness and insights of each tradition, by acknowledging the limitations and excesses of each tradition, theologians of the various churches can aid each other in correctly understanding the relation of Christ and the Christian communities to the neighbor communities of faith within the religions of the world. We need a more intent dialogue among Christians in order to engage more effectively in a dialogue with non-Christians.

This study, then, hopes to be a small contribution to this "dialogue within dialogue". Written from the standpoint of Roman-Catholic tradition, it seeks to evaluate Protestant attempts to understand and encounter other religions. By indicating what Protestant and Catholic theologians have in common and what they might learn from each other, the "greater ecumenism" with the World Religions, will, it is hoped, be clarified and promoted.

In another and more personal sense, this work is the fruit of ecumenism. Its initial stages developed during my studies under the direction of Prof. Juan Alfaro, S.J. at the Gregorian University, Rome. Further impetus came through research under Prof. Karl Rahner, S.J. at the University of Münster. To both, these ecumenical scholars in particular and to the dedicated teachers at the Gregorian University who helped me "lay the foundations", I am deeply indebted. But the bulk of the work took shape under the guidance of Prof. Carl Heinz Ratschow at the University of Marburg, from October 1969 to July 1972. It was submitted as a doctoral dissertation to Marburg University's Faculty of Protestant Theology; on July 14, 1972, the University of Marburg, for the first time in its four-century history, granted the honors of its "Doctor Theologiae" to a Roman Catholic.

I therefore wish to express my sincere gratitude not only to my moderator, Professor Ratschow, and to my second advisor, Prof. Hans Graß, for their ever-ready assistance, but also to the members of Marburg's Faculty of Theology who were so generous with their time and advice, especially to Professors Winfried

Zeller, Werner Georg Kümmel, Otto Kaiser, Heinrich Leipold and Rudolf Bultmann.

A very personal note of thanks is due to Bernd and Renate Jaspert, Marburg, whose "friendship and support", as the dedication of the book states, "stand behind these pages", and to Mrs. Frieda Stiehl whose skill and concern helped prepare the manuscript for final presentation.

Grateful mention is also made of those who aided in the complicated task of publication: Profs. Graß and Kümmel, who accepted the work as an "ecumenical contribution" to the *Marburger Theologische Studien*, and the various organizations which provided financial assistance: The Society of the Divine Word; the "Marburger Universitätsbund e.V."; the Department of Student Affairs of the University of Marburg; the "Landeskirchenrat der Evangelisch-Lutherischen Kirche in Bayern", München; Dr. Adolf Bolte, Bishop of Fulda; St. Peter and Paul Parish, Marburg; the Sisters of St. Elisabeth, Marburg.

Paul Knitter, S.V.D.
January 1974, Chicago, Illinois

Note: References to journals and periodical literature are made with the standard abbreviations found in the RGG[3] and the LThK[2].

Introduction

§ 1. Paul Althaus: A Case Study

In a sense, the primary interest and object of the following pages is *not* Paul Althaus. We are going to be dealing with Althaus not in himself or for himself, but as "a case study for a Protestant Theology of the Non-Christian Religions."[1] This, essentially, is the purpose of this study.

We will analyze Althaus' evaluation of the non-Christian world not because he was an extraordinarily influential thinker who gave shape to modern Protestant theology; on the contrary, he may be considered one of the lesser stars in the theological constellation of this century. We turn to Althaus not because he unfolded new, explosive ideas; as we will see, he did not intend to launch a theological revolution, and whatever he put forth as "new" always had a good portion of the "old" within it. He gathered no theological school around himself, he ignited no theological bombs, he offered no shatteringly new insights. Althaus was a thinker who had something to say, who was respected and listened to; but he was not − like Barth, Bonhoeffer, Bultmann and Tillich − one of the "fashioners" of Protestant thinking of this century.[2]

Our interest in Althaus may be said to be indirect, secondary. He will be for us a means to an end. He offers us, we feel, a well-formed, well-adapted, and therefore meaningful means for answering the question: WHAT KIND OF EVALUATION OF THE NON-CHRISTIAN WORLD IS POSSIBLE ON THE BASIS OF PROTESTANT THEOLOGY? *This* is the *central interest* and *purpose* of this study: if we open our eyes to the reality of the religions (and not all theologians take time or interest to do this) and at the same time if we try to hold true to the basic tenets of the Reformation − i.e. if we try to establish ourselves on a sound but open-minded fidelity to the heritage of the Reformers − what kind of judgments can we make on the religious world which stands "outside" (but today ever so near) Christianity?

---

1 Today, especially in circles of the World Council of Churches, the religions are being referred to as "the living faiths of men". Although this term definitely has its dialogical and ecumenical advantages, it has not yet been fully clarified or accepted in general theological usage. Thus for reasons of terminological clarity, we shall be using throughout this study the traditional terms: "non-Christian religions" or simply, "the non-Christian world". − Cf. C. F. Hallencreutz, *New Approaches to Men of Other Faiths, 1938–1968.* A Theological Discussion (Geneva, 1970), pp. 16–17; *Living Faiths and the Ecumenical Movement*, S. J. Samartha, ed. (Geneva, 1961); *Dialogue between Men of Living Faiths*, Papers presented at a Consultation held at Ajaltoun, Lebanon, S. J. Samartha, ed. (Geneva, 1971). − An outline of Althaus' attitudes towards the religions is offered in: P. Knitter, "Paul Althaus: An Attempt at a Protestant Theology of the Non-Christian Religions", *Verbum SVD*, 11 (1970) 214–235.

2 Althaus' influence was much more pronounced and widespread among the numerous Lutheran Pastors who studied under him and carried his ideas and "spirit" with them into their pastoral work and preaching. Cf. W. Lohff, "Paul Althaus", *Tendenzen der Theologie im 20. Jahrhundert.* Eine Geschichte in Porträts, hrsg. von H. J. Schultz (Stuttgart, 1967²), p. 296.

Tracing Althaus' thought, we shall try to answer these questions. Indeed, Althaus himself presents only *one* answer, his own. Yet it is our conviction that it can be considered a "model answer", a "case study". In presenting his thought we are presenting what is a valid, meaningful attempt at a Protestant evaluation of the religions. Althaus went about his analysis in such a way as to fulfill what would seem to be the necessary *conditions* and *qualities* of a Protestant theology of the religions.

These conditions and qualities are evident in the motivation and goals and in the foundation of his theology of the non-Christian world: 1) The *motivation* and *goals* of Althaus' analysis of the religions were determined and clarified through his critical encounter with Ernst Troeltsch's and Karl Barth's evaluation of the religious world outside of Christ. Both thinkers motivated Althaus to seek a middle path between their extreme positions — a middle path which must be the intent of any Christian theology of the religions. Opposed to Barth, Althaus tried to discover what is the role of the religions in the economy of salvation; but opposed to Troeltsch, he did not want in any way to jeopardize the role which he as a Christian theologian believed Christianity must play. 2) The *foundation* for Althaus' attempt to construct this middle way was that which supports his entire theological program: a firm, determined adherence to the principles of the Reformation, coupled with an openness to and love for the world of man, nature and history. Such qualities, also, must be demanded of any theological evaluation of the religions which claims to call itself Christian and Protestant: the sincere desire to confront the religions and to grasp their God-given meaning on the basis of a theology which seeks to be faithful to the heritage of the Reformation.

In the first two chapters we will present the motivation and the foundation of Althaus' approach to the religions — i.e. his "qualifications" as a case study. In the ensuing chapters (III—VI) we will then study his evaluation of the non-Christian religious world and try to answer our central question as to what kind of an understanding of the religions is possible on the basis of Reformational theology. In order to "test" the conclusions and questions drawn from our case study, we will "apply and verify" it in Chapter VII, within a general survey of contemporary German-Protestant attitudes towards the religions.

Thus, in this case study, we shall not be presenting and analyzing Althaus' thought in itself[3] but as a significant Protestant attempt at a theology of the religions. And our critique shall not be directed to Althaus himself but primarily to his Protestant principles and criteria for judging the religions.

Our case study is thus intended to help Protestant theology reflect on its understanding of the non-Christian religious world — on what would seem to be some for the central questions, demands and difficulties in arriving at a deeper, more integrated understanding of this world. We hope that it will be a small contribution to the further, necessary development of a Protestant theology of the religions.

---

3 Therefore, we shall not be so much interested in the personal *genesis* or *development* in Althaus' thought as in its end-effect and overall judgment concerning the religions. Influences and development will be considered insofar as they elucidate Althaus' *Protestant* attitude towards the religious world.

The fact that this study is being made, unavoidably, from a Catholic viewpoint will enable it also, we hope, to pave the way towards a more expanded and effective *ecumenical dialogue* between Protestant and Catholic theologies of the religions. Such a dialogue, outlined in our Conclusion, is essential for arriving at a truly *Christian* understanding of the religions and at a more engaged dialogue with the religions themselves.

Chapter I

Between Troeltsch and Barth

§ 2. Child of Conflict

Paul Althaus' theology in general, and his theology of the non-Christian religions in particular, was to a great extent the child of conflict. Especially in its early, formative years, it was the result not of quiet, secluded intellectual pursuits, but of resolute struggling for and defense of the truth. Althaus sought to call to task those who, he felt, were betraying or confusing the Christian message; and he sought to provide, as clearly as possible, a counter-position to their errors.

This is not to imply that Althaus' theologizing was totally polemic or apologetic; such an assertion would be both false and unjust. Any reader of Althaus' works will certainly note and marvel at the composure of his presentation, his tolerance of other positions and his genuine pastoral concern.[4] And yet to understand the origin, the general direction and intent of Althaus' theology it is necessary to consider and weigh its polemic "Sitz im Leben". This is especially true for his theology of the non-Christian religions.

For this reason, our first chapter will try to present an overall, yet complete picture of Ernst Troeltsch's and Karl Barth's approaches to and evaluations of the extra-Christian religious world. These two thinkers, more than all others and representing all others, raised the theological (and philosophical) banners which for Althaus were a summons to battle: i.e. to firm opposition and to counterattack. They brought him to direct his full attention to issues which otherwise he perhaps would have treated only in passing; they also were to determine the *manner* in which Althaus dealt with these issues. A theologian, like any scientist, will express himself differently when he is not only proposing his ideas but defending them. This "battle", especially in the case of Barth, was to motivate and influence the entirety of Althaus' theological production.

Troeltsch and Barth, as we shall see, took up their positions at opposite ends of the theological field: diametrically opposed as to the starting point and method of theology, as to the nature of man and his role in salvation, as to the relationship between the human and the divine and between Christian and non-Christian reality. Thus, Althaus was, as it were, fighting on two different fronts. He was flanked by two opponents (and their followers) who were violent opponents of each other. Althaus would, in pursuing and trying to correct the one, constantly have to beware of providing munitions for or even falling into rank with the other. He would have to steer a *middle path* — and this posed both the challenge and the risks of his venture. On the one side: "Die Abgrenzung gegen die Barthsche Theologie" which "überhaupt das ganze theologische Werk von Althaus durchzieht"[5] and which marks him as a shining "Antipode zu Karl Barth"[6] and to

4 H. Graß, "Gedächtnisvorlesung für Paul Althaus", *Nachrichten der evang.-luth. Kirche in Bayern*, Aug. 1966; Lohff, *Tendenzen*, p. 297.
5 Graß, "Die Theologie von Paul Althaus", NZSTh, 8 (1966) 237. Graß goes on to list the wide range of questions in which this "Abgrenzung" expressed itself: "Sie wird vollzogen in der Offenbarungslehre, in der Beurteilung der Religion und der Religionen, in der

4

Barth's Christomonism. And on the other side " ... die Abgrenzung gegen den Relativismus der Religionsgeschichtler – E. Troeltsch u.a. ..."[7] which meant that Althaus' theology developed "in ständiger Fühlung und Auseinandersetzung" with Troeltsch and received "ihre besondere Prägung durch die bewußte und entschiedene Abgrenzung gegen die religionsgeschichtliche Theologie."[8] For Althaus, Troeltsch " ... war der echte Exponent der theologischen Lage, der eigentliche Regent der Jahrhundertwende für die Theologie", – but a "regent" who was leading theology into a dangerous crisis which involved the betrayal of theology's very nature.[9]

By first outlining the attitudes of Troeltsch and Barth towards reality outside of Christ, we will be able in Chapter II to clearly define this twofold "Abgrenzung" of Althaus' own understanding of man's situation, especially in his religion, before or without Jesus Christ.

I. Ernst Troeltsch

§ 3. A Positive and Negative Catalyst

Ernst Troeltsch (1865–1923), standing amid, reflecting and interpreting the turbulence of theological and philosophical thought at the turn of the last century, sought to be the architect of a new view of Christianity and the non-Christian religions. For many he was just that; for many others – including Paul Althaus – he was more a demolition engineer than a builder.[10] Whatever the final and tested

Stellung zum Alten Testament und seiner Auslegung, in der Beurteilung der Konfessionsunterschiede, in der Bestimmung der Aufgabe der Dogmatik...Tiefgreifend ist der Unterschied in der Lehre von der Imago Dei, wie überhaupt in der Anthropologie, in der Frage des Ansatzes und der Durchführung der Christologie, in der Beurteilung der Jungfrauengeburt, in der Frage der Kindertaufe und der damit verbundenen Stellung zur Volkskirche, in der Frage Gesetz und Evangelium, der Stellung und Bewertung der Trinitätslehre, schließlich in der Ethik vor allem hinsichtlich der Zwei-Reiche-Lehre und der Theologie der Ordnungen." (loc. cit.)

6 A. Peters, "Die Frage nach Gott", *Fuldaer Hefte* 17 (Berlin, 1967), p. 80. Peters was speaking here especially of the question of revelation.
7 Graß, "Die Theologie", p. 223.
8 A. Beyer, *Offenbarung und Geschichte*, Zur Auseinandersetzung mit der Theologie von Paul Althaus, (Schwerin, 1932), p. 55, cf. also p. 11; Hans Wilhelm Schmidt, *Zeit und Ewigkeit*. Die letzten Voraussetzungen der dialektischen Theologie (Gütersloh, 1927), pp. 108 ff.
9 A quotation from Althaus as cited in Beyer, op. cit.; cf. P. Althaus, "Die theologische Lage vor 50 Jahren", *Deutsches Pfarrerblatt*, 65 (1965) 744–745.
10 Ernst Benz feels that: "Die bedeutungsvollsten Ansatzpunkte einer wirklichen Neubesinnung auf eine christliche Theologie der Religionsgeschichte, die der tatsächlichen geschichtlichen Situation gerecht wird, liegen auch heute noch bei Ernst Troeltsch." cf. "Ideen zu einer Theologie der Religionsgeschichte", *Akademie der Wissenschaften und der Literatur, Mainz, Abhandlungen der Geistes- und Sozialwissenschaftlichen Klasse* 5 (1960) p. 39. Walter Bodenstein, on the other hand, sums up Troelsch's entire work as more "Demontage als Aufbau", cf. W. Bodenstein, *Neige des Historismus. Ernst Troeltschs Entwicklungsgang* (Gütersloh, 1959), p. 207.

verdict on Troeltsch may be, he cannot be overlooked in a study of the development of Protestant thinking on the religions during this century and especially in an evaluation of Althaus' views of the non-Christian world. Positively or negatively, Troeltsch was a shattering catalyst for a Protestant theology of the religions.

Troeltsch, like Althaus, felt himself shaken and challenged by the findings and the questionings of the non-theological sciences concerning the nature of religion and the religions. His entire work has been called a "theology of crisis" – a reaction to a critical situation which was shaking the very foundations of Christianity.[11] His reaction, however, was entirely different from that of Althaus. A fearless thinker, Troeltsch proposed to take the insights of the new age – with all their doubts, uncertainties, and disturbing discoveries – seriously and let them have their say. This is what makes up "die eigentliche Größe" and the "freie, humane Art seines christlichen Denkens."[12] This was also what gave his approach to the religions such a marked and perhaps uncomfortable difference from that of most of his predecessors who also sought a more positive understanding of the history of religions. German *Idealism* under Hegel and Kant and *Romanticism* under Schleiermacher and Schelling had moved beyond the rather bleak, black-and-white categories in which the Reformers and theologians of the Orthodoxy had viewed extra-biblical religions; instead, they saw the religions and Christianity in a dynamic, complementary, evolutionistic relationship. Yet their "vantage point" for surveying the world of religions remained essentially that of traditional Christian theology; in a sense, they were not looking *at* the religions but *down to* them.[13] Here is where Troeltsch attempted to "refocus" the Christian theologian's point of view. As a theologian himself,[14] he wanted other Christian thinkers to step out of their own "theological skins"– their own traditional categories – in order to understand the religions – and Christianity itself! – from the viewpoint of modern science and according to the mentality of modern man. Troeltsch by no means wished to reject the totality of Christian doctrine and tradition, as many of the Enlightenment thinkers had done in their understanding of the religions. But he did feel that for Christianity to truly encounter and understand the religions, it must remodel its system of thought and its own self-image; it must enter a "new phase"; its "traditional form" must change – not be destroyed or thrown overboard, but radically overhauled. Only by daring to open itself to the age's new "Weltanschauung" and by letting itself change and

11 H. G. Drescher, *Glaube und Vernunft bei Ernst Troeltsch* (Diss. Marburg) (Bochum, 1957), pp. 11–15.

12 Bodenstein, p. 69.

13 For a concise, overall view of the history of Protestant thinking on the religions, cf: C. H. Ratschow, "Religion, theologisch", RGG[3] V, 976–984; Gerhard Rosenkranz, *Der christliche Glaube angesichts der Weltreligionen* (Bern, 1967) pp. 156–197; Benz, op. cit.

14 Troeltsch began his academic career as professor of systematic theology, first at Bonn in 1892 and then in Heidelberg, 1894. But as his intellectual development progressed and as he confronted the philosophical, historical and social problems of his age, he decided that theology was not the foundation on which to work out his great reconciliation. In 1915 he became professor of philosophy at the University of Berlin. – Interestingly, even though Troeltsch constantly occupied himself with the problems of the religions, he never could qualify as a "specialist" in the phenomenology of any one religion. cf. J. Wach, *Types of Religious Experience* (Chicago, 1951), p. 215.

adapt accordingly, can Christianity arrive at a true evaluation of the religions and of itself as a religion; only then is a true reconciliation of the Christian and non-Christian worlds possible.[15] — Whether this new method of evaluating the religions allowed Christianity to remain the faith of the New Testament and of Jesus Christ was a question which pitted Althaus so strongly against Troeltsch and which provoked him to search for his own answers.

§ 4. Troeltsch's New Approach

1. The chief intellectual tools which Troeltsch took over from the modern age and with which he sought to fashion his new understanding of Christianity and the religions can be summed up under three headings:

a) *Scientific historicism* was the dominating hermeneutical principle through which Troeltsch opened his eyes to all reality, especially the religions. He wholeheartedly embraced the intellectual revelation of the nineteenth century (especially in the writings of W. Dilthey) which Karl Prümm terms "einen der größten Fortschritte der Menschheit": historicism.[16] Everything that man is and produces is historical and is subject to the law of historical development. Only by studying him in his historical nature and his historical context can we understand him. Troeltsch outlines the essence of his historical method in three "Grundbegriffe" which must always be present in true scientific investigation of man and his religions: 1) the law of *historical criticism*, which presupposes that in history only "Wahrscheinlichkeitsurteile" are possible and that every judgment must be founded on solid criticism — and ever remain open to further criticism; 2) the law of *analogy* which is "... the only means by which criticism becomes possible" and which insists that the nature of any historical reality can never be established by examining this reality in itself but only by searching for its inborn analogy with other realities; 3) the law of *correlation*, which presupposes the continuous "Wechselwirkung" of all historical phenomena; no historical "event" takes place just for itself; it always, somehow, influences other events.[17]

All other sciences must bow to this historical method. It is forbidden to interpret man according to preconceived, ahistorical, philosophical notions which neglect or subordinate his historical nature. Troeltsch meant this especially — and ruthlessly — for the science of theology (which, as we shall see, he considered a "second-stage" science). He demanded that theology finally shake off its *dogmatic, supernaturalistic* shackles, arguing " ...daß mit der Aufklärungsperiode wie für alle Wissenschaften so auch für die Theologie und Religionswissenschaft eine prinzipiell neue, antisupranaturalistische Grundlage geschaffen worden ist ..."[18]

15 G. von Schlippe, *Die Absolutheit des Christentums bei Ernst Troeltsch auf dem Hintergrund der Denkfelder des 19. Jahrhunderts* (Diss. Marburg) (Neustadt a.d. Aisch, 1966), pp. 9, 26–28, 98.

16 "Offenbarung im Neuprotestantismus vom Aufkommen der Religionsgeschichtlichen Schule bis R. Bultmann", *Divinitas* 8 (1964) 437, cf. also pp. 444–453; Drescher, pp. 34–37.

17 *Gesammelte Werke*, Bd. II (Tübingen, 1913), pp. 731–733. (Troeltsch's *Gesammelte Werke*, Bd. I–IV – 1912, 1913, 1922, 1925 – will be referred to as GW.)

18 E. Troeltsch, "Geschichte und Metaphysik", ZThK 8 (1898) 40.

Nothing can simply be stated, nothing can simply drop from above and demand total intellectual adherence. These are two contrary methods: the dogmatic and the historical. Any attempt at unification would spell loss of integrity.[19] Here Troeltsch was giving a deafening echo to the general tone of Protestant theology at this time; at the end of the nineteenth and beginning of the twentieth centuries, the "historical-critical" method was the star on the stage of Protestant theology.

b) *Individualism* was another of Troeltsch's standards by which he sought to formulate a new view of religious reality. The individual person and the individual culture form, as it were, the building blocks of historical reality and development. One cannot apply and be faithful to the historical method unless one properly esteems and gives full freedom to the individual. This is especially true in the realm of religious reality. Indeed, the individual's personal experience of the divine and the individual's freedom are part of the basic heritage of the Reformers and belong to the central message of the New Testament. The individual must not be violated, but rather must preserve his independence and his "right to be" in the realm of religion and faith. Troeltsch therefore showed a marked "anti-church" attitude throughout his life,[20] and an abiding distrust of authority. The individual, whether in the Christian Church or in the other religions, must be respected, met on his own ground, and never be forced to submit to an extraneous, dogmatic system.[21]

c) *Evolutionism*, closely aligned to his scientific historicism, was also a constant guide in Troeltsch's study of the religions. He felt that an "evolutionary-historical idealism" is "the only possible point of departure" if modern man is to make sense of theology and the history of religions.[22] A universal movement is taking place, an inexorable push towards perfection which, on its pilgrim way, will show various levels of achievement, various stages of lurching forward and slipping backward. And again, this means that the end can never be fully grasped along the evolutionary process. Theology must therefore open itself to the fact of *relativism*. The new historical-evolutionary way of thinking excludes all radicalism, all exclusive absoluteness.[23]

2. In elaborating his new picture of Christianity and the religions according to these three guidelines, Troeltsch marked himself as one of the most enthusiastic and influential spokesmen of a new line of thought in German Protestant Theology which reached its full vigor at the turn of the century: the *Religionsgeschichtliche Schule*. Indeed, our presentation of Troeltsch's new approach to the religions

19 E. Troeltsch, *Die Absolutheit des Christentums und die Religionsgeschichte* (Tübingen, 1912²) (1. Aufl., 1902), pp. 90–91; GW II, pp. 227 ff.; Bodenstein, pp. 16–17; Drescher, pp. 79–85; I. E. Alberca, *Gewinnung theologischer Normen aus der Geschichte der Religion bei Ernst Troeltsch* (München, 1961), pp. 38–52.
20 H. E. Tödt, "Ernst Troeltsch", *Tendenzen der Theologie im 20. Jahrhundert* (Stuttgart, 1967), p. 95.
21 GW II, pp. 116, 125.
22 Troeltsch, "Geschichte und Metaphysik", p. 40.
23 "...sich selbst historisch, psychologisch, als Entwicklungsergebnis objektiv zu begreifen. Das gibt dem Jahrhundert einen zunehmenden Zug des Relativismus und Historismus." GW IV, pp. 617 ff.; id., "Protestantisches Christentum und Kirche in der Neuzeit", *Kultur der Gegenwart*, I. Teil, Abt. 4, 1, 2, hrsg. von P. Hinneberg (Berlin–Leipzig, 1909²), pp. 471 ff.; GW IV, p. 318.

is a presentation of the fundamental creed of this school. He was its "systematic theologian".[24] The "school of comparative religions" had its main camp in Göttingen and invaded theological thinking chiefly under the names of Gunkel and Bousset, who can be termed its founders, as well as of W. Wrede, P. Wernle, A. Eichhorn and H. Greßmann. Their incentive and sustenance were drawn from the same sources as Troeltsch's thinking: the "historical" studies of literary criticism which clearly pointed out the dependence of the Old and New Testaments on their "religious environment". Such studies, these scholars demanded, call for a deep-reaching revision of our ideas on the nature and origin of Christianity as a religion, on the role of other religions in God's dealing with man, and on the relationship and interdependence between Christianity and the religions. Troeltsch was to carry these demands to their limits. His writings are " ... das radikalste und folgenschwerste Unternehmen der religionsgeschichtlichen Schule, das Verhältnis des Christentums zu den übrigen Religionen aus dem Zusammenhang der Religionsgeschichte heraus zu begründen".[25]

To understand fully Althaus' opposition and his response to Troeltsch's "new approach", we first must outline a more complete picture of Troeltsch's views on revelation, religion, and Christianity's relationship to the non-Christian world.

§ 5. God's Message to Man: Troeltsch's Concept of Revelation

1. A theologian's view of the religions is, to a great extent, determined and "preordained" by his understanding of revelation. Revelation, as the reality in which God and man come into contact, in which God communicates the depth of his being and love and man freely opens himself to the force of this communication, — this reality, however it may be understood — is the first step in any interpretation of religion and the religions (and will determine whether this interpretation is positive or negative). The religions' role and meaning will always be in the context and service of revelation. Thus, before taking up Troeltsch's doctrine on the religions, we first must briefly analyze how he understands the reality of communication between God and man. (In the following studies of Barth's and Althaus' evaluations of the religions we will also be starting with their concept of revelation.)

2. Troeltsch's concept of revelation[26] rests on the same foundation he tried to give to the entire structure of his thought: on his *metaphysics*. He states explicitly that his new starting point " ... beruht auf einer Metaphysik des menschlichen Geistes oder stellt vielmehr selbst eine solche dar."[27] Without metaphysics one cannot understand the reality of the Absolute's relationship with the finite; one

24 J. Hempel, "Religionsgeschichtliche Schule", RRG[3] V, pp. 991–994; Bodenstein, pp. 36–41.

25 G. Rosenkranz, "Was müssen wir heute unter Absolutheit des Christentums verstehen? ", ZThK 51 (1954) 109.

26 Troeltsch rarely treats the concept "revelation" expressly. This, for him, would smack too much of the traditional "theological approach" to man's experience of and communication with God.

27 Troeltsch, "Geschichte und Metaphysik", p. 40.

cannot understand religion.[28] This was Troeltsch's enduring goal: to found his reconciliation of Christianity and the religions — of Christianity and modern thinking — on a new, shared metaphysical foundation. But such a foundation, as essential as it is to each department of Troeltsch's thought, is anything but clear. "Der Begriff der Metaphysik gehört mit zu dem Uneinheitlichsten in Troeltschs Werk. Er kann nicht ohne Metaphysik auskommen, aber er kann keinen exakten Begriff davon aufstellen."[29] This is perhaps because Troeltsch was persistently changing his metaphysical wardrobe — or adding to it. Perhaps he was too intellectually omniverous, too assimilative. In any case, the "system" he sought for never became more than an elaborate pattern of metaphysical "preconceptions".[30]

Yet certain of these patterns are recurring and definable enough to determine Troeltsch's view of revelation.[31] One of them is that of *teleological idealism*: Troeltsch himself admits that this was the most delectable and sustaining of the fruits he culled from the field of modern philosophy.[32] Most of his selecting was done from the ideas of Rudolf H. Lotze and Rudolf Eucken. Both of them represented an idealism in which the human "Geist", as expressed in the individual, is the driving force of the evolution of history. On the basis of such an idealism Troeltsch tried to elaborate a metaphysics of *immanent transcendence*. And this, in turn, formed the basis for man's communication with God. The Absolute is both beyond and within the finite world. There is a form of participation, of continuity, of sharing between the finite and the infinite. We might even speak of the "analogia entis" as an essential element in Troeltsch's metaphysics; yet it is more in line with the platonic-augustinian understanding of participation than with the thomistic. Corresponding more to Troeltsch's heritage, we might call this manner of participation a form of "monadology". Here he can trace his lineage, through Lotze, back to Leibniz.[33] The monads are absolute, yet at the same time, because their nature also includes the principle of individualism, they bring about a participation in the Absolute.[34] Two worlds are united here: the finite microcosm, claiming a form of absoluteness, shares in the absolute macrocosm — is in communication with it.[35] Such participation and communication are, theologically, the founding elements for a revelation of the Absolute to the finite.

3. But Troeltsch's understanding of such a revelation becomes fully clear only when he explains the relationship and unity between his metaphysics and *psychology*. The analogy and monadology of being determine and are expressed in man's psychological structures — in his consciousness. In fact, this, for Troeltsch, is the only avenue of approach to metaphysical reality: man's experience of this reality

28 Troeltsch, *Psychologie und Erkenntnistheorie in der Religionswissenschaft* (Tübingen, 1905), pp. 38–49; GW II, pp. 370 f., 479, 724 ff., 764.
29 Schlippe, p. 60; Bodenstein, pp. 48–49.
30 Tödt, p. 94; Bodenstein, p. 17.
31 It is clear that Troeltsch's understanding of revelation is bound to show the same inconsistencies and vagueness that plague his metaphysics.
32 GW II, p. 245.
33 Drescher, p. 48, cf. also pp. 44–49, 25–27; H. Obayashi, "Pannenberg and Troeltsch: History and Religion", JAAR, 38 (1970) pp. 411–412.
34 Schlippe, p. 76, cf. also 42, 103.
35 Schlippe, p. 76.

(or the communication of this reality in man's experience). "Sein" is grasped in "Bewußtsein"; the "Absolute" cannot be proven but only experienced within the consciousness of the "finite" being.[36]

Thus Troeltsch proclaims a dynamic unity between object and subject, between metaphysics and psychology — a basic inner dynamic between both orders. The point of contact between these orders is a concept, old yet explosively revived by Troeltsch: man's *religious apriori*. This is an essential element for understanding Troeltsch's view of God's dealing with man and man's response to God: revelation and religion. It is the point in which the Absolute touches the finite, in which the monad incorporates the individual, and from which the course of history receives its directing force. It is not to be understood simply as an emotion, a feeling, as Schleiermacher held. "Ein Apriori nicht der Seele, wie Rudolf Otto es meinte, sondern der Bewußtseinsstruktur, entsprechend dem transzendentalen Apriori Kants."[37] It is a metaphysical (ontological) reality within man's psychological make-up. In the religious apriori, the "immanent transcendence" of the Absolute brings about man's "transcendental subjectivity".[38] And throughout his works, Troeltsch will always give priority of attention to this subjectivity. In the final analysis, he prefers the psychological — even the mystical — approach to the reality of man's communication with the divine, i.e. to the reality of what theologians would call revelation. To understand revelation, we must look into the mysterious world of man's inner experience.[39]

4. The metaphysical-psychological basis for Troeltsch's understanding of revelation is, as is evident, complex and multi-influenced. Yet the practical "theological" conclusions he drew from this basis were much clearer and, especially for theologians such as Althaus, more provoking. Given this "immanent transcendence", expressing itself in man's religious apriori, one must also hold a universal revelation, affecting all men and all religions. Troeltsch states explicitly: "Das metaphysische Grundverhältnis ... ermöglicht eine Offenbarung Gottes an den menschlichen Geist ..."[40] Because of man's ability to experience and at least partially perceive the "analogia entis", revelation cannot be something special and reserved only to a select few. The religious apriori endows the mystery of communication between the divine and the human with a universal dynamism. Here Troeltsch was striving to offset the restricted, exclusive understanding of revelation as represented in the school of Ritschl; Althaus would certainly second these efforts.[41]

Yet Troeltsch went further: the nature of this universal revelation does not allow it to have, at any point in history, an absolute expression. This would contradict the metaphysical nature of the Absolute which can never be encompassed and fully expressed in a limited, finite form. Even more so, it would go

---

36 Troeltsch, "Die Selbständigkeit der Religion", ZThK 5 (1895) pp. 207 ff.
37 W. Köhler, *Ernst Troeltsch* (Tübingen, 1941) p. 141, cf. 141–155.
38 Bodenstein, pp. 18–20; Alberca, pp. 100–156. Cf. also E. Lessing, "Die Bedeutung des religiösen Apriori für wissenschaftstheoretische Überlegungen innerhalb der Theologie", EvTh 30 (1970) 355–367.
39 Schlippe, pp. 61–63; 76–77.
40 "Die Selbständigkeit der Religion", ZThK 5 (1895) 430 ff.
41 CW, 54.

against the basic and all prevading principles of Troeltsch's method: of scientific historicism and evolutionism. History — and revelation as part of history — is in a progressive movement towards the Absolute; it can never attain it. We can therefore speak only of a "progressive revelation"; to claim an absolute revelation would be to slip back into a primitive supernaturalistic mentality. It would be to violate the laws of history.

The conclusion is clear: Troeltsch not only affirmed revelation outside the visible confines of what has traditionally been defined as Christian revelation. He also stated the basic identity of all forms of revelation and ruled out any essential differences. The historicity of revelation, then, means not that it is mediated through *a* historical expression but that it becomes coterminous with all of history! "Die Geschichtlichkeit der Offenbarung ist umgedeutet in 'Offenbarungsgeschichte' ..."[42] God's revelation in the Old Testament and through Jesus Christ, as unique and special as it may be, is only a "section", a "stage" in the general history of revelation. It cannot be considered absolute.[43]

Bousset summed up Troeltsch's views of revelation — general and Christian — precisely:

> Die religionsgeschichtliche Schule behauptet mit aller Energie eine lebendige und wirkliche Offenbarung. Was wir, Troeltsch und jeder, der sich aus unserem Kreise zu dieser Frage geäußert, verwerfen und worauf unsere Gegner allerdings alles Gewicht legen, ist die Annahme eines absoluten Unterschiedes zwischen der spezifischen Offenbarung Gottes in Christo (resp. der Heilsgeschichte des alten und neuen Testamentes) und der allgemeinen göttlichen Offenbarung in den Religionen der Völker, und die Behauptung, daß erstere von letzterer nicht bloß graduell, sondern *toto genere* verschieden sei.[44]

§ 6. Man's Response to God: Troeltsch's View of the Religions

1. Troeltsch's total view of the religions might be summed up under the two principles of "individual life-forms" and "historical evolution".[45] Both principles, as we have seen, are part and parcel of Troeltsch's "new approach" and of his metaphysical understanding of revelation.

The religions are individual life-forms, i.e. concrete, individual expressions of man's participation in the Absolute. The reality of the Absolute taking hold of the finite being, i.e. the reality of man's "religious apriori", is what constitutes the origin of religion and what makes religion a universal, independent phenomenon. Without this religious apriori we can explain neither the origin nor development of religion.[46] Expressed in other words, the religions are the concrete, varied and independent manifestations of the universal revelation which is at work in all mankind. Thus, Troeltsch could define religion as the "Ergriffensein vom Absolu-

---

42 Drescher, p. 91.

43 Troeltsch, *Glaubenslehre*, N. Heidelberger Vorlesungen aus den Jahren 1911–12, hrsg. von G.v.Le Fort (München, 1925), pp. 71 ff.; Schlippe, pp. 41–42; Althaus, CW, 54.

44 "Die Mission und die sogenannte religionsgeschichtliche Schule", ZMR 22 (1907), 321 ff., 353 ff.

45 P. Althaus, CW, 133–134; MR, 158–159; "Toleranz und Intoleranz des Glaubens", *Theologische Aufsätze* II (Gütersloh, 1935), 108–110.

46 Troeltsch, *Psychologie und Erkenntnistheorie*, pp. 26, 46; GW II, pp. 756, 494.

ten im religiösen Bewußtsein".[47] Religion is born and takes shape within the individual's inner heart, i.e. the individual's encounter with and experience of the Absolute. It is a mystical experience, to the extent that Troeltsch could state that "mysticism is the 'Ur-Phenomenon' of all religion."[48] And because religion is this inner, personal reality, Troeltsch maintained that the tools for the full understanding of this reality must be taken from the science of religious psychology. The psychology of religion "... sucht den Ort, den Ursprung und die Bedeutung der Religion im menschlichen Bewußtsein und kann eben damit allein dasjenige beibringen, was über die Wahrheitsfrage der Religion überhaupt ausgemacht werden kann ..."[49] Again, Troeltsch is faithful to the basic methodology: although religion has its roots in a divine, metaphysical reality, it can be known only by means of positive, scientific investigation.[50]

2. Yet for Troeltsch religion could never be a purely individual, internal, static affair, for it is subject, essentially, to the universal laws of *historical-evolution*.[51] Religion, as an individual life-form, can express itself only in and through history. History becomes the "Durchgangsstadium der Religion".[52]

This means, first of all, that religion will always be culturally conditioned: formed by and having to correspond to the environment and "Zeitgeist" in which it exists. Religions cannot therefore be forced into a "general·concept" or artificially transplanted into another historical milieu. Neither can one pass judgment on one religion from the standpoint of another. History is variegated, and this gives the religious world its kaleidoscopic variety. Even though the Absolute idea behind all religions is "im Kerne ... identisch", "... entfaltet sich auf Grund der geschichtlichen Bedingtheiten die ihnen gemeinsam zugrunde liegende Idee nur verschieden."[53]

Yet the law of historical-evolution also implies that this multiformed religious development has a *common end*. The religions not only spring from the same seed — the absolute religious apriori — they also are in dynamic movement towards the same goal. This absolute goal is the directing and unifying force of all history. The religions, as an essential part of history, are swept up in it and unified in it — even though this unity will become clear only at the end of history.[54]

The more expressly theological conclusions from considering the religions as individual life-forms and according to historical evolution are clear: God is at work in all religions; despite their differences and imperfections, they can never be classified as "foreign" to the divine. Revelation, grace, the possibility of genuine communion with the Absolute are offered in every authentic form of religion. The history of salvation is universal.

3. Yet it is also *relative*. Troeltsch's principles for studying religious reality led him to draw the same conclusion for religion that he did for revelation: there can

---

47 Schlippe, p. 76.
48 GW II, p. 339.
49 Troeltsch, "Selbständigkeit", ZThK 5 (1895) 370.
50 GW II, p. 461, 489; Schlippe, pp. 11–12; 29–30.
51 Ratschow, op.cit., p. 981.
52 Schlippe, p. 30.
53 Schlippe, p. 75; cf. also Benz, op.cit., p. 39.
54 Troeltsch, *Absolutheit*, pp. 32–33.

be no absolute religion; all religions are relative. History not only embraces all religions in a common movement towards a common goal, it also confines them within a universal relativity. This is an iron-clad law of history: it allows no absolutes; it admits only individual, concrete and therefore relative realities. No religion can affirm that it stands above this all-embracing relativity; no religion can claim to be the full and final realization of the general concept of religion. No religion can step outside of history! Every religious phenomenon is always an individual, factual piece in the entire mosaic of history; only as a part of this mosaic can it find its meaning and its value.[55]

But this does not mean that Troeltsch was advocating an "unlimited relativism". Paradoxically, he allows the Absolute to be present and active in the religions *through* relativity. He maintains "nicht das Entweder-Oder von Relativismus und Absolutismus, sondern die Mischung von beiden, das Herauswachsen der Richtungen auf absolute Ziele ..." The history of religions is "... das an verschiedenen Punkten nebeneinander erfolgende Hervorbrechen der auf das absolute Geistesziel gerichteten Kräfte."[56] This, for Troeltsch, is the "unvergängliche Kern des Entwicklungsgedanken".[57] Absolute is the goal towards which the religions are moving; absolute is the inner experience of this goal or this power within each religion; relative, however, are the various stages along the road to this one, absolute goal.[58]

As a theologian, Troeltsch would allow this Absolute to break forth in the course of history in entirely new forms; he can even call this breaking-forth "supernatural". Also, he felt that religious thought and strength has clearly and forcefully "stepped forth only in a few revelations". These are the special revelatory breakthroughs which play a particular role in carrying religious history forwards towards its final goal.[59] But he insists: such "supernatural" occurances or such special forms of revelation can never become "exclusive", as Christian dogma would have it. They can never be so special as to nullify other forms. They can never be limited to one manifestation so as to exclude others. Rather, they are always "inclusive", pertaining to and effecting the entire breadth of the history of religions.[60]

---

55 Benz, pp. 39—40; Bodenstein, pp. 85—91.
56 *Absolutheit*, pp. 58, 72; cf. Köhler, pp. 91—95.
56 *Absolutheit*, p. 71.
58 Rosenkranz, "Was müssen wir", pp. 107—108.
59 *Absolutheit*, p. 75; cf. Benz, p. 43.
60 GW II, pp. 729 ff., esp. 734; Althaus, MR, 156—157. In a similar way, Troeltsch is realistic enough to admit a certain form of absolutism in all religions. Each religion's experience of the Absolute is for that religion absolute — and it must be so. This Troeltsch condescendingly terms a "natural, naive absolutism". It is the deepest and most simple expression of the religious soul. But what the historian and theologian cannot allow is that this "naive absolutism" be transformed into a supernatural, dogmatic absolutism which rejects all other forms of religion; or a rational absolutism which considers all extra-Christian religious experience to be the result of a primitive revelation or the effect of a pre-Christian logos; or evolutionistic absolutism which categorically (without scientific investigation) places Christianity at the top of the evolutionary scale. Such forms of "transformed, artificial absolutism" have taken place in Christianity; indeed, they were stirring already in the New Testament. Troeltsch prefers to imitate the naive absolutism of

4. This helps us to understand that even though Troeltsch adamantly insisted that there could be no absolute religion, no absolute expression of the Transcendent, he did, especially in his early years, allow for a certain classification of religions. Despite the religions' universal relativity and basic sameness, they do show differences; some are closer to the full expression of the Absolute than others. In establishing this gradation, Troeltsch, again, avoids all "theologizing" and "supernatural dogmatism" and resorts to purely scientific, pragmatic criteria. Firstly, to judge a religion's value or the quality of its expression of the Absolute, we must look to its degree of success — its "Erfolg". Has it succeeded in holding the hearts of men? Has it withstood steadfastly the buffeting of history and cultural change? Does it evince a high degree of "Vernünftigkeit" and "Anpassungsfähigkeit" in working for this success? Has it held its ground in the encounter with other religions? Troeltsch felt that there was a certain "struggle" taking place among the religions and that in it norms for judging religions could be detected. Each individual, historical expression of religious value has the ability to encounter other expressions; and in this historical process, certain values will prove themselves superior to others, and thus will be hastened the general evolution of all religions towards the absolute goal.[61] Troeltsch can thus seek to classify religions according to their "inner wealth", i.e. their "simplicity, strength, and depth" — which is sort of a value system based on the products of historical process. This classification, however, will never indicate an area of absolute values.[62]

Secondly, Troeltsch speaks of the *"Beweise des Geistes"*. A religion's "Geistigkeit" will determine its value. Here Troeltsch classifies all religions into nature and spirit religions; the latter are broken down into impersonal and personal. Impersonal religion is represented chiefly by the great pantheistic-monistic eastern religions, especially Buddhism; personal religion is found in the family of prophetic religions: Judaism, Christianity, and Islam.[63] Throughout his studies in the history of religions, Troeltsch always displayed a definite preference for prophetic-personalist religions over their pantheistic-monistic counterparts. For him, the more spiritual and personal a religion is, the closer it is to the Absolute. The Absolute, evidently, must be personal.[64]

Christ, who was intent on living out his relation with God without judging and condemning the experience of others. *Absolutheit,* pp. 109–150; Schlippe, pp. 48–49; Paul Althaus, ER, pp. 13–14; Bodenstein, pp. 46–48.

61 *Absolutheit,* p. 58; Benz, pp. 41–42.

62 *Absolutheit,* p. 52; *Der Historismus und seine Überwindung* (Berlin, 1924), p. 67; Schlippe, p. 50. The value system which is part of Troeltsch's historicism was taken, to a great extent, from the Neo-Kantians, Windelband and Rickert, with whom Troeltsch came into direct contact during his years in Heidelberg. cf. Bodenstein, pp. 23–24; Alberca, pp. 54–57.

63 *Absolutheit,* p. 87.

64 Schlippe, p. 46; A. C. Bouquet, *The Christian Faith and the Non-Christian Religions* (Digswell Place, 1958), p. 355.

§ 7. Christianity and the Religions

1. Troeltsch's *fundamental approach* to the relationship of Christianity to the religions is implied in what we have said above about his understanding of revelation and religion. To grasp the true content of the Christian religion, to relate it properly to other religious manifestations, the scientist — both the historian and the theologian! — cannot begin with Christianity; he cannot consult the pages of the Old and New Testaments. Rather, he must first master the meaning of religion in general and in its manifold manifestations throughout the world. He must first be a historian of religions; only then can he begin to be a theologian. Here Troeltsch shows himself a true disciple of the "religionsgeschichtliche Schule".

A "theology of religions" is therefore essentially subordinated to "Religionswissenschaft". Indeed, Troeltsch calls theology an "ancillary science" for the science of religions. To try to understand the meaning of Christianity from theology alone betrays a naive, mythological mentality. Theology must leave the foundation of its claims to the philosophy of religion; only then can what is "real" and "valid" be established.[65]

All this implies that there is no essential difference between Christianity and the religions. Christianity is in all instances a purely historical phenomenon like all the other great religions. She is always a "relative Erscheinung".[66] "Das Christentum trägt nachweislich Elemente aller umgebenden Religionen in seinem Aufbau und ist selber ein Zusammenfluß der großen Strömungen in dem Zeitalter der Religionswende."[67] "Nirgends ist das Christentum die absolute, von geschichtlicher, momentaner Bedingtheit und ganz individueller Artung freie Religion, nirgends die wandellose, erschöpfende und unbedingte Verwirklichung eines allgemeinen Begriffs der Religion."[68]

2. Was Troeltsch proposing a total denial of Christianity's "Absolutheit"? Althaus, as we shall see, felt he was. Yet in Troeltsch's earlier writings this is not so clear. In his *Die Absolutheit* he held that his historical method does not necessarily exclude the claim that Christianity is the highest form of religion for the individual. Such a claim will always be made on the basis of a personal conviction or confession. Yet this will not be the only ground; it is not simply a matter of "naive absoluteness".[69] On the basis of the historical method itself we can attain to a certain unique place for Christianity within the panorama of religions. Not an absolute, supernaturalistic uniqueness, but a distinct, yes a superior role; not an exclusive absoluteness but an absoluteness "innerhalb der Absolutheit der Religion".[70]

Arguing from his metaphysical foundation for revelation and religion and applying his practical criteria for the worth of a religion, Troeltsch feels he can, as an historian, conclude to Christianity's superior participation in the Absolute which is behind all religions. Having compared the *Christian* religion with other religions, Troeltsch can state:

65 GW II, p. 192; *Der Historismus*, p. 77; Schlippe, p. 59; Drescher, pp. 58—62.
66 *Absolutheit*, p. 52.
67 GW II, pp. 220 ff.
68 *Absolutheit*, p. 35; Köhler, p. 84.
69 Cf. footnote 60; Benz, p. 43.
70 Schlippe, p. 74.

Das Christentum ist in der Tat unter den großen Religionen die stärkste und gesammeltste Offenbarung der personalistischen Religiosität. ... Das Christentum muß nicht bloß als der Höhepunkt, sondern auch als der Konvergenzpunkt aller erkennbaren Entwicklungsrichtungen der Religion gelten ... [71]

It is chiefly in its quality as a purely personalistic religion that Christianity leads the band of religions.

3. But it must be clear: the Christianity which Troeltsch can thus compare with and rank above the other religions is *not* the traditional form of the Christian faith which theologians such as Althaus still held to. It was rather the new, revamped Christianity we mentioned above, a Christianity which the modern mind could grasp and accept and make meaningful in the world of religions. In such a Christianity non-essentials are to be distinguished from essentials — *and* are accordingly to be discarded. Once Christianity is rid of such antiquated, ill-adapted "non-essentials" as the concept of sin (which Troeltsch held to be atavistic), the doctrine of a supernatural, unique revelation, the belief in miracles as proofs for a supernatural order, and "die alten ... Erlösungs-, Alleinwahrheits- und Erbsündentheorien" — then will "die prinzipielle Christlichkeit" shine forth.[72]

The Christian "essence", then, is not a body of doctrines, not a new form of revelation, but a *principle* (a principle whose main content is personalism in man's relation to God). "Mit 'Prinzip' soll dasjenige bezeichnet sein, was einem großen Komplex geschichtlicher Erscheinungen die innere Einheit gibt, was in sich ... Entwicklungskraft enthält, das Grundgeheimnis des geistigen Lebens ..."[73] Only as this principle can Christianity be related to the other religions and be placed among the general evolution of all religions toward the Absolute. It is this principle which is at work and finds a fuller expression in and through the Christian religion.

This principle enabled Troeltsch to attain what can be called a "supra-confessional point of view" — indeed, a point of view which was even "supra-christian".[74] Christianity was liberated from any essential attachment not only to an historical event or to an institution; she was also liberated from an exaggerated attachment to the person of Christ! Thus we finally arrive at a proper, scientific understanding of the person of Christ. He is indeed the means by which we grasp the "principle" of Christianity; he is the "medium";[75] he is an "incitor", "model", "object of cult".[76] But nothing more. He is not to be identified with the

71 *Absolutheit*, pp. 86, 89 ff. Bodenstein feels that Troeltsch, with his idea of all religions moving towards a final goal and point of convergence, really took over "in verhüllter und positivistisch erweiterter Form die von ihm vorher prinzipiell abgelehnte entwicklungsgeschichtliche Deutung der Religionsgeschichte, die in Hegels Religionsphilosophie vorliegt ..." The only real difference is that Hegel is certain that the final point is the Christian religion, while Troeltsch, as we shall see, is not quite so sure. Bodenstein, p. 43. Drescher also feels that Troeltsch was closer to Hegel than he realized. op. cit., pp. 40–41.

72 *Absolutheit*, p. 145; GW II, pp. 837–862; Schlippe, pp. 17–19, 110; Köhler, pp. 71–83. Bodenstein describes Troeltsch's new view of Christianity, especially in the questions of eschatology, grace and faith, pp. 51–60.

73 "Geschichte und Metaphysik", p. 56.

74 Schlippe, pp. 110, 10–11.

75 GW II, pp. 847 f.

76 Troeltsch, *Die Bedeutung der Geschichtlichkeit Jesu für den Glauben* (Tübingen, 1911), p. 9; *Glaubenslehre*, p. 104.

principle; the principle is above him and beyond him. The absoluteness of Christianity cannot rest on the reality of Jesus Christ! Therefore, in relating the Christian religion to other religions, we must as it were prescind from the person of Christ.[77] Jesus Christ must take his place — not an essentially different place — among the other founders of the great religions, eg. Buddha.[78] This, then, is the "supra-christian" Christianity which might be said to be superior to the other religions.

4. "Might be said" — Troeltsch never could make an "absolute", explicit statement about Christianity's absoluteness. Even in his earlier writings, when stating that contemporary scientific investigation points up the superiority of the Christian religion, he always adds that we cannot be certain whether another and higher form of religion — a still greater participation in the Absolute — might still develop. In 1894, in his article on a Christian "Weltanschauung", he opted for the unsurpassability of Christianity.[79] But in his work, Die Absolutheit, (1902, 2nd ed. 1912) he says that we cannot prove "with strict certainty" that a "surpassing" of Christianity is to be excluded.[80] And in Der Historismus und seine Überwindung 1924, he openly holds that the question should not even be posed since it would violate the individuality and uniqueness of all religious experience.[81]

This latter work reflects Troeltsch's final development — his "existential period". It is made up of a series of lectures on "Die Stellung des Christentums unter den Weltreligionen" which Troeltsch was to deliver at Oxford in 1923. His death intervened and the lectures were published the following year under the above title. These lectures constitute what Schlippe terms the "Abschluß" to Troeltsch's gargantuan attempt to formulate a new understanding of Christianity's absoluteness — a period in which he arrived at even more revolutionary (Althaus would say devastating) conclusions.[82] Strongly influenced by Kierkegaard's exaltation of the individual, Troeltsch turned to the individual person and culture to find the final criterion of truth. The "creative act" — the individual deed becomes the sole expression and indication of truth. No longer is it necessary to resort to scientific investigations and proofs for the value of a religion; no longer can one "grade" religions according to their level of success or richness. The "individuelle Überzeugungstat" is alone determinative. Each person and each culture will produce its own "Tat". Truth is thus reduced to act; and act to culture.[83]

The seeds of such extreme individualism were already planted in Troeltsch's earlier works, especially in Die Absolutheit. But in his later period, he clearly admits that in his previous writings he had not sufficiently realized the hidden contradiction between individuality and "objective" evaluation — between the meaning of the individual act for the person who produces it and for the scientist who examines it. It is wrong, therefore, to set one religion above the other, even in a limited way. Each religion is the proper expression of the Absolute for its

77 GW II, pp. 227 ff., 768.
78 GW III, p. 101.
79 GW II, p. 323, p. 317.
80 Absolutheit, pp. 72 ff.
81 Hrsg. von F. von Hügel (Berlin, 1924), pp. 75 ff.; cf. also GW III, p. 119; Schlippe, p. 43.
82 Schlippe, pp. 93.
83 GW II, p. 712; GW III, p. 169.

own historical, social, and geographic milieu. Even though it may appear inferior, it is the true, the only religion for its environment.[84] This is Troeltsch's theory of "polymorphous truth". Truth is always truth for me, for my culture, for my religion.[85]

Christianity therefore can no longer be termed the "point of convergence" or the "goal" for the history of religions. It is merely one form of "Absolutheit", having validity primarily for European cultures. Elsewhere, in other cultures, for other religions, there are other "Absolutheiten" — equally valid, and all moving towards the transhistorical Absolute.[86]

5. These new criteria for truth and for the absoluteness of Christianity were to be for Althaus a call to theological encounter — especially when Troeltsch went on to apply them to the Church's missionary nature and activity. In an article in 1907, Troeltsch boldly stated that the purpose of missionary endeavor is not the "setting up of an absolute religious unity of mankind" or the "salvation of those who are lost in heathendom"; but rather, an "elevation", a "raising to something higher". There is to be no conversion; only a "stepping up" to a higher level.[87] For Troeltsch the motivation which drives the missioner to distant lands is no longer the desire to wrestle with the powers of evil for the souls of men; rather, they go forth because every religion, Christianity included, seeks to convey its ideas to other religions and that in this exchange all religions — Christianity included — are bound to grow richer. Mutual understanding, recognition, and development — these take the place of conversion. In his later period, Troeltsch was to be even more constraining in his understanding of missionary work. Emphasizing polymorphous and cultural truth, he no longer speaks of "elevation" as the purpose of the missions but only of "contact" and "balancing".[88]

*****

This presentation of Troeltsch's views on revelation, the religions and Christianity's relation to the religions — skeletal though it is — provides a necessary backdrop to our analysis of Althaus' theology of the religions. It will aid us in understanding not only the genesis of Althaus' thinking on the religions but also its approach and motivation. Especially in his earlier writings on the non-Christian world, Althaus not only sought after a truly Christian confrontation with the religions; he also endeavored to "correct" Troeltsch's mistakes and infidelities. This will explain a certain harshness which vibrates under the surface of these early articles. He was wielding the sword of faith against its opponents.

---

84 GW III, p. 32.
85 GW II, p. 760; GW III, p. 187; Bouquet, pp. 335–356.
86 Schlippe, pp. 97–98; Drescher presents a short and clear survey of the evolution in Troeltsch's ideas concerning the absoluteness of Christianity, pp. 67–77.
87 "Missionsmotiv, Missionsaufgabe und neuzeitliches Humanitätschristentum", ZMR, 22 (1907) 129 ff., 161 ff.; cf. also GW II, p. 789.
88 *Der Historismus,* p. 80; Schlippe, pp. 94–95; Köhler, pp. 112–119.

§ 8. His Approach: "From Above" – the Divine Transcendence

1. To properly grasp the full content of Barth's evaluation of the religions, we first must situate it within the extended and somewhat complicated evolution of his theological thought. In his early, "immature" years, Barth (1886–1968) followed the lead of his teachers Wilhelm Herrmann and Adolf Harnack and marched quite eagerly in the ranks of liberal theology. Very much like Troeltsch, he felt that the theologian's first steps must be made on the level of the natural-human before he can ascend to the divine.[89] Yet, after the dehumanizing catastrophe of World War I and especially under the pastoral stress of trying to make God's Word meaningful for his congregation in Safenwil, Barth was soon to change his tone.[90] In the second edition of his *Römerbrief* 1922 (to be referred to as RB) and with added vigor in his controversy with Emil Brunner during the 1930's, Barth pronounced a vociferous "Nein" to Troeltsch and liberal-natural theology and all human attempts to grasp the divine;[91] and at the same time he uttered a resolute "Ja" to God's transcendence and priority over all that is human.

This divine transcendence is the pulsing heart behind Barth's mammoth theological production. Within the development of his thought we can distinguish *two main periods*: that of *Exclusive Transcendence*, extending from 1922 to approximately 1940 and that of *Inclusive Transcendence*, which went on till his death.

a) In his first period, Barth presented the divine transcendence in such a way as to "exclude" the human. This was an understandable part of his reaction – or over-reaction – to the exaltation of the human under liberal theology and Neoprotestantism. This first period unfolded in what may be termed a *philosophical* and *theological* phase. In the philosophical phase, which extended roughly from 1922 to 1931 and was represented chiefly by RB, Barth broke clearly with the philosophical underpinnings of Schleiermacher and his followers; but in its place

89 In his article "Der Christ in der Gesellschaft" (1920) he shows traces of a natural theology when he speaks of "eine Schöpfungsordnung, in die wir uns finden müssen" or of "die Analogie des Göttlichen ... im Weltlichen". In *Anfänge der dialektischen Theologie*, hrsg. von J. Moltmann (München, 1966), pp. 4, 20–21, 24, 50. Also in the first edition of Barth's *Römerbrief* (Bern, 1919) we find a positive evaluation of the human, especially when speaking of the knowability of God through sensible creation. Cf. pp. 14–15, 17–19, 97, 245. Barth's anthropological tones come out quite distinctly in "Die Kirche und die Kultur", *Die Theologie und die Kirche*, 1928, pp. 264, 391. Cf. also H. Bouillard, "Karl Barth", LThK[2], II, 5; S.A. Matczak, *Karl Barth on God* (New York, 1962) p. 281.

90 "Jawohl, aus der Not meiner Aufgabe als Pfarrer bin ich dazu gekommen, es mit dem Verstehen- und Erklärenwollen der Bibel schärfer zu nehmen." Forward to *Römerbrief*, 2nd. edition (Zürich, 1940) p. XIII; those who shared Barth's disillusionment with liberal theology and who with him sought a "new way" also began as practical "pastores animarum": Emil Brunner, Eduard Thurneysen, Friedrich Gogarten, Georg Merz.

91 Hans Urs von Balthasar, *Karl Barth, Darstellung und Deutung seiner Theologie* (Köln, 1962[2]), p. 101; H. Zahrnt, *Die Sache mit Gott* (München, 1968), pp. 15–19; K. Barth, *Nein! Antwort an Emil Brunner* (ThEx, 14) (München, 1937).

he took for his starting point and method the dualistic categories of Kierkegaard and Plato.[92] Thus, even though Barth sought to reassert the transcendence and freedom of God and his Word, he still was confining himself within certain philosophical structures. Von Balthasar calls Barth's philosophical method in RB a "conversio ad creaturam" and feels that it obscures and distorts his theological "Sache".[93] Barth could not yet allow God to be God since he was still speaking in human words and according to the insights of human thinkers.

He was soon to realize this. In his *Christliche Dogmatik* of 1927 he attempted to give his thought a more theological foundation and expression. But this first effort was not entirely successful. His book on Anselm in 1931 marks the real beginning of the *theological phase* of his first period: it was the turning point at which Barth clearly affirmed Anselm's "credo ut intelligam" and took his stand soundly on God's Word as the sole foundation and starting point for theology. "Sein Buch über Anselm merzt die letzten Reste philosophischer und anthropologischer Begründungen aus und erfaßt die 'noetische Rationalität' des Glaubens."[94] Gone is his adherence to Kierkegaard, gone are such words as "dialectic", and "paradox", gone is any semblance of flirtation with the "presuppositions" of human nature.[95]

This does not mean that Barth reneged on the fundamental position and purpose of RB and of his philosophical phase. "Der spätere Weg Barths ist eine paradoxe Rehabilitation des *Römerbriefs*, insofern nun klar wird, was dieses seltsame Buch eigentlich sagen wollte: nicht eine theologisch verkleidete Philosophie, sondern eine philosophisch verkleidete und von ihr wieder lösbare Theologie."[96]

b) But even though Barth shed his philosophical trappings and tried to proceed on a purely theological foundation, it still took some time before he began to see God's transcendence as *inclusive* — not only rejecting but affirming and embracing the human. At first Barth emphasized God's Word in such a way that he fell into "a dynamic-actualistic Theophasism or Monism" which still faced a world which was totally cut off from the divine and which touched this world only "im mathematischen Punkt des Wunders der Wende."[97] Only gradually did Barth realize that the transcendence of God and his Word — as revealed in Jesus Christ — did not have to negate man and man's world. Only gradually did he come to the realization "... daß es gut ist, Geschöpf und nicht selbst Gott zu sein."[98]

92 This Barth himself later admitted. Cf. *Credo* (München, 1935), p. 159; "Parergon. Karl Barth über sich selbst". EvTh, 8 (1948–49) 271–272; also, his acceptance speech for the Sonning Award in Kopenhagen, April, 1963, quoted in Zahrnt, p. 29.
93 P. 79. Bultmann expresses similar reservations and feels that Barth unknowingly makes use of "die alte Ontologie aus der patristischen und scholastischen Dogmatik". Cf. *Karl Barth – Rudolf Bultmann. Briefwechsel 1922–1966*, hrsg. von B. Jaspert (Zürich, 1971), pp. 80–82.
94 G. Gloege, "Karl Barth", RRG³ I, 895.
95 Bouillard, p. 6.
96 v. Balthasar, p. 93: cf. also p. 181. Thus Nürnberger calls the theological phase a "Konsolidierungsprozeß" for RB and feels that "... an dieser (RB's) Grundlage (hat sich) fortan nichts Wesentliches geändert". Klaus Nürnberger, *Glaube und Religion bei Karl Barth* (Diss. Marburg) (Marburg, 1967), p. 13.
97 v. Balthasar, p. 102. This, as we shall see, is precisely what Althaus was to term Barth's "Christomonism"; cf. § 14/2.
98 v. Balthasar, p. 99.

This realization is still dormant in the *Kirchliche Dogmatik* (KD) I (1932—38) (perhaps because of the natural theology controversy with Brunner and the menacing "theological implications" of National Socialism), begins to stir in KD II (1940—42), and comes to full form in KD III and ensuing volumes (1945—1967). In his teachings on creation as the "äußerliche Grund des Bundes", in his understanding of human nature as founded in Christ, in his description of the analogy of faith penetrating the finite order, Barth realized that the mystery of the Incarnation, coming "senkrecht von oben", could also affirm and transform that which was beneath.[99]

2. Our summary of Barth's doctrine on the religions will deal chiefly with his concentrated and detailed presentation of this doctrine in the wellknown "Paragraph 17" of volume I/2 of his *Kirchliche Dogmatik* [100] (to be referred to as KD 17). Published in 1938, this volume forms both the termination of his period of Exclusive Transcendence and the bridge to the period of Inclusive Transcendence. Our concentration on Paragraph 17 and on this particular stage in Barth's thought is, we feel, recommended by the following considerations:

a) KD 17 represents the culmination — one might say, the crystallization — of Barth's theological assessment of religion and the religions. Both in its method and its objective presentation, it offers an "einschlägige Behandlung" of religion and "das erlaubt eine für die Arbeit an Barth sonst selten erreichbare Konzentration der Analyse".[101] As implied above, KD 17 contains RB's fundamental statements on the religions — but delivers them in a much more unencumbered, forceful and therefore clearer fashion. In KD 17, Barth speaks of the religions as he wanted to in RB: from God's Word, in the light of Jesus Christ. Indeed, certain philosophical presuppositions remain in KD 17 (this we shall point out), but they are subordinated to and incorporated into God's Word in Christ.

b) It was this Barth — speaking in KD 17 — whom Althaus encountered and sought to reject. True, Althaus took up his theological cudgels against Dialectical Theology right from its very birth and attacked Barth's evaluation of the religions already in its incipient form. But the basic flaw and abiding sin which Althaus pointed out and attacked in Barth's views was something which, although present in RB, came to its full maturity only in KD 17: Barth's Christomonism. Barth's narrow, restricted understanding of Christ, together with the philosophical presuppositions which remained part of such an understanding — this, for Althaus, was the false and "unChristian" foundation for Barth's attitude toward the non-Christian world. This foundation was laid clearly, once and for all, in KD 17.[102]

c) Barth's appraisal of the religions, begun in RB and then clarified and solidified in KD 17, has had a predominating and lasting influence on Protestant attitudes towards the religions — more than any of his subsequent works.[103] Thus in presenting Barth's understanding

99 H. G. Pöhlmann agrees basically with our division of Barth's development. He distinguishes three main periods: a) "vorkritisch" — in RB[1]; "kritisch" in RB[2]; and "nachkritisch" beginning with Barth's Anselm book in 1931. Cf. *Analogia Entis oder Analogia Fidei? Die Frage der Analogie bei Karl Barth* (Göttingen, 1965), pp. 112—113.
100 I/2 (Zollikon—Zürich, 1960[5]), pp. 304—397.
101 Nürnberger, p. 14.
102 Cf. Paul Knitter, "Christomonism in Karl Barth's Evaluation of the Non-Christian Religions", NZSTh 13 (1971) 99—121 for a comparison of Barth's views of the religions in KD 17 and RB, in which it is shown that Althaus' accusation of Christomonism applies primarily and convincingly to KD 17. (A portion of this chapter has been published in this article.)
103 Cf. Peter Beyerhaus, "Zur Theologie der Religionen im Protestantismus", KuD 15 (1969) 100. — Benz holds: "Man findet die Nachwirkung dieser theologischen Betrach-

of the religions in KD 17 we are lining up not only the questions and difficulties which Althaus had to answer and overcome in his efforts to evaluate the religions, but also those which are still facing contemporary Protestant theologians who are accepting the challenge of the religions. This serves the remote purpose of our study.

d) Even though Barth's period of Inclusive Transcendence is brightened with a more positive attitude toward the human and toward the "human effects" of the Incarnation — especially in such questions as Creation (KD III/2, pp. 44–337); Anthropology (KD III/2 pp. 82–241); the "Analogia Relationis vel Fidei", (KD III/1, p. 206 ff. and 220 ff.); the possibility of "other words" and other lights *extra muros ecclesiae* (KD IV/3, pp. 40–187) — his view of the non-Christian religions, as religions, remains, we feel, basically the same: negative and christomonistic. To investigate and substantiate these claims would call for a careful and lengthy study of Barth's later period — which, because Althaus did not explicitly confront this period and its relation to the religions, would carry us beyond the limits of this present study.[104]

§ 9. Extra Christum Nulla Revelatio

1. The sharpest and most constant criticism which Althaus leveled against Karl Barth's views of the non-Christian world was, as we stated above, that of Christomonism:[105] Barth's narrow, restrictive, exclusive understanding of the reality of Christ, which bans all extra-Christian reality into the realm of meaninglessness and godlessness. Althaus, indeed, was not alone in such accusations.[106] He voiced an objection which, he felt, every Christian theologian must make: because Barth's vision of Christ was too narrow, too "monistic", because he set undue limitations on Christ — he missed the breadth of God's plan of salvation and the religions' role in this plan.

This Christomonism, as the starting point and foundation of Barth's entire evaluation of the religions, is found in the first paragraph of KD 17. Speaking of revelation as the reality which expresses the relationship between the divine and the human, Barth states, quite categorically, that this reality is solely in God's hands and absolutely outside of man's reach. In no way can revelation stem from, be prepared for, or be conditioned by the human. Revelation and man — God and man — come from two different worlds, and therefore any kind of "cooperation" between the two is absolutely excluded. Of himself, man has no "organ", no

tungsweise (dialectical theology's) in fast allen neueren missionswissenschaftlichen Werken." Here he refers to E. C. Dewick's *The Christian Attitude to Other Religions* (Cambridge, 1953), pp. 39 ff; cf. Benz, op. cit., 35; cf. also Nürnberger, p. 134.

104 Cf. Excursus: Did Barth Change His Verdict on the Religions? § 12.

105 Cf. especially CW, 56–60, 138; also TG, 741–786, although in this early article Althaus does not use the term "Christomonism".

106 It was the question of God's activity outside of Christ which split the "Zwischen den Zeiten" movement. Brunner's rejection of Barth's narrow views triggered the hefty "Nein" controversy in the 1930's. For Tillich it was Barth's "Supernaturalism" which was untenable; cf. "What is Wrong with the 'Dialectical Theology'?" JR 15 (1935) 127–145, and "Natural and Revealed Religion", *Christendom* (1935) 159–170. In a different context but with the same intent, Bonhoeffer could accuse Barth of "Offenbarungspositivismus" in: *Widerstand und Ergebung* (München, 1951), pp. 170, 184. Other contemporaries of Althaus who rejected Barth's doctrine on revelation were Fr. Brunstäd, H. Schreiner, Fr. Büchsel, Fr. K. Schumann.

"point of contact", no "suitability" or "receptability" for revelation. Both in its "reality and possibility", in its "actuality and potentiality", revelation is entirely beyond man. In viewing (and experiencing) his position before God, man cannot speak of a "Können", "Bedürfen", "Müssen". All that can be said is: "Er kann nicht." (KD 17, 305, 328; cf. also KD I/2, pp. 41–43)

Barth's starting point then is a theme which he heralded throughout his entire theological career: the transcendence of God and the finiteness of man, man's inability to find — even search for — God in and by himself, the necessity of God "doing all", the impossibility of beginning with anything human when speaking of the divine.[107] This starting point might be called a form of "monism": in the mystery of communication between the divine and the human, only God is real; his activity precludes, absorbs, and in a sense negates all human activity.

But why? On what grounds does Barth proclaim this "monistic" understanding of revelation and of the relationship between God and man? The answer is given, indirectly, throughout KD 17 and constitutes a basic building-block in Barth's theology: because of Jesus Christ! Because revelation has become a reality in Christ, it cannot be real anywhere else. The fact that God touched the world at one precise historical, mathematical point means, for Barth, that he comes into authentic contact with the human (and vice versa) nowhere else. Barth's monism is, as Althaus claimed, a Christomonism.

This christomonistic understanding of God's activity is unveiled clearly in the two theological "facts" which for Barth are basic in judging the non-Christian world: God *has* offered his "self-gift and self-presentation" (revelation) (KD 17, 328 ff.), he *has* offered his "grace" (justification) (KD 17, 335 ff.) *once*, in the reality of Jesus Christ. Only in him. *Therefore*, no revelation, no salvation anywhere else. *Therefore*, the total separation of the human and the divine. *Therefore*, the absolute inability of man to know God, to know revelation so "... daß die Versuche des Menschen, Gott von sich aus zu erkennen, zwar nicht auf Grund einer prinzipiellen, wohl aber auf Grund einer praktisch faktischen Notwendigkeit allgemein und gänzlich — umsonst sind". (KD 17, 328, also 335–336) This practical necessity of fact stems from God's revelation in Christ — negating all other forms of revelation. All of man's attempts to know God, outside of Christ, are not only futile but counteractive; they not only miss the truth, but they fall into untruth, into "fiction", into an "opposing god" — all because truth is only in Christ. (KD 17, 330–331)

This, for Barth, is the message of the New Testament: faith and contact with God become possible in Christ. Therefore they are possible nowhere else. Everything else is man's own "works" — the "law" which seals man's sinfulness and separation from God. (KD 17,334–343)

2. Barth interprets the NT texts which frequently have been the basis for a "general revelation" and a positive theology of the religions (Rom. 1, 18 ff.; Rom. 2, 14; Acts 14, 15 ff.; 17, 22) as a support for his Christomonism. Firstly, Barth promptly dispatches the Rom. 2 text about the heathen "doing by nature

---

107 For other references to Barth's rejection of any kind of revelation outside of Christ cf. KD I/2, 334 f.; KD II/1, 67–200, esp. 131 f. and 86 f.; II/2, 541; IV/1, 434 f.; IV/3, 554 f.

what the law requires" as irrelevant since here Paul is speaking about Christian-heathen. (KD 17, p. 332; II/1, p. 131)

Concerning the "general revelation" in Rom. 1, 18 ff., Barth again turns the tables: these statements of Paul must be understood as "... Bestandteil des apostolischen Kerygmas ... nicht gelöst von der Situation der apostolischen Predigt, nicht gelöst von der Fleischwerdung des Wortes". (KD 17, p. 334) Exegetically this may be correct, but Barth goes on to conclude: therefore, this revelation of God through nature can be real for man only *in* and *after* his revelation through Christ. In no way was Paul referring to a "content of revelation" for the heathen, in no way did he wish to "hook onto" ("anknüpfen") a knowledge of God which they had through a form of "Uroffenbarung". "Die Heiden haben eben die Erkenntnis von Ps. 19 prinzipiell nie auch nur im geringsten realisiert." (KD 17,335) Barth even holds that the heathen cannot experience their own sinfulness, i.e. God's wrath, until they have met God's reality in Christ's revelation. (Identification of Law and Gospel.)

These texts therefore are really pointing out man's *total inability* to know God before Christ, i.e. the futility and sinfulness of all his attempts to find the Divine. This, according to Barth, is the intent of Acts 14, 15 and of 17, 22 ff.: Paul, standing in the light of Christ's revelation, could tell the heathen that the God they were seeking is the Creator, the supreme, transcendent Lord of all; this means that all their attempts to know him not only fall short, but fall into idolatry: "Weil Gott der Schöpfer und also der Herr ist — und in Christus ist es für Zeit und Ewigkeit offenbar geworden, daß dem so ist — darum und nur darum können wir sündigen in Abgötterei." (KD 17, 333) In this sense God has not left man without a witness: "Denn eben in und mit der Verkündigung der Gnade Gottes in Christus wird ihnen ja das Zeugnis Gottes aufgedeckt, von dem sie abgefallen, zu dem sie in radikalen Widerspruch geraten sind." (KD 17, 333) Because God's truth has shone in Christ, all previous searchings for truth are "... der Wahrheit ... in einem Winkel von 180° entgegengesetzt ... ein eigensinniges und eigenmächtiges Himmelstürmen ... Gottlosigkeit und Unbotmäßigkeit". (KD 17, 332—334) If God had not chosen to act in Christ, perhaps things would be different; but because he did, we must draw the consequences.

3. *Arguing* from God's unique revelation in Christ, Barth, in KD 17, concludes to the impossibility of any kind of revelation outside of Christ. This line of argumentation is characteristic of his "theological phase".[108] Yet this does not mean that in KD 17 he abandoned the basic position and "presuppositions" of his "philosophical phase" in RB when, arguing from Kierkegaard's "Todeslinie" between time and eternity, he maintained (with Feuerbach) that man is entirely cut off from the divine, and that the finite has no ability to transmit communication from the Infinite.[109] Indeed, in KD 17, Barth seems merely to be reversing his line of argumentation; or better, he seems to redress the philosophical presuppositions in theological garb. In RB Barth begins with his Kierkegaardian immanentism and concludes to Christomonism, i.e. since there is this unbridgeable rift between the divine and the human, *therefore* God can speak only in Christ. In KD 17 Barth starts with Christomonism and concludes to his philosophical immanent-

108 Cf. § 8/1.
109 Cf.. § 14/2; Aagaard, p. 158; Gloege, 895.

ism, i.e. since God has spoken only in Christ, *therefore* he speaks nowhere else and therefore there is the abyss between God and man. In RB, then, Barth begins with the "Todeslinie" and concludes to the "solus Christus"; in KD 17 he starts with the "solus Christus" and arrives at the "Todeslinie".[110]

But there are noticeable differences between KD 17 and RB. Even though Barth's old philosophical presuppositions may shine through his argumentation in KD 17, even though his Christomonism may have been "predetermined" by his philosophical immanentism — from God's Word, in Christ's name - which guides his thought and brings it to its final clarity in KD 17 His "immanentism" in KD 17, even though it is a certain predetermining factor, is not only "redressed" or "reconfirmed"; it is also developed. And the final development is the full elaboration of Barth's Christomonism. His "only in Christ" comes forth all the more clearly, all the more determiningly in KD 17. In KD 17 Barth feels he must pass his negative judgment on the religions not only because of the "Todeslinie" but because of God's sole revelation in Christ. And therefore this judgment is all the harsher, all the more total![111]

§ 10. Extra Christum Nulla Religio

1. From his christomonistic premises Barth draws his conclusions on the religions.[112] Everything he says about the religions is "in the name of revelation", "insofar as revelation steps forth" (KD 17, 335), "measured according to revelation", (KD 17, 332) i.e. revelation as coming exclusively in and from Christ. From this standpoint he can proclaim his sweeping verdict: " ... Religion ist *Unglaube;* Religion ist eine Angelegenheit, man muß geradezu sagen: *die* Angelegenheit des *gottlosen* Menschen." (KD 17, 327) The reasoning is clear: because revelation has

110 In this context Nürnberger shows the strong influence which Feuerbach exercised on Barth at the time of KD 17's composition. Cf. op. cit. pp. 49, 39—45, 50, 59. Beyerhaus goes so far as to claim that under Barth's influence Feuerbach became a "negativer Doctor Ecclesiae", op.cit., p. 89. Benz feels that because of Barth "... hat sich hier Feuerbach mitten in der protestantischen Theologie etabliert ..." op. cit., p. 34; cf. also H. Delhougne, "Karl Barth et la critique feuerbachienne de l'idée de Dieu", MSR, 28 (1971) 121—163.

111 This we have tried to show in our article on "Christomonism in Barth's Evaluation of the Religions", loc. cit.; E. Feil offers a contrary interpretation of the differences between Barth's understanding of religion in RB and in KD 17. He argues that in RB religion is totally opposed to the Gospel, while in KD 17 Barth can allow for the justification of religion. Here Feil seems to have overlooked the preparatory role of the Law which Barth attributes to "religion" in RB (while in KD 17 the Law is to be found only in the Gospel); also he does not sufficiently bear in mind the exclusivity of religion's justification. (cf. Anm. 116). E. Feil, *Die Theologie Dietrich Bonhoeffers* (München, 1971), pp. 326—334. — W. Pannenberg agrees with our understanding of the differences between RB and KD. cf. id., "Die Frage nach Gott", *Philosophische Theologie im Schatten des Nihilismus,* hrsg. von J. Salaquarda (Berlin, 1971), pp. 119—121.

112 In this section we shall be referring to "religion" and "the religions" indiscriminately. All that Barth says here about religion in general can apply to every religion. He makes exceptions or restrictions only when speaking about the "justification" of religion — which is the topic of our next section.

come in Christ and only in him, religion must be seen as man's attempt to do what only Christ can do: reveal and please God.

> Religion von der Offenbarung her gesehen wird sichtbar als das Unternehmen des Menschen, dem, was Gott in seiner Offenbarung tun will und tut, vorzugreifen, an die Stelle des göttlichen Werkes ein menschliches Gemächte zu schieben, will sagen: an die Stelle der göttlichen Wirklichkeit, die sich uns in der Offenbarung darbietet und dar- stellt, ein Bild von Gott, das der Mensch sich eigensinnig und eigenmächtig entworfen hat. (KD 17, 329)

Because the religions seek to do what has been done and can be done *only in Christ*, they are totally opposed to Christ and his revelation (KD 17, 320, 335); they are an abomination to God; in no way can they lead men to God, but only away from him. (KD 17,337—338; 330—331)

Barth at the same time admits that for the human eye there are many similari- ties between the religions and Christ's revelation, that the same "elements and problems" are burning in the interior of all religions. He does not deny that there is human good to be found in the religions, and he refrains from all practical "negative value judgments". Yet despite all these similarities and positive élements he insists that we must allow the "divine judgment" to fall on the religions. If we take revelation seriously, i.e. revelation only in Christ, then all this possible reli- gious good remains essentially and thoroughly *Unglaube.* (KD 17, 306—307; 327) Barth's view of the religions is rooted firmly and incorrigibly in his Christomon- ism.

2. Having stamped the religions as "Unglaube" on the basis of his Christo- monism, Barth draws his practical conclusions. In no way may the theologian or missionary seek a relationship between revelation and the religions; in no way may he look for questions in religion for which revelation supplies the answers; in no way may he look for an "Anknüpfung". Here he is faced with an "either-or". The "slightest giving-in, the slightest concession" in this matter spells heresy. The one and only relationship revelation can have with the religions is that of "Aufhe- bung". (KD 17, 320—331) But concessions have been made. This for Barth is the crying sin of Christian theology: "religionism" — setting religion over revelation, trying to see the positive relations between both, allowing religion to prepare the way for revelation. Expressed in the doctrine of the "analogia entis", it is the heart of the Catholic heresy. In Protestant thinking, it began in the 16th and 17th centuries (exemplified chiefly in the "concessions" made to the religions by Salo- mon van Til and Johann Franz Buddeus) and reached its most ugly expression in the modernism and Neoprotestantism of the 19th and 20th centuries. (KD 17, 308—313)

All this means that a "theology of religions" becomes impossible. Because Barth's Christomonism forbids any "concession" to the religions, the theologian who seeks after the "meaning" of the religions is stepping outside his domain, wasting his time — no longer a theologian. KD 17 by no means offers a *theological* appraisal of the religions. Its purpose is merely to present all that is opposed to God's revelation — to clear the way. For Barth, the religions are only "a negative background to his own unique interest — revelation".[113] To give the religions a theological meaning is to betray the unique (monistic) role of Christ.[114]

---

113 Aagaard, p. 158; cf. also Nürnberger, pp. 105—111, 116.
114 Barth's evaluation of the religions in RB dovetails with that in KD 17 insofar as it brands

§ 11. In Christo Una Religio

1. There are passages in KD 17 which seem to contradict the negative, condemnatory view of religion which we have traced in the preceding section. Clearly, directly, Barth states that God's revelation must have a "human", a "subjective" side. In order to be "an event which encounters man", it must assume "die Gestalt menschlicher Zuständlichkeit, Erfahrung, und Tätigkeit". (KD 17, 305) And this means that revelation must also be a religion. (KD 17, 308) God's revelation becomes his presence in the world of religions. (KD 17, 306—307) Perhaps we have interpreted Barth's christomonistic understanding of revelation too harshly. The "Aufhebung" of religion through revelation also has a positive meaning. It assumes religion; it implies not only "destructio" but also "elevatio".[115] This is implied in Barth's summary of KD 17:

> Gottes Offenbarung in der Ausgießung des Heiligen Geistes ist die richtende, aber auch *versöhnende* Gegenwart Gottes in der Welt menschlicher Religion ... (KD 17, 304, emphasis mine.)

And more clearly:

> Die Aufhebung der Religion durch die Offenbarung braucht nicht bloß zu bedeuten: ihre Negation, nicht bloß das Urteil: Religion ist Unglaube. Die Religion kann in der Offenbarung, obwohl und indem ihr jenes Urteil gilt, wohl aufgehoben, sie kann von ihr gehalten und in ihr geborgen, sie kann durch sie gerechtfertigt ... sein. (KD 17, 357)

Religion, like the sinner, can be justified.[116]

---

the religions as purely *human, sinful*, and thus to be *abolished*. But because Barth's criteria for judging the religions in RB were not yet so clearly and singlemindedly Christomonistic (i. e. he was not yet departing so exclusively from God's singular revelation in Christ) there is also a "brighter" side to Barth's picture of the religions in RB. This picture usually hovers in the background; its lines are not so clearly traced; and sometimes it clashes confusingly with the negative lines. Yet it is there. As to the *origin* of religion, Barth cautiously states that it springs from man's "original but lost union with God". In its *function*, it is the bearer of "impressions of revelation" and plays the negatively necessary role of the "Law" by convincing man of his sinful helplessness and thus preparing him for the onslaught of grace. Barth can therefore speak of a certain *fulfillment* of the "history of religions" in Christ. – In KD 17 this "brighter" side of the religions is no longer to be found; Barth's Christomonism has removed it. Christ is the only light. Cf. Knitter, "Christomonism", pp. 110—113.

115 Aagaard, pp. 164—167; Benkt-Erik Benktson, *Christus und die Religion, Der Religionsbegriff bei Barth, Bonhoeffer und Tillich* (Stuttgart, 1967), pp. 62—63; W. A. Whitehous, SJTh, 14 (1961) 146, stresses the positive content of "Aufhebung" and would translate it with "superseding".

116 Therefore many interpreters of Barth argue that his doctrine of the religions has been misunderstood; Barth can also attribute a positive though subordinated role ro religion. Cf. C. S. Song, op. cit., pp. 40—53, 106—124, 296; J. A. Veitch, "Revelation and Religion in the Theology of Karl Barth", SJTh, 24 (1971) 1—22; H. Strauss, "Krisis der Religion oder Kritik der Religionen?!?", in *Parrhesia*, Karl Barth zum 80. Geburtstag (Zürich, 1966), pp. 305—320, esp. pp. 307—309; E. Feil, *Die Theologie D. Bonhoeffers*, pp. 326—334. But what all these authors seem to overlook is that while Barth allows religion to be justified, he limits this justification — as we try to show in this section — to the "assumption" of religion in Jesus Christ. Cf. also R. Prenter, "Dietrich Bonhoeffer und Karl Barths Offenbarungspositivismus", *Mündige Welt III*, pp. 11—41; A. Szekeres, "Karl Barth und die natürliche Theologie", EvTh, 24 (1964) 229—242, esp. 240 ff.

2. But when Barth goes on to describe this "justification", he reveals it as the epitome of his christomonistic understanding of religion, for he insists that justification of religion can take place 1) *only in the reality of Jesus Christ* and 2) *in a way* in which *nothing* is taken over or *"answered"* from the world of religions. The justification applies only to *a* religion; not to *the* religion*s*.

"Only in the reality of Jesus Christ" — all of Barth's positive statements about religion in KD 17 are tied solely — "christomonistically" — to this condition. Barth clearly admits that for him religion can have a positive value and be "justified" only according to the schema of the *assumptio carnis*. Religion is related to revelation as Christ's human nature to the divine person; the unity between the two is limited to a "determined event". Before this event, before this "assuming", Christ's human nature had no meaning; it existed only as a possibility. The same can be said of religion. (KD 17, 323—324) Only "als Annex der menschlichen Natur Jesu Christi" can it have any kind of positive meaning. (KD 17, 382)

Therefore, if Barth admits that "in seiner Offenbarung ist Gott gegenwärtig mitten in der Welt menschlicher Religion" then this can be said only "in Erinnerung an die christologische Lehre von der *assumptio carnis*", i.e. this presence is limited to "jenem Geschehen zwischen Gott und Mensch". (KD 17, 324) Barth's vocabulary indicates how he jealously limits the justification of religion to the historical, definable, visible reality of the Incarnation. The "... offenbare Gottestatsache des Namens Jesu Christus ... bezeichnet ... ein ganz bestimmtes Geschehen, (!) an dem die Welt der Religionen einen ganz bestimmten Anteil bekommt." Only one religion is justified. "Die Gottestatsache (!) des Namens Jesus Christus bestätigt ..., was keine andere Tatsache bestätigt noch bestätigen kann, die Schöpfung und Erwählung gerade ihrer Religion zur einen, einzigen, (!) wahren Religion." (KD 17, 390—391) "Daß es eine wahre Religion gibt, das ist Ereignis im Akt der Gnade Gottes in Jesus Christus ..." (KD 17, 377) Only that religion which is linked to this "Geschehen", to this "Tatsache", "Ereignis", "Akt" — only that religion which is "Eigentum Christi", and is in his "Bereich und Reich" (KD 17, 322) — only this religion is lifted "aus der Menge der anderen als *die* wahre Religion". (KD 17, 358) Outside of Christ, as Calvin held, religion is only " ... eine Größe x, die ihren Inhalt und ihre Form nur dadurch empfängt, daß sie mit dem Christentum gleichgesetzt, d.h. aber, daß sie von der Offenbarung in sich aufgenommen und zu ihrer Gestalt gemacht wird". (KD 17, 310; cf. Instit. I,3,1 f.; 4,1; 12,1) Here, then, we have Barth's christomonistic interpretation of the religions at its blatant best.

This justification takes place in such a way that nothing really is assumed from the world of religions. If Christianity is justified in Christ, this does not depend on or have anything to do with its quality as "religion". Here we can understand Barth's remarks about Christianity not being different from other religions. The Christian religion's justification in no way implies an "immanent content of truth or value" (KD 17, 369) — a truth it might share with other religions. Nor does it have any kind of "religious self-consciousness as such" (KD 17, 364). If one looks at this "true religion", one surprisingly finds no external differences from the other false religions: the same "divine accusation of idolatry and justification by works", (KD 17, 378), the same sad story of "unfaith and sin", the same "opposition" against God's grace. (KD 17, 389, 369) This true religion is " ... in ihrer Gestalt, aber auch in ihrer menschlichen Wurzel sündige Geschichte, nicht weniger, als dies von der Geschichte des Buddhismus oder des Islam zu sagen ist". (KD 17, 387)

3. *How* then is Christianity the true religion? The answer again lies deep in Barth's Christomonism. The justification of religion is related so "exclusively" to Christ that nothing of religion as religion plays a role in this justification; one can even say that nothing of religion as religion is really effected by this justification. All comes from Christ and, in a sense, remains with him. This is best seen in the image Barth uses to describe the justification of religion: as the light of the sun falls on one part of the earth and not on the other, enlightening one part and leaving the other in darkness, without really changing the earth, so Christ's light falls on the world of religions, making one of these religions light and true and leaving the rest in darkness and falsehood − but without bringing any essential change to the true religion. (KD 17, 388) All depends, simply, on the sun shining here and not there, on the "act of divine election". "Die christliche Religion ist darum die wahre Religion, weil es ... Gott ... gefallen hat, nun gerade sie als die wahre Religion zu bejahen." (KD 17, 384) This is what Barth means when he says that Christianity is the true religion "by the grace of God" or "by the name of Jesus Christ" − simply that God's grace shines on her, Christ's name is spoken over her and therefore she is the true religion. Her sin, her resistance to grace, her "idolatry" remain − but they are forgiven in the sunlight of Christ; God speaks his "Yes" over her. (KD 17, 379−380; 363, 369, 389) This is the essential, the only difference between Christianity and the other religions: Christianity stands in this sunlight. No matter how good and true the other religions may be, they are false, useless − because they are *not* in this light.

Barth gives an example: he compares Christianity with the Buddhistic "grace religions" of Jodo-Shin and Jodo-Shin-Shu. These religions have a remarkable grasp of the basic truth of Christianity − i.e. that all must come from God through grace, that man is totally helpless to save himself. (KD 17, 372−74) But even if their doctrine of grace and faith would be *exactly* the same as that of Christianity, even then, Barth insists, the drastic difference would remain! The grace-religions would be false, useless; only the Christian religion would be true! Why? "Entscheidend über Wahrheit und Lüge ist wirklich nur Eines ... Dieses Eine ist *der Name Jesus Christus*, ... (der) ganz allein die Wahrheit unserer Religion ausmacht!" (KD 17, 376) Only Christianity stands in the light of Christ's name. The truth of a religion, therefore, lies not in its *religious doctrine* of grace, but in the "reality of grace itself" − only through this reality "(wird) die eine Religion von anderen als die wahre angenommen und ausgezeichnet". (KD 17, 371) And only Christianity has this reality!

Stating it somewhat simply, we might say that Christian religion is the true religion because we can place the word "Christian" in front of it. Or as Nürnberger puts it, the justification of religion consists essentially and exclusively in Christ becoming the *subject* of religion without really changing its "Aktinhalt", i.e. without really changing religion itself. Christ "takes over". He becomes, as it were, the new driver; which means indeed that the course of the vehicle is changed, but the vehicle itself remains the same. In the religions, man is the subject; in Christianity Christ becomes the subject; but in the "Aktinhalt" of both, there is no real difference.[117] Christ, in other words, does not really assume religion; religion remains essentially what it was.[118]

117 Nürnberger, pp. 66−70, 123−127; also, id., "Systematisch-theologische Lösungsversuche zum Problem der anderen Religionen und ihre missionsmethodischen Konsequenzen", NZSTh, 12(1970) 16−24.

4. Our initial assertion would now seem to be a valid conclusion: Barth's understanding of the "justification of religion" represents the final and fullest expression of his Christomonism. *Because* religion can be justified in Christ, it has absolutely no meaning, or purpose or value outside of Christ. Only in Christ can the "subject" of religion be changed. To allow this to take place outside of Christ, i.e. outside of the *Christ*ian religion, would be to contradict the reality of Christ as a "Tatsache", as a unique "Geschehen". But even in Christ religion has no meaning of itself; it remains human, immanent. Therefore, there is no possibility whatsoever of relating Christianity to the other religions, of bringing about any kind of encounter.[119] One might compare the contents of Christianity with the contents of other religions and even though one may find some similarity, even identity, one has not yet touched that which makes Christianity the true religion: its subject. This is something entirely beyond the religions, something "incomparable". In his christomonistic understanding of Christianity's "truth" Barth has relativized the Christian religion phenomenologically (as to its "Aktinhalt" there is no basic difference from other religions) but has absolutized it theologically (its subject is totally and absolutely removed from the world of religion).[120]

******

Standing at an 180° angle to Ernst Troeltsch, Barth presented Althaus with the opposite pole of questions which he had to confront and answer in his own attempts to make some theological sense out of the non-Christian religions. On

118 Once it is understood that Christianity's truth does not lie in its quality of religion but only in its having the "Tatsache" of Christ as its subject, Barth admits that certain secondary changes take place in religion. Christianity's justification does include its sanctification. God is "wirklich erkannt und verehrt" and "ein Handeln des mit Gott versöhnten Menschen" takes place. (KD 17, 377) In Christ, Christianity is "ausgesondert", "durch ihn geformt und gestaltet, für seinen Dienst in Anspruch genommen, zur geschichtlichen Erscheinung und zum geschichtlichen Mittel seiner Offenbarung". (KD 17, 393) She is given an "Auftrag", and a "Mission" to step before the other religions "zum Einlenken auf den christlichen Weg einzuladen und aufzufordern". (KD 17, 392, cf. also 395) And yet, Barth continually insists that such positive characteristics in Christianity are only "symptoms", only "signs" of a reality which is constantly beyond her and never identified with her. (KD 17, 372, 377) They in no way can be "proofs" for her truth – of any religion. Truth lies solely in Christ as the subject of a religion – of one religion.
119 Aagaard, pp. 179–180; Nürnberger, pp. 123–124.
120 RB, as would be expected, does not contain such an extended and integrated statement on the possibility of religion's justification as KD 17 does. Still, Barth does speak of religion as a necessary "Begleiterscheinung des Glaubens"; it can be made use of as a subjective expression of faith. But in RB, Barth does not tie this possibility of "justification" of religion so strictly and "Christomonistically" to the analogy of the "assumptio carnis". Therefore he does not speak of "*one* true religion". This leaves the question open as to whether this "acceptance" of religion might also take place outside the Christian religion. (Acceptance always in the dialectical sense of "Erfüllung" through "Aufhebung".) There are many passages – especially where Barth affirms God's absolute freedom and the possible salvation of those outside the covenant – which indicate that he, implicitly, would allow this. cf. Knitter, "Christomonism", pp. 118–121.

every step of his own way, it seems, Althaus was taking up a position against Barth. Rejecting Barth's exclusive understanding of revelation, he proposed his concept of "Uroffenbarung". Unable to accept Barth's branding of religions as "Unglaube", he sought to integrate the religions, both in their negative and positive elements, into the general plan of salvation. And although he agreed with Barth that Christianity is the one true religion, at the same time, he was convinced that a dialogue was possible with the non-Christian world and that the religions could find a certain fulfillment in Christianity. In all these questions, Althaus resolutely discarded Barth's monistic understanding of Christ; but at the same time he himself was confronted with the difficult problems of Christology: especially, how reconcile the Reformers' "solus Christus" with a positive interpretation of the religions? The shadow of Karl Barth will help us understand *how* Althaus elaborated his answer to these questions and *why* this answer is not always totally convincing.

§ 12. Excursus: Did Barth Change His Verdict on the Religions?

There are many who feel that Barth's later development in his period of Inclusive Transcendence enabled him, at least virtually, to take a much different and more positive position towards the religions. The "Theologische Konvent Augsburgischen Bekenntnisses" in 1963 cautioned against making a "Popanz" of Barth's treatment of the religions in KD.[121] W. Andersen feels that Barth perhaps modified his position in later volumes of KD and that a detailed study of this new approach in relation to the religions is "necessary" and "promising".[122] Going further, C. A. Keller attempts a positive reinterpretation of Barth's doctrine on the religions in the light of his anthropology in KD 17.[123] And finally, C. S. Song, in a 1965 doctoral dissertation for Union Theological Seminary, sweepingly affirms that those who criticize Barth's doctrine on the religions for its narrowness have misread its deeper content: Barth's last word on the religions is positive.[124]

No doubt, there is much in Barth's period of Inclusive Transcendence which, if applied to the religions, would cast a quite different light upon them. Thus the various claims for and attempts at a "reinterpretation" of Barth's doctrine. But the *question* remains: can an application of Barth's new and more positive attitude towards analogy, creation and anthropology be made to the religions? And the *fact* remains: Barth himself never seemed to have made — or wanted to make — this application!

The reason why this application seems to be impossible, both for Barth and his interpreters, is that behind all of his positive statements — behind his entire period of Inclusive Transcendence — there remains a God-given fact — a basic, indispensa-

121 Cf. Report by Eugen Rose, *Fuldaer Hefte* 16 (Berlin, 1966), p. 194.

122 Cf. "Die theologische Sicht der Religionen auf den Weltmissionskonferenzen von Jerusalem (1928) und Madras (1938) und die Theologie der Religionen bei Karl Barth", *Fuldaer Hefte*, op. cit., pp. 33–34, 54.

123 Cf. "Versuch einer Deutung heidnischer Religionen (im Anschluß an Karl Barths Lehre vom Menschen)", EMM, 1956, pp. 90 ff.

124 Cf. *The Relation of Divine Revelation and Man's Religions in the Theologies of Karl Barth and Paul Tillich* (Manuscript) 1965.

ble condition for all theologizing; this condition Barth acknowledged and proclaimed in the first volumes of KD and never reneged on it: *only in Jesus Christ!* Hovering over Barth's entire later period is what we might call his "christologische Rückversicherung": all that can be said, positively, about man's and the world's relation to the divine is possible *and* can be *known* and *experienced* only in Christ. Nothing has personal and salvific meaning except in and after the encounter with him. In his descriptions of reality outside of Christ Barth can sometimes allow this "christological however" to remain in the background; sometimes it even seems that he has forgotten it. But always it returns — always it casts all that has been said in an: "however, only if ..."

Barth's "christological however" is especially evident in his doctrine on *analogy* (which, in a sense, underlies his ensuing positive statements on creation and human nature). Barth clearly admits the possibility and reality of the divine mirroring itself in the finite order, both in inanimate nature and especially in interpersonal relationships. (KD II/1, pp. 254 ff.; III/1, pp. 206 ff.) The world is not dumb before God; it can relate the glories of the divine. *But* — and here comes the "however" — it *cannot* do this of itself. The irremovable condition for the finite's ability to be a perceivable analogy of the divine is revelation, i.e. God's unmasking of himself in Jesus Christ. In all the intuitions, concepts, pictures and words we may draw from the world about God, we are always being lead by the Word of God; we are always departing from an act of faith in this Word! What Barth stated so clearly in KD II/1 he never took back:

> Analogie der Wahrheit zwischen ihm und uns *ist* wohl in *seinem,* das unsrige umfassenden, nicht aber in *unserem,* das seinige nicht umfassenden Erkennen. Sondern in unserem Erkennen *wird* diese Analogie der Wahrheit vermöge der Entscheidung seiner Gnade, die eben insofern die Gnade seiner Offenbarung ist. (p. 260; cf. also pp. 90–92, 255–56)

In no way is Barth speaking about an "analogia entis"; but only of an "analogia fidei" (I/1, p. 257), "analogia revelationis" (III/3, p. 59), "analogia veritatis vel gratiae" (II/1, pp. 257–63). It is, in a sense, not an analogy of the creature to the Creator; but only of the Creator to the creature — only because the Creator has revealed his resemblance. Pannenberg sums up Barth's concept of analogy lucidly: "Die von Barth bejahte Analogie der Geschöpfe zu Gott hört nie auf, Gottes Gabe zu sein, wird nie selbständiger Besitz des Geschöpfes und ist deshalb nur im Glauben an Gottes Offenbarungstat erkennbar." As Pannenberg goes on to point out, Barth admits a certain ontological analogy founded in the revelation of God to the world (a relation constituted only in Christ); but he never will allow this analogy to assume a noetic efficacy in itself. Its power to speak comes only in explicit revelation. A relationship exists between God and the world; but God must reveal this relationship before man can know it.[125] "Unter analogia fidei versteht Barth eine Analogie, die in ordine essendi et cognoscendi allein im Glauben, allein in der Gnade, allein in der Offenbarung und allein in Christus, dem einzig gottanalogen Menschen, wurzelt."[126] — To put it more in Thomistic termi-

---

125 W. Pannenberg, "Analogie", RGG³ I, 350–353; also id., "Zur Bedeutung des Analogiegedankens bei Karl Barth", ThLZ 78 (1953) 17–24; also, Zahrnt, pp. 123–124.
126 Pöhlmann, *Analogia Entis oder Analogia fidei?* p. 103 with corresponding references to KD; cf. also op. cit., pp. 101–102, 105, 115–116.

nology, Barth, it seems, constantly rejected Thomas' "primum quoad se est ultimum quoad nos". (ST I, q. 12. a.1; C. Gent. 1.c.10) The "primum quoad se" must always be the "primum quoad nos", i.e. we can never begin with "nos" in our knowledge of God.[127]

This aids us to understand the full content of Barth's doctrine on creation and anthropology. If he can state that creation is "der äußere Grund des Bundes, der Bund der innere Grund der Schöpfung", or that creation is "eine einzige Bereitstellung" for the covenant, " ... nichts anderes als eine Zurüstung für die Gnade"; if he can say that creation is "lauter Verheißung" – all this is not anything which can be found in creation of itself, i.e. without the light of revelation. (KD III/1, pp. 46, 63, 64, 261 f.) In other words, if creation is the "theatrum gloriae Dei", then this "gloria" is not anything that can spring from creation or is inherent in it. The "gloria" is only Jesus Christ! The reality and the activity of creation's relation to the covenant comes from above; there is no counter-movement, of itself, from below.[128] – Or if Barth can speak of an "ontischer Sachverhalt" in *man's nature* which consists "eigentlich und ursprünglich in einer inneren Beziehung (to God), in einer Entsprechung zwischen seiner göttlichen Bestimmung und seiner geschöpflichen Art, zwischen seinem Sein als Gottes Bundesgenosse und seinem humanen Sein" (KD III/2, pp. 244 ff.) – then all this, Barth presupposes, is so and can be *known* only from revelation, only from Christ. Barth speaks of "eine Ontologie des Menschen ... eine Erkenntnis seines wesenhaften Seins" (III/1, pp. 1, 5, 13) only from his christological starting point. The "Phänomene des Menschlichen" are "als solche... neutral, relativ, zweideutig ... Der Mensch ist sich selber nicht das Bekannte und Gewisse, sondern die Frage, auf die er keine Antwort weiß". (III/2, p. 88) Barth insists, therefore, on " ... die Begründung der Anthropologie auf die Christologie", (III/2, p. 50) both ontologically and noetically.[129]

Because Barth, on every page of the ensuing volumes of KD, can appeal to this "christologische Rückversicherung", because he adhered to what Althaus called his "Christomonism" and would never allow any positive value in the human outside of Christ, it would seem both rash and unjust to try to apply his later doctrine on analogy, creation and anthropology to the religions. The religions do not have Christ! They have not yet come into contact with his revelation! Barth himself seems indirectly to warn his interpreters of such a rash application insofar as, throughout his period of Inclusive Transcendence, he continued to admonish against "concluding" to any kind of "Anknüpfung" in the realm of the human outside of or before Christ.[130] Also, throughout his life, he kept up his staunch resistence to any kind of "natural theology" which would try to dig out a form of revelation or contact with God outside of his Word in Christ. In fact, just a few years before his death, he once again railed against natural theology in much the

127 Cf. Matczak, pp. 95, 193–194; F. Flückiger, "Analogia entis and analogia fidei bei K. Barth", *Studium Gen.* 8 (1955) 678–688.
128 Cf. Zahrnt, pp. 118–121.
129 Cf. Hübner, op. cit., p. 134; Heinrich Leipold, *Theorie der Verkündigung. Der Streit um die Frage der 'Anknüpfung' zwischen E. Brunner und K. Barth*, Habilitationsschrift, Marburg, 1969, manuscript, pp. 418–432.
130 Cf. KD III/2, p. 387; also, Gloege, 896.

same way as he vociferated against Brunner in the 1930's. Against Bultmann and Tillich, "an Stelle alles weiteren Herumstolperns in der Sackgasse" he called for new decisions "ähnlich denen, die vor mehr als vierzig Jahren in der Theologie fällig wurden und zu vollziehen waren".[131] Thus Barth in the Forward to KD IV/2 could explicitly state that he was not ready for any "Retractions" ("von Details abgesehen") and that these later volumes of KD did not reveal a "neuen Barth". (p. VIII)

That Barth himself did not make any "positive applications" for the religions — that his basic evaluation of the religions in his later period is not different from that in KD 17 — is clear in KD IV/3. In this volume he takes up the question of the non-Christians — their status and their relation to Christians — more directly than in any of the volumes subsequent to KD 17. The tone and perspective are somewhat different. Looking at the non-Christian world from God's salvific will and activity in Christ, Barth can conclude that the non-Christians are "included in the history of salvation" (405); God "calls man before man hears Him" (559), and therefore also for the non-Christians there is a "schon eingetretene Veränderung und Neubestimmung auch ihrer Situation" (563). Therefore, "alle Zeit ist potentiell Gnadenzeit, alle Geschichte potentiell Heilsgeschichte" (575); and the non-Christian is "virtually, potentially Christian" — "christianus designatus, christianus in spe". (927; cf. also 569). The salvation effected and proclaimed in Christ embraces all men and eventually will win over all men; here we are touching upon the much-discussed question of an *Apokatastasis* in Barth's understanding of final salvation.[132]

However (and here Barth once again resorts to his "christological however") all this remains "in potentia", in God's eternal plan. Without Christ, it cannot become real "in actu"; it cannot be drawn "aus der 'Horizontalen'" or "aus der Kontinuität". (KD IV/3, pp. 581 ff.) It cannot be realized in a religion which does not have Christ! Therefore Barth in this volume conce again gives voice to his previous verdict over the non-Christians and their religions. The non-Christians are those who " ... ohne ihn (Christ), ohne das Licht des Lebens, ohne das Wort vom Gnadenbunde verloren gehen und bleiben müßten" (421). They are in a condition of "verhängnisvollen Selbstmißverständnis und Selbstwiderspruch"; the non-Christian is the "im Tiefsten verwirrte, angefochtene, der tief geplagte, ratlose und betrübte Mensch" (923 f.). Because the non-Christians do not have Christ and therefore cannot respond to God's universal salvific call, they fall into "Not und Angst", which is expressed "vor Allem" in their

> in so vielen, krassen und sublimen Formen, bewußt und unbewußt geübten Götter- und Götzendienst. *Primus timor fecit deos* ... Es wäre eben eine Aufgabe für sich, dies an Hand der Geschichte und Phänomenologie der Religion ... zu belegen. (924)

Thus, in his penultimate section on "Der Heilige Geist und die Sendung der christlichen Gemeinde" Barth can describe the non-Christians and their religions:

> ... befangen in so viel falschem, willkürlichem und ohnmächtigen Glauben, an so viel falsche, weil doch nur ihre eigene Glorie und Misere reflektierenden Götter älterer und neuester Erfindung und Autorität. (1002)

131 *Rudolf Bultmann. Ein Versuch, ihn zu verstehen.* Vorbemerkung zur 3. Auflage, Zürich 1964, p. 6.
132 Cf. 921–928; II/2, pp. 355 ff.; 466–467, 52 f., 181 f., 387 ff.; III/1, p. 212; IV/1, p. 344; v. Balthasar, pp. 186–200.

Even though we must respect the "sogenannten Religionen" and their " ... in ihrer Weise psychologisch, soziologisch, ästhetisch, auch ethisch, überhaupt menschlich nicht nur interessanten, sondern imposanten Gebilde", we must bring the Gospel to these religions "in seiner *radikalen Eigenart* und *Neuheit*" — "in aufrichtigem Respekt und in ebenso aufrichtiger *Respektlosigkeit* gegenüber der sogenannten Religion ..." (1003—1004, emphasis mine) The religions remain the product of man's self-seeking, the result of his sinful refusal of God, the expression of "Unglaube".

That Barth, both theoretically and practically, held to this position to the end is clearly contained in a letter to Georges Casalis in Paris, 18. 8. 1963:

> Die Ergänzung meiner so lichtvollen Darlegungen, die du im Gespräch mit den Kamerunern vorgenommen hast, will mich freilich nicht so recht freuen. Wo findest du in der Bibel auch nur die Spur einer Theorie, laut derer die Tatsache der Religionen für den Glauben ein Zeichen bedeute, daß der Mensch für die Beziehung zu Gott geschaffen sei? Das ist der erste Schritt auf dem Weg zurück in die alte Misere, auf dem du den schwarzen Brüdern auf keinen Fall Beistand leisten solltest.[133]

Thus, there are interpreters of Barth who, in contrast to those who argue for a "new Barth", insist that his doctrine of religion and the religions in later volumes of KD " ... has lost none of its radicalness ..."[134] Hübner feels that Barth's view of religion and the "gottlose menschliche Grundsituation" remains throughout his ensuing development. "Das Urteil des 'Römerbriefs' über sie (religion) bleibt grundsätzlich bestehen."[135] Similarly, Weber argues that while Barth may have given up "einzelne Gesichtspunkte", he retains the "Kern" of RB. "Er findet sich in Bewegung, aber Ausgangspunkt, Gangart und Ziel sind nicht veränderlich."[136] Nürnberger, too, in his thoroughgoing analysis of KD 17 admits that in later volumes there is a certain "Akzentverschiebung ... Auswirkungen, Brechungen, Korrekturen, Anpassungen'; but the foundation which Barth in KD 17 lays for a theological understanding of the religions remains.[137] Aagaard, agreeing with these assessments, explains:

> The fact that this negative line of thought (concerning the religions) is maintained, at the same time as a positive anthropology is developing, is an expression of the fact that the negative view has its origin in his view of revelation and not in anthropology. For the view of *revelation* is unquestionably unaltered in Barth's writings from 1922 till the present day.[138]

Barth's "christologische Rückversicherung" is contained in his doctrine on revelation: only in Christ does God communicate with man; only in Christ can man hear God's voice in the world and in his own nature.

133 Copy in Barth-Archive, Basel.
134 Zahrnt, p. 114.
135 Op. cit., p. 110.
136 Otto Weber, *Karl Barths Kirchliche Dogmatik, Ein einführender Bericht* (Neukirchen–Vluyn, 1963), pp. 283—284.
137 Op. cit., pp. 13—14.
138 Cf. J. Aagaard, "Revelation and Religion" StTh 14 (1960) 166—167. Others who argue that there is no essential change in Barth's later views of the religions are: W. Bühlmann, "Die Theologie der nichtchristlichen Religionen als ökumenisches Problem", *Freiheit in der Begegnung. Zwischenbilanz des ökumenischen Dialogs*, hrsg. von Jean-Louis Leuba u. H. Stirnimann (Frankfurt, 1969) pp. 464, 475; W. H. van de Pol, *Die Zukunft von Kirche und Christentum* (Wien, 1970), pp. 98—99; G. Rosenkranz, *Der christliche Glaube angesichts der Weltreligionen* (Bern, 1967), pp. 216—218.

Chapter II

A Middle Way — A Protestant Way

I. Althaus' Middle Way

§ 13. The Scylla and Charybdis of a Theology of the Religions

Troeltsch and Barth represented, as it were, the Scylla and the Charybdis for Althaus' attempt to evaluate the religions: he clearly saw and pointed out the dangers lurking behind their views, and at the same time he tried to steer a middle course between them.[1] In the first part of this chapter we shall try to indicate just how Althaus chartered this course. We will do this in each of the three major areas of Troeltsch's and Barth's interpretation of the non-Christian world (as outlined in Chapter I): the question of 1) revelation outside of Christ, 2) the general meaning of the phenomenon of religion, and 3) the uniqueness of Christianity. (All of which questions form the chief components for any theology of religions). In all of these areas Althaus clearly stated what he, as a Christian-Protestant theologian, could not accept. In tracing this rejection — this middle course — we have the limits or the poles of his own theology. This will be important for our later treatment of Althaus' own views, when "boundaries" may sometimes appear somewhat nebulous.

Troeltsch and Barth represent the "adversarii" *not only for Althaus.* In a sense they also stand as the Scylla and Charybdis *for any Christian theology of the religions* — also for our present-day efforts to understand the meaning of the history of religions in God's dealing with mankind.[2] Relativism and absolutism, transcendence and immanence, exclusivism and universalism — these are the questions and the opposing poles which Troeltsch and Barth have set up and which must be weighed and balanced off by any theologian who confronts the religions, by a Daniélou and by a Rahner, by a Ratschow and by a Pannenberg. Both poles warn against being "unfair" to either the religions or to Christianity, i.e. to the reality and factualness of religious phenomena and to the claims which Christianity makes on the basis of the Word which has been entrusted to her (and which, it is presupposed, is the basis of the theologian's trade). Althaus was one example of an attempt to remedy this unfairness and trace a middle way — an example which, we feel, can be a help, positively and negatively, in searching for our own way.

---

1 In setting up Troeltsch and Barth as the "poles" or limits of Althaus' thinking on the religions we do not mean that they were his only opponents — the only theologians who "catalyzed" him into a confrontation with the religions. There were indeed others. And yet, all the views of the religious world which Althaus considered to be faulty could be lined up behind either of these two names. This is why the names of Troeltsch and Barth appear more than others when Althaus discusses his "adversarii".

2 H. Waldenfels sees present-day Protestant theology in search for "den Weg zwischen Extremen ... die extrem liberale Position ... die extrem dialektische Position ..." "Das Verständnis der Religionen und seine Bedeutung für die Mission in katholischer Sicht", EMZ, 27 (1970) 151; cf. also G. Cooke, *As Christians Face Rival Religions: An Interreligious Strategy for Community without Compromise* (New York, 1962), p. 150.

§ 14. Between Troeltsch and Barth in the Understanding of Revelation

1. Althaus could endorse Troeltsch's efforts to overcome an all too narrow and restrictive concept of revelation, especially as proposed by Ritschl, (CW, 54) and to seek a more open and universal view of God's revelatory activity in history. Yet because Troeltsch made this effort primarily under the guidance of his historical method he ended up, in Althaus' estimation, by correcting an error with an equally grave error. Troeltsch's mistake can be summed up in one of the most widespread misunderstandings of revelation — that of idealism: "Für den Idealismus aller Zeiten bedeutet die Offenbarung die Auslösung der Selbstbesinnung des Geistes auf sein ursprüngliches wesentliches Gottesverhältnis." (GD/1,47) Such a view of revelation confines God within the structures of human reason and self-experience. It does not allow God to act as he will; especially, it does not allow him to act through history. "Gott wird nur als im Menschengeiste sich erschließender Geist erfaßt, aber nicht als Schöpfer und Herr, der den Menschen in das Gegenüber echter Geschichte zwischen Wille und Wille setzt." (GD/I,48) God must remain God. Here Althaus was on Barth's side.

Further, such an idealistic-rationalistic understanding of revelation does not allow Christ to be the Christ. It excludes an absolute and unique expression of revelation at any point of history. To reduce Christ to merely a "special case" of revelation is to emasculate the content of the New Testament. (CW,54; cf. also Ur,7, GD I,95)

2. But neither could Althaus accept Barth's "confinement" of revelation to the Christ-event. Christomonism is for Althaus the source of Barth's relativizing view of man and the world: his "christomonistische Offenbarungsgedanken" (CW,56), his "exklusiv-christologische These"[3], his "christomonistische Enge" (CW,344), his "monistische Offenbarungslehre". (CW,60) While Troeltsch relativized the finite order by not allowing the supernatural to break through it in its true uniqueness, Barth did the same by so confining the manifestation of the transcendent to one singular point as to render the rest of reality meaningless and totally relative.[4]

Althaus felt that such a christomonistic understanding of revelation was squarely opposed to the content of Scripture and its doctrine of God's historical dealings with man. (CW,57–59, 39)[5] It also contradicted the traditional Reformational doctrines of the "revelatio generalis" and especially of the Law preparing man for an encounter with the Gospel.[6] Althaus maintained that Barth's rejection of any trace of revelation outside of Christ was founded solely on contemporary philosophical presuppositions:

> Der eigentliche Grund für das Außerachtlassen der allgemeinen Offenbarung ist nicht eine theologische Nötigung, sondern eine bestimmte philosophisch-weltanschauliche

---

3 "Durch das Gesetz kommt Erkenntnis der Sünde", *Um die Wahrheit des Evangeliums* (Stuttgart, 1962), p. 168.

4 Althaus attacks Barth's radical relativizing of history in his early article, TG.

5 Cf. also P. Althaus, "Paulus und sein neuester Ausleger. Eine Beleuchtung von Karl Barths 'Auferstehung der Toten'", ChuW, 1 (1925) 20–30, where Althaus again accuses Barth of a "Vergewaltigung" of Paul's thought.

6 "Durch das Gesetz", pp. 169–171; CW, 57, 60; "Bedenken zur 'Theologischen Erklärung' der Barmer Bekenntnis-Synode", in *Korrespondenzblatt der evang.-luth. Geistlichen in Bayern*, 59 (1934) 318–319.

Haltung — also eine Art natürliche Theologie negativen Inhalts —, nämlich das Ja zu dem modernen Relativismus und Skeptizismus, der keine Begegnung mit dem Unbedingten in der Wirklichkeit unseres Lebens mehr kennt. (CW,56)

Such a skeptical-relativistic starting point demands that all non-Christian revelation can show only "einen Götzen, der mit dem Gott, der sich in Jesus offenbart, nichts zu tun hat". (CW,59) It leads to the "total secularization of all human life." (CW,57) What Barth did not realize is that such a view inevitably leads theology itself to be swallowed in skepticism: "Eine Theologie, die vom Skeptizismus ißt, stirbt daran." (TG,753) — In Althaus' mind, a theologian who assumes such a relativistic attitude to the finite order is shirking his responsibility[7] and is digging his own grave. Althaus' staunch resistence to Barth's christomonistic view of revelation was to pit him against the "Übergewicht von Karl Barth" and the "sensus communis" of the time[8] — a clash which assumed uncomfortable tones in Althaus' rejection of the Barmen Declaration.[9]

3. Thus we have a preview of both the content and the tension in Althaus' teaching on revelation in the religious world. In rejecting so clearly and forcefully Troeltsch's and Barth's doctrines on revelation, he determined the tightrope course he had to follow in his own description of God's self-disclosure to man — as he put it: "der schmale Weg zwischen einer 'natürlichen Theologie' und einer christologisch-verengten Offenbarungslehre".[10] Rejecting Barth, Althaus would have to propose a concept of revelation which was universal; yet rejecting Troeltsch, he could not allow himself to jeopardize in any way the centrality of Christ's revelation. Against Barth, he would have to hold that nature and history can be vehicles of God's self-disclosure; but against Troeltsch he would have to show that the human element can never be placed above the divine element and that the revelation through nature and history was essentially subordinated to the historical event of revelation in Jesus Christ.

Already at this point, we should point out what will become more evident in our next chapter: Althaus' efforts to understand revelation in the non-Christian world and in the religions, while tracing a narrow path between Troeltsch and Barth, will tend — in general — to sway closer to Troeltsch's position. While he rejected them both with equal staunchness, he felt that the ultimate solution for the question of revelation lay in Troeltsch's direction. Revelation must be universal. But how? And to what extent?

§ 15. Between Troeltsch and Barth in the Understanding of Religion

1. Althaus could not admit Troeltsch's principles of *individual life-forms* and *historical evolution* for understanding the history of religions. These are the key terms — the principal accusations — with which he summed up all the false views

7 Review of Barth's *Dogmatik im Grundriß*, 1947 and his *Die christliche Lehre nach dem Heidelberger Katechismus*, 1947 in ThLZ, 74 (1949) 611; cf. also W. Lohff, "Paul Althaus", *Theologen unserer Zeit*, hrsg. von L. Reinisch (München, 1960), p. 65.
8 M. Doerne, "Zur Dogmatik von Paul Althaus", ThLZ, 74 (1949) 449–450.
9 Cf. "Bedenken", pp. 318–320; also, Althaus' review of G. Koch, *Die christliche Wahrheit der Barmer Theologischen Erklärung*, 1950 in ThLZ, 77 (1952) 433–434.
10 "Adolf Schlatters Gabe an die systematische Theologie", *Adolf Schlatter, Gedächtnisheft der Deutschen Theologie* (Stuttgart, 1938), p. 34.

of religions during the 19th and early 20th centuries (MR, 155–157; WE, 3–4; ER, 9–11; GD/1, 96–98; CW, 133–134).

All of Althaus' objections against Troeltsch's concept of religion can be boiled down to the same principal difficulty he had with Troeltsch's view of revelation outside of Christ: it leads inevitably to a form of *relativism* which is wholly irreconcilable with the content of Christianity. Troeltsch's attempt to posit an Absolute which is equally beyond and present in all religions obliterates, willy-nilly, all essential differences between religions. There is "keine Mauer zwischen einer angeblich übernatürlichen biblischen Religionsgeschichte und der nur natürlichen Religionsgeschichte – vielmehr steht alles in einem einzigen großen Lebenszusammenhang." (ER, 11) "Das gesamte Gebiet menschlicher Religion ist grundsätzlich als Einheit zu behandeln." (GD/1,95) Althaus would admit a "general context" or "unity" – but not such as removes all differences and totally relativizes all religious phenomena.

2. With equal clarity, Althaus was opposed to Barth's efforts to confine the religions totally to the realm of the human and to classify them as nothing but "un-faith" and "sin". (Cf. esp. TG, 744, 746) Such a position, which could look on the religions as a "Fiktion, die mit Gott selbst nicht nur wenig, sondern nichts zu tun hat" (CW, 138), was founded on Barth's "rein anthropologischer Religionstheorie", which was drawn from the "atheistic positivism" of Feuerbach and Nietzsche. Again, Barth was lending a more ready ear to human philosophy than to the teachings of the New Testament and of the Reformers – whose attitudes towards the religions, Althaus felt, were by no means simply condemnatory. (CW, 138; TG, 744)

Althaus realized that Barth in RB allowed religion and the religions to be an *indirect* witness of God; they make clear that man, in his most noble attempt to find the transcendent, is hopelessly confined to the finite. He is sin and nothing but sin – therefore "sick" and in need of a cure outside himself.[11] Yet Althaus rejected such an indirect witness of God as an *insufficient* assessment of the full reality and meaning of religion. (TG, 744) He would therefore opt for a more direct witnessing – something more than the simple unveiling of man's sinfulness. This we will have to bear in mind when we come to the thorny question of just what positive value Althaus attributes – or can attribute – to the religions.

3. Althaus' middle way between Troeltsch's and Barth's concept of religion will be even more difficult than that between their views of revelation. In refusing to endorse Barth's total "Nein" to the religions, Althaus was asserting the *fact* that they *do play a role* in the economy of salvation, i.e. they are part of God's dealings with mankind. Here Althaus was in basic agreement with Troeltsch. Yet he could not concede to Troeltsch's view that there was no real and fundamental difference between the roles played by Christianity and by the religions in the plan of salvation. Althaus' middle way, then, was to assert that the religions are being used by God (against Barth) but always in a manner which is subordinated to God's activity in Christianity (against Troeltsch).

11 In KD 17 Barth was no longer to admit such an indirect witnessing of man's need of God through the religions. Cf. Paul Knitter, "Christomonism in Karl Barth's Evaluation of the Non-Christian Religions", NZSTh, 13 (1971) 110–113.

The real difficulty will come when Althaus must show how this "subordinate role" is actually carried out in the concrete religions. Against Barth, (at least the Barth of RB), Althaus would not explain this role as *purely negative*, i.e. the religions do more than merely lay bare man's sinfulness, more than merely proclaim the chasm between time and eternity. There is something positive in the religions. Yet against Troeltsch, he would argue that we cannot interpret this subordinate role *too positively*: we cannot claim that God is offering his revelation and salvation in and through them in the same way as in Christ. Nor can the theologian hold, in Althaus' mind, that the subordination of the religions to Christianity can be explained as a merely quantitative difference — as if Christians simply had *more access* to God's love and light, the non-Christians less. There must be a *qualitative* difference. But what is this qualitative difference? And does it permit the religions to play a role in the *salvific* encounter with God? Althaus' middle way will have to answer these questions.

In general — from our analysis of Althaus' reaction to Troeltsch and Barth — we may conclude that his own attempts to answer the questions concerning the religions' subordinate role will tend more towards Troeltsch's direction. He agrees basically with Troeltsch's "first step": that the religions do play a role and that they do have a meaning for the theologian and missioner; he rejected the conclusions Troeltsch made from this first step. — Althaus' own theology of the religions was not Barth's full "no", but a qualified, restricted version of Troeltsch's "yes".

§ 16. Between Troeltsch and Barth in the Understanding of Christianity's Uniqueness

1. Althaus was compelled to renounce Troeltsch's description of Christianity as a "relative Erscheinung" or as a purely "historical phenomenon" together with his reduction of the Christian message to a mere "principle" which could then be compared with the various religions; for Christianity claims to be "die Wahrheit für alle — die letzte Wahrheit". (MR, 171; cf. als ER, 13—14) It brings a "turning point" in the history of religions — a point which is "endgültig ... etwas Totales, das keinen Komparativ verträgt". (GD/I,96—97) — More practically and more personally, Althaus opposed Troeltsch's interpretation of Christianity's uniqueness because it destroyed an essential element in the Church's nature: her *missionary apostolate*.[12] Troeltsch's understanding of the missions brought a change not only in goal and motive but also in spirit and nature of the apostolate. "Es bedarf keines Wortes, daß diese Zielsetzung mit der eigentlich missionarischen nichts mehr zu tun hat." (MR, 164) The salvation which Troeltsch would allow the missioner to preach is not theological but cultural — and that means a salvation not pertaining to all peoples. (MR, 163)[13]

---

12 "Althaus hat sich sehr ernsthaft um eine Theologie der Mission bemüht, aber auf der Basis einer Theologie der Religionen ..." Graß, "Gedächtnisvorlesung", p. 255. For Althaus' understanding of the missions as essential to the Church's nature, cf. WC, 3 ff; *Das Heil Gottes* (Gütersloh, 1926), pp. 230—246; *Die Kraft Christi* (Gütersloh, 1958), pp. 34 ff.; "Um die Reinheit der Mission", EMZ, 10 (1953) 97—99.
13 Cf. also MR, 161—162; "Um die Reinheit der Mission", p. 100.

Because Althaus could not accept Troeltsch's understanding of Christianity's unique place among the religions, he could not go along with the manner in which Troeltsch *related the science of theology* to that of *comparative religions*. For a theologian to accept as his primary criteria of judgment the data of the phenomenology of religions or to consider his science as merely a "Hilfswissenschaft" is to fail in his essential function.

> Das Evangelium erhebt den Anspruch, kraft der Wirklichkeit Jesu Christi die Kriterien für die Schätzung der Religionen in sich zu tragen. Die religionswissenschaftliche Methode der systematischen Theologie wollte umgekehrt aus der religiösen Welt die Kriterien für die Schätzung und Einordnung des Evangeliums gewinnen. (CW, 130)

This does not mean that the religions cannot be studied and understood outside of Christ (cf. GD/I, 95); but for a theological judgment, one can allow "no other criterion ... outside of Christ". (MR, 181; cf. also CW, 5,7) For Althaus, all this corresponds to the rules of the scientific method: the goal of all science is not only to describe but to understand — and that means to judge. But judgment is impossible without certain pre-established norms, certain "Vorurteile". (MR, 189—192)[14] Any scientist, therefore, whether he be a "Religionswissenschaftler" or theologian, must start with certain judgmental givens; and for the theologian, these can be only the givens of the Gospel. (CW, 5) Althaus adds, however, that these given "Vorurteile" should not simply be forced blindly on religious phenomena; rather, they must be verified and must demonstrate their right as valid norms through concrete confrontation with the religions.[15]

2. Although Althaus heartily endorsed Barth's polemic against Troeltsch and Neoprotestantism and held that the Christian religion is *the* true and absolute religion in that it has been assumed and taken over by Christ, he rejected the *exclusivity* — the "only" — which this statement, according to Barth, implies.[16] Althaus did not, like Barth, make an apparent identification of "religion" and the "human nature" of Christ; he did not conclude that before being taken over by the divine person, neither of these two realities can have any significance in God's plan of salvation. Also, Althaus held that when Christ did assume *a* religion, it was not merely by becoming its new "Subject" without changing its "Aktinhalt".[17] He assumed religion as religion; thus Christianity is the true religion not *despite* what it has in common with other religions but *in* what it has in common with them. "Der Glaube an das Evangelium ist auch 'Religion', ja die Erfüllung der Religion." (GD/I, 100) Therefore Althaus also had to reject Barth's view of the encounter between the Gospel and religions as one of total "Aufhebung", without

14 To those who would argue that science can be content merely with descriptive statements without passing any judgment on them or relating them, Althaus answers that in this case, theology cannot be considered a science. "Vom Sinn der Theologie", *Evangelium und Leben* (Gütersloh, 1927), p. 23.

15 "Nicht der Verzicht auf grundlegende Vorurteile und letzte Entscheidungen macht das Wesen wissenschaftliches Geistes aus, sondern die Strenge eines nur durch den Gegenstand bestimmten, die Wahrheit suchenden Denkens. Dazu gehört, daß die Entscheidung, das Vorurteil sich bewähre im Durchdrigen des ganzen Erkenntnisgebietes. Die Kraft, aus dem Chaos eine echte Einheit und Ganzheit zu gestalten, entscheidet (!) über das Recht des Vor-Urteils." "Vom Sinn der Theologie," p. 24.

16 CW, 138; "Um die Reinheit der Mission", p. 100.

17 Cf. § 11/3.

any possible "Anknüpfung".[18] If Troeltsch denied the *necessity* of the missions, Barth committed an equally grave error by falsifying or hamstringing an effective *carrying-out* of missionary work. There must also be a positive relation.

We can thus understand that while Barth looked on a "theology of the religions" as an impossibility, Althaus responded that it is a *necessity*. Forcefully — and contrary to the time's theological good taste — Althaus insisted: "Das Evangelium muß im Lichte der Religionsgeschichte und die Religionsgeschichte im Lichte des Evangeliums verstanden werden." (GD/I, 95) "Die Theologie wäre freilich, verglichen mit der Religionsgeschichte, unwissenschaftlich, wenn sie in ihrer Besinnung auf das Christentum an den anderen Religionen vorbeisähe." (CW, 5–6, cf. also 16) This confrontation consists not merely in passing judgment on the religions but is part of what Althaus said about the necessity of verifying scientific "Vorurteile". [19]

> Das Ja zu dem Selbstbewußtsein des Evangeliums soll und kann nicht etwa durch einen religionsgeschichtlichen Beweis für die Überlegenheit und Einzigartigkeit des Evangeliums begründet werden; es kommt allein in der Entscheidung des Glaubens zustande. Aber diese Entscheidung ist sich ihres Rechtes und Sinnes bewußt; daher sucht sie notwendig ihre Durchführung in konkreter Kritik der Religionsgeschichte. Das Ja zum Evangelium ruht nicht auf dieser Kritik, aber es lebt in ihr. (GD/I, 98)
> Nicht auf die Religionsgeschichte gründet sich der Glaube, aber in ihr wird er vollzogen. (MR, 188)

3. We can sum up the middle path which Althaus (and, we feel, every theologian) must follow between Troeltsch and Barth in arriving at a proper grasp of the uniqueness of Christianity and its relationship to the religions:

a) Against Troeltsch, Althaus sought for a concept of Christianity which would bring out clearly its fundamental distinction from all other religious forms; yet against Barth he would have to show that this distinction did not set Christianity so toweringly above the religions as to remove all similarity and to brand the religions as meaningless. The difficulties in Althaus' middle way lie in determining just what this "something distinct" is. It is qualitative and not merely quantitative. Yet is it a *salvific* quality, which would imply that while revelation can be found in the religions, salvation cannot? Or is it also a *revelatory* quality, which makes Christian revelation entirely different from that in the world of religions?

b) Against Troeltsch, Althaus enforced his claims that Christianity has a right and a duty to carry out the missionary mandate to the religions. She has something to offer them which they do not have. Yet against Barth, he would have to show how this "something new" is not entirely new. Again, Christianity's distinctness does not mean total difference.

c) Against Troeltsch, Althaus demanded a methodology for a theology of religions which was truly theological, i.e. not subordinate to the methods of the science of comparative religions. Yet against Barth, Althaus insisted that theology must confront and understand the religions as objectively and unbiasedly as possible in order to understand her own position. Theology bears an essential relation to the religions and, in this sense, is dependent on them to carry out fully its task of grasping Christ's revelation. The middle line here is not easily defined: objectiv-

18 Cf. § 10/3; also CW, 137, 45–46.
19 Cf. § 16/1.

ity and yet clear "Vorurteile"; lack of subordination and yet dependence. This is the same tension as that of "distinct" and yet not entirely "different".

It should be noted that in the question of Christianity's uniqueness, Althaus works out his own position by tending more in the direction of Barth. He felt that Troeltsch was guilty of the more serious error: he simply denied that Jesus Christ was different from any other religious leader. Barth's manner of claiming Christianity's distinction was true in its basic assertion but sinned through excess. Althaus' own understanding of Christianity's "absoluteness", then, would be a rejection of Troeltsch and a correction of Barth.

II. A Protestant Way

The remainder of this chapter will seek to show that the *foundation* and the *means* for Althaus' efforts to construct a middle way between Troeltsch and Barth qualify him as a reputable and meaningful representative of a "Protestant theology of the religions". Risking the certain danger in general statements, we may describe the sources and the main qualities of Althaus' theology as: 1) *Protestant* — faithful to the traditions of the Reformation and 2) *Incarnational* — open to the world, history and nature. These traits form the fabric of his theology of the religions, the former a balance against Troeltsch, the latter against Barth.

§ 17. Protestant — Fidelity to the Reformation

1. Althaus grew up and pursued his theological career in a familial and intellectual environment which fostered respect for and fidelity to the heritage of the Reformers. The Althaus family, which can trace its origins back to 1557, was in a sense a home for ministers and theologians. It bore its first theologian in 1739 in the person of Philipp Heinrich Althaus who was a Reformed Pastor in Westphalia. Three of his sons studied theology and set an "example" for future generations. Paul Althaus' grandfather, August Althaus, (born in 1807) joined the Lutheran Church (mainly because of the Reformed understanding of the Lord's Supper) and thus established the family's strong adherence to the Lutheran tradition. Althaus called his grandfather's "Verbindung von Erweckungsfrömmigkeit ... und klarer lutherischer Theologie' — überaus sympathisch."[20] — But the influence of his own father, Dr. Paul Althaus, was to be even more pronounced. As a minister in Obershagen and then in Brüggen, he carried on "den Geist eines lebendigen lutherischen Pfarrhauses".[21] And as professor for systematic and practical theology in Göttingen (1897—1912) and for systematic theology and New Testament in Leipzig (1912—1925) he offered his students a theological formation which was rooted soundly in the Lutheran tradition of the Reformation and at the same time open towards new insights and geared towards practical, pastoral application.

---

20 *Die Familie Althaus* (written by Althaus for private use of the family), p. 5.
21 Ibid., p. 6.

Paternal influence on Althaus' theology can be felt more in style and attitude than in any specific ideas or doctrines. The son's intent was to "carry on".[22]

2. Althaus pursued his theological studies in Göttingen and Tübingen. In Tübingen he felt and readily responded to the influence of Adolf Schlatter. Martin Kähler, although Althaus did not study under him, was also to play a formative role in molding his thinking. Both of these theologians, while they were to exercise a very broadening effect on Althaus' theological vision, taught him a deep respect for what they thought was the marrow of Protestant tradition.[23] His doctoral thesis and his Habilitation, both in Göttingen (1913), confronted him, again, with questions of Protestant tradition.[24]

In 1919, after serving as military chaplain in World War I, Althaus at the "tender age" of 31 became ordinary professor at Rostock. His six years there might be considered a "temporary assignment" until he found the milieu best suited to his "way of theology". In 1925 he moved to the University of Erlangen where despite summons from other universities (Leipzig, Halle, Tübingen) he remained until his death in 1966. This dogged fidelity to Erlangen was another sign of Althaus' "fidelity to church tradition"[25] — his determination to seek his answers to the questions which the modern age was throwing at theology (as exemplified in Troeltsch and Barth) without abandoning the basic tenets of his Protestant-Lutheran past. In this sense, he was opposed to the radically new answers of many of his contemporaries and could be considered "conservative".

> Er (Althaus) hat die im 19. Jahrhundert begründete große Tradition der Erlanger Theologie fortgeführt und erneuert, eine Tradition, die gegenüber den großen Auseinandersetzungen, die die Theologie der neueren Zeit erschütterten, gegenüber radikalem Neuprotestantismus (here we could mention Troeltsch) und gegenwartsfeindlicher Neu-Orthodoxie (Barth) entschlossen ihren Weg ging. Es ist der Weg eines kirchlich-konservativen Luthertums.[26]

3. But it was not a "Luthertum" which sought aridly to reproduce the past. Rather, from his base in Erlangen, Althaus became part of a movement which intended to *rediscover* in *Luther* the principles of the Reformation in a way which was meaningful for the contemporary scene (and for a theology of the religions). Althaus was a vital part of the "Luther Renaissance", " ... jener theologischen Bewegung, die gegenüber der Theologie des 19. Jahrhunderts aus ihrer Beschäfti-

---

22 From an interview with Althaus' son, Pfarrer Gerhard Althaus, May 14, 1971; Cf. *Die Familie Althaus,* pp. 9—11; P. Althaus, *Aus dem Leben von D. Althaus-Leipzig* (Leipzig, 1928), pp. 62—69; id., "Paul Althaus, evangelischer Theologe, 1861—1925", *Neue deutsche Biographie,* hrsg. von der Histor. Kommission bei der Bayerischen Akademie der Wissenschaften. I. Band. 1953, pp. 220—221.

23 "Wo steht die evangelische Theologie heute?", p. 1293.

24 *Vernunft und Offenbarung in der deutsch-reformierten Dogmatik um 1600,* Dissertation, Göttingen, 20. Dec. 1913 und Habilitationsschrift 1913 (Naumburg a.d. Saale, 1913) (Teildruck); this was published in full book form the following year as *Die Prinzipien der deutschen reformierten Dogmatik im Zeitalter der aristotelischen Scholastik* (Leipzig, 1914). These works show that already in his early years Althaus was taken up with questions concerning the relationship between revelation and the human condition — revelation and extra-Christian reality.

25 Lohff, *Tendenzen,* p. 297.

26 Ibid., p. 296; cf. also P. Althaus, "Vom Beruf der Universität Erlangen", *Das Bayerland,* 44 (1933) 207—210.

gung mit Luther der theologischen Arbeit neue schöpferische Impulse zu vermitteln versuchte."[27] Althaus was schooled and inspired in this new movement by its Father and Founder, Karl Holl.[28] Holl's sound scholarly research during the years 1903—22 into the total body of Luther's works, especially into many of his much neglected Latin writings,[29] opened the eyes of Althaus and many of his contemporaries[30] to the resources which they could find in Luther and in the "substance of the Reformation" for the perplexing questions of the times.[31]

In 1926, after Holl's death, Althaus was elected his successor as President of the "Luthergesellschaft". This was, as Hans Graß observes, an indication " ... daß er schon damals einen Namen als Lutherforscher hatte". Althaus' personal research in Luther was to be one of the strongest formative influences for his entire theology. "Sie (his studies in Luther) haben seine systematische Theologie aufs stärkste befruchtet und sind mit theologischem, nicht nur mit historischem Interesse geschrieben."[32] Althaus could turn to Luther for guidance in the most variegated questions — from the meaning of Luther's doctrine on the two kingdoms for political questions of the time,[33] to Luther's example for scriptural hermeneutics.[34]

The sheer bulk of his writings on Luther are a striking indication that the Reformer was constantly at Althaus' side in all the stages of his theological development; of the 425 entries in Althaus' bibliography, 68, or 14 %, deal directly with the thought of Martin Luther.[35] In his final years Althaus seemed to direct his attention to Luther all the more enthusiastically. During the years 1959—66, of the 48 titles appearing in his bibliography, 15, or 31 %, deal with Luther. The final flowers of his research in Luther — and, in a sense, of his entire theological

27 Lohff, *Tendenzen*, p. 297.
28 "Wo steht die evangelische Theologie heute?", p. 1294.
29 Published as his "Lutherbuch": K. Holl, *Gesammelte Aufsätze zur Kirchengeschichte* I, 1921. The Renaissance was also fostered by C. Stange's *Die ältesten ethischen Disputationen Luthers* (1904) and by J. Ficker's *Luthers Vorlesung über den Römerbrief* (1908). E. Hirsch, one of Holl's first pupils and a very close friend of Althaus, published his *Lutherbrevier* in 1917 and his *Luthers Gottesanschauung* in 1918 and thus provided further lines for a new picture of Luther.
30 Other notable "pupils" of Holl were H. Rückert, H. Bornkamm, and E. Vogelsang.
31 Graß, "Die Theologie von Paul Althaus", p. 213; cf. also P. Althaus, "Die Bedeutung der Theologie Luthers für die theologische Arbeit", LuJ, 28 (1961), 13—29; also, *Die Theologie Martin Luthers* (Gütersloh, 1963), p. 9.
32 Graß, op. cit., p. 215.
33 Cf. *Religiöser Sozialismus*; also: *Kirche und Staat nach lutherischer Lehre* (Theologia militans 4, Leipzig, 1935); *Luther und die politische Welt* (Schriften der Luthergesellschaft 9, Weimar, 1937); "Luthers Lehre von den beiden Reichen im Feuer der Kritik", *Jahrbuch der Luthergesellschaft*, 24 (1957) 40—68.
34 "Gehorsam und Freiheit in Luthers Stellung zur Bibel", *Luther*, Vierteljahresschrift der Luthergesellschaft, 9 (1927) 74—86; "Autorität und Freiheit in Luthers Stellung zur Heiligen Schrift", *Luther*, Zeitschrift der Luthergesellschaft, 33 (1962) 41—51.
35 A bibliography of Althaus' works from 1911 to 1957 can be found in *Dank an Paul Althaus*. Eine Festgabe zum 70. Geburtstag, hrsg. von W. Künneth und W. Joest (Gütersloh, 1958), pp. 246—272. For the years 1958—1966, cf. Graß' article, "Die Theologie von Paul Althaus", pp. 237—241. A more detailed picture of Althaus' allegiance to Luther is given by W. von Loewenich, "Paul Althaus als Lutherforscher", LuJ, 35 (1968) 9—47.

course — are his two major works, *Die Theologie Martin Luthers* (1962) and *Die Ethik Martin Luthers* (1965).

If Althaus' fidelity to Luther colors many areas of his theology, this is especially the case in his response to Troeltsch and Barth. Here it was not simply a matter of, negatively, trying to be faithful to Luther and the substance of the Reformation but of positively turning to him for guidance along the difficult middle road between Troeltsch's extolling of the non-Christian world and Barth's practical condemnation of it. In an analysis of the "present stance" (in 1950) of Protestant theology, Althaus explicitly states that there were two main reactions to and solutions for the extremes of liberal theology and Troeltsch's "Religionsgeschichtlicher Schule": the dialectical theology of Karl Barth and his followers and "die Wiederbesinnung der evangelischen Theologie auf Martin Luther".[36]

Fidelity to Luther the Reformer, fidelity to the substance of the Reformation — these are trademarks of Althaus' entire theology and are part of the foundation for his evaluation of the non-Christian world.

§ 18. Incarnational — Openness to the World

1. Balancing — which means tempering and directing — Althaus' deep loyalty to the heritage of the Reformation was a genuine and determined openness to the world, to human nature, to the findings and insights of science and philosophy — to the actual, existential moment. Althaus sought to mold his theology not only by appealing to the past but also by confronting and, as much as was possible, accepting the present and the future. If his theology can be called Protestant, it was also incarnational; the qualifications, as should be evident, are not contradictory but complementary.

There were various influences in Althaus' formation which opened his theological vision to the entire breadth of God's creation and which contributed to the "incarnational" quality which was to become one of the hallmarks of his theology:

a) In his "openness", Althaus was, once again, part of the *tradition of Erlangen*. If the atmosphere and history of the University gave him a "confessional Lutheran cast", it also inculcated a "critical distance" to Luther and the Reformation.[37] Erlangen's was what can be called a "freely orientated confessional Lutheranism"[38] — "conservative and at the same time involved in the present moment".[39] In its determination to apply tradition to the demands of the moment, it was not afraid to criticize, to interpret and to correct. Althaus carried on this critical spirit even more than many of his Erlangen predecessors. He did not hesitate to call Luther to task.[40]

Althaus acquired a good deal of his openness from the "Erfahrungstheologie" which was part of Erlangen's tradition. Begun under Adolf Gottlieb Christoph von Harleß (†1879) and

---

36 "Wo steht die evangelische Theologie heute?", p. 124.
37 Lohff, *Tendenzen*, p. 298.
38 Graß, "Gedächtnisvorlesung", p. 253.
39 Lohff, *Theologen*, p. 58
40 Graß, "Die Theologie", p. 213. A case in point is Althaus' readiness to correct Luther's understanding of human nature before the encounter with Christ. Cf. PL, 54—67.

carried forth by Johann Christian Konrad von Hofmann (†1877) and Franz Hermann Rein-hold Frank (†1894), this school of theology turned to "die Erfahrung des frommen Subjekts" as its starting point. These theologians felt that in the experience of rebirth – of the individual and of the community – the basic content of faith and revelation is contained and can be interpreted. Joining this experience to the testimony of Scripture and the Confessions, they produced what was the essential method of "Wiedergeburtstheologie". This method was the immediate continuation of the "Erweckungsbewegung" of the 19th Century (through which, as we have seen, Althaus' family could trace its lineage) but had its deeper roots in Schleier-macher's theology of experience.[41] Although these theologians may not have fully accepted Schleiermacher's system, they did take over his insistence that the human subject must be an essential component in any theological method.

When Althaus arrived in Erlangen in 1925, the "Wiedergeburtstheologie" had already faded, for the most part, from the theological scene. Althaus clearly distanced himself from the exaggerated importance it gave human experience in determining the reality of faith and revelation. This was what he termed "den supernaturalen Psychologismus". (GD/I, 52–53)Yet its influence on his own thinking was both genetically unavoidable and is factually ascertain-able in many areas of his theology. Here the influence of his own father, who was definitely a follower of the Erlangen theology of experience, especially as proposed by F. H. R. Frank and Carl Adolf Gerhard von Zezschwitz, was most evident. The younger Althaus was to give his theology the same "subjektiven Ansatz" which he praised in his father's thought.

His bonds with the Erlangen school endowed him with a deep respect for the person, for the value of the human, and for the role which man plays in the encounter with the divine. After World War I, Althaus, together with Werner Elert (who arrived in Erlangen in 1923) was to revive the Erlangen tradition.[42] Again, he was to call fellow theologians' attention to the necessity of finding the reality of the divine encounter in the experience of the individual – yet not only in the mystery of justification, i.e. rebirth, but in human nature itself. Althaus' teaching on "Uroffenbarung" was, in a sense, a continuation of Erlangen's "Erfahrungs-theologie", but extended beyond and before the moment of Baptism.[43]

b) The paternity for Althaus' incarnational theology is to be found – much more than in the Erlangen tradition – in his Tübingen professor, *Adolf Schlatter*. If every theologian can usually point back to one predominating personal influ-ence in his years of study, for Althaus this would be Schlatter. Speaking of his years in Tübingen, Althaus could write some 50 years later: "Wir haben ihn (Schlatter) gehört; und wer ihn nur gelesen hat, kann noch nicht ganz ermessen, was dieser Mann uns bedeutet hat, im Hörsaal, durch die viva vox, die lebendige Rede."[44]

41 Cf. Schleiermacher, *Der christliche Glaube*, § 15–16, § 32. The Romanticism of Schel-ling, who taught at Erlangen, also played a role in the formation of the University's theological tradition. Cf. Hans Graß, "Erlanger Schule", RGG[3] II, 566–568.

42 "Diese Erlanger gegenwartsmächtige theologische Tradition des Luthertums hat Paul Alt-haus zusammen mit seinem großen Kampfgenossen und Gegenspieler, Werner Elert, über ein Menschenalter repräsentiert." Lohff, *Theologen*, p. 58.

43 F. W. Kantzenbach, "Von Ludwig Ihmels bis zu Paul Althaus, Einheit und Wandlungen lutherischer Theologie im ersten Drittel des 20. Jahrhunderts", NZSTh, 11 (1969) 109.

44 "Adolf Schlatters Wort an die heutige Theologie", *Um die Wahrheit des Evangeliums* (Stuttgart, 1962), p. 131. Interestingly, Ernst Fuchs describes how Schlatter exercised the very same influence on him. *Glaube und Erfahrung*, Ges. Aufs., III (Tübingen, 1965), pp. 136–137.

Even though the first impressions which Schlatter made on his young pupil were through his New Testament exegesis,[45] the deeper and more lasting imprints came through his method of systematic theology. Not content with merely abiding by the traditional methods of theological investigation, not wishing to be tied to any particular confessional system or even solely to God's Word in Scripture, Schlatter pursued a theological method which was "wahrnehmend", "empirisch" – a method of "Beobachtung".[46] He argued that the theologian must observe God's work in its broad entirety. And this meant – as Althaus understood him – that the theologian " ... um die Gewißheit Gottes zu begründen, nicht nur in die Schrift zu blicken hat, sondern auch auf die uns gegebene Wirklichkeit, die Natur und die Geschichte ... Hier stehen wir bei dem, was für den Systematiker Schlatter am meisten bezeichnend ist: er bekennt sich dazu, daß Gott in der gesamten Wirklichkeit sich uns bezeugt und zu spüren ist."[47]

But this "total reality", Schlatter told his students, included not only nature and history but especially, man himself. In man's experiencing of himself, he experiences God; here is where God's reality touches him. Thus, to discover the full reality of the divine, the theologian must open himself to the reality of the human. "Insofern bleibt jede Theologie gerade dann, wenn sie ernsthaft in Gott und nur in Gott ihren Gegenstand hat, anthropozentrisch, weil sie ihren Standort nicht über, sondern im Menschen hat. ... Darum ist die religiöse Anthropologie ein Hauptstück in jeder Gotteslehre."[48] Althaus was to endorse Schlatter's method of initiating his "Theologie" with an "Anthropologie".[49]

Althaus points out that Schlatter proposed his anthropocentric theology as an offset "gegen die gesamte, an Kant anknüpfende – zu seiner Zeit die Ritschl'sche (Theologie)", which tried to limit God's revelation only to Christ.[50] Here too, Althaus explicitly states, we have the tools for a sound correction of dialectical theology.[51]

Years later, Althaus was to describe Schlatter's influence on his understanding of revelation as a "Befreiung". "Diese Weite der Offenbarungslehre ist uns damals und seither immer wieder zu einer mächtigen, frohen Befreiung geworden. Wir gedenken die Freiheit, die uns hier geschenkt wurde, nicht wieder aufzugeben."[52]

---

45 "Schlatters Wort", p. 131.
46 Adolf Schlatter, *Das christliche Dogma* (Stuttgart, 1911), pp. 300 ff.; E. Schott, "Systematische Theologie, Geschichte im deutschen Sprachgebiet im 19. und 20. Jahrhundert", RGG[3] VI, 592.
47 "Schlatters Wort", p. 138; cf. also Schlatter, *Dogma*, p. 13.
48 *Dogma*, pp. 14–15; Stephan-Schmidt describe "die Voranstellung, Länge, und Art" of Schlatter's anthropology which they term the "bezeichnendste" characteristic of his theology: "Sie behandelt das persönliche Leben als das Werk des lebendigen Gottes, die Natur als die Offenbarung der göttlichen Kraft, die Sozietät als Gottes Reich, die Funktion des Erkennens (Wahrheit), Fühlens (Seligkeit), Wollens (Gesetz) als Träger unseres Gottesbewußtseins." H. Stephan und M. Schmidt, *Geschichte der deutschen evangelischen Theologie seit dem deutschen Idealismus* (Berlin, 1960), p. 274.
49 "Schlatters Wort", p. 138.
50 Ibid., p. 139.
51 Paul Althaus, "Adolf Schlatters Gabe an die systematische Theologie", *Adolf Schlatter, Gedächtnisheft der Deutschen Theologie* (Stuttgart, 1938), pp. 31–32.
52 "Schlatters Gabe", p. 33.

c) Although *Martin Kähler* did not have as liberating an effect on Althaus as Schlatter, his influence must be mentioned. From Kähler Althaus learned a lesson similar to the one he gleaned from Holl: that a theology which is to call itself Protestant must be based on and center around the doctrine of justification.[53] "Martin Kählers Kerngedanke war die Rechtfertigung des Sünders durch den Glauben." By taking over Kählers "Kerngedanke" Althaus sought to give his theology what he termed a "protestantischen Grundzug".[54] But Kähler, perhaps more than Holl, also taught him to interpret and apply this doctrine of justification with careful avoidance of "confessional narrowness",[55] and in strict adherence to Sacred Scripture before all other norms.[56] It was such an application of the doctrine of justification which, as we shall see,[57] Althaus used as the final norm for his evaluation of the religions.

Under Kähler's influence, Althaus was also brought to face the question of the meaning of history in the economy of salvation. He felt he had to call Kähler to task for his apparent identification of the Christ of history with the Christ of faith; through such an identification, history seemed to be absorbed into and to lose its meaning within the act of faith.[58] For Althaus the historical Jesus and the historical situation were essential elements in the salvific encounter with God. And yet, in his teaching on faith, Althaus was to take over much of Kähler's concept of the "Übergeschichtlichen",[59] to the extent that it sometimes seems that history is not so essential after all. In the final analysis, Althaus implies that faith depends more on the influence of the transhistorical Christ than on the historical Jesus. The apparent openness and universality contained in Althaus' understanding of history and trans-history will be important in our evaluation of his final verdict on the religions. It will have to be balanced off against his insistence that the uniqueness of Christianity is rooted in an historical reality.[60]

2. All these influences on Althaus' formation and early development contributed to give his theology its incarnational — or to use his own terminology — its *anthropological* quality. Clearly and unmistakably, Althaus demands: "Die Theologie muß also als Anthropologie einsetzen." (CW, 64) The study of God can never be divorced from the study of man; indeed, to know God fully we must first know man.

53 Doerne, p. 453.
54 With this term Althaus describes P. Tillich's theology which also was built on Kähler's "Kerngedanke". Cf. "Die Bedeutung der Theologie P. Tillichs" (Vortrag, 20.5.64), p. 3.
55 Lohse, op. cit., p. 20.
56 Lohff, *Theologen*, p. 58.
57 Cf. § 55.
58 Cf. M. Kähler, *Der sogenannte historische Jesus und der geschichtliche biblische Christus*, 1896[2], p. 194; Stephan-Schmidt, pp. 271–272; Althaus, *Das sogenannte Kerygma und der historische Jesus*. Zur Kritik der heutigen Kerygma-Theologie (Gütersloh, 1958), pp. 10–27.
59 Although, in CW he was to abandon this terminology as too misleading. CW, 115.
60 Cf. § 58/3, § 59/2. Beyer, in his early study of Althaus' theology, lists other theologians whose influence, he feels, molded Althaus' thought: A. Ritschl. W. Herrmann, L. Ihmels, Karl Heim, and the "kenotic" theologians of the 16th and 17th Centuries. (cf. op. cit., pp. 61–67). In all these cases, however, where Beyer speaks of influences, it would perhaps be better to claim only "similarities", or at the most, secondary influences.

That theology must always be anthropological is demanded, *by the nature of God*. He has revealed himself not as a totally transcendent being who is entirely removed and detached from the world of man − but as *the God of man*, the God who shows himself in and through his dealings with man. A God, therefore, who is to be known in and through his creatures.

> Theologie und Anthropologie fallen wesentlich zusammen. Der Gott, von dem die Theologie handelt, ist der Gott des Menschen, der nur erkannt wird, sofern er den Menschen bestimmt, und der Mensch, von dem die Theologie handelt, ist der Mensch Gottes, der nur in seiner Gottesbeziehung als Mensch erkannt wird. (GD/II, 8)

And this creature, whom the theologian can never lose sight of, must be studied not only in himself − in his own inner constitution and dynamism − but also in his relationship to the world around him. The world itself − nature and history − must also have their place in a theology which is to grasp, as far as this is possible, God himself. "Unser Dasein ist wesenhaft ein Sein in der Welt der Dinge ... auch in unserem Bezogensein auf Gott bleiben wir fortwährend auf die Welt bezogen." (LD, 342; cf. also LD 121) Thus Lohff can list as one of the hallmarks of Althaus' theology his "Liebe zur Schöpfung und Offenheit gegen die Welt, die Gott mit sich versöhnt hat".[61]

Because Althaus adhered to what we may call this "anthropological conditioning" of theology, he was " ... ein leidenschaftlich an einer gegenwartsverbundenen Neuformulierung des Glaubens orientierter Theologe",[62] and his theology evinces " ... den entschlossenen Willen zur Gegenwärtigkeit, zur Lebensbezogenheit der Dogmatik".[63] At the beginning of his *Die Christliche Wahrheit*, Althaus proclaims clearly the incarnational character of his theology when he states the necessity

> ... daß die christliche Wahrheit aus ihrer früheren Gestalt heraus in eine neue übersetzt werde, in eine neue Sprache und Geisteswelt hinein; daß sie auf diese bestimmt bezogen, in ihr, für sie ausgedrückt werde. Das Christentum muß in neuer Geisteslage geistig immer wieder neu geboren werden, eine *neue Inkarnation* erfahren. (CW, 9; cf. 8, 15−16)

Because of this necessary, continual "reincarnation", Althaus, throughout his activity as a "systematic", speculative theologian, was constantly relating "systematic theology" to the ethical, social, political questions of the times, (no matter how difficult or "dangerous" this might be). And this was also the real reason why he strove for a "theology of the religions". The world of the religions, at the turn of the century, was being discovered in all its manifold richness and potential. The Christian could not live and incarnate his faith without relating it to this world. (CW, 16)

3. This incarnational-anthropological quality of Althaus' theology has been described − and summed up − by others as a *Vermittlungstheologie* or a "Theologie der echten Mitte".[64] From his middlepoint, Althaus tried to *mediate* between his Protestant principle of justification on the one side and the "forces" of the modern age, i.e. of the human situation, on the other. He evinced a "capacity for

61 Lohff, *Tendenzen*, p. 301.
62 Lohff, *Tendenzen*, p. 297.
63 Id., *Theologen*, p. 70.
64 M. Doerne, pp. 450−451; cf. also F. Konrad, *Das Offenbarungsverständnis in der evangelischen Theologie* (München, 1971), p. 35.

many-sided communication with these forces".[65] Thus his thought can be called a "link" or a "bridge" between the "traditional doctrine of the centuries" and the existential reality of the present and the future.[66] The strength of this bridge rested on the double foundation of what we have called Althaus' fidelity to his Protestant-Lutheran heritage, and his incarnational-anthropological openness.

Hans Graß describes "den Reichtum, die Weite, den anknüpfenden und *vermittelnden Charakter*" of Althaus' theology.

> Seine Theologie war *lutherisch*, aber ohne konfessionelle Enge; *kritisch*, gerade auch in Fragen der Bibelkritik, aber extremen Positionen abgeneigt; *weltoffen*, für eine positive Würdigung des Natürlichen, des Guten, Wahren und Schönen, des Humanen und nicht nur des Christentums.[67]

This "*vermittelnde Charakter*" of Althaus' thought established, according to Graß, the "strength" of Althaus' position, but also "in many respects its weakness".[68] These strengths and weaknesses present themselves most clearly in Althaus' efforts to mediate between his Protestant heritage and a fuller, more positive understanding of the non-Christian world.

§ 19. A Unique Case Study

1. Our analysis of Althaus' reaction to and rejection of Troeltsch and Barth, together with our examination of the Protestant-Lutheran and incarnational-anthropological qualities which run through his theology would seem to substantiate our belief that in his *goals* and in his *foundation*, Althaus presents us with a case study for a Protestant Theology of the Religions.

But he is not only *a* case study — one among many others. He is also, it would seem, a *unique* — we might even say — a singular case study. *Historically*, Althaus seemed to be one of the *first* significant reactions to Barth's theology of the non-Christian world which was clearly outside the camp of dialectical theology and still well within the limits of traditional Protestant-Lutheran thought.

After Karl Barth's thundering prophetic attack on religionism in its every form (especially as typified in Ernst Troeltsch), the religions were, for most German Protestant theologians, "disposed of". In Barth's trail, there reigned a "widespread lack of interest in the outside world".[69] Few theologians saw any need to step

---

65 Doerne, p. 451. Doerne adds:. "Es gibt im deutschen Sprachgebiet heute (i.e. 1949) nur noch einen Dogmatiker, der ihm hierin gleichkommt, den Schweizer Emil Brunner."

66 Ibid., p. 458.

67 Graß, "Die Theologie", p. 237; cf. also id., "Gedächtnisvorlesung", p. 245; cf. also W. Trillhaas, "Paul Althaus", *Luther*, 38 (1968) 49–50.

68 Graß, "Die Theologie", loc. cit. — And indeed, many of Althaus' critics accused him of falling into the pitfalls of the school of "Vermittlungstheologie", as it expressed itself during the period between Schleiermacher and Ritschl. They felt he was too much on both sides and therefore guilty either of betraying certain untouchable truths or of not being clear enough as to just what his own position was. Cf. H. W. Schmidt, *Zeit und Ewigkeit*. Die letzten Voraussetzungen der dialektischen Theologie, Gütersloh, 1927, pp. 108–134; W. Wiesner, "Der Gott der Wirklichkeit und der wirkliche Gott", VF (Theologischer Jahresbericht, 1947–48), pp. 96–97. — Whether such accusation are justified is a question we will have to face in our final analysis of Althaus' theology of the religions.

69 Nürnberger, p. 12.

outside of these confined interests. Althaus, with his concern for the religions based on his doctrine of "Uroffenbarung", stands as a strange species on the time's theological terrain. "Mit seiner Betonung der Uroffenbarung (hat er) am weitesten über die anthropologische Selbstbeschränkung der Religionstheologie seiner Zeit hinausgewiesen."[70]

Other exceptions, i.e. other attempts to criticize and correct Barth's interpretation of the religious world, were few. As Nürnberger points out, *Emil Brunner* was perhaps the only other systematic theologian who, contemporaneously with Althaus, took up a position against Barth's verdict on the non-Christian world.[71] There was, no doubt, a great deal of reciprocal influence between both theologians, but for the most part, as Althaus himself explicitly states, they formulated their positions independently.[72] Similarities in their understanding of revelation outside of Christ and in their description of the religions' role in salvation are extensive. And still, Brunner enunciated and defended his stance against Barth from *within* the camp of dialectical theology. He wished to remain in basic agreement with the principles of Barth's dialectic, especially concerning the transcendence of God and the immanence of all that is human, even though he tried to "qualify" this immanence through his *Eristik*.[73] This pitted him against Barth, but not as clearly and forcefully as Althaus, who from his early years pronounced a sharp "No" to the extremes of the dialectical school. The differences between the two theologians stand forth especially in what, for both of them, is the foundation for their evaluation of the religions: their doctrines of general revelation. Theoretically, Althaus' "Uroffenbarung" is very similar to Brunner's "Schöpfungsoffenbarung"; but phenomenologically and practically, Althaus attributes much more efficacy and independence to his general revelation than Brunner does. Thus, Althaus' "Uroffenbarung" would seem to supply a broader, more "applicable" and more positive foundation for a theological understanding of the religions.[74]

---

70 Peter Beyerhaus, "Zur Theologie der Religionen im Protestantismus", KuD, 15 (1969) 98.
71 Nürnberger, p. 12; E. Brunner, *Religionsphilosophie evangelischer Theologie* (München, 1926); id., *Die Absolutheit Jesu* (Berlin, 1927); id., *Christusbotschaft im Kampf mit den Religionen* (Stuttgart, 1931); id., *Offenbarung und Vernunft* (Darmstadt, 1961²), pp. 73–97; 242–299. – R. Otto and F. Heiler also confronted the problem of the religions but did so more from the basis of comparative religions than of systematic theology.
72 Cf. *Theologische Aufs.* II, p. 173.
73 Cf. Heinrich Leipold, *Theorie der Verkündigung*. Der Streit um die Frage der 'Anknüpfung' zwischen E. Brunner und K. Barth, (Habilitationsschrift, Marburg, 1969), manuscript.
74 In his doctrine of general revelation, Brunner insists on a "von Christus her" much more strictly – and we might say, much more consistently – than Althaus. (cf. § 41, § 48/1) The "Schöpfungsoffenbarung" can become a true revelation only in Christ's light, only "auf Grund des biblischen Zeugnisses von ihr". (*Offenbarung und Vernunft*, p. 77). "Die allgemeine Offenbarung genügt also nicht, nachdem einmal der Mensch ein Sünder geworden, um ihn den wahren Gott erkennen zu lassen." (ibid., p. 91; cf. pp. 73–93) This general revelation, therefore, is a "principium essendi" for man, but *not* a "principium cognoscendi". (ibid., p. 96; cf. also *Dogmatik* I, Zürich, 1960², pp. 24, 28; Leipold, pp. 252–276, 304) Again, much more resolutely than Althaus (cf. § 37/3, § 51/2), Brunner stresses that "die fundamentale Bedeutung der Schöpfungsoffenbarung" is to constitute man a sinner and to let him experience his sinfulness. (*Offenbarung und Vernunft*, p. 92;

Another reaction to Barth's disposal of religion and the religions came from *Paul Tillich*. Tillich shared wholeheartedly Althaus' convictions that Barth's "Supernaturalism" contradicted the content of the Christian message and consequently that his exclusion of the religions from God's plan was unjust.[75] But Tillich's response to Barth went "beyond" that of Althaus. We can say, perhaps, that Tillich's final view of the non-Christian world was formulated *outside* the limits of German Protestant theology. That it was removed from *German* theology was due simply to the fact that National Socialism forced him to immigrate to America in 1933 — an event which, as Tillich admits, was to change the mold of his thinking.[76] That he was beyond Protestant *theology* is to be attributed to Tillich's philosophical-ontological methodology which sometimes seemed to throw theological caution to the wind. Without ignoring the content of Scripture and Protestant tradition, Tillich used more his *philosophy* of religion as the starting point for his understanding of religious phenomena — and of the practical relation between the religions and Christianity.[77] This is *not* to say that Tillich's views are any less valid than Althaus'. Yet they are less adapted and "workable" for a study which seeks to analyze what a theology consciously based on the heritage of the Reformation can say about the non-Christian religious world.

2. *Still today* a case study of Althaus' theology of the religions preserves its significance. For even though Barth's attack on "religionism" has lost its initial,

---

cf. pp. 78–84; *Dogmatik*, p. 27) — On the basis of this understanding of general revelation, Brunner concludes to a theology of the religions in which the negative elements of error and sin far outshine all positive content — even more so than in Althaus' final verdict. (cf. § 63) The religions misuse the revelation offered them; they never come to know the true God; in fact, Brunner seems to detect an evolution in the history of religions away from the true God. (*Religionsphilosophie evangelischer Theologie*, pp. 67, 73–74, 3–8, 22; *Offenbarung und Vernunft* p. 282.) All religions end up as ways of self-redemption. (*Offenbarung und Vernunft*, pp. 298–299) Even though Brunner can speak of the relationship between the Gospel and religions as one of "Erfüllung", it is the concept of "Gericht" which plays the predominating role. (*Offenbarung und Vernunft*, pp. 296–297; *Religionsphilosophie*, p. 66; cf. also Leipold, pp. 171–175.)

75 P. Tillich, "What is Wrong with the 'Dialectical' Theology?", JR, 15 (1935) 127–145; id., "Natural and Revealed Religion", *Christendom*, 1935, pp. 159–170.

76 P. Tillich, "Das Protestantische Zeitalter", *Der Protestantismus, Prinzip und Wirklichkeit* (Stuttgart, 1950), p. 10; cf. Zahrnt, p. 389; Thus it is that Tillich and the meaning of his theology were "discovered" much later in Europe than in America; cf. B. Jaspert, "Zum Werk Paul Tillichs", *Erbe und Auftrag*, 47 (1971) 325–326.

77 Tillich's definition of religion shows its philosophical coloring: "Religion is the state of being grasped by an ultimate concern, a concern which qualifies all other concerns as preliminary and which itself contains the answer to the question of the meaning of our life." Such a definition is, as he explicitly states, "... required both by the Protestant background of my own philosophy of religion and by the present religious situation ..." *Christianity and the Encounter of the World Religions* (New York, 1963), p. 4 — J. L. Adams, in his study of Tillich's early works (till 1945), points out the intimate bonds between a theology and philosophy of religion in Tillich's thought. According to Tillich, there is "no approach to religion at all without what we call theological ontology, the understanding of the Unconditioned or the Transcendent as that which gives meaning to existence, as the transcendent power of being". *Paul Tillich's Philosophy of Culture, Science and Religion* (New York, 1965), pp. 201–202. Cf. also pp. 192–202, 185–188.

sharp impact, even though Barth himself toned down the force of his position, his influence still seems to remain and still seems to impede a vital theological concern for the religions as religions. As is generally admitted, Protestant theology today, especially in Germany, has still not produced an answer to Barth and worked out a complete, pondered theology of the religions.[78] Those contemporary German Protestant theologians and missiologists who have tried to answer the theological question of the religions have well been called "rühmliche Ausnahmen".[79] And yet one can even ask whether these exceptions — once we clear away differences in terminology and tone — have really gone beyond the basic content of Althaus' response to Troeltsch and Barth. It would seem that still today, for better or for worse, Althaus remains a case study for a Protestant theology of the religions. This is a question we shall examine in our final chapter.

---

78 Cf. § 70/2.

79 Beyerhaus, op. cit., p. 100; Hans-Werner Gensichen, "Die christliche Mission in der Begegnung mit den Religionen", *Kirche in der außerchristlichen Welt* (Regensburg, 1967), p. 74; cf. also, Benz, p. 35; Nürnberger, p. 134.

Chapter III

The Religions: Echo of Uroffenbarung

The goals for Althaus' theology of the religions — which, we may say, are or should be the goals for any theology of the non-Christian world — were clear: to avoid what he felt was the relativizing universalism of Troeltsch and the nullifying exclusivism of Barth. The *foundation* and the tools which he used to trace his middle way between these two extremes were the same foundation which Troeltsch and Barth had laid for their positions: *the doctrine of revelation*. Althaus' doctrine of Uroffenbarung[1] forms the basis, the starting point, the guiding light for his entire teaching on the non-Christian religious world. Without his teaching on Uroffenbarung it would be both theoretically and practically impossible to expound and properly grasp his understanding of the religions. In this chapter, therefore, we will lay the foundation for a Protestant theology of the religions, as proposed by Althaus, by establishing and delineating: 1) the relation between religion and revelation, 2) the reality of a general revelation and 3) the manner in which this revelation finds expression.

I. Uroffenbarung: the Foundation and Starting-Point for a Theology of the Religions

§ 20. Religions Originate from and Are Bearers of Uroffenbarung

1. Althaus' concept of Uroffenbarung — general revelation — is an essential part of his general definition of religion. Here we can understand more fully his basic agreement with Troeltsch:

> Religion ist das bewußte Verhältnis des Menschen zu dem ihm sich bezeugenden Gott: der Mensch *anerkennt* die Wirklichkeit Gottes in Beugung und Hingabe und *sucht* bei ihm die Heilung der ihm gegenüber erfahrenen, sonst unaufhebbaren Daseins-Not.
>
> *Wir verstehen die Religion damit als Echo des Menschen auf die Selbstbezeugung Gottes und als Ausdruck seiner Lage unter der Selbstbezeugung ...* Die Religion ist also *theozentrisch* und *anthropozentrisch* zugleich: *Bestimmtsein* von der Wirklichkeit der Gottheit = *Streben* nach Überwindung des Daseins-Widerspruchs durch die Gottheit. (CW, 93–94, emphasis mine)
>
> Religion nennen wir das Ergriffen- und Bestimmtsein des Menschen von der Gewißheit um die sich bezeugende Wirklichkeit des "Heiligen". Das Heilige wird *erfahren* und *vorgestellt* ... (GD/I, 99)

The "reality" of God, his "self-witnessing" — that means a genuinely divine revelation — is behind all religion. In relating this revelation to religion, Althaus employs a recurring twofold terminology: "anerkennt ... sucht", "theozentrisch ... anthropozentrisch", "Bestimmtsein ... Streben", "erfahren ... vorgestellt". Such terminology implies that: 1) Uroffenbarung is the *origin* and creative force of the reli-

---

1 For reasons of stylistic unity, we shall spell the word "Uroffenbarung" without a hyphen ("Ur-Offenbarung") and shall use it in the English text without quotation marks.

gions, and that 2) the religions are the *expression* and the phenomenological form of Uroffenbarung.

2. Throughout his works, in varying yet complementary terminology, Althaus describes how Uroffenbarung constitutes the *origin* of religion. He clearly states "alle Religion (ist) durch 'Offenbarung' Gottes begründet". (CW, 139) " ... sie (religion) entsteht unter der Selbstbezeugung Gottes". (CW, 93) This "founding" and "originating" take place mainly in an *experience* of God in his Uroffenbarung. Because man is "touched, bound, and held" by the only true God in this Uroffenbarung, he produces his religions and gives form to his gods. (CW, 139) This experiencing of Uroffenbarung is not something which took place only at the beginning of history and which, as it were, put the phenomenon of religion into motion, without having to continue itself. Rather, Uroffenbarung must be a continuing life-force which keeps religion in existence. "Wir suchen die Uroffenbarung nicht am Anfange der Geschichte der Religion, sondern überall 'hinter' ihr ..." (CW, 41) "Religion gibt es, weil Gott sich den Menschen nicht unbezeugt gelassen hat, weil ständig Uroffenbarung geschieht." (CW, 141) Only because man is constantly "under pressure" from Uroffenbarung, does he continue to create his religions, in whatever form they may take. "Der Mensch kommt *jederzeit* von der ... Bezeugung der Wirklichkeit Gottes in der Wirklichkeit des Menschen und seiner Welt. Unter dem Druck dieser Wirklichkeit schafft er seine Religion." (WE 2, 282; emphasis mine) Agreeing point-blankly with Troeltsch, Althaus could state: "Das Wissen um Gott ist das *Apriori* aller Religionen" (CW, 138; emphasis mine). "Gott ist das Apriori aller Götzen." (WE 2, 282 f.)

3. Thus, in surveying the vast expanse of religious history, the theologian is faced with a manifold *expression* of Uroffenbarung. No matter how unclear or corrupted the religious form may be, "sie (God's self-revealing) liegt ihr doch zugrunde und bezeugt sich durch alle Entstellung hindurch." (CW, 93) In his definitions of religions, Althaus sees the religions as the "echo", "expression", "recognition" of Uroffenbarung. " ... sie weisen auf Gottes Uroffenbarung zurück" (GD/I, 99). "Wir sehen auf die Religionen mit Ehrfurcht vor der Ur-kunde von Gottes Wirklichkeit."[2] Again, the manner in which God's revelation finds its manifold expressions in the religions is a dynamic process of *experience*. It is the result of man feeling the reality of God in the form of a mysterious question — and then setting out in search of this reality. Uroffenbarung is both behind this quest and is contained in man's feeble, failing attempts to carrying it out. "Die Religionen, theologisch verstanden, sind Versuche der sündigen Menschheit, auf dem Boden der Uroffenbarung die offenen Heilsfragen zu lösen." (GD/I, 102) Both within the meaningfulness and truth of this searching and within its incomplete, faulty answers, Uroffenbarung is finding voice. The dynamism behind the many forms of religion is God's "call" experienced in Uroffenbarung. "Das 'fecisti nos ad te' Augustins muß, so oder so, das innerste Geheimnis aller menschlichen Geistesgeschichte sein."[3]

4. Uroffenbarung finds expression in the religions not only in the individual's personal searching and experience of this call. It is also the force behind the illuminations and utterances of *prophetism*. "Zu der Uroffenbarung gehören auch

2 "Die Wirklichkeit Gottes", *Zeitwende*, 9 (1933) 85.
3 "Christentum und Geistesleben", *Evangelium und Leben* (Gütersloh, 1927), p. 37.

57

die Propheten in der Religionsgeschichte." (CW, 141) Indeed, prophets can be considered to be even more reliable and effective voices of God's revelation in the religions. They are helps — always imperfect in themselves — for the even more imperfect efforts of the individual in his search for the divine reality.

> Gott ist in zweifacher Weise in der Religionsgeschichte gegenwärtig: 1) er steht hinter den Religionen, indem er sich ständig allen Menschen bezeugt; 2) er greift ein in die Welt der Religionen, indem er sich Propheten ruft und durch sie Erneuerung der überlieferten Religion, einen Durchbruch durch ihre Schranken wirkt. Gott schafft, daß überhaupt Religion wird, und Gott ist am Werke in den großen Neuanfängen durch Propheten. (CW, 141)

This claim that God can use prophets in other religions to give expression to his Uroffenbarung was not too clear in Althaus' earlier writings. In CW, however, he can state that he is in basic agreement with Nathan Söderblom's belief that the prophetic religions are more pronounced forms of the general revelation behind all religions. Althaus supports this position clearly: "Die Theologie ist auch nicht gehalten, zu bestreiten, daß ein Prophet wie Zarathustra trotz allem von Gott Wahrheit empfangen hatte." (CW, 98)[4]

Because Uroffenbarung is both the origin and the expression behind every religion, Althaus could view the religious world as a basic *unity*. Despite their variety, despite the varying degrees of perfection with which they give echo to Uroffenbarung, all religions can be considered to play the same role in the economy of salvation. Again, Althaus agrees with Troeltsch: there is a sameness behind all religions. "Überall ist Religion ..., und bei aller Verschiedenheit der Religionen ist ihr Problem und Thema im Grunde das eine und selbe." (CW, 333)

§ 21. Theology of Religions Contained in Theology of Uroffenbarung

Because Uroffenbarung is dynamically present and takes concrete form within the religions, Althaus argues that neither general revelation nor the religions can be fully grasped by the theologian if studied separately. Like matter and form in scholastic terminology, they remain distinct; yet they are not real nor understandable unless joined in a composite unity. "So kann es theologisch nicht befriedigen, daß die Theologie des 19. und beginnenden 20. Jahrhunderts die ursprüngliche Offenbarung anerkennt, solange sie sie nicht auch im Aufbau der Dogmatik zur Geltung bringt, in ihrem Gehalte darstellt und zu den Religionen ins Verhältnis setzt." And the same applies to the religions, for "Religion und Religionen bleiben unbegriffen, werden nur phänomenologisch oder anthropologisch genommen, wenn sie nicht auf dem Hintergrund der allgemeinen Offenbarung Gottes gesehen werden." (CW, 53)

Here, then, we have the *method* of Althaus' theology of religions — the *means* by which he would construct his middle path between Troeltsch and Barth: by establishing and elaborating the relationship between Uroffenbarung and the concrete religions:

---

4 Here Althaus refers to Hanna Wolff, *Der lebendige Gott*. Nathan Söderbloms Beitrag zur Offenbarungsfrage (1938); cf. also N. Söderblom, *Der lebendige Gott im Zeugnis der Religionsgeschichte*. (Nachgelassene Gifford-Vorlesungen, München, 1942), pp. 315–373, passim.

So ist die Aufgabe, in der Grundlegung der Dogmatik die Schöpfungsoffenbarung und die Religion miteinander, in ihrer Bezogenheit aufeinander darzustellen. Die Menschen kommen von den Religionen her zu Christus, und sie kommen von den Religionen trotz allem von der Uroffenbarung her zu Christus. Die Dogmatik muß in ihrer Prinzipienlehre nach der in der Uroffenbarung erschlossenen Gotteswahrheit fragen, welche in aller Entstellung doch der Wahrheitsgehalt der Religionen ist. (CW, 53)

As Carl Heinz Ratschow observes, the basic motive and purpose of Althaus' entire doctrine of Uroffenbarung was "der theologische Begriff der Religion. ... Darauf führt das Kapitel von der Uroffenbarung (in CW) zu ... Es scheint uns eindeutig zu sein, daß es dieses Interesse an den Religionen und ihrer theologischen Beurteilung ist, das Althaus zu seiner Lehre von der Uroffenbarung bewog."[5]

Therefore it is only on the basis of Uroffenbarung that we can fully understand and weigh Althaus' statements on the religions. His works which explicitly treat the religions are, when compared with the bulk of his publications, relatively few and contain a large number of unclarified questions and implications. Their full content can be grasped only when *clarified* and *completed* within the framework of Uroffenbarung. This is what our study seeks to do: to present Althaus' Protestant theology of the religions by analyzing "die Schöpfungsoffenbarung und die Religion miteinander, in ihrer Bezogenheit aufeinander." (CW, 53)

II. The Reality of Uroffenbarung

§ 22. Uroffenbarung – Its Definition and Terminology

1. Althaus' doctrine of Uroffenbarung can well be called the *hallmark* of his entire theology.[6] It played a prominent role in his first appearances on the theological scene in Germany, (especially as a corrective to Barth's influence),[7] and was to develop into one of the primary elements in his theology's "foundation" (CW, 19): it also was an essential hermeneutical tool in understanding the contents of the Gospel (systematic theology) (GD/I, 18; CW 5,4) and in applying it to the contemporary scene (ethics). "Es wird wohl kaum eine gegenwärtige christliche Dogmatik, auch keine römisch-katholische, geben, die der Uroffenbarung eine derart betonte Rolle zumißt, wie diese Dogmatik, (i.e. CW) was nicht nur aus ihrem äußeren Aufbau, sondern auch aus der ... hohen theologischen Relevanz

---

5 C. H. Ratschow, *Der angefochtene Glaube* (Gütersloh, 1957), pp. 285–286; Graß agrees when he points out that Althaus was able to pass judgment on the religions "von seiner Uroffenbarungslehre her". "Gedächtnisvorlesung für Paul Althaus", *Nachrichten der evang.-luth. Kirche in Bayern*, August 1966.

6 "Mit seiner Lehre von der 'Uroffenbarung' hat Althaus seinen charakteristischen Beitrag zur gegenwärtigen evangelischen Theologie geliefert." H. Zahrnt, *Die Sache mit Gott* (München, 1966), p. 77; "Es ist heute vor allem Althaus, der die Auffassung vertritt: Die Christus-Offenbarung als Offenbarung der vergebenden Gnade Gottes (die 'Heilsoffenbarung') setzte eine 'Uroffenbarung' voraus ...". H. G. Fritzsche, *Lehrbuch der Dogmatik.* Bd. I (Göttingen, 1964), p. 291.

7 Cf. TG and "Christentum und Geistesleben", pp. 37–38.

erhellt, die sie ihr zumißt."[8] It can indeed be said that Uroffenbarung determines "the systematic structure of Paul Althaus' theology"[9], and that Althaus bases his theological method on the two pillars of the Gospel and Uroffenbarung.[10]

2. The clearest and most complete definition of Uroffenbarung is found in CW; it contains all the elements which we will have to analyze and apply in order to understand Althaus' final appraisal of the religions:

> Wir unterscheiden von der Heils-Offenbarung Gottes in Jesus Christus seine ursprüngliche Selbstbezeugung oder Uroffenbarung oder Grund-Offenbarung. Das Beiwort 'ursprünglich' bzw. die Vorsilbe 'Ur' haben nicht historischen, sondern prinzipiellen Sinn. Sie sagen von der gemeinten Offenbarung nicht, daß sie ihren Ort am Anfange der menschlichen Geschichte hatte, daß sie nur an das erste Geschlecht der Menschen geschah; sondern, daß sie von der Heils-Offenbarung Gottes schon vorausgesetzt wird, daß sie ihr zugrunde liegt, daß diese sich auf sie wesentlich zurückbezieht. Nicht von einem Präteritum ist die Rede, sondern von einem Präsens, das aber dem Perfectum präsens der Heils-Offenbarung wesentlich immer schon vorausgeht. (CW, 41)

The general content of this definition contains three essential igredients:

a) Althaus makes it absolutely clear that Uroffenbarung is *God's revelation*. It is not simply a human ability to arrive at a knowledge of God, as certain Catholic theologians might hold. It is not only a matter of man experiencing a restlessness, an incompleteness, a questioning and searching, as many Protestant theologians might concede; it is not simply a philosophical "apriori" which is directed towards something beyond man, as Troeltsch would argue;[11] it is not simply an "impression" or a "burnt-out crater" of some long lost revelatory experience, as the early Barth would hold.[12] Although Uroffenbarung may include or make use of all these elements, it is much more — it is *God's* work. It has its origin and its actual existence not only in man but in a divine activity. It is, in Catholic terms, a *supernatural* reality. And this implies that, in this respect, Uroffenbarung is not different from God's revelation in Christ: both revelations share a *divine*, supernatural qualification.

b) In his definition, Althaus also insists that the characterization of Uroffenbarung and Christ's revelation must be such as makes both revelations *clearly distinct* but at the same time sets them both in an *essential relationship* to each other. Althaus stressed that this distinction is not always as clear as it should be in the terminology of many otherwise reliable and commendable theologians. Any description of general revelation is "to be suspected" if it does not sufficiently underline the uniqueness of Christ's revelation and if it allows the impression that the only difference between the two revelations is one of degree — of completion

---

8 H. G. Pöhlmann, "Das Problem der Uroffenbarung bei Paul Althaus", KuD, 16 (1970) 242–258.

9 G. Hillerdal, *Gehorsam gegen Gott und Menschen*. Luthers Lehre von der Obrigkeit und die moderne evangelische Staatsethik (Göttingen, 1955), p. 143; W. Tilgner, *Volksnomostheologie und Schöpfungsglaube*. Ein Beitrag zur Geschichte des Kirchenkampfes (Göttingen, 1966), p. 199.

10 W. Wiesner, "Der Gott der 'Wirklichkeit' und der wirkliche Gott", VF (*Theologischer Jahresbericht 1947/48*), p. 102; cf. also M. Doerne, "Zur Dogmatik von Paul Althaus", ThLZ, 74 (1949) 456–458.

11 Cf. § 5/3.

12 Cf. RB, pp. 67, 225, 105–106, 188, 212, 234.

or fulfillment.[13] And yet the difference must be one which unites both revelations in the unity of God's *one* plan. — Here we have a preview of the difficulties in determining this difference: it cannot be one of *quality*, as if one revelation were divine and the other not; yet neither can it be one of quantity, as if one were more divine than (i.e. the mere fulfillment of) the other. We will face and try to resolve these tensions in our next chapter when we apply the full theological content of Uroffenbarung to the religions.

c) As part of his definition, Althaus also makes it clear that Uroffenbarung *cannot be* considered as something which belongs to the *past* or which derives its present meaning only from the past. In a twofold sense, Uroffenbarung cannot be confined to the past: it is not a reality which took place only at the beginning of time, nor is it something which is real only before Christ. In other words, it continues in its actuality after both the first *and* the second Adam! It is part of the actuality and the continuation of mankind and history: " ... 'Ur' meint die Offenbarung, die unser Menschsein *jederzeit* erst begründet, in der es seinen Ursprung hat. Nicht vom geschichtlichen Anfang, sondern von dem stets *gegenwärtigen* wesentlichen Ursprung des Menschen als Menschen, der Geschichte als Geschichte ist die Rede." (GD/I, 15, emphasis mine) Indeed, Althaus placed the actuality — the "prinzipiellen Sinn" — of Uroffenbarung *within* the actuality of Christ's revelation: just as Christ's revelation continues as a "Perfectum präsens", Uroffenbarung goes on as a "Präsens". In fact, Christ's revelation would not be able to exercise its present reality without the reality of Uroffenbarung. — Thus it is already clear that although Uroffenbarung must be related and subordinated to New Testament revelation, it possesses an existence, a certain independence of its own.

3. From Althaus' definition it is evident that the terminology which he employs to determine this "other revelation" is quite incidental. As long as the concept is clear, he was willing to admit almost any nomenclature. And indeed, throughout his works, the terms do vary. In his earliest writings, the word "Uroffenbarung" does not occur. In "Christentum und Geistesleben", 1925, he prefered to speak of "Grundoffenbarung".[14] By 1929, in the first edition of his *Grundriß der Dogmatik*, this same concept was presented in a much more detailed exposition as "Die Selbstbezeugung Gottes in der Wirklichkeit des Menschen und der Welt". (GD¹/I, 10–14) The term Uroffenbarung seems to appear officially for the first time in Althaus' article, "Die Wirklichkeit Gottes".[15] The expression is not his own invention. Within Catholic theology the term, which has a much different meaning than that of Althaus', has a lengthy history.[16] Among Protestant theologians it turns up for the first time during the 19th Centu-

---

13 Cf. "Die Inflation des Begriffs der Offenbarung in der gegenwärtigen Theologie", ZSTh, 18 (1941) 142 ff.
14 In all probability, Althaus' early predilection for this term stemmed from Tillich's article, "Rechtfertigung und Zweifel" (1924) which, as we shall see, Althaus was to refer to frequently when unfolding his own ideas of a revelation outside of Christ. "Rechtfertigung und Zweifel", *Vorträge der theologischen Konferenz zu Gießen*, F. 29 (Gießen, 1924), pp. 19–32, also in *Gesammelte Werke*, Bd. VIII, pp. 85–100; cf. GW, VII, pp. 93, 95.
15 "Die Wirklichkeit Gottes", pp. 81–92.
16 The Catholic understanding of Uroffenbarung — which, it must be stressed, is *not* part of the official, magisterial teaching of the Roman Church — distinguishes itself from Althaus' concept in that it understands the prefex, "Ur", *literally*. It implies a *first*, "primitive" revelation to Adam which was then passed on through all following generations in

ry in Johann Tobias Beck, but only in passing.[17] August Friedrich Christian Vilmar also makes use of it.[18] In any case, it irrevocably became part of Althaus' theological wardrobe in 1935 in an article entitled "Uroffenbarung". Here he explicitly acknowledged the dangers inherent in this terminology and stated that he had avoided it in his *Grundriß* of 1929, "(um) den weiten Abstand und die Einzeigkeit der biblischen Offenbarung auszudrücken". (Ur 7; GD[1]/I, 10 f.) And although he would allow any name for this revelation, "wenn wir uns über diese Wirklichkeit verständigen können" (Ur 6), he feels the term "Uroffenbarung" is theologically and exegetically founded and expresses the "Wirklichkeit" more precisely than other "names". Thus, in his 1936 edition of GD, the paragraph on "Die Selbstbezeugung Gottes" of the 1929 edition became "Die Uroffenbarung" in a detailed exposition which was to supply the structure for his even-more detailed presentation of Uroffenbarung in CW, 1947.[19]

Although Althaus definitely preferred this term, he by no means limited himself to it. The "synonyms" he makes use of are many and sometimes quite surprising: "ursprüngliche Selbstbezeugung Gottes",[20] "Grundoffenbarung",[21] "allgemeine Offenbarung",[22] "vocatio gene-

various degrees of clarity. It is a mixture of both natural and supernatural revelation, containing preternatural gifts and certain internal illuminations. Its contents embrace both ethical and religious truths, especially concerning original sin and the promise of a redeemer — in other words, the basic content of Genesis 1—3. Although it is difficult to pinpoint just when Uroffenbarung expressly and for the first time appeared in the history of Catholic theology, it was much in evidence in the 15th Century when the New World came into theological view and theologians had to wrestle with the question as to how these newly discovered peoples, who had never heard of Christ, were to find salvation. But it was chiefly during the first half of the 19th Century that the doctrine of Uroffenbarung assumed special importance in Catholic currents, especially under the French school of Traditionalism and then in the Tübingen School (J. S. von Drey, J. A. Möhler, P. Schanz). W. Schmidt and W. Koppers — mixing theology with ethnology, attempted to give Uroffenbarung a scientific basis; but their research, admirable in its scope, is seen today to have been biased by a faulty psychology and philosophy of religions and by too hasty theological presuppositions. Uroffenbarung, for the most part, is no longer held by contemporary Catholic theologians in its traditional or literal sense. Today it is understood "existentially" — i.e. much more in the interpretation given it by Althaus! Literature: J.S. von Drey, "Die Urreligion durch die Uroffenbarung", ThQ, 8 (1826) 237—284; W. Schmidt, *Der Ursprung der Gottesidee*, Bd. I (Münster, 1912), pp. 186—191; Bd. VI (1926), pp. 269—508; W. Koppers, "Uroffenbarung im Lichte profaner Forschung", *Hochland*, 44 (1951)69—72; N. Hötzel, *Die Uroffenbarung im französischen Traditionalismus* (München, 1962); J. Heislbetz, "Uroffenbarung", LThK[2], X, 565—567; H. Fries, "Uroffenbarung", *Sacramentum Mundi*, IV, 1124—1129; J. Götz, "Theorie der Uroffenbarung", *Orientierung*, 21 (1957) 227 ff.

17 Cf. Gloege, RGG[3] VI, 1199.
18 *Dogmatik* I (1874), p. 145; cf. Pöhlmann, "Uroffenbarung", p. 243.
19 Cf. GD[2]/I, 14—27. This exposition of Uroffenbarung was to be preserved verbally in all the following editions of GD. The only change, and a very significant one, is the omission in GD[3] of sub-division 4 of GD[2] (pp. 17—19) in which Althaus had traced Uroffenbarung in the "Ordnungen" of the Third Reich. Cf. P. Knitter, "Die Uroffenbarungslehre von Paul Althaus — Anknüpfungspunkt für den Nationalsozialismus? Eine Studie zum Verhältnis von Theologie und Ideologie", EvTh 33 (1973) 138—164.
20 CW, 41; "Bedenken zur 'Theologischen Erklärung' der Barmer Bekenntnis-Synode", *Korrespondenzblatt der evang.-luth. Geistlichen in Bayern*, 59 (1934) 319.
21 "Christentum und Geistesleben", p. 38; "Die Inflation", p. 143; CW, 41.
22 "Bedenken", p. 319; Ur, 6; CW, 34, 52—53.

ralis",[23] even "manifestatio naturalis" (GD[1]/I, 10) or "natürliche Theologie".[24] Such a wide, varying terminology is an indication of the far-reaching content (sometimes seeming to reach farther than Althaus intended) of his concept of Uroffenbarung.

§ 23. Scriptural Foundation for the Reality of Uroffenbarung

1. Althaus was convinced that his claims for the doctrine of Uroffenbarung had a sound basis both in Scripture and in Protestant tradition. Here we shall study primarily how he established the *existence* — i.e. the fact or reality — of a revelation outside of Christ from God's Word and from Tradition. The theological *content* and *purpose* of the Scriptural doctrine of Uroffenbarung shall be taken up more detailedly in our next chapter when we evaluate Uroffenbarung and relate it explicitly to the religions.

In general, Althaus felt that God's Word in the New Testament in no way claimed to be "die erste und einzige Selbstbezeugung Gottes an die Menschheit und den einzelnen Menschen". (CW, 37) Running throughout the content and method of the New Testament Kerygma is the presupposition that God has already spoken, that man already knows who this God is, that he has already encountered this God. "Das Evangelium meint nicht, das Verhältnis Gottes zum Menschen erst zu setzen, zu begründen ..." (CW, 37) This is the implicit, yet basic attitude of the New Testament concerning the object to which it addressed itself; without acknowledging this attitude, we cannot truly understand the content of the message. Such a general attitude, underlying every page of the New Testament, found an explicit expression for Althaus in the original mission sermons which appeal to and "hook onto" (anknüpfen) a divine self-witnessing, "die jederzeit ergeht, von der die Menschheit in jeder Gegenwart herkommt". (GD/I, 14) These texts, together with the Johannine concept of the Logos, form the main force of Althaus' "argumentum ex Scriptura" for Uroffenbarung.

Rom. 1, 18 ff.

2. In this passage, in which Paul traces the historical and existential context into which the Gospel of justification is and must be spoken, the apostle clearly affirms a revelation of God *before* the announcing of this Gospel. It is, Althaus insists, a *divine revelation* in the true sense of the word. God, his $\delta \acute{v} \nu \alpha \mu \iota \varsigma$ and his $\theta \epsilon \iota \acute{o} \tau \eta \varsigma$ (vs. 20), is the object; and this object is $\phi \alpha \nu \epsilon \rho \acute{o} \nu$ ($\dot{\epsilon} \phi \alpha \nu \acute{\epsilon} \rho \omega \sigma \epsilon \nu$). This is the same word Paul uses in Rom. 3,21 to depict God's revelation in Christ, i.e. his "Heilsoffenbarung". (Ur, 7; GD/I, 14) Both in its object and in its process, then, Paul is speaking about a "revelatio divina". — As we have seen, Althaus rejects any attempts, especially those of Barth, to identify this revelation with that of Christ.[25] That such an identification is impossible is evident from the *addressees* of this revelation. They are neither "man in his original state" (CW, 40) nor are they heathen-Christians. Paul was addressing himself to all men of all times. Be-

23 "Bedenken", p. 319.
24 "Natürliche Theologie und Christusglaube", *Um die Wahrheit des Evangeliums*, p. 34 ff.; Ur, 5; "Das alte Testament in der 'Naturgeschichte des Glaubens'", *Werke und Tage*. Festschrift für Rudolf Alexander Schröder zum 60. Geburtstag (Berlin, 1938), p. 13.
25 Cf. § 14/2.

cause he is tracing the history of mankind in this passage, he may speak about the origins of paganism as a past event. But for him, this history is repeated throughout the ages, as it is indicated by the present form (ἐστίν) in vs. 19. (BR, 21) That this revelation is an ever-occuring reality is also indicated by the twofold means through which it takes place: 1) the visible reality of creation – ἀπὸ κτίσεως κόσμου – ποιήματα and 2) man's νοῦς (vs. 20). Creation remains, and man's power of perceiving and reasoning remains; thus, this revelation remains as a present reality. (CW, 38; cf. also BR, 20–21)

Further, the actuality of this revelation is demanded from the *general context*: Paul was preparing the scene for the arrival of the Gospel, asserting man's guilt and therefore his need of this Gospel. The general revelation he proposes here is necessary for establishing this need and this guilt. Without this revelation man would not be able to experience God's judgment and his own need of redemption.[26] Thus, just as the Gospel is repeated and is real in the present moment, so must this revelation be repeated and be real today. Althaus sums up Paul's understanding of this general revelation: "Diese Uroffenbarung ist Gegenwart". (BR, 21)

By means of this Uroffenbarung, through creation and man's reason, Paul implies: "... der Mensch (kann) Gottes Wirklichkeit in der Schöpfung erkennen ... Die Menschheit hat also eine ursprüngliche Gotteserkenntnis." (BR, 21) But does man de facto make use of this ability? Does he arrive at a true knowledge of God? Althaus felt that Paul is ambiguous in the answer to these questions. Paul's general context implies that man has only an "ahnende Erkenntnis" which does not become a "praktische Anerkenntnis"; thus the "fall" is constituted and constantly renewed so that all men become guilty before God. Yet Althaus went a step further in his exegesis and pointed out that, according to Paul, if men do not know God, this depends on their will or heart and not on their ability. " ... dieses Nicht-mehr-sehen-Können ist willentlich bedingt ... Ihr (mankind's) im Willen begründetes Nicht-Können hebt darum ihr grundsätzliches Können nicht auf." (CW, 38) And Althaus conjectured that Paul would not necessarily exclude the possibility of some men, in their will, making use of this ability and coming to a true knowledge of God. "Paulus spricht hier zunächst von dem grob götzendienerischen Heidentum. Ob es daneben in der Menschheit außer Christus Erkenntnis Gottes auf Grund der Uroffenbarung gibt, liegt außerhalb des Gesichtskreises dieser Stelle. Jedenfalls muß die Frage gestellt werden. Sie ist als unsere Frage nicht schon durch Röm. 1 negativ entschieden." (CW, 39)

Rom. 2,14 ff. – Rom. 7,14 ff.

3. In the reality of the "law written in one's heart", as contained in both these passages, Althaus found a clear, experiential expression of Uroffenbarung. He rejected Barth's attempts to "do violence" to these texts and to identify this law with that of the Gospel.[27] Here Althaus felt he must also call the Reformers to task, for they too, in general, interpreted the positive content of the Law as applying primarily to Paul the Christian and not sufficiently to man without

26 "Durch das Gesetz kommt Erkenntnis der Sünde", *Um die Wahrheit des Evangeliums*, p. 174.
27 "Durch das Gesetz", p. 172; CW, 40.

Christ. (PL, 56—67) In both texts, Althaus argued, Paul was speaking of and to the heathen; this is especially clear from "dem ganzen Zusammenhang und dem Wortlaut" in Rom. 2, 14 ff. "Der Apostel spricht von Menschen, die 'von Natur' (φύσει) die Forderungen des Gesetzes erfüllen. Damit kann nicht das von Christus im Heiligen Geiste bei den Christen gewirkte neue Ethos verstanden sein, sondern allein die 'natürliche' Sittlichkeit der Heiden".[28] To identify this "Sittlichkeit" with that of the New Testament would be to obliterate the traditional Protestant distinction and relation between the "cognitio legis legalis et evangelica". (CW, 59; cf. also CW, 288—289) This law, then, is written in the hearts of religious men not by the Spirit as communicated through Christ but by the Spirit as present in Uroffenbarung.

The *content* of this law is something positive — indeed, it is basically the same as the content of the commandments and of the ethical teaching of the Gospel. In Rom. 2, 14 ff. Paul was acknowledging the "essential ideals of Greek morality" and saw the law of the Gospel as the completion and fulfillment of this ideal. (BR, 21) This passage implies that even though there is "Verdunklung und Verirrung" in the heathens' ethical codes, there is also "mehr oder weniger richtige Erkenntnis des von Gott Gebotenen."[29] The law which Uroffenbarung reveals is not just *a* law, but God's law. "Der Gott des Gesetzes ist der Gott des Evangeliums." Althaus, appealing to Luther, can even describe "das sittliche Gebot als direkte Offenbarung Gottes, daher als Grund des Glaubens, ja als Evangelium." (TG, 751) And because of this basic identity affirmed in Rom. 2, 14 ff., the Gospel will relate itself to the "law of Uroffenbarung" " ... nicht allerorten und nicht primär als ethische Errettung".[30] There is much in this law which will simply be taken over and affirmed. (TG, 752)

4. Throughout his exegesis of Rom. 2, 14 ff. and 7, 14 ff., Althaus associates and even identifies the law written in the hearts of the heathen with the *law given to Israel*. "Nach Paulus kennen die Menschen auch außerhalb Israels, also außerhalb der heilsgeschichtlichen Offenbarung, ein Gesetz, und zwar ein Gesetz, das inhaltlich und als unbedingte Forderung eins und dasselbe ist mit dem Israel gegebenen Gesetz Gottes." (Ur, 13; cf. also BR, 81,75) This would seem to imply that Uroffenbarung in the religions is similar to revelation within the Old Testament — that the religions play a similar role to that of Israel.

A broader and even more significant implication in Althaus' exegesis of Rom. 2 and 7 is that he associates — even identifies — Uroffenbarung with the traditional Lutheran understanding of the "*Gesetz*". As Ratschow comments: "Gottes Gesetz ... ist offenbar das, worum es in der Grund- oder Uroffenbarung geht."[31] This we will have to carefully bear in mind in our theological analysis of Uroffenbarung and of its meaning for the religions. In particular, we will have to ask whether the traditional understanding of the law allows for a really positive evaluation of the

28 "Durch das Gesetz", p. 175; cf. CW, 38.
29 *Grundriß der Ethik* (Gütersloh, 1953[2]), p. 35. This means: "Die außerchristliche Völkerwelt hat in sich Stufen und ethische Bewegungen; sie zeigt nicht überall fortschreitenden Verfall der sittlichen Erkenntnis, sondern vielfach auch Vertiefung und Reinigung durch Reformatoren." loc. cit.
30 *Grundriß der Ethik*, p. 35.
31 *Der angefochtene Glaube*, p. 284.

religions — and more fundamentally, whether Althaus, through his interpretation of Uroffenbarung, especially in its phenomenology, goes beyond this traditional understanding.

Acts 14, 15—17 (also Acts 17, 23 ff.)

5. Althaus finds in these texts[32] a corroboration of Rom 1, 18 ff. and another example of the first heralds of the Gospel affirming and appealing to Uroffenbarung. The apostle states that God has allowed men before Christ "to go their own way", but that through his activity in nature has not abandoned them. (vs. 16—17) Althaus concludes that while Paul and Barnabas implied that the "ways" of the heathen are different from those of Israel, "sich (Gott doch) auch den Heiden bezeugt hat durch sein Schöpferwirken, indem er ihnen die Freude ins Herz schenkt". (CW, 40) This meant for Althaus that the apostles were admitting a "Vorgeschichte, die Gott mit den Völkern gehabt hat". Without this "pre-history", without bringing it clearly into "consciousness", the Gospel — both in itself and in its proclamation — is not at all to be understood. (CW, loc. cit.) The heart of this pre-history is the reality of Uroffenbarung which belongs both to past history and to the present moment.

John 1, 1 ff.

6. John's Prologue was, for Althaus, another mirror of Rom. 1, 18 ff. The same revelation which Paul saw communicated by means of creation and man's reason John incorporates into his *logos-theology*. The Word, which John described as the source of life and light for all men, is not to be identified solely with the incarnate Word. Rather, it is also the eternal Word, before the Incarnation. Before the coming of the God-Man, this Word was already carrying out the function which was to be perfected in the Incarnation: enlightening all men. "Der Evangelist spricht von einer Erleuchtung durch den Logos, von einer solchen, die überall und zu allen Zeiten von ihm ausgeht."[33] The same Logos who is the medium of creation is also a medium of revelation. Here we can understand better the close connection between creation and revelation — why Paul could place his "$\phi\alpha\nu\epsilon\rho\acute{o}\nu$" in the "$\kappa\tau\acute{\iota}\sigma\iota\varsigma$"; it is because of the presence and activity of the Logos within the created order.[34] John, therefore, in this Prologue was clearly asserting a "double revelation", i.e. "die Erleuchtung aller durch das bei Gott seiende Wort und die Berufung der Gemeinde zu Gott durch den Menschen Jesus".[35]

And the function of this "pre-Christian" revelation according to John is the same as of that according to Paul: not only to enlighten all men but to constitute and reveal to them their sinfulness. For as John states: the Word came to his own, but they did not receive him. (vs. 11) Men had the ability and the opportunity to know God, but by an act of their will they refused. (CW, 44) Yet despite this

---

32 He merely mentions Acts 17, 23 f., without offering an exegesis of the text; cf. GD/I, 14.
33 W. Lütgert, *Johanneische Christologie* (Gütersloh, 1916[2]), p. 82, quoted in CW, 41.
34 Here Althaus quotes Bultmann: "Daß darin, daß die Welt Schöpfung des Logos ist, die Möglichkeit der Offenbarung liegt...", *Das Evangelium des Johannes* (Göttingen, 1941), pp. 22 ff.
35 This is a quotation from A. Schlatter, *Die Lehre der Apostel* (1910[1]), p. 110; cf. also op. cit. (1922[2]), p. 163; quoted in CW, 41.

refusal the revelation through the Logos continues. Even though the "κόσμος" did not accept the "φῶς" and decided to remain in the "σκοτία" – the light continues to shine in the world and in the darkness. Throughout the darkness, Althaus interprets, the searching for the "ζωή" goes on. (CW, 41)

In his exegesis of the Johannine argument for Uroffenbarung, Althaus seems to find an even more positive relationship with Christ's revelation than he did in his analysis of Romans. "Die johanneische Logos-Christologie ist ein Ausdruck des Zusammenhanges der Christus-Offenbarung mit der Uroffenbarung." (CW, 44) According to Romans, Uroffenbarung established man's relation with God; in John, it sets man in a genuine relationship with Christ himself, i.e. with the coming Incarnate Word. "Nicht erst durch die Verkündigung seines Wortes entsteht die Beziehung der Menschen zu Jesus."[36] Because the Logos who enlightens all men from the beginning of time is the same Logos who was to take visible, definitive form in Christ, he has from the beginning of time been introducing men to Christ, preparing them for his coming. Thus men already know Christ before their first meeting with him; they have no excuse for not recognizing him. "Weil der Logos jeden Menschen erleuchtet, ist Jesus und sein Wort dem Menschen nicht das schlechthin Fremde ..." (CW, 44)[37] This role of the Logos in Uroffenbarung as "he who brings men to Christ" is similar to the role of the Spirit who bestows the gift of faith. Just as we cannot forget the Spirit in understanding how men approach Christ, neither can we neglect the eternal Logos. (CW, 44)

In another section of CW, where Althaus discusses the relation of the Gospel to Uroffenbarung, he adds, as it were, a footnote to his exegesis of John 1, 1 ff. A concrete example, he feels, of Uroffenbarung through the Logos are *the myths* of the religious world. He states clearly, "daß er (myth) σπέρματα τοῦ λόγου in sich trägt". (CW, 50) This is attested to by the simple fact that the Gospel has made use of such myths. In such religious imagery the Logos is giving voice to Uroffenbarung. Here Althaus shows that in his exegesis of John's Prologue he is following, implicitly but actually, the rich Patristic tradition of the "seeds of the Logos" dispersed in pagan philosophy and religions. This concept of the Logos and its "σπέρματα"[38], together with Althaus' total exegesis of John 1, will be an important and guiding light in our application of his doctrine of Uroffenbarung to his evaluation of the religions.

John 6,44 f.

7. Althaus does not mention this text in his "scriptural proofs" for Uroffenbarung. In his description of the relation of the Gospel to Uroffenbarung, however,

36 Again a quotation from A. Schlatter, *Die Lehre der Apostel* (1910[1]), p. 109 ff., in CW, 44.
37 Here Althaus refers to Lütgert, *Joh. Christologie*, pp. 86, 88. Lütgert feels that because of this preparatory illumination of the Logos, faith in the Christ should be the "normal thing" and disbelief the exception.
38 For the Patristic teaching on the σπέρματα τοῦ λόγου cf. esp. Justin, Apol. II, 10, 1–5; Apol. I, 46, 2–5. Also: P. Gerlitz, "Der Λόγος Σπερματικός als Voraussetzung für eine ökumenische Theologie", ZRGG, 22 (1970) 4–10; G. Thils, *Propos et Problèmes de la Théologie des Religions non chrétiennes* (1966), pp. 96–100; P. Hacker, "The Religions of the Gentiles as Viewed by Fathers of the Church", ZMR (Münster) 54 (1970) 255–256. R. Holte, "Logos Spermatikos", StTh, 12 (1958) 109–168.

he gives it an unusual interpretation which complements his exegesis of the Prologue. He interprets the "drawing" and "teaching" of the Father as applying to men who have not yet encountered the Incarnate Word.[39] "Hier ist von einem Geisteswirken Gottes im Menschen die Rede, das geschieht, schon ehe der Mensch Jesus begegnet; eine Bekundung Gottes ist gemeint, die derjenigen durch das Wort Jesus (i.e. the incarnate Word) vorausgeht." (CW, 46) The enlightening and drawing activity of the Father is similar — if not identical — with the role of the eternal Logos. The Uroffenbarung which takes place through the Logos (as principle of creation and revelation) and through the Creator-Father is not just a making known of the deity but, at the same time, a preparing for and a drawing to the Incarnate Word. Again we see that Althaus' scriptural support for Uroffenbarung from John is much more positive than his exegesis of Paul in Romans.

8. Althaus' scriptural argument for Uroffenbarung has been subjected to frequent criticism, from various quarters. Many feel that his exegetical method is too hasty and facile[40] and too much pre-formed by his own dogmatic position. The wide range of objections can be sifted down to two principal arguments:

a) Althaus' critics argue that he has afforded Uroffenbarung a much greater *efficacy* and *independence* than the texts would allow. In his analysis of Rom. 1, 18 f. he fails to distinguish clearly between the possibility and reality of knowing God. Paul may have admitted the possibility, but not the reality — which can be had only in Christ.[41] The same can be said of Althaus' treatment of Acts 14, 15 f. and 17, 23 f. Here he does not realize that these texts incorporate a "stoische theologia naturalis" which endorses a natural encounter with God which Paul himself would not accept; for Paul such an encounter is only a condition for man's guilt.[42] Althaus also goes beyond the true content of John 1, 1 f. One cannot apply the "ζωή" and the "φῶς" to the "λόγος ἄσαρκος". For John, these terms were "nicht protologische, sondern soteriologisch-eschatologische Begriffe". Also, the drawing and teaching of the Father in John 6, 44 f. does not refer to an Uroffenbarung but to a "Wort-Offenbarung"; it is an illuminating activity confined only to the reality of the Incarnate Word.[43]

b) The critics also object that in his exegesis, Althaus does not remain within the limits defined by the structure of "*Gesetz-Evangelium*": he fails to realize that the Uroffenbarung according to Paul was — or was meant to serve — God's *Zornoffenbarung*. For Paul, Uroffenbarung was merely a "theologisches Nebenmotiv" which is not unfolded any further and whose sole purpose is to bring about man's "Unentschuldbarkeit".[44] Althaus forgets that

---

39 "No one can come to me unless the Father who sent me draws him ... Everyone who had heard and learned from the Father comes to me." John 6, 44, 46.

40 "Althausens Methode (i.e. in exegesis) ist konservativ, die ungeheure Komplizierung traditionsgeschichtlicher Fragen des biblischen Textes, welche die neuere exegetische Forschung erbracht hat, bleibt unberücksichtigt. Die exegetische Begründung ist heute länger, vielschichtiger geworden, als es bei Althaus der Fall zu sein scheint." Lohff, *Tendenzen*, p. 300.

41 G. Koch, *Die christliche Wahrheit der Barmer theologischen Erklärung* (München, 1950), pp. 23 ff.; G. Heinzelmann, "Uroffenbarung?", ThStKr, 106 N.F. 1 (1934—35) 425—427; Althaus "vergißt ..., daß ... in Röm. 7 der Mensch ohne Christus nicht geschildert wird, ... wie er sich selbst sieht, sondern so wie er vom Glauben aus gesehen wird." R. Bultmann, "Christus des Gesetzes Ende", *Glauben und Verstehen* II (Tübingen, 1961³), p. 45.

42 Pöhlmann, "Uroffenbarung", p. 252.

43 Pöhlmann, loc. cit.; Wiesner, pp. 98—120; Gloege, RGG³ VI, 1200.

44 Pöhlmann, op. cit., p. 251.

between the Uroffenbarung and the "Heilsoffenbarung" there rises the dark figure of God's "Zornoffenbarung" which, in a sense, overshadows — even obliterates — Uroffenbarung. The Gospel relates itself and responds only to this "Zornoffenbarung", not to Uroffenbarung, to man's guilt and not to his knowledge of God.[45]

One might ask whether these criticisms of Althaus' exegesis are so soundly exegetical themselves. While they accuse him of interpreting Paul and John too much from his own pre-conceived anthropological ideas concerning human nature and history, they themselves seem to depart just as much from their own "prejudgments" concerning the total separation of the human and the divine. Just as Althaus presupposed that the divine can show itself through the finiteness and sinfullness of the non-Christian order, so do his critics preclude this possibility. It seems to be such positive or negative "preconceived notions" — more than exegetical precision — which determine one's scriptural assessment of Uroffenbarung.

§ 24. Uroffenbarung — Its Foundations in Protestant Tradition

1. Although Althaus' appeal to Protestant tradition for support of his teaching on Uroffenbarung is in no way as extensive as his argument from Scripture, he is convinced that tradition supplies him with an equally solid basis. One of the most impelling reasons for his rejection of the first thesis of the Barmen Declaration was that it ran contrary to what he considered was traditional doctrine in Protestant theology; it "schließt das, was *unsere Väter in der alten Dogmatik* revelatio generalis nannten, einfach aus ... eine vocatio generalis, wie unsere Väter sagten".[46]

Such views of the "Fathers", Althaus was convinced, had their origin and their chief defendent in Luther himself. "Auch außerhalb der biblischen Offenbarung des Wortes, des Glaubens gibt es in gewissem Maße Erkennntnis Gottes. Das stand für Luther außer Frage durch das Zeugnis der Heiligen Schrift. Es bestätigte sich ihm durch den Blick auf die Religionen."[47] Althaus argued that according to Luther, God had given all men "a knowledge about himself" — a knowledge which is "irradicable".[48] But this general knowledge of God is limited; it does not enable man to grasp what is God's will for mankind, i.e. what God has in mind for man's ultimate future.[49] On the basis of these limits, Luther can make the important distinction between two kinds of knowledge of God. "Anderswo unterscheidet Luther ausdrücklich eine allgemeine und die eigentliche Gotteserkenntnis (generalis et propria)."[50] "Generalem habent omnes homines, scilicet quod Deus sit, quod creaverit coelum et terram, quod sit justus, quod puniat impios ..."[51] But the special knowledge, i.e. "quod Deus nobis cogitet, quid dare et facere velit, ut a peccatis et morte liberemur et salvi fiamus, quae propria et vera est cognitio

---

45 R. Walker, *Zur Frage der Offenbarung.* Eine Auseinandersetzung mit Karl Barth und Paul Althaus (Bad Cannstatt 1962), pp. 29–30; cf. also A. Peters, "Die Frage nach Gott", *Fuldaer Hefte*, 17 (Berlin, 1967), p. 100; Pöhlmann, op. cit., pp. 254–256.
46 "Bedenken", p. 319, emphasis mine; cf. also *Die deutsche Stunde der Kirche* (Göttingen, 1934²), p. 9.
47 *Die Theologie Martin Luthers* (Gütersloh, 1963²), p. 27.
48 Op. cit., p. 27; cf. WA, 19, 205, 35; 18, 709, 10; 718, 15; 719, 20.
49 Op. cit., p. 28; WA, 45, 89, 28; 21, 509, 6; cf. also 19, 206, 13.
50 *Theologie Luthers*, p. 29.
51 WA, 40, I, 607 ff., quoted in CW, 139; cf. also WA 19, 206, 8 ff.; 56, 177.

Dei"[52] comes only through Christ's revelation. By means of this distinction be-tween a "generalis" and a "propria" knowledge of God, — Althaus concludes — Luther was implicitly but clearly holding to the doctrine of a twofold revela-·tion.[53] — Only in passing does Althaus appeal to Melanchthon for support of his doctrine of Uroffenbarung; he points out that not only did Melanchthon accept a twofold knowledge of God but that he also stated that God had revealed himself "dupliciter".[54]

2. In CW Althaus presents a sketchy picture of just what the "Fathers" said about general revelation. Although he can claim that it was the old Protestant theology — the Orthodoxy — which first elaborated the "formal" doctrine of a twofold revelation, he has to admit that the terms "another revelation" or "two-fold revelation" were not at all acceptable to a large number of the "Fathers". In the beginning, they took over what Althaus calls the Catholic or Scholastic posi-tion[55] (which is also clearly reflected in his Luther citations): there is a twofold knowledge of God, natural and revealed. The term "revelation", however, is re-served for God's voice in Scripture. An example of this line of thought from the Lutheran Orthodoxy is Johann Gerhard, who explicitly founds his position on Thomas.[56]

52 Cf. WA, 44, 78, 15.
53 For Luther's teaching on "cognitio dei naturalis" cf. R. Seeberg, "Die Lehre Luthers", *Jahrbuch der Dogmengeschichte* IV, 1 (Leipzig-Erlangen, 1917), pp. 141 ff.; O. Weber, *Grundriß der Dogmatik* I (Neukirchen, 1955), p. 221; H. Bandt, *Luthers Lehre vom verborgenen Gott* (Berlin, 1958), pp. 86 ff.; E. Kinder, "Das vernachlässigte Problem 'na-türlicher Gotteserfahrung' in der Theologie", KuD, 9 (1963) 321–322.
54 Althaus refers to H. Engelland, *Melanchthon, Glauben und Handeln* (München, 1931), pp. 222 ff., (cf. CW, 51) but does not give any explicit reference to Melanchthon himself. It should be pointed out that while the young Melanchthon was adverse to a natural knowledge of God, later, especially when as counselor to the universities he came under the positive influence of aristotelian philosophy and of Erasmus, he changed his views. Cf. O. Weber, op. cit., p. 221; F. W. Kantzenbach, *Orthodoxie und Pietismus* (Evangelische Enzyklopädie, Bd. 11/12, Gütersloh, 1966), pp. 32–33. W. Maurer shows Melanchthon's acceptance of a natural theology, even in terms of an "Uroffenbarung": *Der junge Melan-chthon zwischen Humanismus und Reformation*, Bd. I, Der Humanist (Göttingen, 1967), pp. 105–106, 108–109, pp. 99–128 passim; cf. also, op. cit. Bd. II, Der Theologe (1969), pp. 288–289. – Althaus could also have well appealed to Calvin who frequently has been proposed as an advocate of a natural knowledge of the divine. Cf. G. Gloede, *Theologia naturalis bei Calvin* (Stuttgart, 1935); P. Barth, *Das Problem der natürlichen Theologie· bei Calvin* (Th. Ex. 18, München, 1935); P. Brunner, "Allgemeine und beson-dere Offenbarung in Calvins Institutio", EvTh, 1 (1934) 189 ff.; A. E. Dowey, *The Know-ledge of God in Calvin's Theology* (New York, 1952); G. J. Postema, "Calvin's Alleged Rejection of Natural Theology", SJTh, 24 (1971) 423 ff.
55 Althaus feels that the Catholic understanding of revelation is also on his side insofar as the traditional Catholic argument for a natural knowledge of God "der Sache nach" implies a double revelation. This he sees typified in Schmaus' distinction between a "Wortoffenbarung" and a "Werkoffenbarung". (cf. *Kathol. Dogmatik*, I, 1938, p. 59) But even in the later editions of CW Althaus evinces a poor acquaintance with more recent Catholic teaching which has substituted the doctrine of a natural knowledge of God with an explicit argument for a genuine, supernatural revelation outside of Christ. Cf. § 30.
56 Cf. *Loci Theologici*, I, 268, hrsg. von E. Preuß (Berlin, 1863): also I, 277.

In his "Habilitationsschrift", Althaus concludes that the Reformed theologians "im Zeitalter der aristotelischen Scholastik" followed, for the most part, this same pattern: instead of speaking explicitly of two revelations, they referred more to "reason and revelation", "natural and supernatural theology", "das Verhältnis von natürlicher und übernatürlicher Gotteserkenntnis". This was also their interpretation of the relationship between Gospel and Law.[57]

Among the "späteren altlutherischen Theologen" Althaus also admits a varying, sometimes contrasting terminology. Musäus and Baier shy away from the expression "general revelation" and apply "revelation" only to that within the supernatural context of the Bible. Calov, Quenstedt and Hollaz, however, propose — "according to Rom. 1,19", as Althaus approvingly comments — a true revelation of God through nature; they therefore explicitly distinguish a twofold revelation. It is these later Orthodox theologians whom Althaus can call on as explicit defendents for his own terminology; yet he feels that the whole of tradition is on his side. Although there is a considerable "Abweichung im Sprachgebrauche", there is a clearly shaped unity in "sachliche Verständnis". "Die Grundzüge der Lehre von der allgemeinen Offenbarung oder natürlichen Erkenntnis Gottes sind bei den Dogmatikern überall wesentlich die gleichen." (CW, 52)

III. The Phenomenology of Uroffenbarung

Having traced the definition and general characteristics of Uroffenbarung and having established its Scriptural foundations, we can now turn to what Althaus considered to be the expression of Uroffenbarung — the way it shows itself, the way it is confronted and experienced by man in the existential order: its phenomenology. We are intentionally taking up the phenomenology of Uroffenbarung *before* going into its theological meaning, for, we feel, it is only by contrasting phenomenology and theology that we can arrive at an understanding of the full content of Althaus' "Uroffenbarungslehre" — its tensions and unclarities as well as its deeper implications and potentialities. Also, on the basis of Uroffenbarung's phenomenology we shall be in a better position to apply it to the religions; what we are presenting here are the workings and manifestations of Uroffenbarung *within* the religious world.

§ 25. Various Structures for Describing the Phenomenology of Uroffenbarung

1. A certain methodological difficulty arises in describing the various phenomenological expressions of Uroffenbarung. Althaus himself detected the force of Uroffenbarung in an interplay of forms which are not always so easily distinguishable, and in his various works he presents divergent structures for describing these forms.

---

57 *Die Prinzipien der deutschen reformierten Dogmatik im Zeitalter der aristotelischen Scholastik* (Leipzig, 1914), pp. 164–167. For the reformed theologians' manner of speaking of a "religio naturalis" or of a "cognitio Dei naturalis et acquisita", cf. H. Heppe, *Die Dogmatik der evangelisch-reformierten Kirche*, neu durchges. u. hrsg. von E. Bizer (Neukirchen, 1958), pp. 1 ff.

A) In GD^1 (1929), where for the first time he offers an organized picture of the phenomenology of Uroffenbarung, he traces its expressions in:
1) "Leben und Sterben" – i.e. man's experience of the finiteness of life.
2) "Norm und Versagen", which incorporates man's restless seeking after truth, the
beautiful and the moral good,
3) "Das Geheimnis der Natur", especially its teleology,
4) "Das Geheimnis der Geschichte", in which man experiences the relation and the
tensions between:
a) "Natur und Geist"
b) "Schicksal und Tat"
c) "Teleologie und Geheimnis" (cf. GD^1, 11–14)
B) In his article on "Die Wirklichkeit Gottes" (1933) he much more simply limits the
workings of Uroffenbarung in man's experience of:
1) himself,
2) his neighbor,
3) history.[58]
C) The 1936 edition of GD presents the same basic outline as the first edition, but with
altered and expanded contents. Uroffenbarung is described in:
1) Our "Lebendigkeit", i.e. our createdness and our mortality.
2) The "Normen" of truth, beauty-happiness, and moral good and justice (as activated
in conscience),
3) "Die Geschichte", which now includes
a) The community of men in trust and love,
b) The "call" to service
c) "Die Stunde" – the nowness of history's demands
d) "Gericht und Erneuerung" – the present yet hidden hand of justice in history
e) "Schicksal und Verantwortung, Sinn und Geheimnis" – combining 4,b and c,
from GD^1.
4) "Die Natur"
a) The unity and purposefulness of nature,
b) The relation between "nature and spirit", i.e. nature as a means for history's
development. (cf. GD^2, 20–26)
D) The structure for the phenomenological description of Uroffenbarung is rearranged and
elaborated even more drastically in the CW of 1947. Here Uroffenbarung shows itself:
1) "in der Existenz des Menschen"
2) "im geschichtlichen Leben"
3) "an dem theoretischen Denken"
4) "in der Wahrheitsbeziehung des Geistes"
5) "in der Natur". (CW/I (1947), 73–107 = CW, 61–90)

2. In an attempt to tighten the certain looseness and overlapping in these various "structures" of Uroffenbarung's phenomenology, Althaus' critics have done some rearranging of
their own.
A) *F. Konrad* describes the "place" of Uroffenbarung as:
1) "Die Selbstbezeugung Gottes in der Existenz des Menschen", i.e.
a) in man's self-consciousness
b) in his historical existence
c) in his reflection on self and the world.
2) "Die Selbstbezeugung Gottes in der Natur."[59]

58 Op. cit., pp. 83 ff.
59 F. Konrad, *Das Offenbarungsverständnis in der evangelischen Theologie* (München, 1971),
pp. 437–442.

B) *H. G. Pöhlmann* considers the Uroffenbarung to be found in:
  1) "Gott in der Umwelt des Menschen", which includes his presence in:
      a) History
      b) Nature.
  2) "Gott in der In-Welt des Menschen", i.e. in
      a) man's existence
      b) man's theoretical thinking
      c) man's relation to truth.[60]

3. In order to present a picture of Althaus' phenomenology of Uroffenbarung in an organized and clear fashion, but without imposing undue personal interepretations on his own
thought, we can follow the structure which he himself sketched in GD[3]/II. The context was,
per se, not that of Uroffenbarung but of "Die Wirklichkeit Gottes" and the various avenues in
which it encounters man. These avenues provide us with one of the neatest outlines for
organizing his sometimes rambling statements on the many expressions of Uroffenbarung. In
somewhat unusual and perhaps romantic terminology, he speaks of man's encounter with God
as the:
  1) "Ur-Macht" – within man's experience of himself
  2) "Ur-Ich" – within man's experience of others
  3) "Ur-Wille" – within conscience and history
  4) "Ur-Geist" – within nature and man's quest for truth. (GD/II, 13–15)[61]

§ 26. Uroffenbarung in the "Ur-Macht"

1. In this first and perhaps most basic expression of Uroffenbarung, it is evident how closely Althaus' "Middle Way" tends towards Troeltsch's position. In
asserting that God's presence and might is manifest in man's being, Althaus was
adopting – although he did not say so "expressis verbis" – Troeltsch's metaphysical starting point. His entire treatment of "Gottes Selbstbezeugung in der Existenz
des Menschen" presupposes a metaphysics of human nature in which man's being
is open to and dynamically orientated towards the Transcendent. Troeltsch would
call it man's religious apriori. Althaus in general avoids such terminology – which
smacks of rationalism – yet the reality seems to be basically the same.
  This metaphysics of transcendence is contained, first of all, in Althaus' assertion that man's being is a source of Uroffenbarung insofar as this being *is a
relation to God*. Man's "Dasein (ist) in sich selbst Gottesbeziehung ..." (GD/II, 11)
This relation consists of a directedness to and metaphysical call by God. "Diese
Bestimmung zur Gemeinschaft mit Gott macht das besondere Wesen des Menschen aus ... Diese Bestimmung steht nicht nur über dem Menschen, sondern er ist
durch seinen Schöpfer in ihr verfaßt. Er ist in seinem Wesen diese Bestimmung ... Er ist in seiner Existenz angewiesen auf Gott." (CW, 327) We are in
constant contact with an "uns bedingenden Unbedingten". (GD/II, 15) More
simply Althaus also describes this relation to God as the "Gegenwart Gottes bei

---

60 Pöhlmann, "Uroffenbarung", pp. 247–251.
61 As part of the "Ur-Geist", Althaus does not explicitly mention God's presence in nature;
   but that nature may rightly be subsumed under the concept of spirit is clear from his
   understanding of the relation between nature and spirit; because of this relationship man is
   able to perceive the "truth" in nature and seek after it; cf. § 29/1.

uns, nämlich die Präsenz seines Geistes in unserem Menschsein". Both in our "biological being" and in our "spiritual being" the reality of the Divine is present as a preserving and directing force.[62] This relationship and this presence, Althaus adds, remain and are effective even "wenn es dem Menschen noch nicht zum denkenden Bewußtsein gekommen ist" (GD/II, 15), even when man has tried to break the relationship by turning against God in sin. (CW, 328)

Because of this metaphysical definition of man as a relation and directedness to God, Althaus can take the next logical step and claim a *predication* of the divine within the human. All that truly is part of man's being and his activity receives the predication "divine" (which, it must be clear, does not imply an identification). "Wir haben es mit Gott zu tun, wenn wir es mit uns selber zu tun haben ... Mensch sagen heißt: Gottes Wirklichkeit aussagen. 'Seele' sagen heißt: Gottes Wirklichkeit aussagen."[63] Here we have the deepest metaphysical foundation for Uroffenbarung. Althaus can even declare that man's being as relation with God not only is an expression of but *is* Uroffenbarung. "Gottes gewiß werden heißt: die eigene Existenz als im Gottesverhältnis wesend erkennen ... Dieses Wesen des Daseins im Gottesverhältnis ist die Uroffenbarung Gottes, die an alles Menschentum in und mit seiner eigenen Wirklichkeit in der Welt jederzeit gegenwärtig ergeht." (GD/II, 11)[64]

2. Following much the same pattern as Troeltsch, Althaus goes on to describe the workings of these metaphysical realities within the individual. Troeltsch spoke of metaphysics being expressed in the area of religious psychology.[65] Again, Althaus shys away from such terminology; but with Troeltsch he does clearly affirm that the metaphysical-transcendent structure of human existence can be known through *human experience*. Indeed, such experience is unavoidalbe. "Die Unentrinnbarkeit Gottes erfahren alle Menschen..."[66] In our self-consciousness a consciousness of God is "directly" included. (CW, 64) Althaus' many-faceted description of this experience of transcendence[67] can be summarized and clarified as a twofold experience of existence as *given* and existence as *incomplete*.

Man experiences his relationship with God, first of all, in the fact that his being is not his own – it has been *given* to him. The terms which Althaus most frequently employs to describe this experience are: "schlechthinnige Gewirktheit unseres Daseins" (CW, 65; GD/I, 19), "die unableitbare, undurchdringliche, unverfügbare Gegebenheit des Daseins" (GD/I, 19), "die Begabung des Lebens" (CW, 67). Man feels that life is a gift which he has not deserved, and in accepting it he experiences the source of the gift. (CW, 67 f.) – Yet this gift is something over which he

62 "Von der Präsenz Gottes im Menschsein des Menschen", *Mensch und Menschensohn*, Festschrift für Bischof D. Karl Witte (Hamburg, 1963), pp. 17 ff.; for a vibrant review of God's self-manifestation in every aspect of the human cf. *Gott ist gegenwärtig*. Letzte Predigten (Gütersloh, 1968), pp. 112–115 (Sermon, June 16, 1963).

63 "Die Wirklichkeit Gottes", pp. 83–84; cf. also "Von der Präsenz", p. 17.

64 According to G. Zasche the foundation for Althaus' ontology of man as "Verhältnis" is God's "call", the "Personalimmanenz Gottes in der Welt". Yet this is not a static ontology: "Das Wesen des Menschen ist Begegnungsakt, aber nicht Sein." Zasche, *Extra Nos* (Paderborn, 1970), pp. 70–72, also 65–72.

65 Cf. § 5/3.

66 *Das Heil Gottes* (Gütersloh, 1926), pp. 36 ff., Sermon, June 1, 1924.

67 Cf. ibid., p. 250; Peters, pp. 83 f.

does not have full control. Man's existence is exposed to a complex of contingencies — in his own personality, heredity, family, environment, and especially in the uncertainty of the future. He is, in a sense, being led by these contingencies. Admitting his allegiance to Schleiermacher, Althaus feels that man experiences himself dependent on an "alles wirkenden, allgegenwärtigen lebendigen Schicksalsmacht". (CW, 66) A power, however, which in its workings points to a *personal* being.

> Wir können die Macht weder als Willkür verstehen — dazu wirkt sie zu geordnet und gesetzmäßig — noch als starres Gesetz — dazu wirkt sie zu lebendig und „zufällig". Da sie auch unsere Freiheit zur Selbstbestimmung setzt, müssen wir sie nach Analogie unseres eigenen Verfügens denken, das immer zugleich ein geordnetes und ein lebendiges sein will. Wir sind in den Händen eines Herrn über uns. (CW, 66)

The "Schicksalsmacht" is a personal Lord; Uroffenbarung can make known, it would seem, a *personal God*. This is a statement which boldly bounds beyond what many Protestant theologians feel are the limits of a general revelation.

Althaus finds man's experience of his transcendental directedness even more sharply articulated within an existence which is given but *not fully given*. The gift man has received is not totally possessed. And man painfully feels this. Althaus' descriptions of this experience have both an ontological and a modern existential coloring: life shows itself to be a "double-existence" which is "divided" and "alienated",[68] which leads to an "Ungenügen der Lebendigkeit" (GD/I, 19), "gebrochene Lebendigkeit", "Ungeborgenheit und Sinnlosigkeit" (CW, 22—25), "wesenhafte Einsamkeit ... Vergänglichkeit ... Hinfälligkeit" (CW, 70), "Unruhe ... Ungenügen ... Unterwegssein ... Entbehren ... Leiden ... Fremdsein ... Warten".[69] This array of incompleteness can be summed up in a universal "metaphysischen Traurigkeit" and an "ontologischen Heimweh".[70]

Man is gripped by this metaphysical discontent because, as a unique being in God's creation, he can relate to himself; he can distinguish what he is from what he can or should be or wants to be. (CW, 326) Man can therefore painfully distinguish between his "Wirklichkeit" and his "Wesen",[71] between his "Ist" and his "Soll".[72] He is constantly in search of his true being. "Er lebt immer über sich selbst hinaus, er transzendiert seinem Wesen nach sich selbst." (CW, 326) Precisely within this distinction and this search, Althaus concludes, the voice of Uroffenbarung is heard and the one true God is revealing himself. Here man experiences the "Frage nach der Ewigkeit, Frage nach Gott".[73] Here man experiences God as the ever removed and evasive answer to the questions, uncertainties and restlessness of his divided being. (CW, 24 f.) Here man comes to a "consciousness of God". (CW, 70) Indeed, the questions, the torment, the discontent would not at all be possible if God were not already revealing himself to man — if man could not already, in his being, see and feel the divine.[74]

---

68 "Die Wirklichkeit Gottes", p. 83.
69 *Gott ist gegenwärtig*, p. 114; "Von der Präsenz", p. 14.
70 "Von der Präsenz", pp. 13, 15.
71 Ibid., pp. 11 ff.
72 "Die Wirklichkeit Gottes", p. 83.
73 *Gott ist gegenwärtig*, p. 115.
74 "Von der Präsenz", p. 14.

§ 27. Uroffenbarung in the "Ur-Ich"

This form of Uroffenbarung's phenomenology stands somewhat in the shade of the other expressions; Althaus merely seems to state it, without going into any special detail.[75] Yet from what he does state, it is clear that this avenue of God's general revelation is just as effective and meaningful as all the others, for here God is manifesting himself in one of the most deeply felt aspects of man's nature: his interpersonal relationships.

Again, Althaus founds this expression of Uroffenbarung on a *metaphysical* basis. He defines man as a being who can find himself and realize himself only by relating himself to another personal being.[76] Man must open himself to someone else, give himself to and be accepted by someone else if he is to be himself. He must exist in a "community". Thus every human being experiences a "wesenhafte Sehnsucht nach dem Du", a "Sehnsucht, ganz erkannt, ganz verstanden und darin ganz geborgen zu sein ..."[77] A "need to trust" and a "need to love" direct all human exisfence. (GD/I, 22)

Within this ontological communitarian constitution of man, God speaks and gives form to his Uroffenbarung. This is so, Althaus reasons, first of all, because all human self-giving in confidence and love presupposes God as its *"foundation"* and *surity*. In giving himself to someone else, man, in his subconscious, feels the risk and danger of this act; he "presupposes" that the other person will accept him, that the other person will also open himself in confidence and love. Such a presupposition is founded on a source of confidence and love which is more than human. "Vertrauen ist immer ein unbewußtes Bekenntnis zu Gott über und hinter dem Du."[78] "Vertrauen hat seinen Grund in der Gewißheit, daß der andere von dem Unbedingten, aller Treue Ursprung, gebunden und gehalten ist." (GD/I, 21) Therefore: "Wir haben es mit Gott zu tun, wenn wir es miteinander zu tun haben."[79] God is the "Ur-Ich" and the "unbedingte Du" behind every interpersonal relationship. (GD/II, 14—15)

Even more existentially God's presence is felt in the *insufficiency* of such relationships. "Bei allem Reichtum mitmenschlicher Gemeinschaft bleibt ein Ungenügen ... Es bleibt mitten in inniger Gemeinschaft eine unaufhebbare Einsamkeit."[80] Man's metaphysical thirst is greater than any of the finite objects that are within reach, because the "meaning" − the thrust of human love and trust reach beyond the "Wirklichkeit jedes Menschen und der ganzen Menschheit". (GD/I, 22) Therefore, in every finite human being to whom man opens himself in love there dwells the Infinite, to whom, at the same time, man is always opening himself. God is not only the foundation of human love; he is also its ultimate object. "Das Vertrauen, auf dem menschliche Gemeinschaft wie die Ehe ruht, gründet nicht nur in Gott, sondern es meint und sucht zuletzt Gott. Denn es sucht das Du, von dem

---

75 Both Konrad and Pöhlmann in their descriptions of the "Ort" of Uroffenbarung surprisingly do not even mention this expression.
76 "Von der Präsenz", p. 15.
77 Ibid., pp. 15−16.
78 "Die Wirklichkeit Gottes", p. 84.
79 Loc. cit.
80 "Von der Präsenz", pp. 15−16; CW, 70.

ich ganz gehalten, bei dem ich ganz geborgen bin." (GD/I, 22) Again, Althaus can conclude, here we have another example of the workings of Uroffenbarung: the need to love and trust is a "Selbstbezeugung des Transzendenten in unserem Leben". (loc. cit.)

§ 28. Uroffenbarung in the "Ur-Wille"

1. This facet of Uroffenbarung's phenomenology shares the same metaphysical basis as that of the "Urmacht". The Transcendent, which is source and goal of our being, touches us not only in the act of being but also in the concrete acts of *will*. We are confronted by another Will which exerts its influence on our will. Althaus describes this confrontation with such words as "Anspruch", "Gebot", "Inanspruchnahme", "Sollen", "Autorität". (CW, 68; GD/I, 19; GD/II, 14) Man, in the different circumstances of his daily living, feels himself, again and again, obliged by a force which does not originate in himself. Its origin is transcendent. "So werde ich inne, daß der Anspruch von dem ausgeht, der mein Dasein setzt und bestimmt. Die Schicksalsmacht selber ist es, die mich in Anspruch nimmt. Sie ist Herr meines Lebens nicht nur insofern sie es bestimmt, sondern auch insofern sie es beansprucht ... Nicht nur im Sein sondern auch im Sollen ist sie meiner Herr." (CW, 68–69)

Generally, this "Ur-Wille" becomes Uroffenbarung through personal *conscience*. Within our conscience we are "unentrinnbar und unwiderstehlich von einem unbedingten Anspruch getroffen". (GD/I, 20) Yet Althaus is careful to insist that the voice of conscience cannot simply be identified with the voice of God. Conscience is merely a vehicle, serving a force which is separate from and above it. Indeed, the vehicle can often fail in its intended function and blur God's Will. Yet conscience "ist doch die einzige Möglichkeit, Gottes gebietende Stimme zu vernehmen."[81] Thus, Althaus can affirm the revelatory function of all morality. (BR, 21)[82]

2. But the medium of the "Ur-Wille" which Althaus describes most extensively and with particular personal fervor is that of *history* and man's *historical nature*. For Althaus history was not separated from the eternal by the dialectical "Todeslinie". Rather, it was a stage on which man can experience and know God. Eternity and finite history stand "in a relation of immanence". (TG, 748) The Eternal is "the Lord of history", using men as his "tool" so that their own human activity, within each historical situation, serves to realize a divine "Plan".[83] This activity of the eternal within the historical — this experiencing of the divine within the concrete moment — takes place in what Althaus terms "calling" and "responsibility". Within his concrete historical situation man feels obliged to follow a certain course, to take on certain responsibilities, to commit himself. He experiences the "unremitting seriousness" in the "historical moment" (GD/I, 23) — and that his own eternal destiny depends on his reaction to this call. (CW, 69) Also, "in dem Gehorsam gegen den Ruf" he experiences "zugleich die Freude der

---

81 *Grundriß der Ethik*, p. 34.
82 *Grundriß der Ethik*, pp. 17–18.
83 "Christentum und Geistesleben", pp. 40–41; CW, 347.

Lebenserfüllung ..." (CW, 73) Althaus can conclude with somewhat romantic clarity:

> ... in den Verantwortungen ergreift uns die Verantwortung, in den sehr bedingten Aufgaben der unbedingte Herr, in dem Geschichtlichen das Ewige.
>
> ... Wir sind zum Opfer, bis zur Hingabe des Lebens, in den geschichtlichen Verantwortungsverhältnissen gerufen, aber das Opfer gilt Gott. (TG, 748)
>
> Nur lebendiger Wille kann meinen Willen fordern, nur die unbedingte Person kann persönlich, zu personhafter, herzlicher Hingabe binden. Niemandem kann persönliches Leben hingegeben werden außer dem unbedingten Du. Opfer wird allezeit nur der Gottheit ausgegossen.[84]

Again, Althaus is clearly implying that through Uroffenbarung — i.e. before God's full revelation in Christ — man is already encountering and relating himself to a *personal God*.

Yet the "Ur-Wille" is not only the "foundation" of man's involvement in history; he is also its "limit". We experience the "helle Berufung zur Tat", and we feel that there is a purpose — a final goal — to our personal deeds. Also, in viewing the overall panorama of history, we can detect a certain "Ethos" of history according to which nations are held responsible for their deeds and must submit to disasterous sentences when they give way to moral or political degeneration. (GD/I, 23; CW, 74–75) Yet the product of our own activity — as well as the final outcome of world history — is not in our own hands. (CW, 74; GD/I, 23) We are, in the final analysis, helpless to shape history, even though we are called upon to help in this shaping. We experience the "limits" of history; and this implies an experiencing of God. (GD[1]/I, 13)

3. But just what does this "experience" include? This is a question which shall occupy us at greater length in the following chapter. Here we can point out that Althaus was careful to put limits on this presence of God in history. He does not identify time with eternity. God remains beyond the historical, never fully present, never to be experienced with full clarity. Further, it is a manifestation which is mixed with the corruption of a fallen world and ever exposed to the danger of falling from God. Therefore, Uroffenbarung within history, as within all its other modes of manifestation, remains and must remain subordinated to "Heilsoffenbarung". (TG, 749; GD[1]/I, 10–11) — And yet, together with this insufficiency and subordination, Althaus can also maintain: "Niemand kann die Tatsache wegschaffen, daß am Durchleben der Geschichte immer wieder *Gewißheit* Gottes entstanden ist und entsteht." (CW, 71, emphasis mine) This certainty includes, as we already observed, God as a personal being — as a "Du". Althaus adds that through the imperative of history — the call to service and self-sacrifice — God is revealing not only his actuality, his person-ness, but also part of "seinem heiligen Wesen". (TG, 750; CW, 76) And as we shall see in our next chapter, it is a revelation which can even provide the basis for a form of imperfect, subordinated *faith*, faith which is "nicht trügerische menschliche Anmaßung, sondern Antwort auf die Berufung Gottes in der Geschichte ... Beziehung zu dem einen wahren Gott". (GD/I, 23)[85]

Finally, for a full and proper understanding of Althaus' concept of the "Ur-Wille", it must be noted that his description of Uroffenbarung in history was influ-

---

84 "Die Wirklichkeit Gottes", p. 35.
85 Cf. § 44.

78

enced by and received part of its expression through certain *political ideologies* which he inherited from his Lutheran background and which were intensified by his own political involvement with the rise of National Socialism in Germany. Such ideologies form, as it were, a dark cloud over his entire doctrine on Uroffenbarung and supply "the grist" for some of the sharpest criticisms of this doctrine[86].

§ 29. Uroffenbarung in the "Ur-Geist"

1. This final phenomenological form of Uroffenbarung is embodied in the relationship of man's spirit to truth and meaningfulness in the world, i.e. his innate quest for this truth and his ability to respond to it. He is held by a "law of the spirit" which capacitates and propels him to seek truth and to know it. Such a "law" presupposes the reality and enduring activity of an "Ur-Geist". (GD/II, 14)

Once again, Althaus based this affirmation of the intellect as a vehicle of general revelation on an *ontological foundation*. Man's ability to grasp what he feels is truth and meaning in the temporal order is founded on an ontological relationship between *Denken und Sein*, or between *Geist und Welt*. The finite object which is apprehended by the finite intellect was first "thought" by an infinite Intellect or "Geist"; this Spirit injected "thought-ness" or "thinkableness" into the finite order and then enabled finite spirits or intellects to rediscover this meaningfulness. Otherwise, Althaus argues, we cannot explain man's capacity to grasp the "truth" contained in finite objects. (CW, 81) This relationship between "Geist und Welt" was contained, virtually, in Paul's categories of $\nu o \tilde{\nu} \varsigma$ and $\kappa \tau \iota \sigma \iota \varsigma$ in Rom. 1,20; through "die Gabe der Vernunft", man is able to respond cognitionally to the temporal order. (CW, 38; BR, 19)[87]

And because of the "Ur-Geist" who founds this ontological and dynamic relation between "Denken und Sein", Althaus can defend and uphold "das theoretische Denken" as an area in which Uroffenbarung finds expression. Realizing that such a statement was bound to offend the "piis auribus" of many of his compatriots, he first makes it clear that he in no way wishes to propose a sure-fire, rational proof for God's existence. He admits the proud presumption lurking behind the neat array of syllogisms which, wielding the principle of causality, felt they could affirm conclusively the existence of a "first mover".[88] Also, he points out that a true encounter with God is always primarily a matter of the heart and not of the head — of experience and not of rational reflexion. "Die Erfahrung Gottes ist der entscheidende Grund für alle Gotteserkenntnis." (CW, 76; cf. also 79) Admitting this, Althaus can also argue: "Gott bezeugt sich auch dem theoretischen Denken, der Reflexion des Erkennens auf sich selbst, dem Welterkennen." (CW, 77) The so-called traditional proofs for God's existence, despite their syllogistic aberrations, *do* contain an "unaufgebbaren Wahrheitsgehalt". And God is

---

86 Cf. Paul Knitter, "Die Uroffenbarungslehre von Paul Althaus", EvTh 33 (1973) 138–164.
87 Cf. § 23/2. In elaborating this metaphysical basis, Althaus refers to and quotes extensively from A. Trendelenburg, *Logische Untersuchungen*, II (Leipzig, 1862[2]), pp. 430, 463, 469, 490.
88 Althaus feels that Vatican I and the Antimodernist Oath dogmatized such syllogistic argumentation. CW, 77.

known not only "vortheoretisch" — or existentially — but theoretically (CW, 77); " ... Gott läßt sich nicht nur 'hören', sondern auch 'ersehen'. Er bekundet sich nicht nur unserem Gewissen, sondern auch unserer 'Theorie', der denkenden Reflexion und Erkenntnis der Welt." (CW, 79) He reveals himself, indeed, not yet as a "Du" but only as an "Er". And yet this revelation has its own independent value and can serve as preparation for the final and full encounter with the "Du". (CW, 77–78)

The *two particular forms* of the revelation of the "Ur-Geist" in "dem theoretischen Denken" are "die Wahrheitsbeziehung des Geistes" and the study of nature.

2. In describing man's relationship to truth Althaus takes over Augustine's classical presentation of mankind's transcendental thirst to know.[89] Because man is ever in quest of knowledge, because he feels that this quest is worthwhile even at the cost of personal sacrifice, and especially because he suffers and struggles at never being able to lay hands on the full truth — all this is an expression of man's "ursprünglicher Bezogenheit auf die unbedingte Wahrheit" (GD/I, 19) "Das ist die Wahrheit des 'ontologischen' Beweises für das Dasein Gottes." (CW, 80) Any man who thus seeks after the truth is "(von) Gott ergriffen als (von dem) Herrn der Wahrheit, und ... ist hierdurch an Gott gebunden und mit ihm verbunden ..." (CW, 80)[90] Yet never will this encounter with God be complete or satisfactory, for in his thirst for truth, man is seeking to reduce "Geist und Welt", "Denken und Sein" to unity. And this is impossible. Through this constant search for the impossible, " ... werden wir Gottes inne als des Schöpfers, der uns das Denken und Erkennen der Welt gibt und doch darüber bleibt in dem unserem Erkennen entzogenen Geheimnis seiner Schöpfung." (CW, 82)

3. But it is especially within the garden of *nature* that Althaus extolls the ability of man's "theoretischem Denken" to grasp Uroffenbarung. Here again, he realized that he was not "in tune" with a large segment of Protestant theology. Yet he could only chide such colleagues who close their eyes to the richness of creation and refuse to find in it a source of knowledge of — or at least a questioning after — God. Neither could he be satisfied with the half-way concessions of Barth and his followers who admit that nature can speak of God — but only "von Christus her", only "von der biblischen Offenbarung her."[91] Althaus agreed that the full content of nature's message will be unlocked only through the clarity and finality of Christ's light. Yet even before Christ, he insisted, it has something to say. Althaus feels this confirmed through the many natural scientists who, in and through their delving into the vastness and complexity of nature, have been brought face to face with the question of God. He refers especially to Bernhard Bavinck, Max Planck, Max Hartmann, Viktor von Weizsäcker. (CW, 82–84)

Althaus' description of how man's reason can detect traces of the divine within nature follows much the same lines as the traditional "argumentum ex natura". While he refers to the "Reichtum", the "Fülle und Lebendigkeit", the "Erhabenheit und Schönheit" of nature (CW, 310–311), the main brunt of his argument rests on the concept of "Ordnung" — i.e. "Gesetzmäßigkeit und Zielstrebigkeit —

---

89 Althaus explicitly refers to Augustine; cf. *Soliloquia* 1, 15; 2, 2; *De lib. arbitrio* 2, 14, 15.
90 Cf. also "Christentum und Geistesleben", p. 40.
91 Cf. KD II/I, p. 109 ff.

Teleologie." All the world, in its kaleidoscopic complexity, in its "Bestehen und Werden", in its individual entities as well as in its totality — all is governed by laws according to which the "parts" and the "whole" are joined in a harmonious marriage. From the smallest cell to the clockwork of the heavens, there is order, directedness, reliability. Althaus feels that this teleological purposefulness does not lose its awesome effect through "die Dysteleologie der Natur", i.e. through processes which seem to be without purpose or which disrupt the harmony of the whole. All this, he argues, is built into the teleological process — in the service of the parts to the whole. "Kampf und Tod" are directed "auf das Bestehen des Kosmos, auf das Leben ... " (CW, 84–89; GD/I, 24)

As a final note of clarification, Althaus explicitly states that the God who reveals himself through the "Ur-Geist" in nature is not yet the *God of love*. The reality of death hovers like a dark shadow and question mark over all that nature has to say to man. While nature may prevent man from being an atheist, it cannot yet draw back the curtain on a being with whom man can effect a "klares persönliches Verhältnis". Therefore, " ... bedeutet die Natur nicht alles, aber auch nicht gar nichts, sondern etwas". She is not the last word on God but for many men, the first. (CW, 89–90)

§ 30. A Common Starting Point

We must note, briefly but not insignificantly, that the foundation or starting point for Althaus' theology of the religions is, point for point, *basically the same* as that of the "new Catholic attitudes" towards the religious world which have developed during the past decade and have received general (but not total) approval from the Second Vatican Council.[92]

— Karl Rahner — who can be termed the "Father" of the new Catholic thinking on the religions[93] — also bases his theological conclusions concerning the religions on the reality of a general or *universal revelation*. With Althaus (cf. § 20) he would agree that this revelation, which is directed first of all towards the individual, receives a necessary, "social" expression in and through the religions — and thus affords the religions their theological significance.[94]

— There is also basic agreement as to the *nature* of this revelation. Catholic theologians also insist that while it is different from Christ's revelation, is shares a common *divine* quality. (cf. § 22) Catholic theology has for the most part rejected the idea of a literal or historical "primitive revelation" which has been passed on from the beginnings of human history;[95] it has also abandoned the idea of a

92 For literature, cf. Conclusion, ann. 1.
93 P. Hacker, "The Christian Attitude Towards the Non-Christian Religions", ZMR (Münster), 54 (1970) 81; H. Waldenfels, "Das Verständnis der Religionen und seine Bedeutung für die Mission in katholischer Sicht", EMZ, 27 (1970) 143.
94 K. Rahner, "Christentum und die nichtchristlichen Religionen", *Schriften* V, pp. 136–158; cf. also Conclusion, ann. 21. H. R. Schlette appears to have a different starting point than Rahner when he begins his theology of religions with the universality of salvation history instead of revelation. Yet from this history he means to conclude to a genuine and universal divine revelation. H. R. Schlette, *Die Religionen als Thema der Theologie* (Freiburg, 1963), pp. 66–112.
95 Cf. Ch. III, ann. 16.

purely natural revelation or knowledge of God ("theologia naturalis") which would be the product only of man's reason. Rather, contemporary Catholic thought maintains the essential unity (not identiy) between nature and grace – a "supernatural existential" brought about by the Incarnation. Part of this supernatural existential is the possibility of universal, revelatory grace. Revelation outside of Christianity – general revelation – is primarily the product of this grace, not of man's reason or experience. "Uroffenbarung" is always God's work.[96] – And Catholic theologians draw their Scriptural foundation (not proof) for this general, supernatural revelation from the same texts which Althaus made use of, especially the Johannine doctrine of the Logos. (cf. § 29).[97]

–The *phenomenology* of what we may call "Catholic Uroffenbarung", especially as proposed by Rahner, shows the same general lines as Althaus'. It is part of man's "Geistlichkeit", his reaching beyond himself, his "transcendental relation", which through the influence of grace becomes a "Gestimmtheit" by God or a "Grundbefindlichkeit" for the divine. In experiencing himself, man experiences God.[98] A divine revelation is also expressed in the *reality of human love*, of charity, and is behind every authentic interpersonal relationship.[99] And although Rahner does not make use of Althaus' excessively romantic terminology and concepts in describing history as the arena of general revelation, he does see God's revelatory activity, always based on illuminating grace, within the unraveling of profane history.[100] Finally, it is also within man's *cognitional and volitional activity* – his restless seeking after the "verum" and the "bonum" and his ability to perceive and to will – that many Catholic theologians place God as the "conperceived" or "unreflexed" object. A form of revelation can be contained in man's "supernatural intentionality."[101]

96 Cf. Conclusion, ann. 5; also. H. Fries, "Uroffenbarung", *Sacramentum Mundi* IV, 1129; J. Heislbetz, "Uroffenbarung", LThK[2] X, 565; D. O. Brooke, "Natural Religion in the Supernatural Existential", *The Downside Review*, 83 (1965) 201 ff.

97 Denzinger-Schönmetzer, *Enchiridion Symbolorum* 3004, 3015; J. Heislbetz, *Theologische Gründe der nichtchristlichen Religionen* (Freiburg, 1967), pp. 25–30; P. Rossano, "The Bible and the Non-Christian Religions", *Bulletin*, Secretariatus pro non-Christianis (Vatican), 4 (1967) 18–28. The universal interpretation of the Johannine Logos is part of the Catholic acceptance of the logos-spermatikos doctrine; cf. Thils, op. cit., pp. 96–100; also: R. Schnackenburg, *Das Johannesevangelium*, I. Teil (Freiburg, 1965), pp. 203–204, 217–226.

98 This is Rahner's "transcendental method" in understanding both revelation and religions; cf. K. Rahner, *Geist in Welt* (München, 1964[3]), esp. pp. 387–407; id., *Hörer des Wortes* (München, 1963), esp. pp. 47–88; a concise summary of Rahner's transcendental method is found in O. Muck, *Die transzendentale Methode* (Innsbruck, 1964), pp. 197–211, and in J. Alfaro, *Fides, Spes, Caritas* (Romae, 1963, ad usum privatum auditorum), pp. 227–280, 292–321. Cf. also Conclusion, ann. 5. Cf. G. Zasche, pp. 63–64.

99 K. Rahner, "Über die Einheit von Nächsten- und Gottesliebe", *Schriften* VI, pp. 277–298; id., "Gotteserfahrung heute", *Schriften* IX, pp. 166–170.

100 K. Rahner, "Weltgeschichte und Heilsgeschichte", *Schriften* V, pp. 115–135; cf. also id., *Hörer des Wortes*, pp. 161–202.

101 Cf. ann. 99; also J. Maritain, "La dialectique immanente du premier act de liberté", *Nova et Vetera* 20 (1945) 218–235; M. Seckler, "Das Heil der Nichtevangelisierten in thomistischer Sicht", ThQ, 140 (1960) 58–69; Y. Congar, "Salvation of the non-Catholics", *Blackfriars*, 38 (1957) 290–300; M. Eminyan, *The Theology of Salvation* (Boston, 1960), pp. 59–71, passim.

Althaus' attempt at a Protestant theology of the religions and recent Catholic efforts to understand the religions have, it appears, similar if not identical starting points: the admission of a genuinely divine revelation within the non-Christian religious world. From this common starting point do they — or can they — reach common conclusions concerning the religions' positive role and salvific value? — If not, why not? This is the question we will confront in Chapter IV.

Chapter IV

Althaus' Positive Evaluation of the Religions

§ 31. Introduction

1. We are now in a position to examine the central question — the heart — of our case study: trying to trace a "middle way" between the extreme positions of Troeltsch and Barth, seeking to remain faithful to his Protestant-Lutheran heritage, and building on his doctrine of Uroffenbarung — what did Paul Althaus say — or, what was he able to say — about the non-Christian world and its religions?

Our method for answering this question shall be Althaus' own methodology for a theology of the religions: we shall *apply* his doctrine of Uroffenbarung to the reality of religion and examine "ihre Bezogenheit aufeinander". (CW, 53; cf. § 21) In a sense, we shall be *carrying out* and explicitating Althaus' method, for within his treatment of the religions he does not always make clear or explicit the full meaning of Uroffenbarung for them. We shall therefore try to show not only what Althaus *did* say about the relationship between Uroffenbarung and the religions but also what he *could have* said, i.e. what he implied.[1]

In order to make this application and trace this relationship fully we will have to study both Uroffenbarung and the religions in the light of *other elements in Althaus' theology*: his understanding of the Law, of man's divine image, of history, of the act of faith, of God's salvific will.

All this will bring us not only to a deeper theological understanding of the religions but *also* of Uroffenbarung. The full theological content of Uroffenbarung — what it really means for man and whether it can bring him before the face of God — takes shape in the religions. It can be said that the religions are the area where the *phenomenology* of Uroffenbarung becomes the *theology* of Uroffenbarung. They offer the final, theological word on Althaus' doctrine of general revelation. (cf. CW, 93—94)

2. This chapter presents the *positive meaning* of Uroffenbarung for the religions — Althaus' "Yes" to the non-Christian world. This is not the full picture. Uroffenbarung also includes a *negative application* — a "No" — to the religions.[2] This we shall examine in Chapter V. Even though Althaus, for the most

---

1 This does not mean that we will try to impose our own ideas on Althaus by presenting what he "should have" said. We want to remain on the foundation of his "Uroffenbarungslehre" and of his Protestant-Lutheran heritage. "Implications" are to be drawn from *his* thought.

2 F. Konrad holds that Uroffenbarung has only a negative meaning for the religions insofar as they represent exclusively man's abuse of Uroffenbarung. Thus he argues that their "error" blots out the truth of Uroffenbarung (or sends it into a state of "subconciousness") and that they therefore stand only in opposition to the Gospel and Christianity. Throughout this chapter we will try to show that Konrad seems to divide Althaus' doctrines of Uroffenbarung and the religions too strictly, as if the doctrine of Uroffenbarung represents its positive contents while the religions incorporate its negative meaning. Rather, as we have indicated in § 21, Althaus' doctrines of Uroffenbarung and the religions run *within* each other, like matter and form composing one substance. They are, no doubt, different; but not so separable. Therefore the positive *and* the negative are present in Althaus' treatment

part, tried to present these two views together and tried to blend their colors, we are analyzing them separately. And we do this not only for the sake of clarity, not only because we feel that the full content of Althaus' positive picture can be grasped only if studied by itself — but mainly because, in our estimation, these two views are so different that they cannot be satisfactorily harmonized. Their differences even seem to imply opposition. To determine whether this is so (and if so, why so), we first must let then stand by themselves.

I. The Religions Play a Role in the Economy of Salvation

This is the first and more general conclusion which we can draw from Althaus' application of Uroffenbarung to the non-Christian religions: the religions exercise an instrumental role in God's dealings with man, i.e. in what we can call the "economy of salvation" or "salvation history".[3] In this section we shall show how Althaus could assign a role to the religions 1) which is *distinct* from and even partially *independent* of that of the Gospel (and thus he was accused of "natural theology"), 2) which, however, is always a "*supernatural*", divinely-directed role, and 3) which therefore can truly be said to belong to the *history* of salvation.

§ 32. The Religions' Role is Distinct and Partially Independent

1. That the religions play a role in God's plan of salvation which is *distinct* and *different* from that of the Gospel and Christianity is clearly contained in Althaus' definition of Uroffenbarung, as we have presented and analyzed it above.[4] This general revelation, this "ursprüngliche Selbstbezeugung" (CW, 41) which is constantly behind all religions and which gives them their actuality (CW, 141; GD/I, 99) has a reality and function of its own, different from that of "Heilsof-

---

of both Uroffenbarung *and* the religions. His presentation and analysis of Uroffenbarung, for instance in CW, 37—94, shows basically the same negative elements as his study of the religions. (cf. esp. CW, 90—93) And conversely, the same positive side of Uroffenbarung is also clearly asserted within his judgments on the religions. The religions, therefore, *do* represent the misuse of Uroffenbarung, but they also represent its positive content and achievements. As Althaus expressly states in CW, 93, where he "links" his doctrine of the religions to that of Uroffenbarung, the religions have "zwei Pole" — the same two poles which were evident in his study of Uroffenbarung. The religions, in other words, represent the *total* carrying out of the doctrine of Uroffenbarung. And this is one of the central assertions and the method of our study. Cf. § 39/1; § 40/41.

3 Althaus himself makes scarce use of such terminology, mainly because of his concern to limit *salvation* history in the strict sense of the word — i.e. as the full realization of salvation — to Christ and his Word. In our context, we are using this term in a broader sense to describe God's historical plan, in its various stages, of preparing men for and leading them to the fullness of salvation. We do not imply that salvation is necessarily realized at the various stages of this plan. "Salvation history" in this broader meaning corresponds to Althaus' understanding of the historical, progressive nature of God's intervention in the world.

4 Cf. § 22.

fenbarung". The conclusion is simple and clear: this function, which is transmitted through and takes form in the religions, gives them a function and meaning of their own. Thus to ignore the religions, as Barth seemingly did, or to try to minimize their role or absorb it into the role played by the Gospel and Christianity is to perform an undue amputation on God's plan for mankind. Uroffenbarung and the religions are not merely a help or an elective-aid in understanding this plan; they constitute a necessary, distinct part in it. (Ur, 9)

2. But Althaus could go even further in explaining what this distinct role implied. It is not only different and therefore distinguishable from the role of Christ and Christianity, it is also partially *independent*! Here is where he drew sharp fire from many of his colleagues. They could agree with him that Uroffenbarung in the religions is different from Christ's revelation and does perform a distinct task; but they would also insist that this role can be carried out only "von Christus her", only after it is taken up and clarified in the light of Christ. Before this Christian light shines upon it, Uroffenbarung and the religions remain in total darkness.[5]

Althaus would agree that the "von Christus her" is important, even essential for bringing Uroffenbarung to its full light. He by no means wanted to proclaim a total independency of Uroffenbarung. Yet even before the final clarification in Christ, Uroffenbarung can effectively perform its role of giving witness to God. It is "nicht *gebunden* an den Glauben an Christus".[6] It has a meaning and value "durch sich selbst und leuchtet in seinem eigenen Licht". (CW, 61) For many of his contemporaries, Althaus was uncomfortably clear in spelling out what this meant:

Die Wahrheit der Selbstbezeugung Gottes in unserer Existenz ist, welche Bedeutung auch Bibel und Christentum für die Besinnung auf sie haben mögen, nach ihrer Gültigkeit nicht "christlich", nicht an die biblische Geschichte, insonderheit an die Geschichte Jesu gebunden, sondern "natürlich", "menschlich", "vorchristlich". (CW, 62)

Althaus could even say that Christ has only a "heuristische Bedeutung",[7] only a "relative" meaning for the acceptance and grasping of the divine communication which comes through Uroffenbarung. This communication "hat ... ihren eigenen Grund und trägt ihre Gewißheit in sich selbst".[8]

This independent function is also contained in Althaus' threefold and quite novel distinction between Uroffenbarung, "Wortoffenbarung" and "Christusoffenbarung". "Wortoffenbarung" which he defines as "das Gotteszeugnis der Bibel vor dem Evangelium" (evidently, the Old Testament) is basically the same as Uroffenbarung. They "gehören in eins zusammen"; in fact the contents of "Wortoffenbarung" are determined by Uroffenbarung. (CW, 60) The implication is: just as God's "Word revelation" to Israel exercises a function which, although related to Christ, is independent of him, so does Uroffenbarung in the non-Christian religious world.

5 Chapter VII contains contemporary examples of such a "christologischen Rückversicherung"; cf. § 71/2, § 72/5, § 73/5, § 74, § 75.

6 "Adolf Schlatters Wort an die heutige Theologie", *Um die Wahrheit des Evangeliums*, p. 139.

7 Loc. cit.

8 CW, 62 – here Althaus refers to and quotes from A. Schlatter, *Das christliche Dogma* (Stuttgart, 1911), pp. 300 ff.

Given this "independent" function of Uroffenbarung, we can understand how Althaus could maintain that Christianity did not have to bring a new "Gottesgedanken"; it was already present in the "Tatsachen der Religionsgeschichte". (CW, 102–103) Even the deeper content of the Gospel message concerning justification has been grasped by certain religions "without" the influence of Christianity.[9] We shall investigate the full implications of this conclusion in our next sections when we consider "the truth of the religions".

3. Althaus' claim that Uroffenbarung and the religions can carry out a distinct and partially independent role in the plan of salvation is a reflection of his understanding of the *Law and the Gospel*. In his polemic against Barth and in his exegesis of Rom. 2 and 7, Althaus insisted again and again on the difference between Gospel and Law; he warned against identifying or even too closely associating the two; for thus, the distinct and independent function of the Law would be jeopardized or ignored. The "Tatsächlichkeit" of the Law − before the arrival of the Gospel − must be asserted and allowed free play.[10]

The distinction, then, between Law and Gospel corresponds to that between Uroffenbarung and "Christusoffenbarung" and ultimately between Religions and Christianity. There is not a perfect identity here, and we cannot simply equate Law, Uroffenbarung and Religions. Yet all three entities pertain to the same "order" or to the same stage in the economy of salvation. (cf. GD/II, 23) Indeed, Althaus could use the category of the Law as a general definition of this "order". (GD/II, 21) Therefore as we attempt in the following pages to describe the distinct and independent role played by Uroffenbarung and the religions, we will frequently have to return to Althaus' concept of the Law and its counter-role to the Gospel. In the process we shall not only come to a better picture of Althaus' theology of the religions but also of his rich and by no means entirely negative understanding of the Law.[11]

§ 33. "Natural Theology" or "General Salvation History"?

1. By assigning Uroffenbarung in the religions a distinct and independent role within the economy of salvation, Althaus was, in effect, proclaiming another "order" of encounter with God which was "outside" the Christian order − although related to it. Such a proposal smacked heavily of *natural theology*.

9 "Natürliche Theologie und Christusglaube", *Um die Wahrheit des Evangeliums*, pp. 38 ff.
10 "Durch das Gesetz kommt Erkenntnis der Sünde", *Um die Wahrheit des Evangeliums* pp. 169–171.
11 In analyzing Althaus' concept of the Law, we shall be making frequent reference to W. Krötke's fine study "Das Problem 'Gesetz und Evangelium' bei W. Elert und P. Althaus", ThSt(B), 83 (Zürich, 1965). For a more detailed analysis of Elert's concept of the Law, in which it becomes clear that he was much more negative and restrictive than Althaus, cf. L. Langemeyer, *Gesetz und Evangelium. Das Grundanliegen der Theologie Werner Elerts* (Paderborn, 1970). Nürnberger stresses the significance of the Law in determining the differences between Barth's and Althaus' views of the religions and argues that a truly Lutheran understanding of the religions must remain within the category of the Law. cf. *Glaube und Religion bei Karl Barth*, pp. 167–168. In Chapters V and VII we shall try to show that it is precisely a too stringent application of the Law to the religions which seems to hold back Lutheran thinking on the non-Christian world.

Although Althaus himself always looked on natural theology, in its traditional meaning, as a "mortal sin" for any Protestant theologian, and although he constantly sought to avoid this sin, – what he was seeking after was, in effect and even in his own words, "eine 'natürliche Theologie' neuen Stils".[12] This would be a theology which admits and tries to comprehend the "other" order or stage of God's dealing with man. Understood in this way, natural theology could be considered the study of Uroffenbarung and the religions. "Natürliche Theologie ist theologisch zu definieren als der Inbegriff aller in der Menschheit ohne Glauben an Christus wirklichen und möglichen Gedanken über Gott ... Die natürliche Theologie ist nichts anderes als der religiöse Gehalt und Ertrag der gesamten menschlichen Geistesgeschichte."[13] Following Söderblom, he could therefore equate natural theology with the religions.[14]

2. It is understandable, therefore, that Althaus was constantly being accused by fellow Protestant theologians of having fallen into the hersesy of "natural theology". Here we can briefly summarize and outline this very bulky collection of accusations. They will serve to support our own conclusion that Althaus *was* admitting another "order" or "level" of divine history outside of Christ, and at the same time they will help us pose the question as to just what is the nature of this order.

a) Common to all these accusations is that they point to Althaus' doctrine of Uroffenbarung, especially in its phenomenology, as the primary reason for and expression of his "sin" of natural theology. Some of these critics admit Althaus' good will and point out that he tried to avoid such mistakes. And yet in his detailed description of Uroffenbarung and in his application of it to the religions, he proposes "trotz allen Vorbehalten ein Stück 'natürlicher Theologie' in neuer Gestalt".[15] "... die Grenze zur natürlichen Theologie" is not clearly obser-

---

12 "Christentum und Geistesleben", *Evangelium und Leben*, p. 39. For the current state of discussion concerning "natural theology" among Protestant theologians, cf. – besides the manuals (esp. Trillhaas, Weber, Prenter) – the following: H. J. Birkner, "Natürliche Theologie und Offenbarungstheologie. Ein theologiegeschichtlicher Überblick", NZSTh, 3 (1961) 279–295; E. Kinder, "Das vernachlässigte Problem 'natürlicher Gotteserfahrung' in der Theologie", KuD, 9 (1963) 316–333; C. Gestrich, "Die unbewältigte natürliche Theologie", ZThK, 68 (1971) 82–120; W. Lohff, "Zur Verständigung über das Problem der Uroffenbarung", *Dank an Paul Althaus* (Gütersloh, 1958), pp. 151–170; H. Benckert, "Ohne Christus wäre ich Atheist. Zur Frage der natürlichen Gotteserkenntnis", EvTh, 18 (1958) 445–460; R. Hermann, *Fragen um den Begriff der natürlichen Theologie,*BFChTh, Bd. 44, 1950; T. Siegfried, "Was heißt 'natürliche Offenbarung'? Eine Auseinandersetzung mit Tillichs 'Grundoffenbarung und Heilsoffenbarung'", *Der Spannungsbogen*. Festgabe für Paul Tillich zum 75. Geburtstag (Stuttgart, 1961), pp. 87–96; K. Leese, *Recht und Grenzen der natürlichen Theologie* (Zürich, 1954); J. Moltmann, "Gottesoffenbarung und Wahrheitsfrage", *Parrhesia*. Karl Barth zum 80. Geburtstag (Zürich, 1966), pp. 149–172; E. Schlink, "Die Offenbarung Gottes in seinen Werken und die Ablehnung der natürlichen Theologie", ThBl, 20 (1941) 1–13; K. Prümm, "Offenbarung im Neuprotestantismus vom Aufkommen der Religionsgeschichtlichen Schule bis R. Bultmann", *Divinitas*, 8 (1964) 417–523; N. Schiffers, "Natürliche Gotteserkenntnis als ökumenisches Problem", *Catholica*, 21 (1967) 317–328; R. Bultmann, "Das Problem der natürlichen Theologie", GuV II, pp. 294–312; id., "Die Frage der natürlichen Theologie", GuV II, pp. 79–104.

13 "Natürliche Theologie", pp. 34–35.

14 Ibid., p. 34; cf. also p. 38 where Althaus clearly identifies natural theology with the history of religions.

15 M. Doerne, "Zur Dogmatik von Paul Althaus", ThLZ, 74 (1949) 456.

ved.[16] – Other critics are more caustic and accuse Althaus of purposefully and cleverly camouflaging a form of natural theology under the guise of Uroffenbarung.[17]

b) The main brunt of these critics' polemic was that Althaus was proclaiming an order of human-divine history which was too *independent* of Christ and the Christian order. This, as we have seen, was one of the sharpest affronts in the criticism of Althaus' scriptural proof for Uroffenbarung.[18] In his doctrine of Uroffenbarung, especially in its phenomenology, Althaus unfolded the full implications of these "exegetical errors". His very terminology, according to these critics, expresses Uroffenbarung's "insubordination". Lohff feels "daß die Vorsilbe 'Ur' neben der Bedeutung der zeitlichen Priorität eine solche der Herkunft, des Ursprungs in sich trägt und damit auf eine wertmäßige oder kausative Vorordnung der Uroffenbarung gegenüber der Offenbarung Jesu Christi hinzudeuten scheint."[19] Pöhlmann seconds Lohff's reservations and argues that the prefix "Ur" dangerously implies that this revelation is "grundlegend" or that it "'liegt' der Heils-Offenbarung 'zugrunde'".[20] Gloege, too, rejects the prefix, "Ur", since it signifies a revelation which is a "Vorstufe" or a "Vorbedingung" for the New Testament revelation.[21] Althaus, therefore, was running the risk of a "geschichtsphilosophischen Verselbständigung" of Uroffenbarung,[22] of an "Absorbierung und Domestizierung der Christusoffenbarung" in Uroffenbarung.[23] He was proclaiming an order of divine-human relations which carried too much of an "Eigengewicht"[24] and was too "eigenständig".[25] In other words, Althaus "erweckt den Schein, als habe Gott einen *doppelten Weg* geordnet, um sich den Menschen erkennbar zu geben, einmal in Natur und Geschichte *abgesehen von Christus*, und dann im Sohne"[26] – two orders which were much too independent of each other!

c) And because of this natural theology and the "independent order" it implies, Althaus was accused of being more "Catholic" than Protestant, of flirting with Vatican I's "certo cognosci posse",[27] of even outdoing Vatican I by proposing not only the possibility but the actuality of a natural theology. "Römisch-katholische Theologen würden daher wohl die Lehre von der Uroffenbarung bei Paul Althaus als 'modernistisch' empfinden."[28]

16 H. Graß, "Die Theologie von Paul Althaus", NZSTh, 8 (1966) 223; cf. also W. Lohff, "Paul Althaus", *Tendenzen der Theologie im 20. Jahrhundert* (Stuttgart, 1967), p. 301; G. Gloege, "Uroffenbarung", RGG³ VI, 1201; H. Kraemer, *Religion and the Christian Faith* (London, 1956), p. 358.
17 G. Koch, *Die christliche Wahrheit der Barmer theologischen Erklärung* (München, 1950), p. 34; R. Walker, *Zur Frage der Uroffenbarung*. Eine Auseinandersetzung mit Karl Barth und "Paul Althaus", (Bad Cannstatt, 1962), p. 54; W. Wiesner, "Der Gott der 'Wirklichkeit' und der wirkliche Gott", VF (1947–48) 100; E. Hübner, *Evangelische Theologie in unserer Zeit* (Bremen, 1969³), p. 100.
18 Cf. § 23/9.
19 Thus Lohff argues that the theologian should content himself with the expression "Gottes Selbstbezeugung in der Wirklichkeit", – i.e. Althaus' early terminology. Lohff, "Zur Verständigung", pp. 169–170. Cf. § 24.
20 H. G. Pöhlmann, "Das Problem der Ur-Offenbarung bei Paul Althaus", KuD, 16 (1970) 251 ff.
21 Gloege, 1201–02.
22 Lohff, "Zur Verständigung", p. 160.
23 Koch, p. 17.
24 Doerne, p. 452.
25 A. Peters, "Die Frage nach Gott", *Fuldaer Hefte*, 17 (Berlin, 1967), p. 100.
26 G. Heinzelmann, "Uroffenbarung?", ThStKr, 106 N.F. 1 (1934–35) 429, emphasis mine; Wiesner, p. 100; W. Lohff, *Theologen unserer Zeit*, p. 67.
27 Pöhlmann, "Uroffenbarung", p. 254; cf. Denzinger-Schönmetzer, *Enchiridion Symbolorum*, 3004.
28 Koch, pp. 36, 50–51; also Konrad, pp. 435, 639–640; G. Zasche divides the critics of Althaus' Uroffenbarung-doctrine into two groups: those who feel the primary intent of

What all these critics were complaining about was precisely what Althaus, through his doctrine of Uroffenbarung, wanted to uphold: a "Vorordnung", a "Vorbedingung", a "doppelten Weg" – i.e. another "order", distinct from though subordinated to that of Christ, in which the religions were to carry out their own role in the economy of salvation. These complaints, therefore, are "justified", – Yet they are not valid, we feel, when they hold that this "other order" is that of a natural theology. In the following section we will try to show that according to Althaus this order is *by no means* the work of *natural* man. Rather it is a supernatural, a divine order – an order which assigns the religions not only a distinct and partially independent but also a supernatural role.

§ 34. The Religions' Role is Supernatural[29]

1. In our analysis of the *definition* of Uroffenbarung we have shown that although this revelation contains very definite "metaphysical" implications about human nature, it is not simply the product of human nature; it is not a natural revelation or part of a natural order. Rather, it is truly God's revelation – part of a divine order.[30] – Also, throughout our study of the phenomenology of Uroffenbarung we have seen that although Althaus could graphically describe the *effects* of this revelation within human nature, history and creation, the *cause* always remained beyond these "natural" realities. It is the "Ur-Macht", the "Ur-Ich", the "Ur-Wille", the "Ur-Geist" which is the generator of what might seem to be man's natural ability to experience the divine in himself and the world around him. All this implies that the knowledge of God which might result from Uroffenbarung is something entirely different from the "cognitio Dei naturalis" as it has traditionally been understood (or *mis*understood).

Althaus frequently makes this implication explicit. He distinguishes strictly between Uroffenbarung and what he calls man's "tatsächliche Gotteserkenntnis" or "natürliche Theologie". (CW, 42) Such a knowledge of God is made up of the

this doctrine is to allow *exceptions* to man's general sinfulness, and those who argue that it establishes a necessary *condition* for this sinfulness. Zasche (who does not mention the extensive criticisms of Heinzelmann, Wiesner, Doerne, Koch, or Walker) concludes that the first group predominates. Zasche himself, surprisingly, holds that Althaus goes "too far" and allows Uroffenbarung a too effective role. *Extra Nos* (Paderborn, 1970), pp. 136–143.

29 This is the central intent of Zasche's detailed study of Althaus' theology: to show that Althaus, especially in his distinction of Uroffenbarung and "Christusoffenbarung" " ... 'auf evangelisch' sagt, was der katholische Begriff vom 'Übernatürlichen' meint" (p. 227); here the Catholic theologian " ... findet... das Anliegen seines Übernatürlichkeitsbegriffes voll und ganz wieder". (p. 119; also pp. 28, 90–91, 60–65). Although Zasche's study labors under a confusing complexity (in method *and* language) and sometimes draws incomplete conclusions, (cf. ann. 46) its general conclusion is correct: Uroffenbarung and Christusoffenbarung represent two distinctly different phases within the one supernatural order of Christ's grace (cf. pp. 17–19). Althaus' rejection of the supernatural as a "Denkform" rested on a false picture of the new Catholic understanding of the relationship between nature and grace. Cf. Zasche, pp. 121–130; K. Rahner, "Über das Verhältnis von Natur und Gnade", *Schriften* I, pp. 323–345; J. Alfaro, "Transcendencia e immanencia de lo sobrenatural", *Gregoriana*, 38 (1957) 5–50; Conclusion, ann. 5.

30 Cf. § 22/2.

"Gottesgedanken unserer theoretischen Vernunft", the thoughts of God which are prompted by or forced upon us by the world. (CW, 33) Even though this would seem to square with Althaus' description of Uroffenbarung in man's "theoretischem Denken", he insists that such a knowledge of God differs not only from Christ's revelation but also from Uroffenbarung, for *all* revelation, both special and general, must come from a transcendent source. "Sie (revelation) ist in diesem Sinne übermenschlich, transzendent, Geschenk, Gnade, Charisma, *super rationem* – *auch die 'allgemeine Offenbarung'* ... " (CW, 34, emphasis mine) Thus he intended the following remarks, made in the same context, to apply also to Uroffenbarung: "Das Subjekt der Offenbarung ist in strenger Ausschließlichkeit Gott selbst ... Im Blicke auf uns kann das Geschehen der Offenbarung allein durch Passiva ausgedrückt werden, die unsere Aktiva erst begründen." (CW, 32–33) – What is clear is that according to Althaus Uroffenbarung expresses and constitutes an order in which God is active, in which He takes the initiative – in Catholic terminology, an order of universal, illuminating grace.[31]

2. Because the religions, as the products of Uroffenbarung, are part of this supernatural order, Althaus insists – and here we have the theological basis for his rejection of Barth – that they cannot be considered merely the "works of man". We cannot find "... den Sinn der Religion ... in der Lösung irgendeiner natürlichen Problematik des Menschentums, seiner Daseinsnot, seines Kampfes um Freiheit von der Natur, um Geistigkeit und dergl(eichen)" as if the religions were only expressions of the "menschlichen Persönlichkeitsideale".[32] "Es ist schlechterdings unmöglich, die Gedanken der Religionen nur als Phantasiegebilde menschlichen Lebenshungers hinzustellen."[33] "Die Religionen sind nicht freie Schöpfungen des Menschen im Dienste seines natürlichen und idealen Lebenswillens ..." (GD/I, 99) Even though there is certainly much within the religions which is the product of human phantasy, much that is purely profane, the fact stands: because Uroffenbarung remains behind all religious phenomena, the religions remain part of a divine order and carry out a God-directed, supernatural role.

3. We can further apply the supernatural character of Uroffenbarung to the meaning and role of the religions: just as Althaus repeatedly referred to the universal activity of the Spirit to explain the phenomenology of Uroffenbarung, so, too, we can look upon the Spirit as part of the dynamism behind the role of the religions. Althaus himself does not elaborate this "application", yet he certainly indicated the work of the Spirit within the religions when he stated: "Wo immer es Erkenntnis Gottes gibt (and as we shall see in our next section he *does* assert a knowledge of God in the religions), und sei es im Bruchstück oder selbst in der Entstellung, da ist Gottes Geist am Werke." (CW, 344) All this is consistent with Althaus' general theology of the Holy Spirit which affirms "das allgemeine Geisteswirken Gottes" – an activity which takes place "schon ehe der Mensch Jesus begegnet". (CW, 44–45; cf. also 345) The universal, "pre-Christian" workings of the Spirit Althaus finds particularly in man's divine image. "Die Gottesebenbildlichkeit des Menschen wird durch Gottes Geist gewirkt". (CW, 344; PL,

---

31 Cf. Conclusion, ann. 3.
32 "Christentum und Geistesleben", p. 33.
33 "Die Wirklichkeit Gottes", *Zeitwende*, 9 (1933) 85; cf. also "Christentum und Geistesleben", pp. 42–43.

66; Ur 20) The fact that man feels himself a part of the family of God, that he experiences a relation to God and searches after the fulfillment of this relation – in other words, the phenomenology of Uroffenbarung as the "Ur-Macht" – all this, Althaus insists, is real and comprehensible only as the fruit of the Spirit. And it is precisely this "Gottesebenbildlichkeit" which is expressed and searched for in the religions. (CW, 494; PL, 41–67)[34]

4. Even more clearly, we can draw conclusions concerning the presence of the divine *Logos* within the religions as part of their supernatural role. We have already seen that Althaus acknowledged the activity of the Logos within *religious myths* outside of the Gospel[35]. This is a clear indication that the Logos, as well as the Spirit, which are operative in Uroffenbarung will also receive an expression within the social forms called *religion*. According to Althaus, the Logos, the Spirit – the entire phenomenology of Uroffenbarung – cannot be confined to the individual's religious experience; it also can and does find a social-religious expression. The illuminating force of the "ewigen Wort Gottes" will carry out its role not only in "jedem Menschen" but also "in der menschlichen Religion",[36] not only in nature and history but also in the "Religionsgeschichte"[37]. – And where the Logos is at work, we are moving on a more-than-human level.

§ 35. The Religions' Role: Part of the History of Salvation

In this section we wish to illucidate an important facet of the conclusion we have already drawn: because the religions play a distinct and supernatural role in "another order" outside of but always related to the order of Christ, they can truly be said to be part of "Heilsgeschichte". The "other order" to which the religions belong is not outside God's historical plan for mankind's salvation, i.e. it is not outside salvation history.

1. One of the reasons why Althaus rejected Barth's Christomonistic view of revelation was its "Epochelosigkeit".[38] It maimed the historical nature of God's dealing with mankind and failed to grasp its full expanse. Therefore through his own doctrine of Uroffenbarung Althaus sought to show that "Sein (God's) Handeln mit der Menschheit hat Stationen" (CW, 59) and that there are "Epochen in Gottes Handeln mit der Menschheit, ein echtes Nacheinander".[39] Within this "Nacheinander" we can distinguish "Anfang ... Fortgang ... Höhe ...". (CW, 59) God's "Handeln" – i.e. salvation history – therefore is not one-dimensional. Like all history, it is extended, it has stages, it possesses "Tiefendimensionen".(CW, 59) Althaus would not be adverse to characterizing the first "epoch" of this history as its "general stage", just as he would allow Uroffenbarung to be called a "revelatio *generalis*" as long as such terminology did not jeopardize the necessary subordina-

34 *Die Kraft Christi*, Predigten (Gütersloh, 1958), pp. 115–117.
35 Cf. § 23/6.
36 *Politisches Christentum* (Leipzig, 1936), p. 25.
37 Here Althaus was approvingly describing Tillich's "Logos-Christologie", "Die Bedeutung der Theologie Paul Tillichs" (Vortrag, 20.5.1964), pp. 11–12; cf. also CW, 56. Even G. Koch could praise Althaus' "Logos-Christologie". Cf. Koch, pp. 31–33.
38 "Durch das Gesetz", p. 176.
39 "Durch das Gesetz", loc. cit.

tion and relation of Uroffenbarung to Christ's revelation.[40] Thus he is in basic agreement with contemporary Catholic theologians who locate the religions within "the general history of salvation", as distinguished from the "special history" within the Old and New Testaments.[41]

2. This understanding of salvation history and its stages is related to Althaus' *theology of history in general*. Or, we might say: his claim that salvation is always historical is a reflection of his equally clear claim that history as a whole is related to salvation.[42]

Althaus held, firstly, that *God makes use of the entirety of history* to realize the final goal of his love. (GD/II, 34) This is what is implied by belief in Christ as the Lord of history.

> Weil wir ihn bei Gott wissen, der der Herr der Geschichte und unserer persönlichen Schicksale ist, sind wir im Glauben gewiß, daß der Gang der Geschichte und die Einzelschicksale der Herrschaft Jesu dienen müssen, d.h. seiner lebendigen Begegnung mit den Völkern und mit den Einzelnen. Natur und Geschichte liegen in seiner Hand. Es herrscht in ihnen kein anderer Wille als die in Jesus offenbare Liebe Gottes. (CW, 492)

God is also making use of the history of the "Völker"! The fact, then, that he elected a certain segment of history among the Jewish people did not mean that he cut off his activity among the nations. On the contrary — what he was doing through and for Israel was to serve as a representation of what he is doing, in different forms and stages, among all peoples. (GD/I, 70) God's universal activity in history gives all history a certain unity, a single "Thema" which is "die Beziehung zu Gott".[43] God is making use of "Weltgeschichte" to serve the purposes of his "Heilsgeschichte". Just how he is doing this will become clearer in the following pages.

Corresponding to God's use of "Weltgeschichte" — or better, as a result of it — there is a *dynamic orientation* in all history towards the coming kingdom. Althaus is not always clear and consistent in describing this orientation; as we shall see, he stressed that God's activity in world history is hidden and that therefore it is impossible to propose a clear-cut metaphysical teleology of history.[44] Yet his positive statements are clearly articulated and unmistakable. He strongly rejects an "hamartiocentric" view of history's meaning and dynamism — as if the Fall cut it off entirely from God's coming kingdom and propelled it solely in the direction away from this kingdom.[45] Despite the weight and movement of sin away from

---

40 Cf. § 22/3; CW, 34.

41 Cf. H. R. Schlette, *Die Religionen als Thema der Theologie* (Freiburg, 1963), pp. 66–112. Again, we must here recall the distinction we presuppose in our use of the word, "salvation": it signifies God's salvific dealings with mankind, not the actual achievement of salvation for the individual. cf. footnote 3.

42 Here, it should be noted, we are not treating the more precise and much more complicated question of how Althaus understands the mediation of salvation through history, i.e. how revelation is related to history and whether the act of faith must always have an historical mediation. This question we shall consider in § 45.

43 "Heilsgeschichte und Eschatologie", ZSTh, 2 (1924–25) 606–607.

44 Ibid., p. 607; GD/II, 35; LD, 361; CW, 673–84, passim.

45 "Gestalt dieser Welt und die Sünde. Ein Beitrag zur Theologie der Geschichte", *Theologische Aufsätze* II, pp. 45 ff.

God, there remains in all of history as a whole a thrust towards him, as towards its inherent goal. (CW, 683) "Insofern ist alles durch Christus als das ewige Wort Gottes und auf ihn hin als den 'Herrn' der Gemeinde geschaffen, hat in ihm seinen Bestand und sein Ziel." (GR/II, 34) This inner orientation will express itself in what Althaus sums up under the concept of *promise*; throughout its development history as a whole is constantly giving form to "Verheißungen", "verheißendes Gleichnis", "Vorschmack", "heißes Verlangen" towards that which is its God-given goal. He even holds that history can contain a call to faith and justification — "die Berufung der Gnade und Liebe Gottes zum Einsatz, zum Sterben, zum Ganzopfer". The world "ist auf den Glauben und auf das Opfer hin geschaffen."[46] — And this God-bound "orientation", with its "promises" and with its "call" is expressed not only in the "Einzelnen" but also among the "Völker" (CW, 492) — not only in man's heart but in his religions.

3. Therefore, in scattered remarks, Althaus explicitly spoke of the religions as part of God's history with man. In his commentary on Acts 14, 15–17 he concludes that the "Völker" and the "Heiden" make up the *Vorgeschichte* to the special and the final stage of God's dealings in the Gospel. (CW, 40) Elsewhere he describes the religions as the "von Gott gesetzte *Vorstufe*, ein 'Noch nicht' des Evangeliums". (CW, 137, emphasis mine)

He also sees God making use of the religions in much the same way as He makes use of history in general. The religions are God's "Werkzeuge" — the "von ihm benutzten 'Vertreter' seiner wahren Wirklichkeit". (CW, 139–140) This, Althaus feels, is the deeper sense of Gal. 4, 1 ff. when Paul reminds the Galatians that as pagans they were under the στοιχεῖα — the "Urwesen", much the same as the Jews were under the Law. God himself had placed them under these "Weltmächte" — cosmic spirits which are not forces of evil any more than the Jewish Law was. Even though these forces or spirits are not yet the true God, even though they can distort the face of this one God, they are still *willed* and *used* by God. Such imagery is found also in Deut. 4, 19 where Jahweh is said to have placed the nations under their respective stars. "Sie (the "Gestirnmächte") sind die 'Aufseher', die Gott über die Unmündigen gesetzt hat. Durch sie *übt er*, obgleich hinter ihnen verborgen, seine Herrschaft aus und verwahrt die Völker bis auf und für den Tag der Mündigkeit, der die Befreiung vom Knechtsdienste bringt, die Einsetzung in den Sohnesstand." (CW, 137)

Therefore, even though Althaus so persistently rejected Troeltsch's theory of evolution, he himself could admit a definite historical *evolution* behind all religious phenomena. "Man kann in der Religionsgeschichte mit Recht von Entwicklung sprechen, nicht nur im Sinne eines ununterbrochenen Flusses des Werdens, sondern auch im Sinne eines weithin offenkundigen Aufstiegs von niederen zu höheren Stufen." (GD/I, 96) Against Troeltsch and as part of his general understanding of history's orientation towards the Kingdom, Althaus insists that this evolution is not unilinear or able to be programmed by the historian of religions; it cannot of itself evolve into the kingdom. On the other hand, neither is it an evolution which is simply a scattered movement, without a goal, constantly turning in the wrong direction. "In die Religionsgeschichte gehört gewiß der Begriff

---

46 Ibid., pp. 63–64, cf. also pp. 51–56.

der Entartung hinein, aber auch der der Entwicklung."[47] As part of this evolution Paul could propose " ... die Ansätze zu einer Theologie der Religionsgeschichte als einer Geschichte auf Christus hin." (MR, 181) The history of religions, we can conclude, is part of God's history of salvation with mankind.

II. The Nature of the Religions' Role: Their Content of Truth

Having shown that Althaus, by means of his doctrine of Uroffenbarung, could assign the religions a distinct, partially-independent, and supernatural role within the history of salvation, we naturally face the next question: *what* is this role and *how* is it carried out? This section will try to give this question at least part of an answer. It will show that in the religions — again, through Uroffenbarung — a communication of truth is offered to man. Such truth is contained primarily in the possibility of knowing the one, true God.[48]

§ 36. In the Religions Man Can Know the One, True God

1. We have already pointed out that in his exegesis of Rom. 1 Althaus was uncomfortably hesitant about stating that man, under the influence of Uroffenbarung, does come to a clear knowledge of God. While he was absolutely certain in claiming the *possibility* of knowing God through this general revelation, he was not that adamant in affirming man's ability to translate this possibility into an *actuality*.[49]

Yet in his phenomenology of Uroffenbarung Althaus seemed to be unmindful of his exegetical "hesitancy". Even though he nowhere states or implies that in Uroffenbarung the veil is drawn back as much as it is in Christ, even though he is persistent in insisting that man's encounter with Uroffenbarung is imperfect and in need of fulfillment in Christ, he does frequently and explicitly affirm that in the various manifestations of God's "Selbstbezeugung", a true knowledge of God does result. We could sift through § 26—29 and underline the instances where Althaus — not haphazardly but "with full consent of the will" — speaks of knowing God or knowledge of God. He describes man's experience of the "Ur-Macht" in such a way that this experience does not remain buried "incognito" beneath consciousness but expresses itself in the concept of a Supreme Being and in the search after him. In Althaus' phenomenology of Uroffenbarung in history, the concept of the Transcendent seems to assume even clearer, more certain lines. Experience becomes knowledge — so much so that Althaus can sum up: "Niemand

47 Cf. "Heilsgeschichte", p. 614.
48 In this section we shall be treating the cognitional level, i.e. what man can and does know. For the most part, we shall avoid any further questions or conclucions concerning the operational level, i.e. what man can or does do with this truth. Such questions usher us into the heart and final significance of the theological content of Uroffenbarung and of Althaus' theology of the religions. We shall confront these questions when we study the religions as "viae salutis" and when we analyze Althaus' negative reservations concerning the religions.
49 Cf. § 23/2.

kann die Tatsache wegschaffen, daß am Durchleben der Geschichte immer wieder *Gewißheit* Gottes entstanden ist und entsteht." (CW, 71) In man's searching after truth and in his readiness to submit to truth wherever he may find it, "hat (er) darin Gott *ergriffen* als Herrn der Wahrheit". (CW, 80, emphasis mine) And through his study of nature and the world, man can, according to Althaus' description, arrive at a concept of the Creator-God which although it may not present the personal God, although it may not be the "letzte Wort" about God — can be "ein erstes (Wort)" which is not "zu entwerten und zu verachten". (CW, 90)

All these remarks about a knowledge of God, which are scattered throughout Althaus' phenomenology of Uroffenbarung, are crystallized and magnified in his summary statements concerning the nature and purpose of Uroffenbarung. He maintained that by means of his doctrine on Uroffenbarung he intended to carry on Schlatter's efforts to establish an "Anspruch für die *Erkenntnis Gottes,* die Begründung der *Gewißheit Gottes*" outside of Christian revelation.[50] In the last major paragraph of his phenomenology of Uroffenbarung in CW he states: "Unter der Selbstbezeugung (Gottes) ist Erkenntnis Gottes grundsätzlich *möglich* und *wirklich.*" (CW, 90, emphasis mine)

Althaus was therefore asserting more than a merely *potential* knowledge of God. This was precisely what he rejected in his critique of Barth's *Römerbrief*, i.e. that Barth's "Offenbarungseindrücke" remained in the realm of pure possibility: "Ihre Bedeutung besteht im Grunde nur in dem Hinweis auf die unmögliche Möglichkeit, daß das Nicht-Gekannte Gegenstand der Erkenntnis werden könnte." (TG, 746)[51] In Althaus' doctrine of "Offenbarungseindrücken", the "Nicht-Gekannte" *does* become an object of knowledge. Limited and limping though it be, it *is* known. — His critics are correct: "Althaus spricht keineswegs nur von einer reinen Potentialität" (in the knowledge of God).[52] "Es ist wirklich ganz erstaunlich, was wir kraft der Uroffenbarung bereits alles wissen sollen."[53]

2. So we can draw our conclusion: this possibility of knowing God which can and does become an actuality is also both possible and actual within the religions. "Das *Wissen* um Gott ist das Apriori aller Religion". (CW, 138—139) Despite an unavoidable deformation and insufficiency, and taking into consideration the different grades of clarity in different religions, a definite knowledge of the true God is to be found in all religious phenomena. (WE 2, 282; CW, 139)

In numerous — but again somewhat scattered — statements, he expressly admits a knowledge of the true God within the religions. With Luther, he maintains: "Omnes, qui idola constituerunt et coluerunt et Deos vel Deum appelaverunt, item immortalem esse Deum, i.e. sempiternum, item potentem et adjuvare volentem, certe ostenderunt se notionem divinitatis in corde habuisse ... certissime sequitur, quod notitiam seu notionem divinitatis habuerunt quod certissime ex

50 "Adolf Schlatters Gabe an die systematische Theologie", *Adolf Schlatter.* Gedächtnisheft der Deutschen Theologie (Stuttgart, 1938), p. 32, emphasis mine; cf. also "Schlatters Wort", p. 138.
51 Althaus refers to Barth's RB, pp. 55, 64, 72.
52 Koch, p. 14.
53 Ibid., p. 15; cf. Hübner, pp. 99—100; Heinzelmann, pp. 421—422. Althaus can state flatly: "Außer Christus gibt es ... Selbstbezeugung Gottes, daher auch Erkenntnis Gottes ..." in "Die Inflation des Begriffs der Offenbarung in der gegenwärtigen Theologie", ZSTh, 18 (1941) 143.

Deo in illis est ..."[54] Or: "Wir sehen auf die Religionen mit Ehrfurcht vor der Ur-Kunde von Gottes Wirklichkeit, die trotz allem in ihnen wirklich ist ... Wieviel von Gottes Wirklichkeit hat sich in ihnen bezeugt!"[55] He can even point to specific religions or religious doctrines where a knowledge of God is certainly to be found: "Auch der Theismus Indiens, 'Indiens Gnadenreligion', wie Rudolf Otto sie genannt hat, auch der Mahayana-Buddhismus Chinas und Japans sind Möglichkeiten menschlicher *Gotteserkenntnis* auf Grund der Uroffenbarung."[56] Such "possibilities"can lead to a content of "echter Erkenntnis Gottes" among the "heathen"[57] which is founded "in echter religiöser Erfahrung"[58]; it can produce an "echtes gottesfürchtiges Heidentum".[59] The followers of the religions can confront the "Ernste Gottes als des Herrn" (CW, 45); they can be dealing "mit dem wahren lebendigen Gott".[60]

§ 37. In the Religions Man Can Know the Personal God and His Offer of Love

1. The God whom man can know through Uroffenbarung in the religions is not only the one and true Supreme Being, the source and goal of all creation; he is also God as Person, the personal Being who approaches his creatures as persons and communicates his offer of love. In showing that such a communication is possible for religious man, we are progressing another step deeper into the theological content of Uroffenbarung.

Althaus argues for such a personal communication through Uroffenbarung in § 3 of CW, "Das Wesen der Offenbarung und des Glaubens", in which he expounds the general characteristics of *all* revelation. At first reading, one might have the impression that in this paragraph he is refering only to biblical revelation. Yet from context and contents it is clear that Althaus here is dealing with revelation in general — i.e. both "Ur- und Heilsoffenbarung".

A"Wesenszug"of both revelations is: *Personhaftigkeit*: "Offenbarung heißt, daß das Ewige mir als Person, also auf personhafte Weise begegnet." (CW, 25) "Offenbarung heißt: Gott stiftet ein Personverhältnis und handelt mit uns innerhalb desselben." (CW, 28) This means, first of all, that the source or origin of revelation must always, somehow, be a person or refer to a person. Revelation may be transmitted through a "naturhaftes und geschichtliches Geschehen" but it must always point to a person. It may communicate "Wahrheit", "Gedanken", "Tatbestände", "Sinn", but they must be the truth, the thoughts, the reality and purpose of a person. (CW, 26—27; cf. also BR, 15) And therefore, all revelation must always touch the *receiver* in his "Personhaftigkeit"; "die Offenbarung ist niemals nur ein objektives Geschehen, außer mir, mir gegenüber, sondern sie ist, objektiv und subjektiv zugleich, immer Offenbarung an jemanden, in Richtung auf ihn, für ihn, bestimmt, von ihm empfangen zu werden und damit in ihm zu geschehen." (CW, 26)

2. Althaus affirms the personal God within Uroffenbarung when he insists that it does not bring about a "theoretisches Welterkennen" but always an "existentiel-

54 WA, 56, 176, 29, as quoted in CW, 139 and in *Die Theologie Martin Luthers* (Gütersloh, 1962²), p. 27. Althaus adds that Luther's arguments for a knowledge of God outside of biblical revelation were "bestätigt ... durch den Blick auf die Religionen", loc. cit.
55 "Die Wirklichkeit Gottes", p. 85.
56 Ibid., p. 86.
57 "Das Kreuz Christi", ZSTh, 1 (1923) 122.
58 "Christentum und Geistesleben", p. 37.
59 "Völker vor und nach Christus", *Das evangelische Deutschland*, Aug. 15, 1937, p. 280.
60 "Durch das Gesetz", p. 177.

les oder personales Erkennen". Uroffenbarung does not bring its recipient to Kants' theoretical knowledge but to a person who speaks to my person. It includes "eine Begnadung unserer Existenz, die zu danken, ... (eine) Bindung, die zu achten, ... (einen) Anspruch, der zu erfüllen ist". (GD/I, 89–90) — Althaus argues further that Uroffenbarung is never *demonstratio* but always includes *confessio* or *appellatio*. Through Uroffenbarung God does not confront us as "eine bedingte Wirklichkeit oder Wahrheit" which is demonstrated through our "theoretisches Denken". Rather, as "der unbedingte lebendige Herr ... bezeugt (er) sich (through Uroffenbarung) unserem Bewußtsein durch seinen Geist unmittelbar und wird in *personhafter Anerkennung* erkannt." (GD/I, 19, emphasis mine) God is giving witness of himself as person, "in unmittelbarem Innewerden, in lebendiger Erfahrung ... in lebendigem Ergriffensein". (CW, 62) Uroffenbarung *always* has "den Charakter des Zeugnisses und der Anrede" (GD/I, 19). It makes up "Der Anspruch Gottes vor und außer dem Evangelium ..."[61]

Now we can understand the full content and implications of Althaus' frequent — but never perfectly clear — references to the divine "Du" in his phenomenology of Uroffenbarung: that man can surmise a personal will and purpose behind his experience of himself, that he is searching for a greater "Du" in all his interpersonal relations, that he confronts the personal Lord of history in his envolvement in his own historical situation, and that even in his innate pursuit of truth he feels that this truth can be personal. In all this, the "appellatio", the "Anrede", the "Anspruch" of the personal God is being voiced and experienced.[62]

And this voice, this summoning, this loving hand of a personal God — we can rightly conclude — can be found via Uroffenbarung within the religions of mankind. It will be present in various degrees and always in distorted, sometimes false tones. But if we take Althaus' teaching of Uroffenbarung seriously, then we can also look for the one personal God within the non-Christian religions.

3. We can also argue for a confrontation with the personal God in the religions from Althaus' understanding of the *Law*. As we have pointed out, the relationship between Law and Gospel is a necessary guideline for expounding the nature of Uroffenbarung and its effective presence in the religions.[63]

According to Althaus, the first meaning of the Law is to present man in the pre-Gospel order with a *personal* God who offers a person-to-person relationship to his creatures. "Die Offenbarung Gottes in Gestalt des Gesetzes bedeutet zunächst, daß die Beziehung des Schöpfers zu seinem Geschöpf den Charakter eines

---

61 "Durch das Gesetz", p. 175. Graß rightly remarks that Uroffenbarung is never "ohne den Anspruch und Erfahrung Gottes". "Gedächtnisvorlesung für Paul Althaus", *Nachrichten der evang.-luth. Kirche in Bayern*, August, 1966, p. 255.

62 Cf. § 26/2, § 27, § 28/2, § 29/2. A certain difficulty arises in relating this characteristic of personalism to Althaus' phenomenology of Uroffenbarung in nature. He stated that in this particular form of God's general revelation, man does not yet confront the divine being as a person. (Cf. § 29/3) One may ask: if personalism is a necessary trait of Uroffenbarung, then how can this impersonal knowledge of God through nature qualify as part of this revelation? Althaus would probably reply that nature remains a valid avenue of Uroffenbarung because the knowledge of God which it offers serves as a preparation for encounter with the personal God by arousing a longing for and searching after a personal Deity. Cf. CW, 89–90.

63 Cf. § 32/3, also § 23/4.

persönlichen Verhältnisses hat." Through the Law God communicates his personal Will to man as "Gebot", "Anspruch", "Forderung". (GD/II, 21—22) The purpose of the Law, then, is not simply to proclaim man's sinfulness by plunging him into the frustration of trying to observe the Law on his own; it is not simply to cut him off from the living God, but to keep this personal God ever before man and to continue his offer of friendship.

Althaus gave special attention to this positive content and purpose of the Law in *Gebot und Gesetz. Zum Thema "Gesetz und Evangelium"* (1952).[64] Here he carefully distinguishes between "Gebot" and "Gesetz" in an effort to make clear the *full* nature and abiding purpose of the "Law". The "Gebot" represents God's call to man in the "Urstand" and the offer of a personal relationship of love; it belongs, therefore, to the so-called "supralapsaric" state. After the fall, however, the "Gebot" became the "Gesetz" and the "infralapsaric" state intervened. Here man experiences his inability to observe and accept the "Gebot" — which thus becomes the "Gesetz" — and here he constitutes his rebellion against God in that he tries to wield the "Gesetz" as a means of self-justification.[65]

All this is fine and clear — the traditional Lutheran interpretation of the Law in somewhat new terminology. But Althaus goes on to add a twist to his distinction: having distinguished and separated the two realities, "Gebot" and "Gesetz", he then, as it were, brings them back together again! Not as if the "Gebot" continues, as in the "Urstand". By no means, for we are in an infralapsaric condition; the "Gesetz" holds sway. And yet, within the "Gesetz", the "Gebot" is *still contained* and still *offered* to man. "Seinem entscheidenden *Inhalte* nach ist das Gesetz allerdings mit dem Gebot identisch. Auch in ihm drückt sich der eine unveränderliche Wille Gottes an den Menschen aus."[66] And the essential content of the "Gebot" is God's personal love: "Das Gebot lautet völlig personal: Gottes Liebe sucht in ihm mich zur Gemeinschaft mit ihm."[67] Indeed, the "Gestalt" of God's personal will in the "Gesetz" is essentially different than in the "Gebot", which means that the "Gebot" is shrouded — hidden — within the "Gesetz". And still, Althaus argues, it can be grasped: "Daher klingt mir auch nach dem Fall durch das Gesetz immer noch das *Gebot* der Liebe Gottes hindurch ... Kein Mensch steht also nur unter dem Gesetze, er steht immer auch noch unter dem ursprünglichen Gebote der Liebe Gottes."[68] One example of this is the fact that man can still rejoice in the Law, as Paul graphically describes in Rom. 7, 22; he is rejoicing in the "Gebot" of divine love.[69] Within the Law therefore, man can know not only God's wrath but also his love.[70]

---

64 BFChTh, Bd. 46, Heft 2. We will be quoting from its reprinting in: Gesetz und Evangelium. Beiträge zur gegenwärtigen theologischen Diskussion, hrsg. von E. Kinder und K. Haendler (Darmstadt, 1968), pp. 201—238. Krötke offers an excellent analysis of this work in his comparison of Althaus' and Elert's teaching on the Law, cf. ann. 11.

65 "Gebot und Gesetz", pp. 206—215.

66 "Gebot und Gesetz", p. 210.

67 Ibid., p. 211.

68 Ibid., p. 216.

69 Ibid., p. 217.

70 Krötke, p. 29. In his earlier works Althaus did not draw this distinction between "Gebot und Gesetz". This in no way signifies that in 1952 his doctrine of the Law took a different, more positive turn. Really, the distinction only explicitates his view of the Law

This understanding of the Law as contained in "Gesetz und Gebote" enables us to apply Althaus' doctrine of Uroffenbarung to the religions all the more clearly and securely. It answers the question we posed in § 23/4 as to whether his doctrine of the Law allows for a *positive* evaluation of the religions. The *twofold* mission of the Law is carried out by Uroffenbarung within the religions. This means that even though the original or intended content of Uroffenbarung may be deformed or shrouded within the religions, even though the religions may "misuse" Uroffenbarung and try to make it a means of self-justification (as we shall see in the following Chapter) the "Gebot" of God's love, the knowledge of God as a person and his summons to friendship can still be preserved and experienced.

§ 38. In the Religions Man Can Know His Need of Redemption

1. In conformity with his understanding of the Law, Althaus also allows Uroffenbarung to bring the non-Christian to a knowledge and realization of his own sinful, helpless state before God — of his alienation from God and of God's wrath against him; and thus it leads him to the realization that if he wants to find salvation, he must seek it outside of himself!

Rejecting Barth's insistence that the Law can "take effect" and bring knowledge of sin and divine wrath only in the Gospel,[71] Althaus affirmed that even before the proclamation of the Word, "die Offenbarung des Zornes" is "für jeden (ein) offenkundiges Geschehen". (BR, 18) The realization of the divine wrath does not come "zum Bewußtsein ... erst durch das Evangelium".[72] Indeed, Althaus can even hold that through Uroffenbarung God's "Geist" works on the non-Christian's conscience and can reveal to him the "Persönlichkeit" behind the contradictions and alienations of life; the non-Christian can realize that all this is the judgment of a personal God. (CW, 408) Naturally, a clear knowledge of this "wrath" and "judgment" will come only through the Gospel. Yet even before the Gospel it can be imperfectly and, still, effectively known.

Knowing God's "wrath", the non-Christian can also know his own *guilt* and *sinfulness*. The full "Radikalität und Tiefe" of sin will stand forth only in the shadow of the cross of Christ; and for many men, Althaus also points out, a true knowledge of sin and guilt will come only through the Gospel.[73] And yet it still remains possible that man arrives at a true self-knowledge even without the Gospel. "Der Mensch kann seiner innewerden, bevor das Evangelium an ihn herantritt ..." (CW, 408)[74] In this case, all Christ has to do is clarify and confirm this

from his early years — when he stated that the Law expresses an "echte Beziehung" and a "persönliches Verhältnis" to God (GD/I, 17; GD/II, 22); when he accused Luther of having a too negative attitude towards the Law (PL, 56–57); or already in 1924 when as part of his critique of Barth's *Römerbrief* he argued that if we distinguish between knowing and keeping the Law we can call the Law "direkte Offenbarung Gottes, Grund des Glaubens ... ja Evangelium ... Der Gott des Gesetzes ist der Gott des Evangeliums". (TG, 750–751)

71 "Durch das Gesetz", pp. 170–172; cf. Barth, KD IV/1, pp. 400–403.
72 "Durch das Gesetz", p. 174.
73 Ibid., p. 169; cf. CW, 409.
74 Cf. Krötke, p. 22.

self-knowledge — this realization of human sinfulness. "Der Radikalismus der Selbsterkenntnis von Röm. 7 ist die Vollendung, die höchste Steigerung und Klärung einer Erfahrung, von der man in aller Menschheit etwas weiß." And Althaus, to remove any doubt, stresses that such an experience and knowledge is not limited to "Judentum" but is found "auch im Heidentum". (PL, 40—41)

2. Althaus frequently waxes quite eloquent in his descriptions of *how the religions* can and do *grasp man's sinful, needy state* — as if he forgets his own reservations about the clarity of this knowledge! Quite unequivocally, he states that "die menschliche Religion, die jüdische wie die griechische und jede andere" possesses "einen Geist" which brings them to an understanding "von dem Ernste Gottes ... von der Verantwortung, von der Schuld und dem Gerichte." (CW, 45) The religions "wissen auch in ihrer Weise etwas von Sünde und Schuld".[75] There is "außer und vor Christus lebendiges Sündenbewußtsein und Sündenerkenntnis" which Althaus calls the fruit of Uroffenbarung and "menschlicher theologischer Reflexion ... unter der Leitung des Geistes Gottes".[76] The religions grapple with the contradictions and frustrations of life, especially with the staggering mystery of death, and through this reflexion conclude to man's fallen state. Something has happened — or man has done something — to estrange himself from God. (CW, 140) Such a living awareness of sin is part of the "Tatsachen der Religionskunde bzw. Religionsgeschichte". Phenomenologically, we cannot deny "die offenkundigen Analogien zwischen dem Christentum und den Religionen, zwischen der Sündenerkenntnis hier und dort".

And through this experience and knowledge of sin the religions can also grasp another element in the picture of man's actual situation: they can realize that before man can again find himself and his God a *redemption*, a *new birth* must take place which will inaugurate a new era. Not only that — they can even come to "Ahnungen" and "Schatten" as to *how* this redemption must take place. They realize that somehow man must die and God must take over. This is the fundamental content behind the idea of *sacrifice* as it is found throughout the religious world. The theologian cannot ignore the truth contained in this idea for "in seiner Mitte steht das Wort von dem Opfer Christi." (CW, 140) Some religions have carried this insight to even further — almost perfect — clarity: they teach that man is totally incapable of saving himself and that salvation must come only from God. Man has only to open himself in faith and trust to God's redeeming intervention. This is the case, as we shall see, especially in the so-called "Religions of Grace".[77]

§ 39. Summarizing: The Religions Are Instruments of God's Truth

1. The knowledge which the religions can attain of the one, true and personal God and of man's condition before this God can be summed up in what Althaus frequently termed the religions' "Wahrheitsgestalt". The religions *do contain truth* — which means God's truth. And they can thus be considered instruments for making this truth existentially real and comprehensible for their followers.

---

75 Sermon for the "Jahresfest der Leipziger Mission", Feb. 3, 1957, in *Die Kraft Christi*, p. 35.
76 "Durch das Gesetz", p. 180.
77 Cf. § 64.

Is this going too far in our interpretation of Althaus? Would he really allow the religions to make this existential translation of the truth of Uroffenbarung into the factual, comprehensible truth of a religious system? Franz Konrad, who understands Althaus' doctrine of the religions as "the failure of Uroffenbarung", would say no.[78] Weighing Althaus' many negative statements concerning the necessary deformation and misuse of Uroffenbarung within the religions, he concludes that there can be no practical, "useable" truth in the religions. The truth of Uroffenbarung becomes so corrupted that it loses all practical positive content. Indeed, Konrad feels, Althaus proposes truth within the religions *only* as a condition for the denial of this truth and thus for man's guilt. Therefore, truth and falsehood in the religions are not to be considered "als positiver *und* negativer Ausdruck der Uroffenbarung ... sondern die Wahrheit als das Apriori der Lüge ..."[79] The only positive content which Konrad would concede to Althaus' understanding of truth in the religions is that in this "entstellten Wahrheit" there is "das Bewußtsein von der ursprünglichen, von Gott geschenkten Wahrheit". And in this sense, the religions are "ansprechbar" – not because they contain elements of truth but because they have misused the truth of Uroffenbarung![80]

In Chapter V, when we consider Althaus' "No" to the religions, we shall see that Konrad indeed has grounds for such an appraisal. Althaus *does* hold to such a negative content of truth which ends up in "Lüge" within the religions. Yet this does not remove the fact that he also affirms a positive truth, a truth which can be grasped and made use of. This is part of his "Yes *and* No" to the religions. We must admit both. Only then can we determine whether there is opposition between the two, whether one wins out over the other.

Althaus' program for a theology of religions and his definition of religion imply a *content of truth* which is *positive* and *actual* and not just a left-over from an "original truth": "Die Dogmatik muß in ihrer Prinzipienlehre nach der in der Uroffenbarung erschlossenen Gotteswahrheit fragen, welche in aller Entstellung *doch* der Wahrheitsgehalt der Religionen ist." (CW, 53, emphasis mine) "Wir verstehen die Religion ... als Echo des Menschen auf die Selbstbezeugung Gottes und als Ausdruck seiner Lage unter der Selbstbezeugung. *Darin besteht ihre Wahrheit.*" (CW, 93, emphasis mine) And this truth, despite and throughout its "Entstellung", continues to "give witness to itself". (CW, 93) The truth of Uroffenbarung is passed on, finds an "echo", an "expression", a "witness", within the religions. The religions "zeugen nicht nur von Trug und Niederhalten der Wahrheit, (as Konrad maintains) von ihrer Entstellung und Zerreißung zu vereinzeltem Bruchstück, sondern eben damit *auch* von der Wahrheit selber."[81] There is truth in the religions which is willed by God and has a definite *value* in his eyes. "Gott will insofern die Furcht der Götter, die Ehrfurcht, die Demut, die vertrauende Erwartung, wie die Religionen das alles kennen. Er will sie als in aller Gebrochenheit ihm selbst geltend. Die Religionen haben eben darin Wahrheit." (CW, 140) Althaus even singles out the phenomenological, useable forms of this "Wahrheitsgehalt" in the history of religions: within their 1) concept of the "Holy", 2) their acknowledgement of God's will within the Law and the "Ordnungen", 3) their insights into the "Verfallenheit" of human existence, 4) their realization of the necessity of some kind of sacrifice, even "Sühneopfer", and 5) their various forms of "Heils- und Erlösungsgedanken". (WE, 7–9) Here the theologian has no right

---

78 Cf. ann. 2.
79 Konrad, p. 448.
80 Ibid., pp. 446–447.
81 Sermon for the opening of the second "Deutschen Theologentag" in Frankfurt a.M., October 9, 1928, *Der Gegenwärtige* (Gütersloh, 1932), p. 146.

to hold that within such non-Christian religious doctrines there is only "Lüge" or suppression of the truth. Here we can find genuine "religiöse Werte", a "wertvolles Erbe".[82]

2. That the religions' content of truth is, according to Althaus, something positive and something "useable" is further indicated in his understanding of the *questions and answers* in them. Here he goes beyond the widespread Protestant attitude that the religions contain genuine questions but no real answers; the one and only answer comes in Christ.[83] Althaus responds that not only can the religions formulate genuine questions which have a dynamic orientation towards the answer — and in this sense, build an "Einheit" with the answer[84] — but also that within the religions' anwers there can be a real element of truth. "Daher hat die Menschheit nicht nur die religiöse Frage, auf die allein das Evangelium Antwort gäbe; sondern auch in den Antworten der Religionen ist Wahrheit. Frage und Antwort haben Wahrheitsgehalt." (WE 2, 288) Althaus illustrates this in the phenomenon of sacrifice within the religious world. There is truth not only in the religions' questioning after a solution for the limitations, frustrations and "unredeemedness" of existence but also in the answers they supply through their sacrificial rites; they realize that the answer demands a dying to self and a coming to life of the deity. Thus: "Die Antworten ... haben Wahrheit, soweit sie die Richtung ausdrücken, aus der das Heil kommen muß ..." (CW, 146—147) Althaus, of course, will stress that within the truth of such answers there slumbers much error. But this, it seems, would not destroy the reality of this truth and the necessity of making use of it. — This will be clearer in the next section when we consider how the Bible and Christianity can make and have made use of this truth.

III. The Positive Relation between Christianity and the Religions

In presenting Althaus' understanding of the positive relation between the Gospel and the religions, we will be clarifying the contents of the previous two sections: in this relation the religions' *role* can never be totally distinct or independent from Christianity's and their *truth* can never be set above Christ. Althaus was by no means ready to compromise Christianity's "Absolutheit"; here, as we have seen, he remains close to Barth. Yet at the same time, his doctrine of Uroffenbarung permits him to place Christianity and the religions in a relationship of cooperation and dialogue. — All this is seen especially in his concepts of "Anknüpfung" and "Erfüllung".

---

82 "Schlatters Wort", p. 137. Doerne, quite grudgingly, would also agree with our evaluation of the "content of truth" within the religions. He observes that while Althaus states that the religions represent the deformation of Uroffenbarung, his practical theology of the religions in § 16 of CW goes well beyond this and allows a real possession of truth within the religious world. Cf. Doerne, p. 456. – H. Kraemer also criticizes Althaus for the much too positive implications in his concept of the religions' "Wahrheitsgehalte"; cf. *Religion and the Christian Faith*, pp. 348—349.
83 We will consider such attitudes in Chapter VII.
84 "Christentum und Geistesleben", p. 37.

§ 40. The Possibility of "Anknüpfung"

1. Konrad feels that Althaus' frequent mention of "Anknüpfung" or "Erfüllung" concerning the religions implies only a *negative* relation to Christianity. Continuing his argument that the truth of "Uroffenbarung" becomes so deformed in the religions as to be rendered ineffective and hidden, Konrad concludes that according to Althaus, the only way Christianity can relate to the religions is by correcting and condemning them; the only way she can fulfill them is by totally opposing them. "Noch indem das Evangelium die Religionen richtet, erfüllt es sie, und indem es in einen radikalen Gegensatz zu ihnen tritt, weist es einen Zusammenhang auf." The religions are "ansprechbar" only in that they represent man's "Verlorenheit und Sünde".[85] These quotations reflect Althaus' own terminology, (cf, MR, 192–193; GD/I, 99) and indeed, as we shall see in Chapter V, Althaus' concept of "Anknüpfung und Erfüllung" do have a negative content. Yet, our contention is that he also gives them an equally positive meaning, which cannot be ignored. Again, just how the two are to be balanced off is a question we will have to face below.

In describing the various ways in which the Gospel relates to Uroffenbarung, Althaus, after stating that Christ's Word first takes up and forgives man's guilt, goes on: "Damit nimmt das Evangelium die in der ursprünglichen Offenbarung empfangene Wahrheit auf; es bestätigt sie und will sich an ihr als Wahrheit bewähren." (CW, 42) This implies that although the "Bestätigung" takes place within and through the "Vergebung", it is something more than the negative act of correcting and forgiving. There is a positive confirmation and acceptance of something which was really there! So Althaus concludes, the Gospel is always a process of "Anknüpfung" (loc.cit.) and one can certainly assume that he was well aware of the positive connotation which this word acquired during the controversies of the 1930's and 40's.[86] Still within the same passage, Althaus makes an application for the religions: Christ's message can also carry out an "Anknüpfung" with the truth which "trotz allem" is "wirksam" in the *religions*. (loc. cit.) "An die aus Gottes Selbstbezeugung stammende Wahrheit *in* den Religionen, soviel oder sowenig ihrer ist, knüpft die Verkündigung des Evangeliums seit Paulus an, sie nimmt sie auf, macht sie frei aus Entstellung und Lähmung." (CW, 141, emphasis mine) The liberation and the "Anknüpfung" then, are effected not simply through rejection but also through acceptance!

Althaus could allow this "Anknüpfung" to take place not only with the "truth of Uroffenbarung" within the religions but also with the "religious traditions" themselves, with the phenomenological forms of the religions. "Wir meinen auch nicht, daß das Evangelium sich einfach an die Stelle aller religiösen Tradition der Völker setze; es tritt in Beziehung zu ihr, und zwar nicht immer nur in die negative des Gerichts."[87] It is not only unjust but theologically unfounded to

85 Konrad, pp. 446–447; 465. Yet Konrad also admits, in passing, that Althaus "im konkreten Aufweis der ursprünglichen Selbstbezeugung Gottes" does not always speak of "entstellter Wahrheit". (p. 465) We feel that he should have given greater attention to such "konkretem Aufweis" and its meaning for Althaus' theology of the religions.

86 Especially that between Barth and Brunner, and later between Barth and Bultmann in the question of "Anknüpfung" on modern philosophy. Cf. E. Brunner, *Natur und Gnade. Zum Gespräch mit Karl Barth* (Tübingen, 1934); K. Barth, *Nein! Antwort an Emil Brunner* (ThEx 14, München, 1937); *Karl Barth–Rudolf Bultmann, Briefwechsel 1922–1966*, hrsg. von Bernd Jaspert (Zürich, 1971), pp. 169–202.

87 "Um die Reinheit der Mission", EMZ, 10 (1953) 100; cf. also CW, 140.

demand of the non-Christian who approaches Christ that he give up everything which he brings from his own religious traditions and practices. (CW, 45)

The possibility of "Anknüpfung", if taken seriously and carried out properly, leads to the possibility of *"Erfüllung"*. "Das Evangelium stellt sich selbst dar als Erfüllung der Heils-Erwartung, nicht nur Israels, sondern auch der außerbiblischen Menschheit." (CW, 46;cf. also 42) "Der Glaube an das Evangelium ist auch 'Religion', ja die Erfüllung der Religion." (GD/I, 100) Althaus can even substitute this concept of fulfillment for the term "Absolutheit" in explaining just what is the superiority of the Christian religion — not a superiority which destroys but which preserves and perfects. (MR, 178) Here we see, clearly, the positive meaning of both "Anknüpfung" and "Aufhebung": what is taken over is not simply destroyed or changed; it is lifted up, elevated, brought to itself.[88]

This fulfillment will bring to perfection the *"letzte Einheit* von Christentum und Religionsgeschichte" — a unity originating in Uroffenbarung.[89] This fulfillment will satisfy the inner movement and longing and "evolution" within the religions and will reveal "die Herrlichkeit des Einen, die alle Völker suchen, von der sie alle ahnend und betend einen Strahl erschaut haben ...".[90] It will satisfy the "Geist" which is present in Uroffenbarung and the religions and which leads the non-Christian "nicht an Jesus vorbei und gegen ihn, sondern ihm zu". (CW, 45) Althaus can even picture the history of religions as an edifice which finally finds its unity when the one and only cornerstone is added in Christ.[91]

This "Erfüllung" can even work two ways! The religions also have something to offer Christianity; through the dialogue and the "Anknüpfung" Christianity herself can grow richer. Althaus would certainly not propose that the religions can offer anything beyond Christ's revelation, but through their questions, their own insights, they can lead theology and the Church to a deeper penetration of the Gospel. "Sie (Christian theology) gibt nicht nur Antworten, sondern sie hört auch Fragen, die sie selber zu neuer Besinnung auf den ganzen Reichtum des Evangeliums rufen".[92]

2. Althaus builds his argument for the possibility of "Anknüpfung" and "Erfüllung" on the New Testament's "dialogue" with the religions. A brief review of his analysis of the New Testament argument shows that his program is by no means limited to a negative encounter. He assembles various examples of how the biblical revelation drew from the religious world around it in order to clearly formulate and then meaningfully articulate its message: Iranic Parsismus which strongly influenced both late-judaic eschatology and, indirectly, the New Testament message; further Iranic influences in the title, "the Son of man"; the understanding of Jesus as the "$\kappa\acute{\nu}\rho\iota\sigma\varsigma$" or the "$\sigma\omega\tau\acute{\eta}\rho$" as taken over from hellenistic thought; Paul's use of Greek redemption myths — especially in the mystery religions, to express the content of the cross and resurrection; and John's Gospel with its use

---

88 H. Schreiner emphasizes the positive content of the term "Aufhebung" in Althaus' theology. Cf. Review of H. W. Schmidt's *Zeit und Ewigkeit*, ThLZ, 55 (1927) 405.

89 "Christentum und Geistesleben", p. 37.

90 Sermon for "Rostocker Missionsfest", July 9, 1922, *Der Lebendige* (Gütersloh, 1924), p. 68

91 Sermon on May 31, 1925, *Das Heil Gottes*, p. 218–219.

92 "Christentum und Geistesleben", p. 45

of early Gnosticism, representing "eine einzige große 'Anknüpfung'". (CW, 46—48)

We can summarize Althaus' evaluation of such "facts" in three assertions: a) Christianity can establish a definitely *positive* relation to the religions: "Alles in allem: Das Evangelium steht in *positiver* Beziehung auch zu dem vorchristlichen Mythus" ... There is a "*positive* Anknüpfung". (CW, 49, emphasis mine; cf. CW, 46; WE 2, 281) Althaus admits that in taking over this contribution from the non-Christian world there is always a "Korrektur", a "Wandlung" (CW, 49); these concepts must "do penance" before they can be incorporated into the Gospel. (WE 2, 282) Yet all this does not obliterate the truth they contain nor does it rule out the fact that this truth, as it is, can be accepted. "... man darf aber auch über dem Bedeutungswandel der Begriffe die Kontinuität nicht vergessen." (CW, 49) This continuity, this "Zusammenhang zwischen der biblischen Wahrheit und den Religionen", (WE 2, 281) this "heimliche Synthese"[93] can be searched out and then accepted. The necessary "no" to the religions and their myths does not obstruct a possible "yes".

b) The "Anknüpfung" can be carried out with the *religions themselves* and with their concrete forms and doctrines. Here the dialogue is not directed, as Konrad seems to hold, only to the truth behind the erroneous forms, or to the question behind the question — i.e. not only to "Uroffenbarung" in the religions but to the religions themselves. Althaus asserts here that Christianity can take over the religious myths themselves, their concepts and teachings. (CW, 49) He argues that the example of the New Testament proves that there is a positive relation "zwischen dem Evangelium und einer *Gestalt* außerbiblischer Religion". (CW, 47, emphasis mine) What he usually refers to as the Gospel's relation with *Uroffenba-rung* within the religions now becomes a relation with the actual *Gestalt* of the religions.

c) The New Testament teaches us, finally, that Christianity's relationship of "Anknüpfung" and "Erfüllung" is one which is *part of her own nature* and that of the *religions*. She is to relate herself to the religions not simply as part of a technique of linguistic adaptation or pedagogical preparation which does not really touch her nature. (CW, 48) Rather, in dialoging with the religions she is exercising an essential function of her nature and mission; it is part of preaching her message — *even* of understanding the full content of this message. "Die Wirkung Irans" was a decisive factor in helping late-judaic eschatology understand the transcendence of redemption; Jesus and the early Christian preachers took over this understanding. "So sind auch sie *bedingt* durch die iranische Religion." (CW, 46—47) On the other hand, the religions, by their very nature, contain questions and voice longings which the Christian message cannot ignore. The "Heilsverlangen des Hellenismus" inspired by the eternal Logos, (CW, 49) calls for fulfillment in the incarnate Logos. The dialogue and relationship between Christianity and the religions, therefore, as we find it in the New Testament, is determined by a dynamism and by needs within their very natures. We shall see in the next paragraph that this means that the dialogue is one of *necessity*.

3. Further support and clarification for the possibility of a positive "Anknüpfung" with and fulfillment of the religions is found in Althaus' doctrine of the

93 Ibid., p. 36.

Spirit and *man's divine image*. We have already seen that in the religions the Creator Spirit is present, forming man to God's likeness;[94] but it is not yet man's divine likeness in Christ. Following Paul, Althaus feels he can propose a twofold divine image in man: "Er ist Ebenbild in seiner wesenhaften Bestimmung für Gott;" (CW, 337)[95] "er ist Ebenbild, wenn diese Bestimmung an ihm erfüllt ist." (CW, 342)[96] This "first image" — which Althaus describes as human nature's *call* to God and its ability to respond to this call *freely* — cannot be ignored in the redemptive process of becoming the second and perfected image of God. Rather, the preacher must take over and make use of — "anknüpfen" — all that this first image possesses: "Hier waltet ein positives Verhältnis, hier geschieht Anknüpfung, hier ist Kontinuität zwischen dem Menschen ohne Christus und dem Menschen in Christus." (PL, 65) The first image is thus to be fulfilled; man, and all that he brings with him in cultural and religious values, is to find his true unity and integration: "Er ist ganz Mensch geworden (i.e. in Christ), nämlich nicht nur Mensch für Gott und vor Gott (the first image), sondern Mensch Gottes." (CW, 342) In bringing man's divine image to fulfillment, the Redeeming Spirit is fulfilling the work of the Creator Spirit. (CW, 345) Althaus again admits that the work of the redeeming Spirit implies correction of the "first image", breaking with the past but at the same time *fulfillment*. And he comments: "Beides ist gleich stark zu sagen. In der überlieferten Lehre wird von dem zweiten (i.e. fulfillment and "Anknüpfung") zu wenig und ungenügend geredet."

4. We can also trace the theological foundation for the possibility of a positive relation between Christianity and the religions in Althaus' teaching on the *Law*. This is but the explicitation and application of his distinction concerning the Law as "Gesetz" and as "Gebot".[97] If the Law, even after the fall from the "Urstand", continues to be "Gebot", i.e. if it still offers man the possibility of experiencing the personal God and his offer of love, then it is clear that when it comes time for Gospel and Law to encounter each other, they will have much in common, much about which they can dialogue, much that the Gospel can relate to and accept — "anknüpfen". As Krötke rightly observes, this was one of the principle intents of Althaus' teaching on the Law as "Gebot": to assert and clearly trace not only the difference and opposition between it and the Gospel, but also their "Zusammengehörigkeit". It is this offer of divine love which is the "gleiche Intention" or the "Konstante" among all the variables[98] between Law and Gospel and which makes possible not only a "gegenseitige Geltungsbestätigung"[99] and a "wechselseitige Stützung" (CW, 302) between them, but which ties them together — despite all "Abstand" and "Gegensatz" — in an underlying "Einheit". (BR, 82) Therefore, when the "Gottesgedanken des Evangeliums" confront the "Gottesgedanken des Gesetzes", the latter cannot be discarded merely "als niedere, überwundene Religionsstufe, ein 'Idol', eine 'Fälschung' der christlichen Gottesidee" (GD/II,

---

94 Cf. § 34/3.
95 Here Althaus refers to I Cor. 11,7; Jam. 3,9; cf. CW, 337.
96 References are: II Cor. 4,4; Col. 1,15; Rom. 8,29; II Cor. 3,18.
97 Cf. § 37/3.
98 Krötke, pp. 45, 54.
99 Cf. CW, 598, 302; Krötke, p. 45.

24)[100] rather, it must be shown that the two thought patterns are representing — in their different ways — the same God.

This basic unity between Law and Gospel will allow not only "Anknüpfung" but "Erfüllung". The offer of God's love — his "Gebot" will be *fulfilled*. Christ is "zwar des 'Gesetzes', aber nicht des 'Gebotes' Ende."[101] "Durch das Evangelium kommt das im Gesetze sich selbst entfremdete Gebot wieder zu sich selbst, wie es ursprünglich von Gottes Liebe ausgeht und verstanden sein will."[102] This means, then, that in the confrontation between the Gospel and the Law — i.e. between "Heilsoffenbarung" and Uroffenbarung, *and* between Christianity and the religions — there is not only "Ablösung" and "Aufhebung" but also "Erfüllung". (BR, 82; GD/II, 23) What the New Testament accepted and fulfilled in the "Mythus" and the "Begriffe" of the religions was this offer of God's love in the "Gebote".

§ 41. The Necessity of "Anknüpfung"

1. The ability to "anknüpfen" on the religions, together with its possibilities of fulfillment, is not only a possibility but a *necessity*. "Alles, was wir bisher sahen, bedeutet die Möglichkeit *und Notwendigkeit* positiver Anknüpfung der missionarischen Botschaft an den religiösen Besitz der nichtchristlichen Religionen." (WE, 10, emphasis mine) Here we reach the full implications of Althaus' insistence — as a correction of Barth's position — that Christianity cannot bypass the religions and that a theology of the religions must be part of all dogmatic or systematic theology.

Althaus speaks of the relation between "Heilsoffenbarung" and Uroffenbarung in such a way as to demand, quite clearly, the *necessity* of a *positive* relation to the religions: a relation in which Christianity not only must save the religions from sin but also *must* take over and confirm the good which they contain.

This is seen in the *very nature of "Heilsoffenbarung"* and of the Gospel itself. We have already noted that Uroffenbarung holds a central place in Althaus' entire theology precisely because the Gospel bears an essential relation to it.[103] Such a relation is both necessary and *positive*! "Das biblische Wort von Gott bedeutet nichts anderes als dieses, daß die Uroffenbarung Gottes in der Wirklichkeit des Menschen und der Welt ins Licht gesetzt und ausgesprochen wird." (GD/I, 16) The "hearing" and "speaking" of God's Word by the Church must always hear and take into consideration all that man already knows through Uroffenbarung (GD/II, 135) and through his religions. The Gospel is "ganz und gar bezogen auf" the truth of Uroffenbarung (CW, 45); there is an "unlösliche" connection between the two. (GD/II, 11) "Das Schöpfungswort und das Christus—Wort zeugen gegenseitig füreinander und setzen sich ins Licht."[104]

This, according to Althaus, is what is demanded by Christ's revelation insofar as it is a *word-revelation*. Revelation through word implies that it must always be

---

100 Althaus is referring here to Ritschl's understanding of Law and Gospel.
101 "Gebot und Gesetz", p. 218.
102 Ibid., pp. 222–223.
103 Cf. § 22.
104 *Die deutsche Stunde der Kirche* (Göttingen, 1934²), p. 43; *Grundriß der Ethik*, p. 36.

108

spoken to a concrete person and into a concrete situation and positively relate to this situation: "Wortoffenbarung (ergeht) im Zeugnis von Gott" and therefore "bezieht ... (sie) sich immer auf eine bestimmte Wirklichkeit des menschlichen Daseins und seiner Welterfahrung." (GD/I, 15−16) Therefore "Das Kerygma ist nicht geschichtslose Offenbarung, sondern gehört in eine lange Geschichte der Besinnung auf das Verhältnis zwischen Gott und Mensch unter der Leitung des Geistes Gottes hinein."[105] This, in Althaus' estimation, is what Paul meant when he wrote to the Corinthians: "We proclaim the truth openly and commend ourselves to every man's conscience before God." (2 Cor. 4,2) Althaus by no means understands "conscience" merely as the experience of sinfulness: "Das Gewissen ist hier das Bezogensein des Menschen auf die Uroffenbarung, sein Wahrheitsbewußtsein." (CW, 45; cf. also GD/II, 12; GD/I, 17) This makes it undeniably clear that this necessary "Bezogenheit" of the Gospel is directed to the positive content − the "religiösen Werte", the "wertvolle Erbe", the truth of Uroffenbarung and the religions; all this "... muß ins Verhältnis gesetzt werden zu dem Wort des Neuen Testaments, und zwar in ein positives Verhältnis."[106]

2. Althaus emphasizes the necessity of this positive relation to Uroffenbarung and to its presence in the religions by a striking repetition of the particle nur. "Gottes Offenbarung im Evangelium ... wird nur in dieser Beziehung auf die Uroffenbarung als Wort Gottes erkannt." (GD/I, 17) He even can argue that God's revelation can exist only in this relation, i.e. "daß der Sohn Gottes und das Wort Gottes Offenbarung nur sind durch die Offenbarung in der Schöpfung."[107] It can be "ergriffen" "nur in Beziehung zu der Wirklichkeit" of Uroffenbarung. (GD/II, 135) Also the translation of revelation into the personal reality of faith is dependent on this "nur": "Die Gewißheit des Glaubens kommt nur so zustande, daß die neue Wahrheit in Christus sich der alten Wahrheit, von der wir immer schon herkommen ... bezeugt. Die neue Wahrheit und die alte Wahrheit treten in ein Gespräch miteinander. Dieses Gespräch ist der Weg zum Glauben." (Ur, 21) This "nur" also determines the possibility of Christ being recognized for what he is: "Christus wird erkannt nur im Zusammenhang mit der Uroffenbarung Gottes in unserer Existenz, in unserer Lebenswirklichkeit und Lebensfrage; nur im Zusammenhang mit der 'Religion', in der wir zuvor schon auf Gott bezogen sind." (GD/II, 77)

This led Althaus to formulate this necessary relationship with Uroffenbarung and the religions in a way which triggered the consternation of many of his Protestant colleagues: in a sense, Christ and his revelation must allow themselves to be measured by the revelation in man's nature and his religions! Christ and the New Testament, of course, will always remain the final measuring stick of all reality; and yet, before he can carry out this role − or better, while carrying out this role − he must enter into dialogue with the religions. He must submit to and be measured by the questions and truth which Uroffenbarung has instilled into them, for such truth is God's truth and to deny it or to avoid being measured by it would be to deny the unity of God and the unity of his one Work in Christian and non-Christian reality: "... indem sie (Christusoffenbarung) der Uroffenbarung Maß ist, bezieht sie sich zugleich auf diese, bezeugt sich in dieser Beziehung, läßt sich mit ihrem Offenbarungs-Anspruch in dieser Beziehung messen, in der Einheit einer einzigen Gotteswirklichkeit, des einen Wortes Gottes." (GD/II, 12, emphasis

---

105 "Durch das Gesetz", p. 180.
106 "Schlatters Wort", p. 137, emphasis mine.
107 W. Lütgert, Schöpfung und Offenbarung (Gütersloh, 1934), p. 178, in CW, 55; Lütgert repeats this position in op. cit., pp. 394−397, passim.

mine) "Indem er (Christ) sich *messen läßt* an aller vorgegebenen Wirklichkeit unseres Lebens, wird er selber das Maß." (GD/II, 77—78, emphasis mine).[108]

3. Not to remain on the level of theory or general principle, we can consider a practical example of this "Anknüpfung". In his understanding of the *cross* of Christ and redemption, Althaus describes a dialogue between God's Word and the religions which illustrates impressively not only the necessity of this dialogue but its truly positive significance for both Christianity and the religions. Althaus first stresses what any theologian would admit: that the cross of Christ is something totally unique − "eine ganz neue, vertiefte Offenbarung" − in the history of religions.[109] Therefore the theologian cannot hold that the religions, with all their longings and "promises", could ever of themselves arrive at a true knowledge of the "Wesen" of Christ's cross.[110]

And yet Althaus also adds that the cross in itself, as it stands in the New Testament Kerygma, cannot fully be grasped. The reality of Easter was necessary to bring meaning to the cross, but even Easter, Althaus can say, was in itself not enough to clarify fully what is the nature *and* the necessity of the cross. The cross, therefore, must be "measured" and be set in relation with realities outside itself; and such realities are to be found in the history of religions: "Die Erkenntnis des Kreuzes als Heilsgeschehen, als Tat der göttlichen Gnade hat eine innere Vorgeschichte...eine lange biblische (i.e. Old Testament) and außerbiblische Vorgeschichte, ohne die das neutestamentliche Kerygma vom Kreuz Christi nicht zu denken ist."[111] To comprehend the cross not only "als ein nur Tatsächliches" but also as "ein um Gottes und der Menschheit willen Notwendiges" we must bring it into contact and dialogue with the "Begriffe" and "Bilder" stemming from the history of religions: "ἱλαστήριον, Opfer, Hohepriestertum, ... Sünde, Sühne, Vergebung ..."[112] "Der Todesgang Jesu wird in den umfassenden Zusammenhang des Gottesverhältnisses und der Gottesgeschichte der Menschheit eingeordnet *und so* als *notwendig* begriffen."[113] It is clear that Althaus here is speaking of a dialogue which, on the part of the religions, includes more than their negative content of frustration, sinfulness, error, − and takes up also their understanding of their own needs, the possibility and necessity of approaching the divinity through sacrifice, through death to oneself. Also, he sees this dialogue not merely as something which pertains only to the "religionsgeschichtliche" development and formation of New Testament concepts − as if only the New Testament authors had to turn to the religions to clarify their message of redemption. The necessity of this dialogue continues as a challenge to present-day theology: "Es gilt immer wieder. die Wechselbewegung zu vollziehen: die Religionsgeschichte im Lichte des

---

108 Such a position supplied further grist for the criticism we heard above (§ 33). Lohff: Althaus allows Uroffenbarung to become "*Maßstab* und Rahmen" for Christ's revelation. (Lohff, "Zur Verständigung", p. 164) Gloege: Uroffenbarung is a "*Vorbedingung*" for New Testament revelation. (1201−1202) Pöhlmann: Uroffenbarung is too "*grundlegend*". ("Uroffenbarung", p. 152) Walker: Uroffenbarung becomes the "*hermeneutische Voraussetzung* der Heils-Offenbarung". (pp. 24−25) Heinzelmann: Uroffenbarung is the "*Norm*,... an der die wahre Gotteserkenntnis gemessen werden ... soll." (p. 422) Wiesner: Uroffenbarung thus becomes "das letztbestimmende *Prinzip*". (p. 102; cf. also pp. 104−105) Even C. H. Ratschow, who in general is quite conform with Althaus' doctrine of general revelation, feels that Althaus, without wishing to do so, slips into excesses and presents "das Wissen der Grund-Offenbarung als die Gegebenheit und das Wissen der Heils-Offenbarung nur als seine Modifikation ... " *Der angefochtene Glaube* (Gütersloh, 1957), pp. 284−285.

109 "Das Kreuz Christi", p. 110.

110 Ibid., p. 110.

111 "Durch das Gesetz", pp. 179−180.

112 "Das Kreuz Christi", p. 109; "Durch das Gesetz", p. 179.

113 "Das Kreuz Christi", p. 109, emphasis mine.

Kreuzes und das Kreuz im Lichte der Religionsgeschichte zu verstehen..." The two partners must take each other seriously: "... die uns überlieferten Tatsachen der Geschichte Jesu einerseits, die Grundzüge und Möglichkeiten aller religiösen und Gewissenserfahrung andererseits. Beides so tief und vollständig wie möglich aufeinander zu beziehen und ohne Gewaltsamkeit nach hier- und dorthin die Einheit zu finden, das ist das theologische Ziel."[114] A very bold program, indeed, for a dialogical theology of the religions! We will have to ask whether Althaus, in his concept of the cross and of justification, has the theological means to carry out this dialogue fully.

IV. The Religions as "Viae Salutis"?

§ 42. A "Catholic" Question

Here we stand before the most crucial, and at the same time, the most delicate question in our analysis of Althaus' theology of the religions: if the religions have their own role to play in God's plan for mankind, if they can help bring man to a knowledge of God and of his own unredeemed, God-needy situation, if they can enter into a positive dialogue with Christianity and be fulfilled within the Gospel − would all this allow the religions − in given instances, imperfectly, and still implying subordination to the Gospel − to be "ways of salvation"? Might their role be salvific? Might the God whom they make known also be the God of love who takes man into his love and saves him? Might their attempts to search for redemption or to allow God to intervene receive a divine saving response? And might the dialogue between them and Christianity not only be that between those who are searching and those who have found − but also between those who have seen the light and those who have its fulness? Might the religions be instruments − always God's instruments − in bringing the non-Christian to salvation? A salvation which would not be as clearly understood as that coming through Christ, perhaps not as easily attained, a salvation still requiring "fullfillment" − and yet, the same salvation offered and realized through Christ and his Word? In other words: is the role which God has assigned to the religions only that of *bearers of revelation*? Or can they also bear *salvation*? [115]

Such questions, we might say, are "typically Catholic". They usually stand, quite toweringly either at the beginning or at the end of any Catholic evaluation of the religions, determining the entire fabric of this evaluation. Can the non-Christian find salvation "extra Ecclesiam" through their own religions? [116] Among

114 Ibid., pp. 110−111.
115 When we speak of the religions as "ways" or "instruments" of salvation, we mean this *only in the sense* in which Christianity (i.e. Word, Sacraments, Community) or any human means might be *used by God* to communicate *his gift* of redeeming grace. We do not imply that the religions could be means to effect or to merit salvation by themselves.
116 Cf. K. Rahner, "Christentum und die nichtchristlichen Religionen", *Schriften* V, pp. 139−143; H. R. Schlette, *Die Religionen als Thema der Theologie* (Freiburg, 1963), pp. 11−20; J. Heislbetz, *Theologische Gründe der nichtchristlichen Religionen* (Freiburg, 1967), pp. 17−69, 111−143; G. Thils, *Propos et Problèmes de la Théologie des Religions non Chrétiennes* (1966), pp. 14−28; H. Maurier, *Theologie des Heidentums* (Köln, 1967), pp. 14−20. For the general question of salvation for the "heathen", cf. especial-

Protestant considerations of the religions this entire problematic is, for the most part, remarkably absent. They can speak of God's ways within the religions – which imply "revelation", "truth", "Anknüpfungspunkte" – but the question whether the religions can be "Heilswege" is not confronted. It seems to be either superfluous (for salvation comes only through Christ) or improper (for salvation outside of Christianity is hidden in the mystery of God's will). Either it is not raised at all or it is taken for granted.[117]

Althaus, too, did not take up explicitly the question of salvation in and through the religions. And yet, perhaps because his starting point and many of his general principles are close to those of Catholic theologies of the religions[118] this issue is not entirely silent within his exposé of Uroffenbarung and the non-Christian world. Indeed, the question of salvation through the religions seems frequently to raise its voice on its own. It takes shape by itself and stands before Althaus. In such situations, his responses (when offered) vary. They are not at all clear and consistent.

In this section, then, more than in the preceding three, we shall be "applying" and "explicitating" Althaus' doctrine of Uroffenbarung within the religions. And also more than in the other sections, we shall have to turn to other aspects of his theology (eg. God's salvific will, the nature of the act of faith) to clarify this application. We will not simply be drawing our *own* conclusions. Throughout, we shall try to be guided by Althaus' own statements and his "Protestant principles". We want to draw out their deeper content and meaning for the religions – a meaning which he, frequently, only alluded to.

§ 43. The Certainty of God's Universal, Salvific Will

1. Before the question of the possibility of salvation through the religions can even be broached, a *foundational issue* must be settled: God's universal, salvific will. Only if a theologian accepts the reality of this will – not only *theoretically* (as every theologian, it would seem, must) but *practically* – will his vision be cleared for the issue of the salvific significance of the religions. Only if he accepts this will, will he have a necessary tool (just one of them) for working out a response to this question.[119]

ly: L. Capéran, *Le Problème du Salut des Infidèles*, Tome II: Essai théologique (Toulouse, 1934²); M. Eminyan, *The Theology of Salvation* (Boston, 1960); H. Nys, *Le salut sans l'Evangile* (Paris, 1966).

117 This is a question we shall expatiate on in Ch. VIII, § 70/1.

118 Cf. § 30.

119 This is why Catholic interest in the religions developed only after the matter of God's universal salvific will was affirmed, not only theoretically but practically, i.e. after it became clear that the age-worn dictum, "Extra Ecclesiam nulla salus", could not be applied literally. Only then did the mystery of God's ways in the religions take on meaning. Only then did the possibility of a new, more positive understanding of the religions become real. This is also the reason why contemporary Catholic studies of the religions always begin with, or at least include, a reaffirmation of God's salvific will and universal offer of grace. Cf. footnote 116; also L. Capéran, *Le Problème du Salut des Infidèles*, Tome I: Essai historique (Toulouse, 1934²); R. Lombardi, *La salvezza di chi non ha fede* (Roma, 1948); Y. Congar, *Außer der Kirche kein Heil* (Essen, 1961),

Althaus definitely laid this foundation and could wield this tool. For him, there was no doubt about the theoretical truth of this doctrine and its *practical realization*: God *wills* the salvation of all men and he *can* and *does* put this will into practice. Althaus points out "... das klare Zeugnis des Evangeliums von Gottes *unbedingtem, allumfassendem Gnadenwillen*; er reicht so weit wie die Verlorenheit des Menschengeschlechtes, d.h. er trifft *alle* Menschen." (CW, 618, first emphasis mine). The crystallization of this "clear witness of the Gospel" is 1 Tim. 2,4. Because Althaus would not allow any practical explaining-away of the truth of this text, he had to reject both Augustine's and Luther's restrictive interpretation – especially Luther's view of a "hidden will" of God which can decree "the death of the sinner".[120] God's "Heilswille" runs throughout history. (CW, 273) "... von Anfang an ist dieser Gnadenwille Gottes da ..."[121]

2. Althaus therefore argues that since this salvific will is real and since the theologian must take it seriously, a Christian may never hold, or even imply, that the followers of the *non-Christian religions* are on a one-way road to *hell*. Whoever has heard the message of God's love for all men in Christ "... kann die anderen, die vorchristliche Menschheit, die nach Christus von der Mission nicht erreichten Völker und Generationen ... nicht als verloren ansehen". (CW, 481) The Christian may not use the Gospel as a dividing line which neatly and all too proudly separates us, the "electi" from the others, the "damnati", "... als stände uns, den Gehorsamen, einfach Ungehorsam gegenüber,"[122] as if we were the "faithful" and the non-Christian the "unfaithful". Althaus expressly limits the concept of "damnatus" and "infidelis" only to those who have seen Christ and then turned their backs on him: "... die Vorchristen, die außerchristliche Menschheit, die Heiden ... sind nicht die Ungläubigen. Der Unglaube, der einen Menschen verlorengehen läßt, entsteht gegenüber dem Evangelium, aber nicht ohne das Evangelium." (CW, 481; cf. also LD, 187)

3. Althaus does not hesitate to explicitate the implications of such an understanding of God's salvific will: salvation is *not tied* to the *Gnadenmittel* of Christianity or to the preaching of the Word; it cannot be confined within the limits of the Church! The theologian, therefore, may never interpret the dictum "extra ecclesiam nulla salus" literally, for there *is* salvation outside the Church.[123] "Allen Menschen wird die Möglichkeit der Rettung gegeben." (CW, 480) This is the

pp. 107–156, for bibliography cf. pp. 157–163; id. *Heilige Kirche*, Ekklesiologische Studien und Annäherungen (Stuttgart, 1966), pp. 434–464; H. Küng, *Die Kirche* (Freiburg, 1967), pp. 371–378.

120 Although Augustine originally held to the universality of God's salvific will (cf. *De spiritu et litt.* 33, 58), he later put "restrictions" on the assertion of this will in 1 Tim. 2,4: it means only that God wills to save men from all classes (*Enchir.* 103); or that whoever is saved is saved by the divine will (*Contra Julianum* IV 8, 44, *Enchir.* 103); or that God makes us desire the salvation of all men (*De corrept. et gratia* 15, 47). – Althaus' comment on Luther's understanding of God's hidden, unsalvific will: "Sie zerstört die Glaubwürdigkeit des Evangeliums in Verkündigung und Sakrament." CW, 618; cf. WA, 18, 685. Cf. also Althaus' presentation of Luther's doctrine of the "Deus revelatus" and "Deus absconditus", *Die Theologie Martin Luthers*, pp. 238–243.

121 Sermon on December 26, 1961, *Gott ist gegenwärtig*, p. 74.

122 "Toleranz und Intoleranz des Glaubens", *Theologische Aufsätze* II, p. 117.

123 "Christentum und Geistesleben", p. 44.

interpretation which Althaus gives the doctrine of Christ's "descent into hell" as described in 1 Pet. 3, 19 ff; 4,6.[124] Althaus by no means intends to interpret this passage literally, as if we could conclude to a historical happening between the death of Christ and his resurrection. (CW, 484–485) Rather, we are dealing here with "einer zeitbedingten mythologischen Gestalt", whose contents, however, are clear and an essential part of all Christian dogma: "... die Gewißheit des Glaubens über die Reichweite von Christi Heilandsamt ... Diese Gewißheit ist auch für unseren Glauben wesentlich." (CW, 481) His dogmatic commentary on these texts, it might be said, relativizes the "Heilsnotwendigkeit" of Christianity and gives God's salvation a truly universal presence: "Gott kann und wird auch Menschen, die den geschichtlichen Gnadenmitteln in ihrem Leben nicht begegnet sind, selig machen, jenseits dieser geschichtlichen Bedingungen." "Unbedingt nötig zum Heile sind die Gnadenmittel für uns, die wir ihnen begegnen. Für uns gilt: außerhalb der Kirche ist kein Heil. Aber was für uns gilt, ist nicht auch eine Notwendigkeit für Gott, nicht eine Beschränkung seiner Freiheit, Menschen auch ohne die Gnadenmittel selig zu machen, *wo er will*." (CW, 545)

4. "Wo er will" – this is the question which flows from such an understanding of God's salvific will and which, actually, occupies us in this section. Might this "Wo" be found in Uroffenbarung and its activity within the religions? Might God be making use of the religions, not only to carry on his Uroffenbarung, but also to carry out his salvific will for those who, through no fault of their own, have never heard of Christ? If God is not tied to the "Gnadenmittel" of Christianity, might he make use of those provided by the religions, especially since the "Mittel" of the religions are already animated by the "grace" of Uroffenbarung?

Many Catholic contemporaries would hold that the affirmative response to these questions is a natural conclusion. In his understanding of the divine salvific will, Althaus sets up the very same first premises which they use to conclude to the religions as "ways of salvation": God's salvific will which is not only a possibility but a reality within the existence of every individual, the universality of Christ's redemptive activity extending beyond the Church (the "supernatural existential"),[125] and thus the universality of God's offer of grace. From these presuppositions, they conclude to the presence of grace and salvation *within* the religions.[126]

Even though Althaus does not articulate this conclusion, even though, as we shall see in Chapter V, he masses statements which oppose it, he also, frequently, seems to imply it or to allow it. It is almost as if he wanted to draw it, but feared to do so. Such *implications* and *allowances* that salvation can be found in and through the religions can be summed up and studied in his understanding of: 1) a *"form of faith"* in Uroffenbarung and the religions, 2) the possibility of the Spirit

124 "It was in the spirit also that he went to preach to the spirits in prison ... The reason the gospel was preached even to the dead was that, although condemned in the flesh in the eyes of men, they might live in the spirit in the eyes of God."

125 Cf. § 30.

126 With God's universal, salvific will as their first premise, Catholic theologians apply their "second premise": "man is esentially a social being", and conclude: therefore God's salvific will will necessarily find an expression in man's social-religious forms – in his religions. While Althaus would not deny this second premise, it is questionable whether he would apply it so absolutely and universally; cf. § 78/2, d.

effecting an act of *faith beyond the historical conditions of Christ*, and 3) the reality of Christ carrying on his salvific mission *"transhistorically"* but still *within history*.

§ 44. A Form of Faith within Uroffenbarung and the Religions

1. We have already seen that, according to Althaus, Uroffenbarung meets all the necessary requirements to fulfill the definition of a true, divine revelation.[127] If this be so, then we can conclude that Uroffenbarung *must have an essential relation to faith*, for faith belongs to the reality of revelation and cannot be separated from it. "Offenbarung und Glaube *gehören so zuhauf*, daß man jene nicht für sich nehmen und in ihrer Objektivität behandeln kann. Ihre 'Wirklichkeit' wird nur von dem Glauben erkannt, den sie 'wirkt', und nur daran, daß sie zum Glauben drängt."[128] Konrad and Albrecht Beyer, in their studies of Althaus' concept of revelation, conclude (Konrad drawing the same conclusion, 39 years after Beyer!) that for Althaus revelation can come into being and can be investigated by the theologian only in relation to the act of faith.[129] This was the main point in Althaus' critique of Wolfhart Pannenberg's *Offenbarung als Geschichte*:[130] Pannenberg's concept of revelation is divorced from the act of faith: he forgets that the two cannot be separated.[131] All this applies primarily to Althaus' understanding of "Christusoffenbarung" and therefore cannot simply be equated with Uroffenbarung. And yet, if Uroffenbarung does qualify as revelation, then we can expect it, too, "zum Glauben drängen" and to bear an essential relation to the act of faith. – In his theological unfolding of Uroffenbarung, Althaus meets such expectations.

2. Within his doctrine of Uroffenbarung – or we can even say, *forced* by this doctrine – Althaus developed what Koch rightly terms *"einen zweifachen Begriff des Glaubens"*.[132] He definitely did admit a "form of faith"[133] belonging to and being demanded by the process of Uroffenbarung. To the reality of Uroffenbarung belongs "die Wirklichkeit von 'Glaube' und 'Gewissen', schon abgesehen von Christus".[134] And although Althaus always tried to point out the differences between faith through Uroffenbarung and faith through Christ, the distinctions are not always so convincingly clear.

Althaus states that Uroffenbarung leads to a *"faith in the wide sense"*. While it is not salvific faith, it still remains faith in the *theological* sense of the word. "Glaube im allgemeinen theologischen Sinne (hier ist noch nicht von dem speziel-

---

127 Cf. § 22/2; § 37.

128 "Theologie des Glaubens", ZSTh, 2 (1924–1925) 306.

129 Konrad, op. cit.; cf. also § 45; A. Beyer, *Offenbarung und Geschichte*. Zur Auseinandersetzung mit der Theologie von Paul Althaus (Schwerin, 1932), pp. 55–68.

130 Hrsg. von W. Pannenberg in Zusammenarbeit mit R. und T. Rendtorff und Ulrich Wilckens (Göttingen, 1965³).

131 "Offenbarung als Geschichte und Glaube. Bemerkungen zu Wolfhart Pannenbergs Begriff der Offenbarung", ThLZ, 87 (1962) 321–330.

132 Koch, p. 21.

133 This is *not* Althaus' own terminology.

134 "Schlatters Gabe", p. 33.

len Rechtfertigungsglauben die Rede) bedeutet: personhaftiges Empfangen perso-
naler, personbezogener Wahrheit." (CW, 29; GD/I, 89–90) Such faith is a "confessio" (CW, 62), an "existentiales Erkennen" and leads to a "Sich-selbst-Erfassen
des Menschen in seiner sittlichen Freiheit, Verantwortung, Normbestimmtheit";
and although it is not "Offenbarungsglaube", it definitely "belongs" (zugehört) to
this salvific faith and is related to it. (GD/I, 90–91) That it "belongs" to salvific
faith is clear; but one is left somewhat perplexed as to what really separates the
two.

This perplexity thickens when Althaus explains how this faith through Uroffenbarung comes about. In the "modus" in which it comes into being, it is in no
way different from salvific faith; it, too, must be the result of an interior, divine
illumination – of a "Reden Gottes":

> Auch die Geschichte in Jesu Christi und das Neue Testament läßt sich ungläubig
> verstehen. Hier (i.e. in Uroffenbarung) wie dort ist das rechte Sehen *Gnade und ge-
> schieht im Glauben...* Es steht auch nicht so, daß Gott in Christus leichter und wider-
> spruchsloser erkannt würde als in seiner Uroffenbarung. Nicht der *Modus,* sondern der
> *Inhalt* der Gotteserkenntnis unterscheidet die Wirklichkeit Christi von der Wirklichkeit,
> auf die wir hier hinzeigen... Das Erkennen Gottes in Christus steht unter *genau* den
> gleichen Bedingungen wie das Erkennen in der Uroffenbarung. (CW, 63, emphasis
> mine)

Thus, the historical reality of Christ cannot of itself lead to faith any more
readily than the various historical realities which communicate Uroffenbarung –
history, nature and, we might add, the religions. Both can become faith – and do
become faith – only through the illuminating activity of the Spirit. The difference, then, between salvific faith and faith through Uroffenbarung is not in the
"modus credendi" but in the object. Yet theology has traditionally seen the
essence of salvific faith, as described in the New Testament, ("supernatural faith"
in Catholic terminology) not in the object believed but in the manner of believing,
i.e. through God's gift and illumination.[135] This illumination, however, is according to Althaus already to be found in Uroffenbarung. One is tempted to conclude
that the difference between the two is not essential.

Althaus' description of a "form of faith" in Uroffenbarung appears strikingly similar to
the Catholic understanding of "faith before faith",[136] of an "aconceptual, existential
faith",[137] of the "intentio fidei",[138] or of an "embryonic faith".[139] All such views insist that
such "pre-faith" is different from the fullness of faith in Christ; yet they do not deny that it
can lead to a personal decision for God and thus to salvation.

3. The question whether faith through Uroffenbarung and the religions can
bring man to a salvific encounter with God – and thus whether Althaus really
implied more than what he actually said – is even more pronounced in his allu-

---

135 K. Rahner und J. Ratzinger, *Offenbarung und Überlieferung* (Freiburg, 1964), p. 19;
   M. Seckler, "Das Heil der Nichtevangelisierten in thomistischer Sicht", ThQ, 140
   (1960) 57; cf. Conclusion, ann. 36.
136 J. Ratzinger, "Kein Heil außerhalb der Kirche", *Das neue Volk Gottes.* Entwürfe zur Ekklesiologie (Düsseldorf, 1967), pp. 355 ff; Y. Congar, *Außer der Kirche kein Heil,* pp.
   120–127.
137 Eminyan, pp. 59–60; Seckler, op. cit. in ann. 135, pp. 58–69.
138 Y. Congar, "Salvation of the non-Christians", *Blackfriars* 38 (1957) 290–300.
139 P. A. Liégé, "Le Salut des autres", *Lumière et Vie,* 18 (1954) 741–749; M. Seckler,
   "Nichtchristen", *Handbuch theologischer Grundbegriffe* II, p. 241.

sions to faith within his *phenomenology of Uroffenbarung*. This is especially the case in his description of *history*. We have already seen that Althaus could allow man to respond to the "Berufung", the "Verantwortung" and the "Ruf" of the historical moment only because man was thus experiencing God and responding to God's personal call — subconsciously — within this historical summons.[140] "... das Opfer gilt Gott". (TG, 748) "... nur die unbedingte Person kann persönlich, zu personhafter ... Hingabe binden."[141] Within history there is "Gottesbegegnung" and encounter with "dem Heiligen und Unbedingten". (GD²/I, 18) Is not all this faith? Althaus *explicitly* admits that it is. "Es gibt kein echtes geschichtliches Handeln ohne solchen Glauben." (CW, 73) And although he throws in qualifications that this faith is not salvific faith in Christ, he brings the two into an amazingly close relationship. Theology must evaluate such an historical faith "mit dem gleichen Ernste" as faith in Christ, for it is an "*echte* Beziehung zu dem Herrn der Geschichte, dem *einen lebendigen Gott,* (loc. cit.) ... zu dem einen wahren Gott". (GD/I, 23) Such a faith is not "heidnischer Trug", (CW, 73) "trügerische menschliche Anmaßung". (GD/I, 23) Although it will have to be purified in Christ, it will also be fulfilled. Althaus can even allow this act of historical faith to contain an explicit knowledge of God; it is not just a surrender of self to a subconscious, aconceptual "something": "Weil die Geschichte voll des Willens Gottes ist, schenkt sie Erkenntnis Gottes. Diese Erkenntnis ist wie die Bejahung des göttlichen Willens in dem vergehenden geschichtlichen Augenblicke, 'Glaube'." Such a knowledge-in-faith is not the product of reasoning but comes about in the same fashion as knowledge through salvific faith: through divine onslaught and human surrender: "Sie erschließt sich nur dem Ja der freien Hingabe ... Der Inhalt des Willens Gottes enthüllt sich uns in der Geschichte. Gewiß nur so, daß der Geist uns das Auge öffnet." (TG, 749)[142]

4. Similar allusions to the possibility of a salvific faith through Uroffenbarung within the religions are found in many of Althaus' statements concerning faith through *creation* and within man's quest for and surrender to *truth*. — For Althaus, "creation" is a concept which cannot flow from man's rational processes; it can be arrived at only through an act of faith. "Der Gedanke 'Schöpfung' ist nicht eine Hypothese des Welterkennens, sondern ein Akt des Glaubens (Heb. 11,3). Schöpfung bedeutet die Grenze alles menschlichen Denkens und Begreifens. Schöpfung kann von dem Geschaffenen nur glaubend anerkannt, aber nicht gedacht und nicht begriffen werden." (GD/II, 31) And yet, Althaus can allow this concept of creation, with its implications of a personal (and salvific?) faith — to become real for man in the non-Christian religions. He rejects as "krampfhaft und unhaltbar" any thesis which insists on a "christological foundation" for the "Schöpfungsglaube". "Jesus und das Neue Testament setzen den Schöpfungsglauben voraus. Er lebt schon im Judentum, auch im Parsismus. Er gründet ... darin, daß man *Gottes als des Herrn innewird.* Das ist nicht an die Begegnung mit Jesus Christus gebunden, sondern kann ihr vorausgehen." (CW, 301) Althaus questions whether, without Christ, such a faith is "durchzuhalten" since it is always "under attack" through man's own sinfulness and the contradictions of life. So the line of separation between such a faith and that through Christ is there — but, especially when one considers the essential "Angefochtensein" of Christian faith (CW, 601; 611–612) — the line seems rather thin!

When speaking of man's *quest for truth*, Althaus makes similar remarks (which in this case almost seem like "slips") about possibilities of a personal faith and union with God. "Wer

140 Cf. § 28/2–3.
141 "Die Wirklichkeit Gottes", p. 85.
142 Cf. Beyer, p. 24.

nach unbedingter Wahrheit fragt und ihr sich zu beugen bereit ist, den hat darin Gott ergriffen als Herr der Wahrheit, und er ist hierdurch an Gott *gebunden* und mit ihm *verbunden*, wie fern von ihm er auch sonst in seinem persönlichen Leben sei." (CW, 80) Although Althaus is careful to add that despite this union man *may* be far from God in his personal life, he does state that this encounter with God effects a "Gebundenheit" and "Verbundenheit" with him. But this is precisely the distinction he will later use to argue that Uroffenbarung is unsalvific: it can bring about "Gebundenheit" but not "Verbundenheit" with God. "Verbundenheit" means salvific union.[143] Is our reference merely a terminological slip? Or perhaps what we might call, in the theological sense, a "Freudian slip" in that it reveals what Althaus throughout his doctrine of Uroffenbarung was, without full realization, implying or allowing?

5. All these scattered statements about a form of faith possible through Uroffenbarung and the religions reflect and in a sense sum up the "implications" which ran through our presentation of Uroffenbarung in Chapter III. This general revelation was making known and summoning man to a personal God — and frequently man seemed to be able to make use of this knowledge and respond to this summons. This was always an unclear knowledge and imperfect response, for man did not yet see the full expression of God's love — "quod Deus vellit" — in Christ. Therefore, an imperfect faith. And yet, it seemed to allow a real, though imperfect, union with God. Althaus insists that this is not yet salvation. The reader, however, who takes Althaus' description of Uroffenbarung in the religions at its word, can ask: why not? Can there be a "form of salvific faith" outside the historical reality of Christ and his revelation? We can insist on these questions, as we now consider Althaus' understanding of the relation between "history" and "Spirit" in the act of salvific faith.

§ 45. Does Faith Require Knowledge of the Historical Reality of Christ?

1. If this direct question were posed to Althaus, he would no doubt have answered in the affirmative. Such an affirmative reply, as we shall see, is contained in his doctrine of justification.[144] At this juncture, however, we would like to hear the answer he gives within his doctrine of revelation — or more precisely, of the *relationship between revelation-faith and history*. This entire issue — whether faith and revelation are communicated primarily through the power of the Spirit *or* through history — is one of the most complex and penumbral aspects of Althaus' theology. It has already been the subject matter of two doctoral theses — Beyer and Konrad[145] — and of a lengthy study by Hans Wilhelm Schmidt.[146] The common conclusion of these different studies — different both in viewpoint and tone[147] — leads us a step further in our own question concerning the possibility of salvific faith through Uroffenbarung and the religions.

143 Cf. § 51/3, b.
144 Cf. § 58, § 60.
145 Cf. ann. 129.
146 H. W. Schmidt, *Zeit und Ewigkeit*. Die letzten Voraussetzungen der dialektischen Theologie (Gütersloh, 1927), pp. 108—156.
147 The differences stem not only from Beyer's and Schmidt's Protestant viewpoint and Konrad's Catholic approach, but are also found in their "tone". Beyer and Konrad build their argumentation on a much more scientific, objective foundation, while Schmidt's reasoning seems darkened in the smoke of personal polemics; the same might also be said

2. There *seems* to be no doubt as to where Althaus stood within the "historical Jesus" controversy which swept over the theological terrain after World War II. In his *Das sogenannte Kerygma und der historische Jesus* (1958) he reenuncitated his previous position and rejected Bultmann's so-called "Kerygmatheologie" or "Existenztheologie". Stated succinctly: faith and revelation presuppose and must be founded on historical reality. "Die Frage nach der Wahrheit des Evangeliums schließt die Frage nach seiner Geschichtlichkeit, d.h. nach seinem Grunde in der Geschichte ein ... Das Bekenntnis zu Christus setzt seine Geschichtlichkeit unbedingt voraus." (CW, 116–117) The "kerygma", therefore, is not only "Word" but also "witness" to historical realities.[148] Therefore, theology and faith cannot run away from the question of the historical Jesus and the uncomfortable probings of historical-critical research, for here the validity and the content of the Christian message are at stake. (CW, 120; 128–129)[149]

3. But just as much as Althaus could find fault with Bultmann's "Kerygmatheologie", he also had to reject — as we have seen — Pannenberg's extreme version of what seemed to be a "Geschichtstheologie". "Beides, Geschichte und Erleuchtung durch 'Reden' Gottes zu dem menschlichen Geiste, gehört zusammen."[150]

Thus Althaus seems to represent an understanding of revelation-faith as originating from "Kerygma" *and* "Geschichte" — from "Geist" *and* "concrete fact". Indeed, this is the position or solution he *strove for*. But the critics mentioned above have ferreted out and revealed the impression which the attentive reader feels but cannot always put his finger on: that Althaus' synthesis between "history" and "Spirit" is not that clear. The precise "Ort" in which revelation and faith take place is not so evident. What Konrad terms Althaus' "Und-Formeln" do not achieve a synthesis: "Glaube *und* Geschichte ... Geschichte *und* Wort ... Manifestation *und* Inspiration ..." Where do we construct this "und"? For Althaus "der Ort der Begegnung zwischen Gott und Menschen" is "nicht eindeutig zu bestimmen."[151]

4. This unclarity originates from the fact that although Althaus insisted on the necessity of the historical Jesus and his work for the act of faith (especially within his doctrine of justification), he seems to give *more and decisive importance* to the *role of the Spirit* and his *interior illumination*. What determines the act of faith is the "Erleuchtung durch Reden Gottes", much more than "Geschichte".[152] This is

---

of E. Peterson's article, "Über die Forderung einer Theologie des Glaubens. Eine Auseinandersetzung mit P. Althaus", ZZ, 3 (1925) 281–302.

148 *Das sogenannte Kerygma und der historische Jesus* (Gütersloh, 1958), pp. 15 ff; cf. also pp. 27 ff.

149 Althaus admits that with this assertion he is "going beyond" the position he held in the 1936 edition of GD (§ 9) "zu klarer Einsicht in die Bedeutung der historischen Forschung an den Evangelien für unsere Gewißheit um die Echtheit des Evangeliums und seines Christusbildes". CW, 120. For the question of the historical Jesus, cf. CW, 116–130, GD/I, 36–46; "Der 'historische Jesus' und der biblische Christus", *Theologische Aufsätze* II, pp. 162–168; Graß, "Die Theologie", pp. 220–221; Konrad, pp. 483–523.

150 Cf. ann. 131. Here Althaus quotes from GD/I, 30–31.

151 Konrad, pp. 626–627; Beyer, p. 117; H. W. Schmidt, pp. 108–134.

152 This "priority of the Spirit" expressed so clearly in Althaus' critique of Pannenberg was

also implicit in Althaus' insistence that what really makes Uroffenbarung and "Christusoffenbarung" revelation in the true sense of the word — i.e. faith — is not their "Inhalt" but their "Modus", i.e. the Spirit which enlightens the contents of both.[153]

The decisive role of the Spirit and its internal illumination in the act of salvific faith is, negatively, set in even sharper relief by Althaus' apparent *devaluation of history's influence* on man's "I believe". Even though he held that all revelation and faith must happen "in geschichtlichem Handeln" (GD/I, 33), this "Handeln" seems to lose its essential role when it comes to the production of the individual's act of faith — and the Spirit takes over. It is almost as if history becomes merely a "conditio sine qua non" for faith — but does not exercise any kind of real causality. Here Althaus was holding true to the "common ground" he shared with Barth: although he allowed the Divine to step into history, the two remained separated; history could not be a cause by which the divine is brought into the existence of the world or of the individual. The "schmerzliche Schranke" remains.[154]

For Althaus, history *in itself* — even Christ's history — was an *impediment* to the act of faith, for all history remains a "Verhüllung" of God's love and salvation; Christ himself could not escape being such a "veil". This "historical hiddenness" of God becomes meaningful and can be "overcome" only in the act of faith, i.e. only through an internal light; yet it *always remains*. "Was Verhüllung ist, wird dem Glauben Offenbarung, indem es ihn fordert und schafft; aber es bleibt zugleich Verhüllung".[155] "Die Offenbarung ist wehrlos dem Zweifel ausgesetzt: Gott läßt sich nicht 'sehen'. Was 'sichtbar' ist, das ist weltlich: was ewig ist, das ist 'unsichtbar'." (Shades of Barth!) (CW, 25) "Nur wo Verhüllung ist, da ist Glaube an die Offenbarung Gottes."[156] Within Althaus' dialectic of "Offenbarkeit und Verhülltheit", "(liegt) der entscheidende und damit die Dialektik sprengende Akzent auf der Verborgenheit Gottes."[157]

Therefore Althaus' critics can, from their various standpoints, reach a common verdict: Althaus may propose a salvific faith (or revelation) as the product of the historical and the more-than-historical, but the decisive and really essential element is always the more-than-historical: the Spirit. "Diese eigentümliche Geisteswirkung ... ist die grundlegende Bedingung des Glaubens, neben der die geschichtliche Beobachtung nur sekundäre Bedeutung beanspruchen kann."[158] Konrad feels that Althaus places so much emphasis on the Spirit within the act of faith that "die geschichtliche Erkenntnis einseitig zu einer Funktion des geistgewirkten Glaubens gemacht wird";[159] history seems to become a "rein gegenständliches Phänomen" and is not really a "Medium der personalen Offenbarung Gottes".[160] Schmidt pushes this charge to its extremes when he argues that the personal or spiritual aspect of faith

also contained in his early articles, "Theologie des Glaubens" (1924–25) and "Christologie des Glaubens", *Theologische Aufsätze*, I, pp. 206–222.

153 Cf. § 44/2.
154 "Heilsgeschichte und Eschatologie", p. 646; cf. Konrad, p. 604.
155 "Theologie des Glaubens", p. 313.
156 Ibid., p. 301; cf. also TG, 767 ff.
157 Konrad, p. 509; cf. also p. 604.
158 Beyer, p. 66, cf. also pp. 40–48; Konrad, pp. 492–500, 558–571; Schmidt, pp. 135–140.
159 P. 577.
160 Ibid., pp. 604–605.

attains, according to Althaus, an "unabhängige Selbständigkeit von der verhüllenden und Ärgernis erregenden Geschichte",[161] — which seems to imply "daß die Theologie des Glaubens ihrer ganzen Struktur nach geschichtslos ist".[162] Although we cannot accept some of the extreme formulations in such evaluations of History-Spirit in the act of faith (eg. that Althaus' understanding of faith is "geschichtslos" or that history for him becomes a "rein gegenständliches Phänomen"), their central assertion seems correct: as much as faith and revelation must have a historical foundation, history does not enter into the *causality* of the act of faith.

5. Our application: In the light of his understanding of the relationship between history and Spirit within the act of faith, Althaus *could allow* the possibility of salvific faith in Uroffenbarung and the religions. Such an "allowance" could be constructed in three steps:

a) If the *Spirit* and his *internal illumination* play the essential and determinative role in the act of faith, why can't this Spirit carry out his role through Uroffenbarung and, therefore, within the religions? As we have seen, the Spirit *is* clearly present in and through Uroffenbarung. Althaus frequently referred to the Spirit being behind the various phenomenological manifestations of Uroffenbarung, providing them with their reality and dynamism. And it is the Spirit which transforms these manifestations into authentic revelation by enlightening their recipient — just as he has to enlighten the recipient of Christ's revelation.[163] Why cannot the Spirit illumine Uroffenbarung salvifically?

b) One may answer: because this salvific illumination is limited, as Althaus implies, to a specific *Inhalt*, i.e. to the historical content of Christ's revelation. (CW, 63) Only this piece of history can be illuminated salvifically. Yet it would seem difficult to press such an argument since as we have just seen, Althaus admits that even Christ's history plays, as it were, a non-causative role in the act of faith; in other words he admits that the reality of faith is determined not by the "objectum credendum" but by the "modus credendi". Althaus even states that the "Inhalt", the historical element in Christ's revelation, labors under the same deficiencies — albeit to a lesser degree — as the historical element in Uroffenbarung: it, too, is shrouded in a "Verhüllung" of God; it, too, is an "Ärgernis"; it, too, is exposed to "Zweifel". Only through the Spirit can one overcome these "obstacles". Yet the same Spirit is present in Uroffenbarung, confronting similar if not the same obstacles. Can Althaus logically insist that the salvific illumination is limited only to Christ's historical content?

c) According to Althaus' concept of faith, the historical element, even though it may not be causative, is still *necessary*: the Spirit requires the historical element in order to operate. — Still, we can ask: why cannot the Spirit draw this necessary element from the historical expression and content of Uroffenbarung and the religions? Indeed, he would not be able to make such facile, certain and universal use of the historical content of Uroffenbarung as he does of Christ's revelation. Differences remain — very important differences. But if the Spirit needs "the historical", if the historical is offered in Uroffenbarung and the religions, and if the Spirit is already present within Uroffenbarung — why cannot he make use of the "history" of Uroffenbarung and despite its "Verhüllung" and "Ärgernis" bring

161 Schmidt, p. 152; cf. also p. 156.
162 Ibid., p. 140.
163 Cf. § 34/3; § 44/2.

the non-Christian to salvific faith? Proceeding from Althaus' "premises" concerning the nature of history and Spirit in faith, such an allowance *seems* possible — almost logical.

§ 46. The Universal Christ — Working Salvation within History

1. In the preceding two paragraphs we have shown that Althaus *could allow* the Spirit to make use of Uroffenbarung and the religions in order to effect a "form of salvific faith" outside Christianity. In this paragraph we will collate and analyze the statements in which he indicates that this *actually does take place*: salvation outside the Gospel and within the religions.

Such statements are based primarily on Althaus' understanding of the *universal, salvific activity of Christ*. He describes this activity in § 13, "Das Evangelium", of CW: (CW, 102—107)

> Obgleich an einem historischen Punkte erschienen, ist Jesus in seiner *Vollmacht* allen Geschlechtern der *Geschichte* von Gott her als gleichzeitig gesetzt. Das heißt: aller Menschen Gemeinschaft mit Gott trotz und in ihrer Sünde lebt verborgen von seiner, des Gekreuzigten und Auferstandenen, Vollmacht. Wo es vor und außer dem Evangelium und der Christenheit irgendwo in der Menschheit, z.B. im Alten Testamente, *wirklich* von Gott gewährte *Gemeinschaft* der Sünder mit ihm gibt, erfahrene *Vergebung* und *Nähe Gottes*, da wird sie um Jesu willen, 'in Christus' geschenkt — ob 'vor' ihm oder 'nach' ihm, historisch genommen. In diesem Sinne ist Jesus Christus auch vor seiner historischen Zeit schon *überall* gegenwärtig, in der Gemeinde des Alten Testamentes, aber *nicht nur in ihr*. Wie Luther es ausgesprochen hat: Christus etiam ab initio mundi occisus est pro peccatis totius mundi; ... (WA, 39 I, S. 49) Das ist die neue Sicht der Menschheitsgeschichte von dem Glauben an Jesus Christus her. (CW, 107, emphasis mine)

An analysis of this passage reveals the following ingredients:

a) This universal presence and activity of Christ demands the *universal possibility of salvation*. This is contained in Althaus' understanding of the concept, "Vollmacht Christi", which he defines in the following pages as the power by which guilt-laden man is brought back "in die Gemeinschaft mit Gott ... durch heiliges Vergeben". (CW, 108) In this passage he already speaks of this "Gemeinschaft" of sinful man with God, which is already "wirklich" — a union worked by God, through his "Nähe" and "Vergebung". — The universal presence of Christ, in other words, becomes a synonym for the universal salvific will.

b) This salvation which is universally possible always remains a Christian salvation, i.e. although it takes place "extra Christum", it is always "propter Christum", stemming from his unique "Tat" and "Vollmacht". Thus we can say that Christ and his Incarnation have a *cosmic efficacy*. This is what Althaus terms Christ's "übergeschichtliche Gegenwärtigkeit"[164] which he received after the resurrection (CW, 492), or more simply, the "Gegenwärtigkeit der Geschichte Jesu" (CW, 115), "die allezeit gegenwärtige Geistesmacht Gottes über die Herzen".

164 In CW Althaus expresses reservations about the term "übergeschichtlich" which in earlier writings he had adopted from Martin Kähler. He feels that it tends to detach the universal power of Christ from its historical source. Christ, indeed, can effect his salvation at any moment of history only because he entered history at one precise moment. CW, 115.

(CW, 492) The Incarnation affects "die Weite und Länge samt allen geschehenen und zu erwartenden Wendungen und Wandlungen in der Geschichte." (CW, 107)

c) More important for our study, Althaus states here that this salvation can be and is effected not only beyond history — at the end of time — but *within and through history*. The universal Christ can penetrate the historical moment and the historical means in which the non-Christian finds himself. This provides an answer to the questions posed at the end of our last paragraph: the Spirit *can* make use of other, non-Christian historical realities to effect the act of faith. Althaus could therefore endorse Tillich's concept of grace as "souverän" and "nicht gebunden an irgendeine endliche Form" and able to work through various "kairoi" within history.[165]

d) Althaus further implies that salvation through the universal Christ is worked out especially in history's *religious phenomena*. When speaking of the "irgendwo" of this salvation, i.e. where it is concretely to be found, he mentions the religious community of the Old Testament, but immediately adds, "nicht nur in ihr" — also within other religious bodies; the implication is: also within other religious "Gnadenmittel". —

On the basis of the universal Christ, then, we can conclude that this Christ can and does use the religions as "viae salutis"; his Spirit can work through them and bring men to a form of salvific faith.

2. We must point out that nowhere does Althaus expand these "conclusions" into a *doctrine* of the religions as ways of salvation. Even within § 16 of CW — his concentrated study of the religions — there is no clear, direct statement on the salvific instrumentality of the religions.[166] But in various other and somewhat isolated contexts, Althaus does make explicit assertations that salvation *can be* and sometimes *is* communicated to the non-Christians *by means of their religions*. We can group such assertions into three complementary categories:

a) When confronting the question as to what will be the lot of those who step before the *last judgment* without ever having had the opportunity to know Christ and his Word, Althaus first emphasizes that they definitely cannot be packed off to hell according to a theory of predestination calling for a "doppelten Ausgang". Then, after stating that their eternal lot is a "mystery" hidden in God's will, Althaus still ventures an answer: "Wir können tastend einige Gedanken wagen." (LD, 187) He feels that the salvation of the non-Christians will "perhaps" be decided by the use they made of Uroffenbarung in their religions! "An alle Menschen ergeht fortwährend Gottes 'vocatio generalis' (one of his synonyms for Uroffenbarung) ... Diese 'allgemeine Berufung' stellt jeden Menschen vor das Entweder-Oder der Gottesfurcht oder ungebrochener Weltlichkeit, der Selbstbehauptung oder des Dienstes. *In aller Religion* ist ein Schatten der großen Entscheidungsfrage Gottes, die in Christus den Menschen trifft. *Vielleicht* wird Gott die von Christus nicht erreichte Menschheit *nach ihrer Haltung* gegenüber der ihr jeweils kundgewordenen Wahrheit richten." (LD, 187, emphasis mine) Althaus dared to make this very same statement in his article on Christ's descent to hell: "*Vielleicht* macht Gott sie selig ohne eine andere Entscheidung als die, welche

---

165 "Die Bedeutung der Theologie Paul Tillichs", p. 8, cf. also p. 17.
166 On the contrary, as we shall see in the next Chapter, he has much to say about the religions' "Heillosigkeit".

durch Gottes vocatio generalis auch ohne die Begegnung mit dem Evangelium sich in ihrem *irdischen Leben* vollzog."[167] – Here Althaus is saying that "perhaps" the religions are ways in which the non-Christians can work out their salvation.

b) Such "perhaps-statements" take on greater probability when Althaus, in CW, remarks: "... in den Religionen empfängt man ... das *relative Heil*". (CW, 139) And when he explains this "Heil", the "perhaps" seems to become a certainty. He compares the use the non-Christians make of their religions "mit dem irrenden Gewissen": although the religions may not contain the full truth, although there is much error mixed with the truth they have – still, like conscience, they are a "bindendes Gesetz"; the non-Christian *must* obey the truth as he feels he finds it in his religions. "Auch mit einem irrenden, begrenzten Gewissen soll man gewissenhaft sein."[168] And if the non-Christian does accept and bow to the truth which his religions offer him, he will find a genuine "Bezogensein auf Gott". They will offer him not a "Gottes-Ersatz" but will be for him "'Vertreter' seiner (God's) wahren Wirklichkeit". (CW, 139–140) Therefore God *wills* that the non-Christians follow their consciences as formed in their religions: "er will, daß die Menschen vor ihm ganz die sind, die sie sein müssen."[169] The decisions man makes through his religions are decisions made for or against the one, true God. "Er will sie (the religions) als in aller Gebrochenheit ihm selbst geltend." (CW, 140) In this sense they are his instruments which he uses to lead men to decisions which will decide their salvation. This would seem to be the content of the "hohen Sinn" of God's "Führungen" within the history of the individual and of the religions, which Althaus alludes to elsewhere. (CW, 629) This would also seem to be the way in which the "universal Christ" effects "seine lebendige Begegnung mit den Völkern und mit den Einzelnen". (CW, 492) The "relative Heil" is relative in that it is worked out imperfectly, through a cloud of truth mixed with error, by means of an "erring conscience" – yet in the end effect, it is eternal salvation.

c) In another context Althaus renders this "perhaps" and this "relative salvation" even more concrete in that he states explicitly that God can make use of the historical forms of the religions to grant his "Gnade" and "Vergebung" and thereby his "Gemeinschaft" to the non-Christians. In a 1923 article on the Cross of Christ he states that redeeming "forgiveness" must always be communicated through historical realities (the essential relation between history and revelation!) and such realities can be provided by the religions:

> Es ist freilich weithin in der Religionsgeschichte, wo die Sünde mächtig war, auch die *Gnade Gottes* mächtig gewesen. Die Erkenntnis des Widerstreites gegen Gott und das Sühnebegehren ist durch den Bann des Zornesverhängnisses immer wieder durchgeschlagen. Die Religionsgeschichte ist ein *Denkmal* nicht nur des Zornes Gottes, sondern *auch der Vergebung Gottes.* Aber diese Vergebung hat sich sehr konkret betätigt. Was *in den Religionen* an echter Erkenntnis Gottes, an echter Buße und Freudigkeit zu ihm

---

167 "Niedergefahren zur Hölle", p. 370. In CW, it should be noted, Althaus seems to have lost this courage; it is precisely this sentence which he jettisons in the otherwise verbatim reprinting of this article on pp. 479–485; in CW, he is satisfied with the comment: „Zu postulieren ist hier nichts." CW, 482 (also in CW[1]/II (1948), p. 265) – And yet in later editions of LD he lets this "daring statement" stand; cf. LD, 187.

168 "Toleranz und Intoleranz des Glaubens", p. 117.

169 Loc. cit.

124

da ist, was also mitten unter dem Walten der Menschheitssünde in ihrer religiösen Gestalt als *wirkliche Gemeinschaft Gottes* mit dem Menschen wirksam wird, das geht immer auf Stifter und Propheten, auf konkrete Bundesschließungen und Gerichtsbekundungen Gottes zurück. Nirgends ist das so ausgeprägt wie in der Religion Israels.[170]

Is not this salvation? God's "Gnade", his "Vergebung", his "Gemeinschaft" possible through the historical forms — "Stifter, Propheten, Bundesschließungen" — not only in Israel but in the "Religionsgeschichte"?

Such an early statement — perhaps somewhat "unguarded" — is repeated in its essential content in *Grundriß der Dogmatik* where Althaus, speaking of the relation between pre-Christian history to Christ's history, states that within the "verheißenden Vorbilder" of Israel and other religions there is genuine "forgiveness". In this passage he directly relates such redeeming forgiveness to the influence of the "universal Christ": "Auch im *Gleichnis und Zeichen* (both in Judaism and in "der Menschheitsgeschichte") kann Herrschaft Gottes durch *Vergebung wirklich* sein, weil Christus in alledem übergeschichtlich schon gegenwärtig ist... Alle Erfahrung von Vergebung galt und gilt 'in Christo'." (GD/II, 105, emphasis mine)

4. All these statements concerning the universal Christ and his salvific "Vollmacht" together with the possibility of this "Vollmacht" being realized within the religions, do not, we must emphasize, form a unified, clear whole — i.e. a doctrine of salvation through the religions. Such statements are scattered, frequently hesitant. Yet they *are* to be found within Althaus' evaluation of the non-Christian world. We cannot ignore them, or explain them away in the light of other, more negative ennunciations.

Yet, we must also ask why they appear only in this "half-hearted" manner, why Althaus did not or could not develop them — and especially, whether they can be reconciled with what he also said about the "Heillosigkeit" of the religions. These are the questions to be treated in Chapters V and VI.

170 "Das Kreuz Christi", p. 122.

Chapter V

Althaus' "No" to the Religions: Dialectical or Contradictory?

§ 47. Introduction

In a sense, it would be much easier — and preferable — if we could omit this present chapter. Althaus' positive picture of the religions could be accepted as it is; we could add our own critical comments and suggestions as to where it might be better clarified, balanced and perhaps developed in order to form a more rounded, integrated view of the religions. In its substance, though, it could stand as it is.

But it does not. As self-sufficient as this positive picture may appear, Althaus, as we have mentioned above,[1] could not allow it to stand by itself. Even though his favorable view already contained a clear limitation of the capabilities of the religions and a definite subordination of their role to that of the Gospel, Althaus felt this was not enough. He had to articulate these limitations and reservations even more clearly. Thus we have what we may call his "no" to the religions. It is not as extensive and many-faceted as his positive view; indeed, this chapter appears to be merely an "appendage" to the preceding. And yet its basic message and demands are just as clear and just as meaningful (if not more so!) as those of his positive view.

Althaus by no means intended his negative, restrictive assessment of the religions to be entirely different from his positive appraisal. Rather they were to be two dimensions of the same picture. In adding his "no" he did not wish to rescind his "yes". Like the majority of Christian theologians, both Catholic and Protestant, he felt that any evaluation of the non-Christian religious world must be dialectical.

Yet here is the difficulty — and the purpose — of this chapter. Can Althaus' "no" be pronounced together with his "yes" — as he tries to do? Can the negative dimension of his picture of the religions be blended with the positive?

In the first section of this chapter we shall trace Althaus' "no" as it runs parallel to the divisions of our preceding chapter — i.e. to the religions' distinct role in the plan of salvation, their content of truth, their relation to Christianity and their capacity to be "viae salutis". In the second section, we will explicitly confront the question which, we hope, will have taken form within the first part: did Althaus' attempt at a theology of religions succeed? Does his dialectical "Yes-No" present a balanced picture — or is it, ultimately, contradictory?

I. Althaus' Parallel "No" to the Religions

§ 48. Concerning the Religions' Role in the Plan of Salvation

1. While Althaus assigns Uroffenbarung in the religions a role which was "nicht gebunden an den Glauben an Christus" and which could function "durch sich selbst ... in seinem eigenen Licht" and which therefore had a "Gültigkeit" which

1 Cf. § 31/2.

126

was "natürlich, menschlich, vorchristlich" (CW, 62)[2] he also warns, repeatedly, that he is not thereby proposing a *natural theology*. Yet it is not always clear just what is contained in this warning! In it, he not only rejects a revelation which is purely human and natural (thus affirming that all pre-Christian revelation must be from God and therefore be supernatural) but also, frequently, he seems to be denying any real *value* or *efficacy* to this revelation. In GD, he defines what he understands as "den Begriff der natürlichen Theologie": "Er bezeichnet die dem natürlichen Menschen trotz seiner Sünde *auf Grund der Uroffenbarung* kraft der relativ unversehrten Vernunft mögliche Erkenntnis Gottes; sie wird, als unvollständig und vor allem zum Heile nicht ausreichend, von der übernatürlichen Offenbarung wohl ergänzt, aber auch bestätigt." (GD/I, 25—26, emphasis mine) At first impression, one would say that this pretty well sums up the picture of the role of Uroffenbarung which we presented in the preceding chapter. Yet Althaus immediately adds: "Dieser Begriff ist abzulehnen." And the reason that he gives for this rejection is that this revelation and the knowledge it brings, although it stems from Uroffenbarung (and therefore is not just "natural"), although it is "unvollständig" and must be "ergänzt" — still grants man before Christ too much of an independent function. It does away with the total sinfulness of man. Althaus therefore insists that this function cannot be "in sich selbst gültig"! (ibid.) Is there not a certain contradiction here between "natürliche Gültigkeit" and "nicht in sich selbst gültig"? Just how much validity is left for Uroffenbarung?

This unclarity becomes even more perceptible through Althaus' repeated insistence that Uroffenbarung can be "recht erkannt *erst* im Lichte der Offenbarung Christi". (GD/I, 13) Again, the full meaning of "recht erkannt" or "ins Licht gestellt" is not always evident. And it seems to involve a certain contradiction. Although Althaus labeled Barth's "nur von Christus her ... nur von der biblischen Offenbarung her ..." a "verkrampfte theologische Rede", (CW, 83—84; 301)[3] he himself continually resorts to what we can call his own form of a "christologischen Rückversicherung": to almost every facet of Uroffenbarung he adds the reminder that true knowledge of Uroffenbarung can come only from Christ. (Cf. CW, 84,147; GD/I, 29; MR, 179; Ur, 24; WE 2, 277—278; PL, 39) He admits explicitly that the clause, "'nur von Christus her' ... natürlich in letzter Hinsicht richtig (ist)."[4] Just what does "in letzter Hinsicht" mean? If it implies that full and clear knowledge can come only in Christ, fine. This could be well integrated into Althaus' positive picture of Uroffenbarung. But frequently the reader has the impression — which we shall bear out in the following pages of this chapter — that Althaus intends more.

It appears that the "illuminating power" which he would allow Uroffenbarung by itself, i.e. "vor Christus", is not so effective and useable after all. This is indicated when, at the beginning of his treatment of Uroffenbarung in GD, he emphasizes that although he may be commencing with Uroffenbarung, he is defi-

---

2 Cf. § 32/2.

3 In this particular criticism of Barth, Althaus is speaking of his attitude towards nature and creation; cf. KD II/I, pp. 109 ff.

4 In "Warum schreiben wir?" Veröffentlichung des Verlags Bertelsmann, Gütersloh, Weihnachten, 1949, as quoted by G. Koch, *Die christliche Wahrheit der Barmer theologischen Erklärung* (München, 1950), p. 49.

nitely not using it as his "Standort"; he will be presenting Uroffenbarung "durchaus von der Offenbarung in Christus her". Thus, while the theologian may (and must) *begin* with Uroffenbarung, he "darf ... nicht von der vorbereitenden Offenbarung *ausgehen*." (GD/I, 13) This would imply that all of Althaus' impressive phenomenological description of Uroffenbarung is possible only from the standpoint of biblical revelation. Yet if Uroffenbarung has a "validity" and "light" of its own, why cannot the theologian start with this light and *then* submit it to Christ? – Also, how can Althaus argue, "es gibt keinen Maßstab für die Vergleichung der Religionen, der außerhalb Christi läge", (MR, 181) if he also holds, as we have pointed out, that Uroffenbarung is a "measure" in itself for Christ's revelation[5] and especially that the Cross of Christ *must* be measured within the religions in order to clarify its total content?[6] If the religions are indeed a "Maß", then this demands that they have a value and cognitional efficacy even before the "von Christus her".[7]

Althaus' insistence on his own "von Christus her" leads one to ask just how effectively and positively Uroffenbarung and the religions can carry out their role before Christ.[8]

2. Further, Althaus' conclusions concerning Uroffenbarung's and the religions' place within the *history* of salvation are thrown into a confusing light when we consider his *negative assertions* about the role and effectiveness of *history itself*. While he could claim that God is making use of history to serve his plan of love and that therefore history contains an orientation towards and a promise of the coming kingdom[9], he also insisted that history must be thoroughly *broken* and *removed* before the kingdom can be realized. The kingdom in its final form is something entirely *beyond* history. "Zwischen der jetzigen und der kommenden Welt steht Ende, Abbruch, dem Tode des Menschen zu vergleichen." (LD, 361) " ... Gott muß die jetzige Weltgeschichte und Weltgestalt zerbrechen" (CW, 677; cf. also LD, 43; GD/II, 21). Therefore, all that history contains cannot really serve as "building blocks" for the coming salvation; the new world will be entirely new. (CW, 362) This seems to exclude not only a "unilinear development" towards divine redemption but any "Entwicklung" whatsoever. " ... von Adam zu Christus, vom alten zum neuen Menschen führt *keine Entwicklung*." (LD, 42, emphasis mine) " ... die vollendete Erlösung ist Erlösung von der Geschichte ... sie besteht in der Aufhebung der Geschichte durch die Ewigkeit."[10] This conforms to Althaus' understanding of the "eschata" as coming from *beyond* history and as introducing a "new world" – an eschatology which does not really possess "den Blick auf den Zusammenhang zwischen der menschlichen Heilszukunft und der gegenwärtigen menschlichen Geschichte, den Blick auf die Heilsgeschichte."[11]

5 Cf. § 41/2.
6 Cf. § 41/3.
7 Cf. F. Konrad, *Das Offenbarungsverständnis in der evangelischen Theologie* (München, 1971), p. 444.
8 Koch also finds an incoherency between Althaus' affirmation of Uroffenbarung's distinct role and his insistence on a "von Christus her", cf. pp. 31, 34–35.
9 Cf. § 35.
10 "Heilsgeschichte und Eschatologie", ZSTh, 2 (1924–25) 646, 668.
11 L. Wiedenmann, *Mission und Eschatologie.* Eine Analyse der neueren deutschen evangelischen Missionstheologie (Paderborn, 1965), p. 43, cf. also pp. 39–42. – In the earlier

Can this negative view of history be reconciled with an understanding of the religions as part of a genuine "Vor*geschichte*" to Christ? If we take these negative statements seriously — i.e. if the goal of history is essentially "beyond" and if it can arrive only after a radical "Bruch" — what *real, positive* meaning do the orientation, the promises, the preparation, the certain "Entwicklung" within Ur-offenbarung and the religions really have? — These questions will be reinforced below when we consider Althaus' reservations concerning the relationship between religions and Christianity.[12]

§ 49. Concerning the Religions' Content of Truth

1. Running parallel to Althaus' very clear assertions that a knowledge of God is not only "possible" but "actual" (CW, 90) and that man can, through Uroffenba-rung, attain a "Gewißheit" about God's existence, (CW, 71)[13] are numerous reservations in which he, again, seems to deny any real and practical value to this knowledge. And such valuelessness, in turn, appears to blot out the very existence of this knowledge. Following Paul in Rom. 1, he shows that man does not take God's revelation seriously "in *praktischer* Anerkenntnis des überweltlichen Gottes". (BR, 21, emphasis mine) This precisely is what makes up man's guilt: that he "wissen müßte" but that he "*tatsächlich* nicht mehr darum weiß". (CW, 42, emphasis mine) Man refuses. (BR, 18) This is the distinction we mentioned in our analysis of Uroffenbarung: through this revelation man has the ability to know God in his *Vernunft*; but in his *heart* he doesn't use this ability.[14] Yet from this "does not will" Althaus concludes, implicitly, to a "cannot" — i.e. to a "Nicht-mehr-sehen-können". Although it is "willentlich bedingt", it still remains an inability. The "tatsächliche Nicht-mehr-Erkennen" (CW, 43) leads to a "Nicht-mehr-können". (CW, 38—39) One can ask, what good is an ability if by using it, one loses it? And if it is lost, is it not a contradiction to speak of an "actual" knowledge of God through creation?

---

editions of LD, Althaus held more to an "axiological eschatology" which emphasized the experience of eternal life within present values. In the 4th edition of LD (1933), however, he gave the "Endgeschichte" "eine prinzipielle Bedeutung" and reaffirmed that the final kingdom must be "beyond". Cf. H. Graß, "Die Theologie von Paul Althaus", NZSTh, 8 (1966) 277 f.; id., "Gedächtnisvorlesung für Paul Althaus", *Nachrichten der evang.-luth. Kirche in Bayern*, August, 1966, p. 254. Also: F. Holmström, *Das eschatologische Denken der Gegenwart* (1936), pp. 279—322, 338—348, 401—416; Pallas, "La Eschatologia de P. Althaus", *Scriptorium Nitoriense*, 11 (1964) 7—17; P. Cornehl, *Die Zukunft der Versöhnung*. Eschatologie und Emanzipation in der Aufklärung, bei Hegel und in der Hegelschen Schule (Göttingen, 1971), p. 325; G. Sauter, *Zukunft und Verheißung*. Das Problem der Zukunft in der gegenwärtigen theologischen und philosophischen Diskussion (Zürich-Stuttgart, 1965), pp. 96 ff. A doctoral dissertation on the development and significance of Althaus' eschatology and its influence on his entire theology is presently being prepared by Walter Wimmer under Prof. Dr. Juan Alfaro for the Gregorian University, Rome.

12 Cf. § 50.
13 Cf. § 36.
14 Cf. § 23/2.

Althaus seems to voice the same negation when he explains that in rejecting a "natural theology" he wishes to deny a "mögliche Erkenntnis Gottes" which would be possible "auf Grund der Uroffenbarung kraft der relativ unversehrten Vernunft". He rejects "eine zwar ergänzungsbedürftige, aber in sich selbst gültige Gotteserkenntnis". (GD/I, 25—26) Again, he is denying a knowledge of God which might have any real validity before Christ. Elsewhere he explicitly states that what he means by his distinction between Uroffenbarung and natural theology is the distinction between it and "der tatsächlichen Gotteserkenntnis". (CW, 42) Does Uroffenbarung therefore exclude a "factual knowledge of God"? But if this knowledge is not "factual", nor "valid", how can it be *real*?

2. Even more questions arise when we compare all that Althaus said about Uroffenbarung placing man before a *personal* God and his *offer* of love[15] with his statements concerning the situation of *despair* which is the end-result of this general revelation. In his experiencing of Uroffenbarung, man becomes all the more painfully aware of the limitations, contradictions, and unanswered questions in his own existence — and in Uroffenbarung itself. The realities of death, evil, unsatiated desire, imperfect knowledge, "der grauenvolle Daseinskampf, die Zerstörung und Nichtigkeit" in Nature, the "dunkle, notvolle Gesetz des Lebens-Widerstreites" in history (GD/I, 28; CW, 90) — all this, as it were, is put into the spotlight by Uroffenbarung. This brings about "die Frage und Angst um die mögliche Sinnlosigkeit des ganzen Daseins, des Einzellebens und des großen Geschehens in der Geschichte". (CW, 92) "So findet der Mensch unter der Selbstbezeugung Gottes sich in einem tiefen Widerspruch vor ... Er bedeutet aber zugleich einen *Widerspruch Gottes selbst*." (CW, 92) Man feels himself called by God and then excruciatingly left in the lurch. Luther's question: "Quid Deus velit erga nos?" rings out with delirious intensity. (ibid.) Althaus concludes not only: "Hier kommen wir nicht über den Zweifel hinaus" but also "Damit endet sie (Uroffenbarung) in der *Verzweiflung*." (GD/1, 29) In fact, he sees this despair as one of the purposes — not only an effect — of Uroffenbarung: "Man kann nicht ohne Gott verzweifelt sein, man ist immer nur durch Gott verzweifelt ... Weil ihm (dem Menschen) Uroffenbarung geworden ist, ist seine Lage verzweifelt." (Ur, 23; cf. also 11) Can man live before or seek union with such a personal God? "Wer von der Uroffenbarung lebt, der weiß wohl zuviel von Gott, als daß er ihn ganz vergessen könnte, aber zuwenig, als daß er *mit ihm, vor ihm leben* könnte ..."[16] The non-Christian stands before a personal God whom he cannot love.

From this situation of despair, Althaus again attests man's inability to know God. Uroffenbarung leads to a "*Nicht-Wissen um Gott*"; it is the "Voraussetzung" for the "*Verborgenheit* Gottes". (CW, 93) His reasoning is the same as in the previous section: from a basic and real ability he concludes to a practical and very actual inability — a non-knowledge of God. "Nur als der Deus revelatus — im Sinne unseres Begriffes der Selbstbezeugung — ist Gott für uns der Deus absconditus, nämlich der, dessen Wille über uns verborgen ist." (ibid.)

3. This unclarity and lurking contradiction is what Konrad terms "eine der größten Schwierigkeiten" in Althaus' doctrine of Uroffenbarung — his "merkwürdige Stellungnahme" in which he opts "für eine natürliche Gotteserkenntnis (i.e. a general revelation) und gegen

15 Cf. § 37.
16 "Die Wirklichkeit Gottes", *Zeitwende*, 9 (1938) 86.

eine natürliche Gotteserkenntnis" (i.e. what we called the "gültige, tatsächliche" knowledge of God).[17] What Althaus maintained against those who reject Uroffenbarung, he seems to renege in what he holds against those who propose a natural knowledge of God. And Konrad feels that in the final analysis, Althaus cancels out any real knowledge of God outside of Christ.[18] Rolf Walker concludes: "Die Lehre von der Uroffenbarung mündet bei Althaus ein in die Lehre von der Verborgenheit Gottes – damit hat Althaus seine Lehre von Uroffenbarung selbst ad adsurdum geführt."[19] Günther Koch and Gerhard Heinzelmann also accuse Althaus of a "Schwanken in der Feststellung der wirklichen Erkenntnis der Uroffenbarung", a continual teetertottering "zwischen dem subjektiven Vorhandensein und Nichtvorhandensein der Uroffenbarung".[20] "Was ist eine Uroffenbarung, die nirgends offenbar macht, was sie offenbar machen soll?"[21] – Such critics, whatever their final appraisal, were perplexed, as we are, by Althaus' "parallel" statements concerning man's ability-disability to know God through Uroffenbarung.

4. As is to be expected, this parallelism and this perplexity spilled over into his understanding of the "*Wahrheitsgehalt*" ot the religions themselves. We have seen that Althaus held to an unavoidable "Entstellung" of the truth in the religions, and yet he still could affirm that a content of truth remains and can be made use of.[22] Yet in other passages, where he describes this "Entstellung", one is forced to ask just how much real, useable truth is left in the religions. For instance, there are passages where he seems to say that the decisive outcome of the religions' use of Uroffenbarung is a *misuse* of it.[23] "Überall in der Menschheit ist Gottes Uroffenbarung ergangen und ergeht sie fortwährend. Alle Völker kommen von ihr. Aber überall wird sie auch beim Empfangen verkannt und entstellt in den Religionen." (CW, 98) " ... Religion ist nach Paulus zustande gekommen durch Abfall von dem lebendigen Gott, von der Wahrheit, die er in seiner ur-offenbaren Wirklichkeit ist." (CW, 136) The misuse of Uroffenbarung in the religions ends up in "sündhafter Verkennung Gottes". (CW, 141; cf. also 94; GD/I, 29)

Also, in his descriptions of the union of truth and error within the religions he frequently implies that it is *error* which *determines* the quality of the mixture. There are only "pieces of truth" within the religious world, which, when fit into the whole of any particular religion, become falsehood: "Die Teilwahrheit, als das Ganze genommen, wird Lüge." (WE, 10) The "Bruchstück, vereinsamte Teilwahrheit (ist) von Lüge überschattet und überfremdet, ein Träumen statt des Wachseins vor Gott ..."[24] The pieces of truth, then, are part of a whole which in the end stands opposed to God's truth in the Gospel. (CW, 146) Althaus even implies that it is impossible to pick out these pieces of truth and make use of them; there is not "minder und mehr" but only an "entweder-oder". (WE 2, 279) Thus the

---

17 Konrad, p. 436.
18 Ibid., pp. 461–466, esp. p. 463.
19 R. Walker, *Zur Frage der Uroffenbarung*. Eine Auseinandersetzung mit Karl Barth und Paul Althaus (Bad Cannstatt, 1962), p. 39. He continues: "Auf dem Weg, den Althaus beschritten hat, konnte er sein Versprechen von Selbstbezeugung Gottes in der Wirklichkeit des Menschen und der Welt zu lehren, nicht halten." loc. cit., cf. also pp. 35–39.
20 Koch, pp. 13, 17.
21 G. Heinzelmann, "Ur-Offenbarung?" ThStKr, 106, N.F. 1 (1934–35) 429.
22 Cf. § 39.
23 It is particularly with these passages that Konrad constructs his argument that the religions incorporate only the failure of Uroffenbarung. Cf. § 39/1; § 40/1.
24 "Kirche und Volkstum", *Evangelium und Leben*, p. 123.

religions stand before the Gospel as *darkness*. "Heidentum und Dienst des wahren, lebendigen Gottes stehen in ausschließendem Gegensatze. Sie verhalten sich nicht etwa wie Dämmerung zum Tageslicht, sondern wie Finsternis und Licht." (CW, 137)[25]

Just as Althaus could give an imposing practical description of how truth is expressed in the doctrines and rites of the religions,[26] he can offer an equally impressive — and perplexing — view of their falsehood. He feels that all religions, basically, show themselves to be "Trug" in that they do not grasp: 1) the person-hood of God and the personal quality of man's relation to him and 2) "als die tiefste Not des Menschen seine Sünde und Schuld" which call for redemption through "die Gottes-Tat der Versöhnung". (CW, 141) He sees this general failure and deception expressed in the two "großen Hauptmöglichkeiten der Religion": *mysticism*, which erodes the personality of God and easily falls into a "Selbstver-gottung des Menschen", and *law-religion* which feels it can overcome the distance between God and man through human performance. (GD/I, 100–101) Elsewhere — forgetting that he allowed a faith in God the Creator within the religions — he claims that "die Religionen ... Gott nicht klar und unbedingt als Schöpfer der Welt (kennen)" which leads to a dualistic or damonistic interpretation of the world; also, the religions "wissen nicht um Gottes Gottheit als die freie heilige Liebe" and therefore they must turn to the law for justification.[27] Althaus concludes, "alle Religionen sind Wege der Selbsterlösung. Freilich nicht alle in gleicher Wei-se." (CW, 142)

Whereas he once termed the religions' searching after salvation through sacri-fice and cult true roadsigns, he now sees them only as products of human phan-tasy: "Denn Heilsweg und Heilsgewißheit der menschlichen Religionen ... sind nicht in göttlicher Offenbarung begründet, sondern von dem Menschen in seiner Not und Sehnsucht erdichtet." (GD/I, 28) Therefore, to his former judgment that the gods of the religions are "Vertreter" and "Werkzeuge" of God, willed by him, he now adds what he feels is the New Testament verdict: the pagan gods do not have any kind of a "göttlichen Wirklichkeit" (Gal. 4,8); compared with the living God they are "nichtig". (Acts 14,15; Jer. 2,5; Rom. 1,21) He even seems to place the religions under the decisive dominion of "evil spirits". (Acts 26,18; Col. 1,13; Eph. 2,2; 6,12) (CW, 136) "In den Religionen und ihren Kulten sind Geister von übermenschlicher Mächtigkeit am Werke ... Von dem Kultus gehen dämonische Kräfte aus und halten die Völker in der Lüge gefangen." (CW, 390)

Can all this be interpreted merely as a balancing dialectical "no" to Althaus' earlier "yes" to the religions' content of truth?

§ 50. Concerning the Relation between Christianity and the Religions

1. From this apparent denial of real, useable truth within the religions, Althaus also could formulate negative statements on the relation of Uroffenbarung-religions to Christianity which seem to call into question much of what he said

25 Here Althaus is referring to Acts 26, 18; Eph. 5,8; 1 Pet. 2,9. Cf. also *Gott ist gegenwärtig. Letzte Predigten* (Gütersloh, 1968), p. 135.
26 Cf. § 36/2; § 39/1.
27 *Grundriß der Ethik* (Gütersloh, 1953²), pp. 35–36.

about "Anknüpfung und Erfüllung".[28] Such reservations may not be as numerous as his positive statements, but their rigor makes them just as impressive. They stem, first of all, from certain categorical remarks on the *fundamental opposition* between *Uroffenbarung* and *Christ's revelation*. Despite all the two may have in common, Althaus implies that once man tries to make use of the "natural knowledge of God" offered him by Uroffenbarung, it becomes basically opposed to Christ. "Sie (knowledge through Uroffenbarung) kann daher durch das Evangelium nicht ergänzt, sondern nur bekehrt (werden) ..." The Gospel demands "Bruch mit der natürlichen Gotteserkenntnis der sündigen Menschheit". (GD/I, 26) And when Althaus describes this "break" in terms of the Law, it becomes total. Even though the Law implies a "unity" with the Gospel, as soon as it is used, it falls into "Gesetzlichkeit" and becomes "Gegensatz". The final relation between Uroffenbarung-Law and the Gospel is negative: " ... es gibt zwischen dem gesetzlichen Wahne des Menschen und dem Glauben an das Evangelium keine Vermittlung, kein Teils-Teils, sondern nur Entweder-Oder ... Jedes noch so leise und noch so begrenzte Ja zur Gesetzlichkeit verneint das Evangelium ganz ..." (BR, 82–84) This opposing character of "Gesetzlichkeit" runs through the entirety of Uroffenbarung. Thus: "Der Charakter dieser Uroffenbarung im Verhältnis zu der Heilsoffenbarung in Christo ist im wesentlichen negativ. Von 'Anknüpfung' kann daher nur sehr bedingt gesprochen werden..."[29]

2. This indication of Uroffenbarung's fundamental opposition to Christ is echoed frequently and quite somberly in Althaus' description of the *religions'* relation to Christianity: Although he spoke about a basic "synthesis" and "unity" between the two,[30] he also seems to argue that because Christianity brought something which was so entirely new and caused such a radical "Wende" in the history of religions, (GD/I, 97) there is an excluding difference between the two. Therefore, Christianity's "unerschütterliches Bewußtsein" not only "der Einzigkeit" but also "der Ausschließlichkeit". (CW, 13) Therefore, in confronting the religions, Christianity demands a basic "Entweder-Oder", (CW, 133) a basic "intolerance". "Diese Intoleranz abtun heißt die Substanz des Evangeliums verletzen."[31] Christianity *is* in the final analysis "fremd".[32] Although Althaus calls the Gospel a "religion – indeed the fulfillment of religion" (GD/I, 100) he also can state " ... das Evangelium ist nicht eine Religion unter anderen."[33] And together with his claim that Christianity must be "measured" by the religions[34] he can write "Das Christentum läßt es nicht zu, an irgendeinem außer ihm liegenden Maßstab der Humanität, des einheitlichen Weltverständnisses *oder sonst* gemessen zu werden."[35] He also seems to qualify his admission of a certain "Entwicklung" within the religious world towards the Gospel[36] when he does not allow the

---

28 Cf. § 40, § 41.
29 C. H. Ratschow, *Der angefochtene Glaube*, p. 282. Therefore Ratschow expresses a certain bewilderment that Althaus can speak so positively of "Anknüpfung". Loc. cit.
30 Cf. § 40/1.
31 "Toleranz und Intoleranz des Glaubens", *Theologische Aufsätze* II, p. 113.
32 "Kirche und Volkstum", p. 123.
33 *Gott ist gegenwärtig*, p. 135.
34 Cf. § 41/2.
35 "Christentum und Geistesleben", *Evangelium und Leben*, p. 34, emphasis mine.
36 Cf. § 35/3.

Gospel to really be part of this development, as if in the decisive moment this development comes to a dead-end. (GD/I, 96) "Nicht um Entwicklung, sondern um Enthüllung und Entscheidung geht es, also um etwas Totales, das *keinen Komparativ* verträgt ..." (GD/I, 97; cf. also MR, 179)

3. Such statements on the difference between Christianity and the religions, if "stretched", might still allow a minimum of useable common content. Yet Althaus' descriptions of the "Bruch" which must take place in the dialogue between the two seems to call for fulfillment *solely* through "Aufhebung": "Indem das Evangelium zu den Religionen ein *ganzes, nicht ausnehmendes Nein* sagt, befreit es die dort isolierte, vereinseitigte und damit zur Lüge gewordene Wahrheit ..." Fulfillment can come only "in *völliger Preisgabe* der heidnischen Religion ... nur in wirklicher *Zerstörung* durch das schlechthin gegebene Evangelium selber, in *ganzer Antithese*, Buße und Bruch. Damit ist gegeben, daß die *herrschende Kategorie* des Verhältnisses zwischen Evangelium und Religionen immer die des *unbedingten Gegensatzes* bleiben muß." (MR, 192—193, emphasis mine) Althaus even states that fülfillment is something which can take place only *after* this first categorical "no"; the fulfillment *results from* and is *subordinated* to the rejection: "Der Übergang ist Entscheidung, Bruch. Erst von hintennach, in theologischer Besinnung, mag sich dann die Bekehrung als Erfüllung, das Gericht über die Lüge des Heidentums als Befreiung der in ihr vereinsamten und damit verzerrten Wahrheit darstellen." (MR, 194; cf. also 179) Since the "pieces of truth" in the religions had been swallowed into the totality of error, "der Übergang von der Religion zu Christus ist *nicht ein teilweiser*, sondern ein *totaler* Bruch." (WE 2, 279, emphasis mine) — Such brutally harsh descriptions of the "Bruch" and of fulfillment only through rejection appear chiefly in Althaus' early articles on the religions, when he was more occupied with an offensive against Troeltsch's relativism; in later works, the tone is mellowed. And yet, he never retracted these verdicts; and in his later works the same total "no" frequently breaks through.[37]

If such a description is taken seriously, can one still allow any kind of a "continuity", any kind of a practical "positive relation", any "Anknüpfung" on the "Begriffe" and on the "Gestalt" of the religions? Can there be a real, positive dialogue between Christianity and the religions?

§ 51. Concerning the Religions as Viae Salutis

1. It is here that Althaus' "no" to the religions assumes its clearest and sharpest tones. If in the other sections of this chapter we were dealing with reservations and partial negations which *seemed* irreconcilable with his "yes", here, in the question of salvation, there can be no doubt about the impossibility of a compromise. Indeed, as we shall see, all the other reservations are but *reverberations* of this central and quite vociferous "no".

---

37 Cf. GD/I, 97, where he again insists on "Krisis", fulfillment only through eschatological "Aufhebung", no comparison, a "Wende gegenüber allem sonstigen religiösen Verhältnis"; CW, 146, where the truth contained in the religions' idea of sacrifice, because it is misused as a means of self-redemption, must in the end be abandoned; CW, 137: "ausschließender Gegensatz", exclusion of "Entwicklung", only "Wendung", "Bruch".

Categorically, Althaus states that man *cannot make use* of Uroffenbarung in his religion to attain salvation. He cannot find or construct any kind of a real answer to his questioning after salvation. "Kein Gedanke und Wort über Gott (i.e. through Uroffenbarung) kann umhin, die *Heilsfrage* zu beantworten, stillschweigend oder ausdrücklich." (GD/I, 26) "Sie (Uroffenbarung) selber bringt das Heil nicht, sie ist heillos. In Bezug auf die Heilsfrage bleibt das Reden Gottes in der Uroffenbarung ein Schweigen ..." (Ur, 24) God's witness to himself before Christ " ... macht nicht gerecht und hebt unsere Heillosigkeit nicht auf."[38] Any attempt man makes to use Uroffenbarung to achieve salvation only plunges man deeper into a state of unredemption. "Ein neutrales Empfangen der Uroffenbarung gibt es nicht. Das Vernehmen der Uroffenbarung ist immer schon entweder zum Götzendienste und selbstgemachter Heilslehre entstellt oder es ist erfüllt im Glauben an das Evangelium. Eine dritte, gegenüber diesem Entweder-Oder neutrale Möglichkeit menschlicher Religion gibt es nicht." (GD/I, 26) Therefore, "Wir kommen von der Uroffenbarung her immer nur als solche, die schon an ihr *schuldig* geworden und daher *heil-los* sind. Wir stehen vor der Uroffenbarung als solche, die zugleich unter dem Zorn Gottes stehen wegen der Verleugnung seiner Wahrheit." (GD/I, 27) We can conclude: the error mixed with the truth of Uroffenbarung renders the religions totally unsalvific.

This is, in essence, Althaus' understanding of the Law. Even though through the Law man is definitely able to know the personal God, his Will and his offer of love[39], man *cannot make use of* this lofty gift in order to find union with the Giver. In the Law man has "das Ohr und Herz für seinen (God's) Willen. Aber der Höhe dieser Würde entspricht die Tiefe der Not des Menschen: er kann eben dieses Gebot, an dem er sich freut, nicht verwirklichen." (BR, 77) We must distinguish clearly between the Law as containing an "Offenbarung des Wesens und Willens Gottes ... von dem, was der Mensch aus dem Gebote macht ..." What he does with the Law leads him into the doldrums of despair. (TG, 750–751) The Law therefore "hilft nicht zur Rechtfertigung, nicht zur Überwindung der Sünde ..." The Law may be "die Vorbedingung für das Heil ... aber es ist selber alles andere als Heil. Es ist der letzte Schritt des alten Weges, nicht der erste des neuen." (BR, 31–32; cf. also CW, 288–289)[40]

2. An *essential purpose* of Althaus' entire doctrine of Uroffenbarung is to *constitute* man a sinner and to bring him to the *realization* of his total sinfulness. And from Althaus' descrption of this purpose and, more so, from its very nature, one must ask whether it is not only *a* but *the* essential mission of Uroffenbarung and of the religions. Our previous chapter has shown that Althaus indeed granted a positive function to Uroffenbarung, yet this negative role of rendering man a sinner seems almost constitutional to this doctrine — so that the positive content of Uroffenbarung, as important as it is, becomes *only* a means to this negative end. Man must know God, he must know him clearly, personally, *in order to* reject him and sin against him! Althaus therefore accuses Barth of not really holding to man's total sinfulness because he rejected Uroffenbarung. Without

---

38 "Bedenken zur 'Theologischen Erklärung' der Barmer Bekenntnis-Synode", *Korrespondenzblatt der evang.-luth. Geistlichen in Bayern*, 59 (1934) 319.
39 Cf. § 37/3.
40 Cf. also *Die Herrlichkeit Gottes* (Gütersloh, 1954), p. 201; Ratschow, op. cit., p. 284.

Uroffenbarung and its positive content, "... verliert das Wort der Sündigkeit des Menschen jede Bestimmtheit und jeden Ernst". (Ur, 11; cf. also 9–12) "Um der gegenwärtigen Uroffenbarung willen sind wir Sünder und Heillose." (GD/I, 27; cf. also CW, 43–44) That this is Uroffenbarung's central role is probably the reason why he placed it as the *first* of the three ways in which the Gospel relates to Uroffenbarung: man must first become "schuldig ... ständig schuldig"; only then does the Gospel "anknüpfen" and "erfüllen". (CW, 42) Althaus himself thus takes over what he felt was Paul's main reason for speaking of a general revelation: unlike judaic tradition in Wisdom 13 and 14, Paul did not wish merely to proclaim a positive revelation through nature. "Bei Paulus steht der Gedanke der Erkennbarkeit Gottes aus seinen Werken *ganz und gar* im Dienste der Anklage." (BR, 20, emphasis mine) Althaus can even imply that Uroffenbarung, carrying out the mission of the *Law* in Rom. 2, 9–20, "hat ... *keine andere Wirkung*, als zur Erkenntnis der Sünde zu führen ... es zeigt dem Menschen, was Sünde ist, und läßt ihn erfahren, daß er unter der Sünde ist." (BR, 31, emphasis mine)[41] If this be the main task of Uroffenbarung, we can only ask how much positive value can any other role have.

This central, condemnatory role of Uroffenbarung is also contained in Althaus' insistence that Uroffenbarung always *leads to* and therefore includes God's *Zornoffenbarung*. Only with the proclamation of the Gospel does the revelation of God's "Gerechtigkeit" begin; before that, despite all possible positive contents and hopes, there is revelation of his "Zorn". (BR, 18; cf. also 16) Uroffenbarung and "Zornoffenbarung" indeed "sind und bleiben zweierlei" and therefore "wohl zu unterscheiden"; but they also remain "unscheidbar" and therefore are contained "in einem". (GD/I, 13–14) Because of this unbreakable unity, the religions can never escape the cloud of God's wrath. As soon as they try to make use of the Uroffenbarung within them, they become objects of this wrath: "Das Heidentum als Gottesverhältnis steht unter dem Zorne Gottes." (MR, 179) "Außer Christus ist der Mensch unter dem Zorne mit allem, was er hat und denkt, auch in und mit seiner Religion, und wenn sie sich noch so hoch entwickelt hätte." (WE 2, 280) And it is the reality and inescapability of this wrath which plunges the religions even deeper into a state of unredemption: "Davon wird seine (man's) Religion eitel und leer: das natürliche Menschentum, unter Gottes Zorn, kann nicht anders als sich selbst, seine Bedürfnisse und Begehrungen zum Maße Gottes, zum Sinn der Gottesbeziehung zu machen." Because of this divine wrath, Althaus can even give his "placet" to Feuerbach's critique of religion (shades of Barth!): "Der Mensch ist mit sich selbst allein, auch in seiner Religion ... Feuerbach's Religionsauffassung und Kritik ist in ihrer Art der Kommentar zu Röm. 1. Er hat scharf gesehen und ist dadurch ein *Zeuge von Gottes Zornesverhängnis* geworden."[42] We ask again: can such an understanding of God's wrath over the religions allow even the slightest possibility of a "form of faith" or of a "Vergebung" and "Gemeinschaft mit Gott" as Althaus himself, in other contexts, did allow?

3. Throughout his presentation of Uroffenbarung, Althaus, in different terms and in different contexts, *distinguishes* strictly between Uroffenbarung and salvation − and *separates* the two:

41 For a similar treatment of Uroffenbarung-Law in Rom. 7, 7–13 cf. BR, 73–74.
42 "Das Kreuz Christi", ZSTh, 1 (1923) 117–118, emphasis mine.

a) *Immanence* and *personal nearness.* — "Diese 'Immanenz' Gottes in der Existenz des Menschen muß *streng unterschieden* werden von der 'Nähe' oder Gegenwart Gottes in personhafter Gemeinschaft der Liebe." God can be present within man's being and yet be "distant" from his heart. (CW, 15) — Yet elsewhere Althaus could speak of a personal nearness to God for non-Christians by means of Christ's universal presence.[43]

b) *Verbundenheit* and *Gebundenheit* — Uroffenbarung constitutes man within a definite and indissoluble "Gebundenheit" with God, yet it does not bring about a "Verbundenheit". Indeed, the fact that man cannot be "los von Gott" is the basis for his personal "Gottlosigkeit". (CW, 58) — Here Althaus seems to forget that he could also allow a certain form of "Verbundenheit" with God through man's acquiescence to the "truth" of Uroffenbarung.[44]

c) *Relation* and *community* with God. Althaus cautions against confusing "das Gottesverhältnis, in das Gott jeden Menschen hineingeschaffen hat", "und die Gemeinschaft Gottes" which brings about personal union. (CW, 67) — Yet here, too, he fails to remember that he explicitly spoke of "Gemeinschaft" with God, through forgiveness, outside of Christ's revelation and within the religions![45]

d) *Condemning knowledge* and *evangelical knowledge* of God. There is the knowledge of God through Uroffenbarung which establishes sin and the "evangelische Erkenntnis" which bestows the Spirit. (CW, 58) — But elsewhere he could point out an "echte Erkenntnis Gottes" in the religions which founds "echte Buße" and "wirkliche Gemeinschaft Gottes".[46]

e) *Revelation* and *salvation.* This, essentially, is the distinction which underlies all the others and which both relates but strictly separates Althaus' doctrines of Uroffenbarung and "Heilsoffenbarung". Although the presence of salvation always demands the presence of revelation, the reverse is not the case. Revelation is not *coextensive* with salvation. It can exist and be active and bring forth fruit in a context where salvation does not yet exist. In his 1941 article against "Die Inflation des Begriffs der Offenbarung",[47] he adamantly rejected the then current usage of the term "revelation" to cover the entirety of Christ's work; revelation does *not* necessarily include redemption as an act of atonement and forgiveness. "Außer Christus gibt es zwar Selbstbezeugung Gottes, daher auch Erkenntnis Gottes, aber nicht zum Heil... Die Grundoffenbarung führt nicht zur Gemeinschaft zwischen Gott und Mensch, durch des Menschen Schuld."[48]

Summing up, then: "Unsere Kirche lehrt, daß es *nur eine* Heilsoffenbarung gibt ..."[49] The terminological distinction between "Heils-" and "Ur"-Offenbarung must be taken *literally*. Salvation is limited to only one form of revelation — to only one historical expression of God's self-witnessing: Christ's.

4. Althaus' refusal to allow Uroffenbarung to become a means of salvation is matched by his *reluctance* to allow God's salvific will and final redemption to be

43 Cf. § 46/1.
44 Cf. § 44/4.
45 Cf. § 46/1.
46 Cf. § 36/2, § 46/2; cf. "Das Kreuz Christi", p. 122.
47 "Die Inflation des Begriffs der Offenbarung in der gegenwärtigen Theologie", ZSTh, 18 (1941) 134–149.
48 Ibid., p. 143.
49 "Bedenken", p. 319, emphasis mine.

mediated through any history outside that of Christ. This reluctance stands opposed to the scattered statements in which, as we have seen, he "ventured" to trace salvation in and through non-Christian historical forms.[50]

Resolutely, Althaus refuses to locate this salvific will *within history*; to do so would be to violate the *mystery of God's ways.* "Der in seinem Worte bezeugte eine Heilswille Gottes ist allerdings unter seinem Walten in der Geschichte tief verborgen." (CW, 273; cf. MR, 180) We must bow humbly before this will (ER, 22) and accept the impossibility of determining its "wo und wie". (GD/II, 163—164; CW, 482) "Eine Theologie der Geschichte, welche das Geschehen durchleuchten und die großen Sinn-Linien göttlichen Berufens und Übergehens aufzeigen könnte, ist uns, solange wir selber unterwegs sind, versagt." (CW, 629) — Thus, while Althaus could trace the effects of God's Uroffenbarung within history, he felt he did not have the right to do the same for God's salvific will.

Because of this "mystery" not only does Althaus refuse to locate salvation within non-Christian history, but in general he tends to push its realization *beyond history.* Rather than "dare" to allow salvation to be mediated through any historical form outside of Christ, he prefers to give it a mediation which is outside this earth's confines. Thus, when asserting that Christ's "power of redemption" cannot be restricted to the "irdischen Heilsmittel", he adds that it will be carried out "über die Geschichte hinaus". (CW, 673) This universal salvation is to be found "jenseits der Grenzen unserer Geschichte". (LD, 188) "Die vor unseren Augen liegende Geschichte" is not "das Ganze und Letzte der Geschichte Gottes". God will have another salvific history beyond these earthly borders. (GD/II, 150) Thus, while Althaus could not allow God's "Heilsoffenbarung" to extend into the realm of pre-Christian Uroffenbarung, he does explicitly allow it to be stretched the opposite direction and to be found beyond "der irdischen Geschichte". (LD, 188)

Just *how* this trans-historical salvation of the non-Christians will be effected is not perfectly clear in Althaus' descriptions of it. What seems to be certain is that it will generally take place *without any relation* to the earthly history of these non-Christians. Althaus' "perhaps-statements" concerning a final salvific decision on the basis of the use they made of Uroffenbarung in their religions[51] seems to have been only a passing reflection. The normal procedure, he maintains, is that all men who during their lifetime had only Uroffenbarung to work with and have never known Christ " ... werden alle noch einmal vor ihn gestellt werden. ... Jeder Mensch wird jenseits seines Sterbens Christus noch einmal begegnen." (CW, 672—673) In various contexts, he proposes three possible and somewhat contradictory ways in which men will react to this encounter: a) It is possible that God will simply justify the non-Christians who have never known Christ by an act of his omnipotent will — *without any personal decision* on their part. (CW, 482) " ... er kann andere ohne die Entscheidung des Glaubens in das Schauen und damit zum Heile führen... Vielleicht wird Christus sich den auf Erden von ihm nicht Erreichten und den Ungläubigen einfach in seiner Herrlichkeit offenbaren und dadurch den Unglauben richten und tief beschämen." (CW, 672) b) Or, God himself will *bring man to a decision* and "take over", as it were, his free will.

---

50 Cf. § 46.
51 Cf. § 46/2, a.

Where the Gospel has not yet been preached, " ... da wird Gott ... den Menschen *jenseits des Todes,* am *Tage Christi,* vor die Wirklichkeit Christi und seiner selbst stellen und ihm den Willen schenken, ohne den die Verwandlung seines Wesens allerdings magisch wäre." (LD, 225) (Yet Althaus seemed to permit such a "magical act" above when he allowed salvation "without a decision of faith".) c) Elsewhere, Althaus states that in this trans-historical final encounter with Christ, those who have not known him on earth will have to *make their own decision.* "Christus wird *jenseits der Grenzen* unserer Geschichte (wo und wann, ist uns verborgen) allen, die er in der Geschichte mit dem Evangelium nicht erreichte, noch begegnen und sie zur Entscheidung und Scheidung vor sich stellen." (LD, 188)

All these quite nebulous and contradictory efforts to locate salvation-for-the-non-Christian beyond history bear out, we feel, Althaus' reluctance and fear to situate this salvation within history − i.e. within Uroffenbarung and the religions. We can only ask: would it not be easier and more consistent to allow the "Spirit" within Uroffenbarung to bring the non-Christians to a "form of salvific faith" here on this earth, − rather than to resort to such transhistorical speculations?

The final result of this fear and of this determination to place non-Christian salvation beyond history is a limping theory of *apocatastasis.* In order to reconcile the reality of God's salvific will with the fact that multitudes of men have never known his "Heilsoffenbarung", Althaus appeals to faith in a final, universal salvation beyond this world. He does not propose this faith as a certainty; the "possibility" of a "doppelten Ausgang" for history, i.e. the possibility that many will be lost, must remain a very real possibility; we need it as a sobering reminder of the necessity and gravity of faith in Christ. And yet, it is a "zu überwindende Möglichkeit". (LD, 194) Because we believe in the love God has shown in Christ and his desire to bring all men to himself, we can dare to believe that in the end, beyond history, all will be saved. (CW, 671) This possibility of damnation turns out to be, it appears, only a hypothetical possibility, for we can believe that God's grace will save all. "Dieser Glaube (an Gottes allmächtige Gnade) wagt den Ausblick der Apokatastasis und so ist es gewiß zuletzt ein Gedanke, in dem wir enden." (LD, 196)[52] We can believe that in the world beyond all men will be united in Christ's community. "Wir glauben, daß die Einheit der heiligen christlichen Kirche, die wir allsonntäglich bekennen, und die Einheit der Menschheit in dieser Kirche einmal Ereignis, Gestalt, greifbare Wirklichkeit sein wird."[53]

As beautiful and as founded as this hope for universal final salvation may be, it dispensed Althaus from having to place the possibility of salvation within non-Christian history; and it indicates, again, that he preferred to grant the non-Christians salvation on the "Last Day" rather than within their own religions.

52 Cf. also "Theologie des Glaubens", ZSTh, 2, (1924−25) 321. − Yet Althaus adds that such a "final belief" is possible only for those who have really been shaken by the possibility of damnation. CW, 671, cf. also 630; "Wiederbringung", RGG[3] VI, 1694−1695.
53 "Toleranz und Intoleranz", p. 119. We should point out that Althaus ventures this belief in an Apokatastasis not only to explain the fact that so many men have never known Christ but also − and perhaps primarily − the fact that so many have rejected him. CW, 628−631.

§ 52. Althaus' Central, Summarizing "No" to the Religions

Althaus' "no" to Uroffenbarung and the religions as "Viae Salutis" — in its intensity and its clarity — *sums up, motivates* and, also, *clarifies* the other expressions of this same "no". It is his central and regulating reservation about the "order of things" before Christ. All the other forms of his negative picture of the religious world seem to have this one purpose: to make sure that Uroffenbarung or the religions could not become instruments of salvation. As soon as it appeared that his "yes" was approaching the boundary line between unredemption and redemption, Althaus had to sound a sudden — and frequently confusing — "Halt". The "yes", as positive and promising and encouraging as it may be, had to remain "on its own side".

— The purpose behind his anxious warnings against a *"natural theology"* was to assure that this "order before Christ", which he himself established through his teaching on Uroffenbarung, did not have any real *value* or *efficacy* in removing the fundamental corruption and sinfulness of man. Therefore, the necessity of his *"von Christus her ... in letzter Hinsicht"*; the "letzte Hinsicht" would be the order of redemption where the religions and all they contain can make sense only in the light of "Heilsoffenbarung". Here there can be no "Entwicklung" from one order to the other; without the "von Christus her", the first order comes to a dead stop.[54]

— Also, the *praktische Anerkenntnis* which the non-Christians sought to draw from Uroffenbarung had to end up as a "Nicht-mehr-sehen-können" and as non-knowledge because in it they were trying to make "practical" use of Uroffenbarung in order to find God and his redemption. For the same reason he had to establish *despair* as the end-effect of this attempt, for if man could break out of despair and, through Uroffenbarung, really find the living God, he would be in possession of "Heil"; he would be crossing the forbidden boundary. Thus God remains "hidden"; and the *Wahrheitsgehalt* of the religions, because it is engulfed in the "error" and "deformity" of unredemption, remains in a prevading darkness.[55]

— *Anknüpfung* and *Erfüllung* are possible only where the religions are searching for salvation and suffering under this search; but because they think they can find salvation, there is only "Bruch", "no comparison", "unconditional opposition" between them and Christianity. As soon as the religions try to cross over into the territory of redemption, a wall has to be erected.[56]

— Finally, it was this central "no" which did not allow Althaus to speak of more than a "form of faith" or of a "relative salvation" within the religions and which rendered his statements about "Gemeinschaft" and "Vergebung" among the non-Christians so scattered, isolated, and in the final analysis, so contradictory.[57]

54 Cf. § 48/1.
55 Cf. § 49/1–4.
56 Cf. § 50/1–2.
57 Cf. § 51. – In his study of the "supernatural" within Althaus' understanding of Uroffenbarung, Zasche reaches much the same conclusions we drew in Ch. IV, §§ 43–46; there is a real possibility of salvation within Uroffenbarung (but again, Zasche fails to make any references to this possibility within the religions). His argument is in part similar to ours:

II. Dialectic or Contradiction?

§ 53. A Dialectical View

We have presented Althaus' "yes" and "no" to the religions as two parallel verdicts. For him, however, these two parallel words, each with its own content, could be joined togehter into one, dialectical word — a final, unified verdict. He sums up his "theology of the non-Christian religions" thus: "Wir haben ein *doppeltes Wort* über die Religionen im Lichte des Evangeliums sagen müssen." He goes on to describe the components of this dialectic in terms we have become familiar with in these last two chapters: "Wahrheitsgehalt – Lüge", "Anknüpfung – Bruch", "Getroffensein von Gott – Gottlosigkeit", "Verlangen nach Gott – Flucht vor Gott". (CW, 146) The very last sentence of CW § 16, "Die Religionen im Lichte des Evangeliums", brings the dialectic to its culmination in Christ: "In dieser *Erfüllung* und diesem *Gerichte* erst lernen die Religionen sich selbst ganz verstehen, im Glauben an Christus." (CW, 147) The "double word" is to be *one* word; the contrasting components stand not opposed to but within each other as one verdict: "Wahrheit und Unwahrheit, Würde und Unwürdigkeit liegen (in den religions) nicht nebeneinander, sondern ineinander. Sie sind ineinander da." (WE 2, 283)

The reason and foundation for such a dialectical view, he feels, is to be found in God's Word, especially in the New Testament's verdict on the religions: "Das Wort des Neuen Testamentes über die Religionen ist *mehrsichtig* und *dialektisch* ... Dementsprechend muß unsere dogmatische Lehre von den Religionen mehrsichtig und dialektisch sein." (CW, 138, emphasis mine) Yet this foundation runs deeper and is rooted in what Althaus feels is an *essential characteristic* of all systematic or dogmatic theology. There is a "Notwendigkeit des dialektischen Redens" which pervades "alle großen Themen der Dogmatik". (CW, 242) He describes this dialectical method in a manner which seems to mirror the sequence of our last

a) If Uroffenbarung reveals God as a "*liebendes Du*", it also includes the possibility of "Gemeinschaft" with him. (*Extra nos*, pp. 77–79) b) Man's "*Gottesebenbildlichkeit*" implies the salvific presence of Christ in the pre-Christian order. (pp. 86–92) c) The *universal activity* of the *Spirit* makes possible the "Präsenz der einmaligen Tat Christi für jeden Menschen". (p. 112, also 109–110) Yet Zasche notes that such conclusions stand against many opposing statements, especially those in Althaus' "Sündenlehre" (p. 77). Thus he concludes that this possibility of salvation within Uroffenbarung remains, according to Althaus, "in der Schwebe" (p. 91), only a "Wahrscheinlichkeit". (p. 118) – As our Ch. IV illustrated, we would agree with Zasche that salvation in Uroffenbarung is a "Wahrscheinlichkeit" (even a certainty!); but in our opinion, Zasche does not give sufficient attention to the opposition between this probability and the many contradicting statements we have listed in this Chapter (esp. § 51). There is not only tension here – but clear contradiction! And if Zasche would have examined the roots of these opposing statements within Althaus' "Rechtfertigungslehre" (as we shall do in Ch. VI), he would have seen that the "probability" of salvation in Uroffenbarung is turned into an impossibility. Thus, while Zasche's conclusions concerning the "Wahrscheinlichkeit" of salvation in Uroffenbarung are *true* in themselves, they are not *complete* insofar as they are not sufficiently weighed on the scale of Althaus' "Rechtfertigungslehre". (An example of such overhasty judgments is found on p. 118, ann. 512 where Zasche brushes away the possibility of unbelievers encountering Christ beyond time as "ein biblisch kaum nachvollziehbares Theologumenon". For Althaus this was not only a real but a preferable possibility.)

two chapters: "Dialektisch ist ein Denken, das jedem Satze einen Gegen-Satz zur Seite stellt und den Satz nur im Zusammenhange mit dem Gegen-Satze als Ausdruck der Wahrheit anerkennt." The truths contained in God's revelation can be grasped "nur in je zwei Gedanken, zwei Worten, die einander widerstreiten und einander zugleich fordern ..." (GD/I, 107) Althaus points out that this necessary dialectic is not an "ontologische Dialektik" which, according to Barth, is based on a "reine Exklusivität von Ewigkeit und Zeit" (GD/I, 109); rather it is a theological dialectic, dictated by the fact that God remains God and can never be fully grasped by man, and that man remains a sinner, whose knowledge is always an "angefochtene Erkenntnis", a "theologia viatorum", always exposed to contradictions and unclarities. (CW, 241–242)[58] Since the theologian must construct his understanding of the religions "in the light of the Gospel" this necessary dialectic would also apply to them, even though they are not a direct object of divine revelation. Althaus' dialectical doctrine of the religions, we might say, has both a theological and natural foundation: it is called for by his general theological method and by the nature of the religions themselves.

§ 54. A Contradictory View

1. We can agree with Althaus that a certain contradictory dialectic belongs to the warp and woof of any Christian theology of the religions — simply because there is a basic dialectic running throughout the fabric of redemption. In bending to the world and then in entering it through the Incarnation, God pronounced both a "yes" and a "no" to man and all that is human; he came both to accept and to contradict. This, indeed, calls for a necessary dialectic in all "the major themes of theology". (CW, 242) A theologian therefore is never allowed to pronounce only a "yes" to the religions; also required is a definite "no" — which implies an undulating dialectic.[59]

But the suspicion and the question which pursued us throughout this Chapter (and which already began to find voice in Chapter IV) is whether Althaus' dialectic of the religions is so constructed as to *end up* in a *basic and bewildering*

---

58 That Althaus drew heavily from Barth's school of dialectical theology is clear in a letter to Barth from Rostock, 13.6.1925, in which he confesses "die Nähe zwischen uns (d.h. Ihnen, Brunner, z.T. Gogarten und mir), die *trotz allem* da ist..." (Original in Karl Barth Archive, Basel); H. W. Schmidt, in his early study of Althaus' theology, accuses him of still adhering too closely to Barth's dialectical method, based on the exclusive difference between time and eternity — thus, in the long run, an ontological dialectic. (Cf. *Zeit und Ewigkeit. Die letzten Voraussetzungen der dialektischen Theologie*, Gütersloh, 1927, pp. 109 ff.) Yet Schmidt fails to see that Althaus, while admitting a certain "exclusivity" between human and divine, did not intend it to be "pure exclusivity" which leads to the total "Ohnmacht und Nichtigkeit des Menschen" before God; cf. GD/I, 109. Yet the fact that Althaus clearly based his dialectic on the necessity "daß Gott Gott bleibt und der Mensch Mensch" (CW, 241) indicates that his method, too, had an ontological foundation — even though, as he felt, it would be an ontology dictated by God's Word. — Schröer also points out the affinity between Althaus' and Barth's dialectic. Cf. H. Schröer, *Die Denkformen der Paradoxalität als theologisches Problem* (Göttingen, 1960), p. 172; cf. also A. Beyer, *Offenbarung und Geschichte*. Zur Auseinandersetzung mit der Theologie von Paul Althaus (Schwerin, 1932), pp. 77–78, 89, 93. For an early presentation of his dialectical method, cf. P. Althaus, "Die Theologie", cf. Schweitzer, *Das religiöse Deutschland der Gegenwart*, Bd. 2, Der christliche Kreis (Berlin, 1930), pp. 121–150, esp. p. 136.

59 Cf. Konrad, pp. 478–482.

contradiction. As many of Althaus' critics argue, his "Satz" and "Gegen-Satz" seem to be so formulated that they cannot achieve a balanced synthesis.[60] Their "einander widerstreiten" seems to be much more predominant than their "einander zugleich fordern". (cf. GD/I, 107) Thus we can say that the two sides of his dialectic are "parallel" instead of "complementary"; they run alongside each other, independently. They do not call for a meeting in synthesis; indeed, they seem to exclude such a meeting.

The *fundamental reason* for this contradiction and impossibility of synthesis seems to be, simply, that his two positions *go to such extremes* as to *lose each other*: his positive view is so positive as not to support his extreme negative view — and vice versa. This is the pervading impression when we place Chapter V alongside Chapter IV. The contradiction — or at least, the extreme confusion — can be detected in the following summarizing line-up:

Eigenes Licht – Von Christus her: Althaus' description of the independent function and meaning of Uroffenbarung contradicts what he later says about the necessity of the "von Christus her" for this role to be meaningful and "gültig".
(§ 32 – § 48/1)

Vorgeschichte – Endgeschichte: It is extremely difficult to reconcile Althaus' understanding of the religions as making up a "Vorgeschichte" in the plan of salvation, in which God uses them as his "instruments" to effect his "scheme of love" – with what he later states about the basic "Diesseitigkeit" of history. The "end" – final salvation – will break into the present order but it will be something entirely new.
(§ 35 – § 48/2)

Erkenntnis Gottes – Unkenntnis Gottes: Althaus can speak of a real, actual knowledge of God within the religions through Uroffenbarung and also of a "Nicht-Mehr-Sehen-Können" and a "Nicht-Wissen um Gott". Real knowledge which is no knowledge.
(§ 36 – § 49/1)

Gott-als-Du – Totale Verzweiflung: Within his phenomenology of Uroffenbarung and frequently in his remarks about the religions, Althaus allows the non-Christian to know the personal God and his offer of love and thus to search for this God; yet he also

---

60 Koch notes a confusing "Schwanken...zwischen der Anerkennung und der Nichtanerkennung der menschlichen Religion". (Koch, p.19) Doerne, generally favorable towards Althaus, observes this same contradictory trend in his attitude towards the religions and blames it on his dialectical method of "Satz und Widersatz". M. Doerne, "Zur Dogmatik von Paul Althaus", ThLZ, 74 (1949) 456, also p. 454. Schröer points out a threefold paradox undergirding all of Althaus' thought: a christological, soteriological and ecclesiological paradox or dialectic. He feels that this paradox becomes an excuse to appeal to faith instead of working out a clear synthesis. (Schröer, pp. 172–175) Wilhelm Koepp traces a lack of unity in Althaus to "die These von dem paradoxen Charakter aller Glaubensaussagen". W. Koepp, *Panagape*. Eine Metaphysik des Christentums, 1. Buch (Gütersloh, 1928), p. 38. – Cf. also Beyer op. cit., p. 76. – Konrad also finds an unresolved dialectic running throughout Althaus' method: "... der Grund unserer Kritik an Althaus...liegt...in einer inneren Unausgeglichenheit, bzw. in dem Verzicht von Althaus, das Dialektische seiner Theologie denkbar zu machen." Althaus is guilty of an "ungerechtfertigter Mangel an gedanklicher Durchdringung". (pp. 601–602) Finally, Zasche concludes from the dialectical contradiction in Althaus' "Sprache": "Es zeigt sich...daß es schwierig ist, Althaus beim Wort zu nehmen." (p. 21, also pp. 20–24, 40–49).

insists that Uroffenbarung and the religions can lead only to despair. How personal and loving is a God who can foster only frustration?
(§ 37,38 – § 49/2)

Wahrheitsgehalt – Nur Finsternis: Althaus claims a truth which can be known and made use of within the religions; yet he also argues for "Lüge'' and "Trug'' which swallow up the "Teilwahrheit'' in what seems to be total darkness.
(§ 39 – § 49/4)

Kontinuität – Unbedingter Gegensatz: Although Althaus insists on an "Anknüpfung'' and fulfillment and "positive Beziehung'' to the religions, which he illustrates very positively in his picture of the New Testament's use of the religious world, he also claims "ganze Antithese'', "völlige Preisgabe'', "totalen Bruch''.
(§ 40 – § 50/1-2)

Messen lassen – Nur messen: Christ's revelation must allow itself to be "measured'' by Uroffenbarung and the religions (n.b. the example of the cross being measured by the history of religions!) yet Christianity does not permit any other "Maßstab'' outside itself.
(§ 41 – § 50/2)

Relatives Heil – Heillosigkeit: Althaus claims that the non-Christian can find God through following his conscience, though erroneous, within the religions; yet man always stands before Uroffenbarung as "heillos''.
(§ 46/2 – § 51/1,3)

Vergebung – Zorn: Althaus allows "Vergebung'' and true "Gemeinschaft'' with God in the religious world, yet insists that Uroffenbarung is always overshadowed by God's Zornoffenbarung which confines the religions under God's "Gericht''.
(§ 46/2, also § 44 – § 51/2)

Allzeit gegenwärtiger Christus – Heil jenseits der Geschichte: Christ has a universal presence within history and effects salvation within history; yet Althaus, for the most part, can allow salvation for those who have not known Christ to be effected only beyond history.
(§ 46/1, also § 45 – § 51/3)

2. Because of this final unclarity, tension and contradiction, it would seem that Althaus' attempt to trace a *middle way* between Troeltsch and Barth was *not entirely successful*. His own way is not clearly marked, and therefore it becomes *unviable*. As we have shown, his goals, intentions, yes, even his first steps in marking this middle way were laudable and quite acceptable. His "positive view of the religions'', with both its clear assertions and its potential conclusions, seemed to offer a sound path between Troeltsch and Barth. For the most part, it corrects the exaggerated relativism of Troeltsch without resorting to the exclusivism and negativism of Barth; it draws out the "positive'' from both sides. Yet Althaus could not remain content with this middle path. After having extracted what was acceptable from Troeltsch's position, he returns, as it were, to Barth. The result, it seems, is that he has too much of both.

It is as if Althaus, within his theology of the religions, tried *to say* – or actually *did say* – *more than he felt he could*. Thus, he was continually backtracking, correcting himself, rescinding in one context what he had quite clearly affirmed in another. In his view of the non-Christian world Althaus very much resembles a helmsman who casts out into new waters, and then finds he does not have the means to navigate them. Althaus wanted to do more than he could, and when he tried, he found himself floundering. Karl Barth, in a personal letter to Althaus (1927), described these efforts with amazing perspicacity: "Alles ... was mir bei Ihnen imponiert und zugleich unheimlich ist: die Fähigkeit nach allen Seiten offen zu sein und bewegt mitzugehen, die, von mir aus gesehen, dann doch auch die Fähigkeit ist, allzu Vieles zu schlucken und gutzuheißen, als daß ich den *ganz* deutlichen Ton Ihrer eigenen Trompete immer hören würde."[61] Althaus seemed to assert more than his own position would allow; and when he did sound "his own trumpet" he called into question much of what he had already accepted.

More concretely: with his doctrine of Uroffenbarung, especially in its phenomenological presentation, Althaus tried to lay a foundation for a more positive evaluation of the non-Christian world, and to a great extent he carried out this evaluation in his explicit teaching on the religions. But in the end, the foundation turns out to be broader than the actual edifice Althaus could build on it. The foundation remains but is in glaring disproportion to the structure it supports. With his doctrine of Uroffenbarung, Althaus laid a foundation on which he could not build. – He proposed a positive evaluation of the non-Christian religious world which he himself could not fully accept.

3. Why? What is the fundamental reason for these contradictions, these unclarities? Why did Althaus have to continually backtrack? Why could he not finish what he so promisingly began? Why could he not fully build on the foundation he laid in his doctrine of Uroffenbarung?

And the more important question: does his negative view win out over his positive evaluation? Are we to resolve the contradictions in favor of his "antithesis"? Simply: is his "no" stronger than his "yes"?

The general direction in which we must search for an answer to these questions has already been indicated in § 52 where we observed that all of Althaus' reservations about the religions circled around and stemmed from the question of "Heil". This indicates that Althaus' *doctrine of salvation-justification* is the source of his dialectic. The contradictions between these last two chapters arise from the tension between Althaus' positive evaluation of Uroffenbarung in the religions and his understanding of justification.

For the ultimate verdict on the religions, then, we must now place both his positive and his negative evaluations before the "judgment seat" of his "Rechtfertigungslehre" and ask whether it becomes the "articulus stantis 'et' cadentis religionis".

---

61 Letter from Münster, September 19, 1927. Original in Paul Althaus Archive of G. Althaus, Traunstein.

Chapter VI

Justification — the "Articulus Stantis et Cadentis Religionis"

§ 55. Introduction

1. The final touchstone for all of Althaus' theology was the doctrine of justification. This for him was indeed the "articulus stantis et cadentis ecclesiae" — the shibboleth of his strongly Lutheran and Reformational thinking,[1] the middle point from which all theological speculation and conclusions must depart and to which, for final resolution, they must return. It was part of the inheritance he accepted from Martin Kähler, who had established the "rechtfertigenden Glauben" as the common denominator for his theological system.[2] But especially, it was ingrained immoveably into Althaus' own system by the Luther-Renaissance which, especially in the voice of Karl Holl,[3] inspired him in his early years and guided him throughout his life: theology must return to its center of gravity — to the doctrine of justification as contained in Paul and reasserted in Luther.[4] From this middlepoint, theologians must confront the demands of the times. What cannot be brought into the gravitational pull of this doctrine — no matter how beautiful and promising its construction — must be allowed to drift away.

And this, Althaus states explicitly, applies especially to a theology of the religions. Every theological interpretation of the non-Christian world must be brought into harmony with the reality and meaning of Christ's act of redemption and with the way he justifies sinners: "Es ist die Rechtfertigung des Sünders in Christus, von der aus wir die Religionen zu beurteilen versucht haben." (MR, 205) Luther's principle remains: "Der Glaube an die Versöhnung und Rechtfertigung ist Standort und Maßstab seiner Kritik aller Religion." (ibid.) The "Wort vom Kreuz", and the mystery of justification which it proclaimed, must remain the final "Maßstab aller Religionen".[5] Althaus even calls the mystery of "Christus crucifixus et resurrectus" the "religiöse Apriori" necessary for the final understanding of the religions. (WE 2, 277—278)

The terminology used in these quotations indicates that Althaus was speaking here primarily of the act of judgment: "beurteilen ... Standort der Kritik ... Maßstab". This helps us distinguish the roles played by the doctrine of Uroffenbarung and that of justification in his theology of the religions. Althaus made use of the reality of Uroffenbarung to *understand* the non-Christian religious world — to grasp how it came into being, what is its nature and content. But he feels he must turn to the doctrine of justification to *judge* this world, — to measure its value and its real meaning in the eyes of Christian theology. In Althaus' theology, then,

---

1 Cf. § 17.

2 Cf. § 18/1, c; also B. Lohse, "Martin Kähler", *Tendenzen der Theologie im 20. Jahrhundert* (Stuttgart, 1967), pp. 20—21. Stephan-Schmidt, *Geschichte der deutschen evangelischen Theologie* (Berlin, 1960), p. 271.

3 H. Rückert, "Karl Holl", *Tendenzen*, op. cit., pp. 103—105.

4 Cf. G. Koch, *Die christliche Wahrheit der Barmer theologischen Erklärung* (München, 1950), p. 34; M. Doerne, "Zur Dogmatik von Paul Althaus", ThLZ, 74 (1949) 451.

5 "Das Kreuz Christi als Maßstab aller Religion", *Evangelium und Leben*, p. 64.

Uroffenbarung, as it were, presents the defendant and its case; but the doctrine of justification is the sole − or ultimate − source of a verdict. The verdict has the final word, for true knowledge is achieved only when one arrives at judgment.

2. In this chapter, therefore, we wish to examine this verdict, weigh its full and decisive content, and thus let it ring out over all that we have so far presented about Althaus' "understanding" of Uroffenbarung and the religions. We must ask what this verdict means for Althaus' "positive picture" of the religions, as traced in Chapter IV. In the light of his "Rechtfertigungslehre", can the religions carry out the positive role which he granted them within the history of salvation? Can they be "instruments" in the salvific encounter between God and men? In other words, does Chapter IV *or* Chapter V present the final verdict of Althaus' theology of the religions?

What we are also asking: Does Althaus' final verdict conform to the "case" he presented? Is the judgment he draws from the doctrine of justification − i.e. from "Heilsoffenbarung" − in conformity with the evidence he presented from the doctrine of Uroffenbarung? Or is there a clash between evidence and verdict − and is this clash the source of the contradictions and tension which we noted between his positive and his negative pictures of the religions?

In the following pages, we shall construct our analysis of this final verdict according to the pillars of the Reformational doctrine of justification: the "sola fide" (containing the "sola gratia") and the "solus Christus". What do these two "soli" mean according to Althaus for the non-Christian religions?

I. Sola Fide − Establishes the Religions in a State of Sin and Condemnation

§ 56. Means that God is God and Man is a Sinner

1. The fact that man can be justified *sola fide* means simply that he must acknowledge and accept *God as God*. In the encounter between God and man, God must be allowed to be what he is: the Transcendent, the Almighty, he who works all and before whom all creatures are nothing and can do nothing. Man steps back and permits God to be what he is and must be. This is what Althaus means when he asserts that "Gottes Gottheit" is the "Sinn der Rechtfertigungslehre".[6] The "sola fide", then, permits God to be the "Creator ex nihilo" also in the mystery of justification.[7] Also, it establishes the *first commandment* as the essential demand in the process of justification and for the proper observance of all the other commandments; the first commandment, fulfilled in the mystery of justification, becomes the core of the Gospel.[8]

Althaus insists that the necessity of justification by "sola fide" cannot be interpreted "hamartiozentrisch". Man must step back and let God take over, he must allow God to do all not simply because he himself is a sinner and through his sin has been robbed of the ability to make a contribution to his justification. Even

6 "Gottes Gottheit als Sinn der Rechtfertigungslehre Luthers", *Theologische Aufsätze* II, pp. 1−30.
7 Ibid., p. 25.
8 Ibid., p. 29.

if he had the power to make such a contribution, i.e. even if he could perfectly fulfill God's will and obey his law — he still would, as it were, have to toss away these means and let God be the sole operator. The "sola fide" is based solely on a theocentric necessity: God's nature and his will demand it — and that determines all: "Das 'allein durch den Glauben' ist in Wahrheit nicht nur für den Sünder die einzige Möglichkeit, vor Gott zu leben — es ist darüber hinaus und zuvor, von der Sünde abgesehen, die einzig mögliche Ordnung zwischen Gott und Mensch". (CW, 605) The "sola fide" " ... ist nicht erst Gottes zweiter, durch den Fall bedingter, sondern sein ursprünglicher, erster Wille". (CW, 606)[9]

The act of "sola-fide", therefore, is nothing else but the "Erfüllung des Gottesverhältnisses". (CW, 355) It can be a justifying salvific faith only when it acknowledges this relationship perfectly, i.e. only when it is nothing else but "sola". Althaus' description of such an act of faith shows how rigorously he interprets the "sola"; the least attempt on man's part, consciously or subconsciously, to add something to this "sola" and to offer God something out of which he can "create" justification destroys the entire process and renders salvation impossible:

> Die Rechtfertigung geschieht also *sola fide*. Wer sich des *sola* weigert, der hat das Ganze zerstört und preisgegeben. Denn Glaube heißt eben: nichts als empfangen, nichts als: das an sich geschehen lassen, was Gott tut. Wer in Sachen der Geltung vor Gott zum Glauben etwas hinzusetzt, der hat die Dimension des Glaubens überhaupt verlassen. Hier ist kein Platz für ein sowohl-als auch, sondern hier gilt die *particula exclusiva*: *sola fide*! (CW, 603) Das bedeutet...: ganz und gar darauf verzichten, sich selber die Ehre bei Gott zu erwirken; in dieser Sache alle Aktivität preisgeben, von sich selbst nichts erwarten; sich nicht mehr auf sich selbst stellen ... Glauben ist ein Wollen, aber ein Wollen der reinen Passivität ... Als solche ist er die einzig mögliche Haltung, mit welcher der Mensch Gottes Tat sich zueignen und sie damit für sich wirklich machen kann. (CW, 600)

Such rigorous conditions for salvific faith places, as is clear, heavy demands on the religions. Might the "form of faith" which Althaus allowed the religions[10] ever attain such clarity as to the "sola"?

2. Althaus' answer is clear: man of himself — and his religions by themselves — can never attain such clarity. And this is precisely what *constitutes* man and his religions in an *inescapable state of sinfulness*. In a sense, we can say that the theocentric foundation for the "sola fide" brings about its "hamartic" necessity: "Das Rechtfertigungsverhältnis (i.e. sola fide) gilt nicht erst um der Sünde willen, sondern die Geschichte des Menschen in seiner Sünde geschieht um der Rechtfertigung willen."[11] It is not that man cannot perform an act of "sola fide" because he is a sinner, but he is a sinner because he cannot meet God "sola fide". (CW, 145) He cannot give God the glory, he cannot allow God to be the "Creator ex nihilo", he does not permit God to be God — and therefore he is a sinner. Naturally, because man is a sinner his inability to elicit an act of "sola fide" is intensified; we can therefore speak of a certain reciprocal causality in Althaus' understanding of "sola fide" and man's sinfulness. But the starting point is not man's sin but the demands of the "sola fide" and his inability to meet these

---

9 Cf. ibid., pp. 15, 23, 28; also, "Sola fide numquam sola — Glaube und Werk in ihrer Bedeutung für das Heil bei M. Luther". *Una Sancta*, 16 (1961) 228; Doerne, p. 452.

10 Cf. § 44.

11 "Gottes Gottheit", p. 15.

demands. His sinfulness lies essentially in his inability to observe the first commandment.[12]

And because man and his religions cannot keep this first commandment, their observance of all the other commandments is corrupted and itself becomes sinful. Thus, while man is capable of good and does produce, especially in his religions, a quantity of ethical good — this entire production is penetrated by sin. It is part of an improper relation to God; it does not fulfill the whole Law concerning the way man must relate to God — and therefore it is sinful. "Wer das Gesetz nicht ganz erfüllt, der ist Sünder." (CW, 359) "'Ethisch' gesehen mag der Mensch böse und gut sein — in der Gottesbeziehung ist er ganz böse, denn er verweigert in seiner innersten Haltung Gott immerdar seine Ehre, die Furcht, die Liebe, das Vertrauen über alles; und gerade sein Gutes, seine ethische Gerechtigkeit, wird ihm zum Mittel, von sich selbst her, statt von Gott her zu leben ... Im Blick auf die Sünde wider das erste Gebot hat die Absolutheit und Monotonie des reformatorischen Urteils über den Menschen als ganz sündig recht." (GD/II, 56–57; cf. also BR, 21, 25–26)

Althaus here speaks of an "innerste Haltung" which is the source of man's inability to produce the "sola fide" and therefore of his total sinfulness. "Nicht weil er Sünden tut, neben denen er Gutes aufweisen kann, ist der Mensch Sünder, sondern er tut Sünden, weil er wesentlich, in seiner *Grundhaltung* Sünder ist." (GD/II, 56) Within man there is an "innere Gegenbewegung" against God, a drive to place himself above God. (CW, 360) "Der Mensch ist nicht nur in einzelnen Akten, sondern in seiner ständigen Grundhaltung gegen Gott sündig." (CW, 362)

3. But just what is the *cause* of this "Grundhaltung", this "Gegenbewegung"? Why cannot man and his religions keep the first commandment and produce an act of "sola fide"? To determine the tangible cause of man's sinfulness and of his inability to elicit the "sola fide", Althaus admits, is impossible; the cause is "inconceivable" and "inexplicalbe". And yet, to locate it, we must turn to the concept of the *"Urstand"* and the *"Urfall"*: "Wir bekennen uns zu der *Unbegreiflichkeit* der Sünde, indem wir den Ursprung der Sünde in einer *unerklärbaren* Tat finden. Damit ergibt sich die Notwendigkeit, den Gedanken des Urstandes zu bilden." (GD/II, 62, emphasis mine) The only really "conceivable" content offered by the idea of the original state is the certainty that the cause of sin is not to be found in God. (ibid.)

The "Urfall" cannot be dated; it is both past and present together. It represents "eine *tiefere Dimension* der Wirklichkeit, die in unserer Menschheitsgeschichte nicht faßbar ist, aber ihr zugrunde liegt. Die ersten Menschen und wir heute und die letzten Menschen stehen in ihrer Sünde als ein Mensch, ein Wille vor Gott." (CW, 384–385) There was not *one* sin which determined all the others. Rather, the "original" represents an "Einheit und Gleichzeitigkeit" which pervades all mankind and all history. "Der Fall erscheint in der Geschichte, aber er ist in ihr nicht zu lokalisieren, sondern allgegenwärtig und gleichzeitig." (ibid.)

Original sin therefore brings out what Althaus feels are the two necessary aspects of man's essential sinfulness: "Wir sind Sünder mit dem uns allen einen und selben Wesen der Gattung Mensch, das wir erben; wir sind mit eigenem Willen Sünder." (CW, 368–369) The "Gattung Mensch" which we inherit is something "überindividuell"; and the "eigener Wille" is something "individuell". (GD/II, 62) Yet the "überindividuell" represents a decision which is "schon vollzogen" — an "immer schon vor mir entschiedener Gesamtwille". The individual then makes this "already decided" his own free decision — "als echte Tat des innersten Willens".[13] But he is not free to decide anything else than that which is already decided. Man

---

12 "Zur Lehre von der Sünde", ZSTh, 1 (1923) 318.
13 Ibid., pp. 329–334; CW, 369.

is no longer free to decide for God, to allow God to be God. He preserves a "Willentlichkeit", yet it is contained within an "Unentrinnbarkeit seiner Selbstbestimmung zur Sünde". (CW, 343) "Unverloren und unverlierbar ist die wesensmäßige Bestimmung des Menschen für Gott ... Verloren ist die Freiheit für Gott als Kraft der Hingabe an ihn ..." His "Willentlichkeit" can be exercised only to rebel against God.

Here we are dealing with the mystery of human freedom and of the "personalism" of original sin — problems which neither Protestant nor Catholic theologians have solved — or can solve.[14] And yet we can only comment that Althaus' presentation of the "cause" of man's sinfulness within "original sin" seems to be merely a restatement of the "Grundhaltung" we mentioned above. Original sin is simply this "Haltung", this "tiefere Dimension" in its historical and existential, its transindividual and individual forms. This attitude of man is there, both in the first man and in all mankind; it did not come from God, that is certain. But just where the "Unentrinnbarkeit", the "Unwillkürliche", the loss of freedom originated is not clear. It is simply man's "Haltung". — This leads us to ask whether the ultimate cause of this attitude and the impossibility of breaking out of it might be found in Althaus' understanding of the "solus Christus". Man does not possess freedom for God because he does not possess Christus.[15]

4. From his understanding of the "sola fide" and of the demands it places on man, it is clear that Althaus had to lock the religions in an inescapable state of sinfulness and basic rebellion against God. For especially in the religions, man asserts his "Grundhaltung" and his "Gegenbestimmung" against God; he does not give God the honor; he does not step back. And therefore the religions remain inescapably sinful. We can now understand that while Althaus could acknowledge "ethical good" in the religions, while he could praise their doctrinal systems and insights into the nature of God and the situation of man — he still had to "backtrack" and reaffirm the total sinfulness of it all — for the religions do not observe the first commandment.

We will understand *why* the religions cannot arrive at the "sola fide", why they continually put themselves above God when we relate the "sola fide" to the "solus Christus".

§ 57. Means that God is Judge and Man the Condemned

1. The nature of the "sola fide" demands that man bow before God not only as the "Creator ex nihilo" but also as the *Judge*. Here we have the same relation of reciprocal causality as between "sola fide" and man's sinfulness: because man cannot and does not acknowledge God as God in an act of "sola fide", God becomes the judge and enemy of man. Man's "Grundhaltung", therefore, establishes not only the reality of his own sinfulness but the reality of the divine

---

14 For a concise and clear presentation of literature and opposing opinions in the present-day Catholic controversy concerning original sin, cf. "Neuere Entwicklungen in der Erbsündenlehre", HerKorr, 25 (1971) 485–490; "Zur Diskussion um die Erbsünde", HerKorr, 21 (1967) 76–82.

15 G. Zasche summarizes Althaus' doctrine of sin and original sin, but does not confront the question of man's freedom and the cause of his sinfulness. *Extra nos*, pp. 93–97. That Althaus' understanding of original sin and man's total sinfulness agrees essentially with the doctrine of the Lutheran Confessions, cf. H. G. Pöhlmann, *Rechtfertigung* (Gütersloh, 1971), pp. 95–111. Cf. § 60/3.

"Zorn" and "Gericht". Man *must* be a sinner; and God *must* condemn man and be his "enemy".

Althaus describes this "must" as a divine — almost ontological — necessity. "Das ewige Ja der Liebe Gottes zum Menschen muß dessen Nein gegenüber zum Nein Gottes wider des Menschen Nein werden." (CW, 396) As man cannot escape his state of sin, so God cannot escape this necessity of pronouncing a "no" to man and all that man does. He owes it to his own nature, especially to his holiness and his justice, to place man under his "Zorn".[16] "Der Zorn kann nicht weggenommen werden, weil er Gottes Zorn ist, aus heiliger Notwendigkeit verhängt."[17] God's love, as it were, must give "the right of way" to his wrath and declare war on man: "So schließt die Liebe den Zorn, den Kampf mit dem Menschen ein." (CW, 277) This "Kampf" calls for "Gottes Widerstand"against man (CW, 396—344). "Der Widerstreit zwischen Gott und Mensch" (CW, 465) will be carried out against all of man's attempts to find God and save himself, for all these attempts are riddled with his "Grundhaltung". They all stand under a divine "no" and rejection.

Althaus points out that because of this "Zorn" and "Gericht" God's love for man does not cease; indeed, it remains behind and within his wrath. (CW, 396; 277—289) Yet Althaus seems to see this love as "incapacitated".[18] It cannot really assert itself, it cannot really embrace man before the divine "wrath" is asserted. God's love is not really effective until something happens to remove his wrath — or to enable his love to overcome his wrath. Before that something happens, man remains inescapably under this wrath; he remains condemned.

2. God's necessary wrath not only holds back his love but, according to Althaus, *actively drives* man ever deeper *into his state of sin and rebellion*. As a decree of his just "Gericht", God abandons man to his self-seeking and turns him over to the power of Satan, thus widening the gap all the more between himself and his creatures: "Denn es ist Gottes Gericht, daß er das Leben der Menschheit unter das Gesetz des 'Reiches der Sünde' stellt und dem Satan in ihm Macht gibt ... Die eigentliche Macht des Verderbens ist der Zorn Gottes (!) ... Der Satan ist nur Werkzeug des Zornes Gottes." (CW, 470, 478) "Das *servum arbitrium*, die Verknechtung des Willens ist Gericht Gottes ... Gott hat den Sünder an das *regnum diaboli* preisgegeben." (CW, 399) Althaus sees the condemnation to sin expressed in a "Wirkenlassen einer Gesetzlichkeit des Lebens" which prevades with its corrupting poison all aspects of life and history. (CW, 396—398, 400—405) He even can call it a "Dualismus der Welterfassung" according to which, although the world remains in God's hands, it is also turned over to the "Gesetzlichkeit der Sünde und des Todes". (GD/II, 41)[19]

3. Therefore, for the act of "sola fide" to be salvific and to have the one, true God as its object, it must be *directed* towards the *just* and *angry Judge* and it must *experience* the *full vigor* of his condemnation and demands. Again, any slighting of this Judge and his demands renders the act of faith worthless and unsalvific. In his act of faith and encounter with God, man may never merely throw himself into the arms of a loving father; he may never seek unity directly. Rather he first must experience this "distance" and the necessity of forgiveness. "Die Einheit mit Gott wird nie anders wirklich als in einer Gemeinschaft, die mit

---

16 "Das Kreuz Christi", ZSTh, 1 (1923) 117.
17 Ibid., p. 121; cf. also GD/II, 26.
18 This is not Althaus' terminology.
19 "Das Kreuz Christi", pp. 117—118.

Vergebung der Sünde nicht nur begann, sondern dauernd nur durch sie besteht ..."[20] Yet it is not sufficient merely to seek forgiveness from God by acknowledging his love (as the religions, for the most part, may do). Forgiveness can come only by first acknowledging and feeling his *wrath*. Man must experience "die Unmöglichkeit Gottes ... zu vergeben, ohne daß seine Ordnung und sein Zorn über die Sünde geheiligt wird." (GD/II, 115) Man therefore must tremble under the genuine demands of God's wrath before his faith can bring him forgiveness. It is not sufficient to see the divine wrath merely as an instrument of his love, as if God first threatens only to love. His wrath makes real and terrifying demands: "Eine theologische Theorie, daß alles Strafen Gottes nur werkzeuglich, d.h. erzieherisches Handeln sei, entspricht nicht dem Glauben, der auf Erden nur in ständiger Überwindung der Furcht lebendig ist."[21]

Man's act of "sola fide" must realize that there can be forgiveness only by satisfying God's wrath. "Sühne" is the "Bedingung heiligen Vergebens." (GD/II, 117) No "Überwindung" of the judgment unless the judgment is "bestätigt" and "vollzogen". (LD, 177) No "Vergebung" without "Vergeltung": "... die Vergeltung ist die ständige Voraussetzung, der bleibende Hintergrund der Vergebung ... (Vergebung) wird in ihrem heiligen Ernst nur von dem Menschen verstanden, der um die Vergeltung ... weiß. Das Bild des vergebenden Gottes kann also niemals dazu dienen, das Bild des vergeltenden Gottes zu verhängen."[22]

All this means that for an act of "sola fide" to be truly salvific it must be penetrated by what Althaus calls a "durchlaufende *Spannung*" – a *tension* between God's love and his judgment, between forgiveness and punishment, between hope and fear.[23] "So gibt es keinen Offenbarungsglauben ohne in der Spannung zur Anfechtung des 'Ärgernisses' (Matt. 11,6), keinen Heilsglauben ohne in der Spannung zur Furcht."[24] As soon as man, in his religious pursuits, ignores or does not experience this "tension" he is standing before a false god.

4. Once again, we can see how such an understanding of justification through the "sola fide" must establish the *religions* and all they contain under God's *wrath and judgment*. Because the religions, like man in general, can never attain a genuine act of "sola fide", because they end up putting themselves before God as expressions of man's "Eritis sicut Deus", God must pronounce his "judgment" over them, he must be angry with them. They *cannot escape* this *wrath* and this *condemnation*. Now we can understand why Althaus, despite all the good and truth which he allowed Uroffenbarung to produce in the religions, *had* to constantly remind himself and his readers that this positive content could lead only to the "Zornesoffenbarung". It is also understandable why, in his negative picture of the religions, he *had to* end up condemning all the "laudable" achieve-

20 "Theologie des Glaubens", ZSTh, 2 (1924–25) 289.
21 "Vergeltung", RGG[3] VI, 1354. Yet God's wrath and judgment, as real and serious as they are, are not God's final intent. By satisfying his wrath, God seeks to bring man to his love. In this sense, Althaus can also call God's wrath an instrument of his love: "Gottes Widerstehen widerspricht seinem Willen zum Heil des Menschen nicht, sondern ist mit ihm notwendig gegeben... Gottes Richten ist von ihm nie als Ziel, sondern als Mittel gemeint." CW, 396.
22 "Vergeltung", op. cit., 1353.
23 "Theologie des Glaubens", p. 319.
24 Ibid., p. 302, cf. also p. 289.

ments — their "Wahrheitsgehalt", the "Anknüpfungspunkte", their "form of faith" — for nothing can escape the divine "Gericht".

It now also becomes clearer why Althaus, in the final analysis, *had to* be so *critical* of all the *theories of redemption* which he found in the religions. Although, as we have seen, he could allow the religions to come to an understanding of the rift between God and man as a "Gericht" of the living God, although in their cult the religions frequently achieved startling insights as to the necessity of sacrifice and reparation,[25] Althaus rejected all these doctrines and rites as unsalvific because they do not realize or experience the necessary "Spannung" which must be part of salvific faith. They do not allow "Versöhnung" to play the "beherrschende Stellung". (GD/II, 108; cf. also CW, 145) They live from a "Naivität, d.h. davon, daß ... (ihnen) der Streit mit Gott, die Feindlichkeit Gottes, die Macht des Satans in der Welt verhüllt ist". (GD/II, 34) Just why this is so will become fully clear as we now take up Althaus' concept of the "solus Christus" in the mystery of justification.

II. Solus Christus — Deprives Religions of All Possible Escape from This State of Sin and Condemnation

The intent of this section will be to show that while Althaus' understanding of the demands of the "sola fide" establishes the religions in a state of sin and enmity with God, the "solus Christus" closes all possible doors by which man could escape (or better, by which he could be enabled by God to escape) from this state. At the same time we shall gain a clearer insight into what we feel is the "causality" behind the negative effects of the "sola fide". The ultimate reason behind the necessity of the "sola fide" is God's transcendence — God must be God. Yet the reason why man cannot allow God to be God and is thus constituted a sinner, and, once constituted a sinner, the reason why he cannot allow God to be Judge and is thus driven deeper into his state of sin and condemnation is because he *does not have Christ*. The demands of the "sola fide" can be met only within the "solus Christus".[26] It is on the basis of the "solus Christus", then, that Althaus formulates his final and overriding "no" to the religions. It is a final word which points to Chapter V as Althaus' real picture of the non-Christian world.

25 Cf. § 38.
26 In Scholastic terminology we might say: the nature of justification *quoad se* is found in the "sola fide", i.e. man can be justified only if he abandons himself totally and passively to God as the transcendent Creator and as the demanding Judge. But the nature of justification *quoad nos* is contained in the "solus Christus", i.e. only in Christ can we understand this nature of justification and only in Christ are we enabled to participate in — i.e. to passively receive — the mystery of justification. Thus, in the first section of this chapter, we were "presuming" the "solus Christus", i.e. we were presenting "quoad se" that which we could know — "quoad nos" — only in Christ.

§ 58. Necessity of the "Solus Christus" – Physically-Objectively[27]

1. Althaus first of all admits that it is impossible for the theologian to penetrate fully and rationally the necessity of the "solus Christus", i.e. to grasp why God effects and communicates his justifying love at only one point in history: the cross and resurrection of Christ. The theologian must simply accept this as a given fact and then *try* to show why such a necessity is fitting. (GD/II, 117)[28] – In his own attempts to found this necessity he interprets the necessary instrumentality of Christ in such a way that the religions are excluded from any possible participation – even a remote, imperfect participation – in its effects.

Here we can present only a summarizing outline of how Althaus understands the causality of the "solus Christus" within they mystery of justification and redemption. It is an understanding which, we must emphasize, he felt reflects the Reformational "Rechtfertigungslehre".

2. Althaus seems to locate the necessity and causality of Christ principally in his acceptance and incorporation of God's "Zorn und Gericht". Christ stands between God and man as the spokesman, as it were, for both sides: "für Gott unter der Welt ...mit der Welt für Gott." (GD/II, 116–117) As God he experiences and proclaims the reality and the inescapability of God's wrath and the demands of his judgment; a price must be paid; something must be done. As man, he feels and suffers under the weight of sin and rebellion. This means "... daß er (Christus) den Widerstreit zwischen Gott und Mensch ganz an sich selbst erfährt, sowohl der Menschen Stehen wider Gott wie Gottes Stehen wider die Menschen und eben in diesem Widerstreite an Gott und an den Menschen festhält." (CW, 465) And because he stands between God and man, taking serious the wrath which God feels towards the sinner and the consternation which the sinner feels under this divine wrath – he *must suffer*. Here, Althaus stresses, both *as God and man* Christ must suffer. *As man* because God's "Gericht" must be "bestätigt und vollzogen" (LD, 177), his "Zorn" must be "geheiligt" (GD/II, 115); there must be "Geltungsmachung des Gesetzes ... i.e. Sühne" (ibid.); the "Strafanspruch des Gesetzes" must "in seinem Ernste durch den Gehorsam und das Leiden Christi herausgestellt werden". (CW, 477) "Um seiner Treue gegen Gott willen muß er leiden. Er zieht den Widerspruch gegen Gott auf sich." (CW, 466) *As God*: because God himself must suffer under the distance which man has sinfully put between himself and the divine. "Alle Vergebung fordert wahrhaftiges Durchleben des Risses. Von wem? Zunächst von dem Vergebenden rein für sich. Sein Handeln ist ja kein Vergeben, wenn er die Tiefe nicht spürt, über die er die Hände streckt. Es kann

---

27 This somewhat unusual terminology best expresses, we feel, Althaus' understanding of Christ's instrumentality in redemption and justification, as we present it in this section: the Christ-event is understood as containing a necessary physical efficacy in bringing about justification; only where there is physical-express contact with this event, through Word or Sacrament, can justification be effected and realized throughout history and for the individual.

28 H. Graß rightly observes that Althaus has difficulty in making clear the necessity of the "solus Christus" because of the primarily theocentric foundation he gave to the "sola fide". "Allerdings wird bei einer theozentrisch begründeten Rechtfertigung die *Funktion Christi* in der Rechtfertigung nicht ganz deutlich." ("Die Theologie von Paul Althaus", NZSTh, 8 (1966) 215) This is why Althaus, in analyzing the necessary role of Christ, refers much more to the "hamartic" nature of justification than to its theocentric demands. The "solus Christus" seems to be more necessary for satisfying God's demands as "Judge" than as transcendent Creator.

keinen Vergebenden geben, der nicht litte."[29] "Die Liebe Gottes steht nicht über der Not der Menschheit, sondern trägt sie; sie ist leidende Liebe. Gott leidet in Jesus unter der Sünde und Verfallenheit der Menschheit. Nur als Leidender kann Jesus erlösen." (CW, 297–298)

And in this individual who stands for God and man and suffers for them both under the divine wrath, salvation and justification are effected. (CW, 665) – But just *how* is this salvation effected? Althaus warns firstly that we should not think that Christ's cross *causes* God's love – as if this love did not exist beforehand, as if God hated and punished before he actually loved. Such an idea Althaus terms "ein heidnischer Gedanke". God's love was already being expressed on the cross. (CW, 471–472; GD/II, 114) – In the same line, he rejects all the "satisfaction theories" – expecially those of Anselm and the early Protestant theologians, which rationalize redemption into a business transaction. (GD/II, 109–111, 117)[30] Christ's sufferings were not simply the payment of a penalty, after which all could be normal again. "Jesu Leiden unter Gott bedeutet ... nicht, daß er eine kommende endgültige Strafe vollgültig abgebüßt hätte." (CW, 476)

Justification and redemption are not a "payment" or a legal procedure but a *miracle*. Althaus defines this miracle chiefly with the concept of *Durchbrechung*. God's love breaks through his wrath; his desire to save man and to bring him to an act of "sola fide" "overcomes" his judgment. "Die Liebe 'durchbricht' und 'überwindet' den Zorn". (CW, 477; GD/II, 117–118) It is a miraculous "Überwindung Gottes durch Gott." (GD/II, 25) God's love is thus able "das Gericht von Grund aus zu wandeln". (LD, 177). God's wrath and judgment are not done away with; they remain – but at the same time are overcome, broken through, transformed. This is the miracle which takes place through Christ.

And yet, although Althaus tries to avoid all rationalization of the mystery and miracle of justification, the above description would seem to imply that in the end he sees Christ as what we may call, in the wide sense of the word, an *efficient cause* of salvation. What takes place is indeed a miracle, but it can be effected – or permitted – only *by* Christ's taking God's wrath and judgment upon himself, only by his suffering. These sufferings may not be a "price to be paid", yet they are the necessary element for bringing about the miraculous transaction. Without a "Heiligung" of the judgment, there can be no "Aufhebung" (GD/II, 25). Without an "Anerkennung" of God's wrath, there can be no "Durchbrechung". (GD/II, 118) Therefore, "Gottes Liebe, die versöhnen will, kann ... nur den Weg des Kreuzes Christi gehen." (CW, 472) This seems to mean: the divine love cannot be asserted unless divine wrath is "satisfied" through the cross.

Althaus can summarize: Christ's "power" to save (i.e. his instrumentality in salvation) is to be found in his suffering. "Wir verstehen, daß an diesem vollen Durchleiden der Not der Menschheit unter Gottes Zorn seine (Christ's) Vollmacht zu versöhnen hängt." (CW, 471) – It may be argued that Christ's sufferings are more a "conditio sine qua non" rather than an "efficient cause". Perhaps. Yet the borderline between cause and condition would seem to be meandering and vague.

29 "Das Kreuz Christi", p. 131.
30 Cf. Anselm, *Cur Deus Homo* (MPL, 158); also, Y.M.J. Congar, "Regards et réflexion sur la christologie de Luther", *Chalkedon*, Vol. III (1954), pp. 457–486; W. Pannenberg, *Jesus God and Man* (London 1968), L. L. Wilkens and D. A. Priebe, tr., pp. 42–44, 274–280.

What is clear: God's justifying love, according to Althaus (and what he feels is the traditional Protestant doctrine of redemption) can be "released" and become effective and thus embrace man only through the instrumentality of Christ's death and resurrection.[31]

This is what we mean by the physical or objective necessity of the "solus Christus": salvation and justification can be effected only within the physical-historical reality of the Christ-event. They can be *real* and *present* for the individual only where there is some kind of physical-direct connection with this event.

3. Because Althaus tied salvation and justification to Christ's deed as an efficient cause (or "conditio sine qua non"), we can understand why he was so *reluctant* to allow salvation to be *mediated* in any other historical form outside of Christ. God's love is enabled − or permitted − to overcome his wrath only in Christ, − "nirgendwo außer ihm". (LD, 29) "Die Rechtfertigung ... hat ihren Grund ausschließlich in der Freiheit der Gnade Gottes, die aber als heilige Liebe allein in Christus, dem Gekreuzigten und Auferstandenen, also 'um Christi willen', für den Menschen da ist." (GD/II, 144−145) This is the real reason for the basic and ineradicable difference between Uroffenbarung and "Heilsoffenbarung", which we pointed out above,[32] −why salvific revelation can never be found within the territory of Uroffenbarung:

> ... die erlösende Offenbarung kann nicht ein allgemeiner, überall erlebbarer Gehalt alles geschichtlichen Lebens sein ... Die Hilfe (i.e. salvation) kann hier *nur* als das gar nicht Allgemein-geschichtliche, als ganz konkreter, nicht zu erwartender kontingenter Akt kommen. Dieser geschieht in dem geschichtlichen Leben, aber *nicht überall*, sondern in einer bestimmten, begrenzten, einmaligen, abgeschlossenen Geschichte, an einem von Gott erwählten räumlichen Orte. (GD/I, 34, emphasis mine)

Although God's love is free, it can be communicated only in the event of Christ; that means only where this event is again made present throughout the course of history by means of the Word. The "nur 'propter Christum'" means "Nur im Zusammenhang mit dem Worte vom Kreuz wird die Rechtfertigung der Sünder verkündigt". (CW, 599) Thus, while Althaus could boldly claim that the effects of Christ's redemption are "transhistorical" and extend beyond the event of Christ,[33] he is bound to have difficulty in allowing these effects to be mediated through other historical realities. This is why, we feel, he had to "postpone" or transpose salvation for those who had not come in contact with Christ to a point beyond history where this event could more easily be proclaimed to them and thus salvation be effected. While he could speak of "Vergebung" and "Gemeinschaft" within the religions, his doctrine of "solus Christus" did not allow him to explain just how this forgiveness and salvation is mediated.

Expressed in the terminology of causality: because Althaus interpreted the "solus Christus" as the sole efficient cause − or the sole "conditio sine qua non" − of justification, he *could not allow* this causality *to be shared* by anything outside of Christ.

---

31 And this raises the question whether in the end Althaus' understanding of redemption does bear a certain "legalistic character". He insists that Christ's sufferings were not a price to be paid; God did not consider them a price. And yet, without these sufferings, salvation and justification could not take place.

32 Cf. § 51/1,3.

33 Cf. § 46.

However, where Christ is understood as the sole final cause of justification — as is the case, for instance, with many contemporary Catholic theologians — a subordinated participation in this causality is not only allowed but presupposed. Christ is the final expression of salvation which gives other causes their meaning and effectiveness, and their goal. For Althaus, it would be extremely difficult, if not totally impossible, to allow the effects of the "solus Christus" to be found anywhere outside its immediate and sole cause.[34]

That this is so will become even clearer, we hope, in § 60 where we will show that Althaus restricts salvation to the fact of Christ not only physically-objectively, but even more so, psychologically-subjectively.

§ 59. The Final "No" to the Religions — Physically-Objectively

1. Because of his understanding of the "solus Christus" as "physically-objectively" necessary for justification, Althaus *had* to pronounce a final, general verdict on the religions which excludes or seriously compromises the positive content and function he had granted them on the basis of Uroffenbarung.

For if salvation and justification are to be found only in the physical reality of Christ — and in physical contact (through Word or Sacrament) with this reality — the religions do *not* possess and are *not* in contact with this reality. "Das Gemeinsame der nicht-christlichen Religionen ist, daß sie Christus nicht haben, und das schlechthin Unerreichbare, Neue des Evangeliums ist, daß Christus da ist, Christus, in dem *allein* wir Gott nahen können, durch den allein wir versöhnt sind. Das Neue des Christentums ist einfach die *Tatsächlichkeit*, die *Kontingenz* der Wirklichkeit Christi." (WE, 11, emphasis mine) This is really what makes up the uniqueness of Christianity — "das schlechthin Einzige, Einsame des Christentums": the fact that she alone is in possession of the physical, factual event of Christ; which means that she alone is in possession of God's redeeming "Vollmacht". (ibid., cf. also ER, 16)[35] Christianity alone possesses "das einmalige Wunder göttlichen Eingreifens", — a "Wunder" which does not take place anywhere else "...einsam, einmalig, ausschließlich — nicht ein Wunder, sondern das Wunder". (GD/I, 97; MR, 204) And this means that Christianity is *totally different* from the religions. Even though Althaus could enthusiastically speak of what the religions and Christianity have in common, of their "Anknüpfungspunkte", the fact that the religions do not have the physical event of Christ means that they and the Gospel are worlds apart. "Das ganz Andere ist Jesus Christus selbst".[36] There can be no bridge between the two, for Jesus Christ and his salvation are only on this side; this is why Althaus could not allow any positive "Entwicklung" of the religions towards Christ, why he had to insist on a basic intolerance, why he ended up placing them in a total "Gegenüber"[37] why, in the final encounter between reli-

---

34 Rahner assigns Christ's death and resurrection a sacramental causality: the Christ-event is the "sacramentum", while salvation is the "res sacramenti". Just as the "res sacramenti" can be realized outside the "sacramentum" itself — but always dependent on it and directed toward it, so, too, salvation outside of Christ. Cf. "Erlösung", *Sacramentum Mundi* I, 1159–1176, esp. 1171–1172; Conclusion, ann. 17.

35 "Natürliche Theologie und Christusglaube", *Um die Wahrheit des Evangeliums*, p. 41.

36 "Das Christentum — Religion unter Religionen?" *Universitas*, 11 (1956) 1134.

37 Cf. § 50.

gions and Gospel, there can be no real give-and-take dialogue but only "Enthüllung und Entscheidung ... eine Wende gegenüber allem sonstigen religiösenVerhält-
nis der Menschheit". (GD/I, 97) Even though Althaus could allow the religions to
be part of God's "historical dealings" with mankind, even though he tried to give
them a positive role in these dealings — he could not allow them to be part of
salvation history in the true sense of the word; their role was doomed to failure. —
All because salvation can be found only within the "physical-objective" confines
of the "solus Christus". And the religions do not have Christ.

2. The application of the physical-objective necessity of the "solus Christus" is
further illustrated by the fact that, in the end, Althaus sees the religions' doctrines
and their attempts to find salvation as *empty, ineffectual thoughts,* as "Ideen", as
the products of *imagination* and *phantasy* (GD/I, 29), of "menschlicher Sehnsucht" (WC, 15; CW, 142), whereas only Christianity has the *fact* and *reality* of
salvation. "Das Neue Testament und die christliche Botschaft verkündigen nicht.
den Gedanken, die Idee der Gottesliebe, sondern ihre konkrete Wirklichkeit und
geschichtlichen Tat in Jesus Christus."[38] Indeed, as far as the "thoughts" themselves go, there may be no difference between the religions and Christianity; Althaus
repeatedly stresses that Christianity does not bring "einen neuen, besonderen
Gottesgedanken".[39] The real difference is that, because salvation is found only in
the physical-objective reality of Christ, the religions' ideas are empty, while Christianity's have "reality", a new "Gottesverhältnis" (GD/II, 25; WE 2, 280), the
divine saving "Vollmacht" (CW, 103), "nicht eine legendäre Gestalt, sondern einen wirklichen geschichtlichen Mensch", not empty speculation, but "echte Geschichte".[40] The "solus Christus" means that "saving truth" can never be simply
truth which man, under God's guidance, comprehends; it must be truth which he
receives and grasps in a unique historical event: "... die erlösende Wahrheit ist
dann nichts anderes als die freie Tat der vergebenden Liebe Gottes ... seine
(Christ's) Geschichte in ihrer Bestimmtheit und Einmaligkeit ..." (GD/I, 48) Truth
which is not founded on this unique event remains human, unredeemed speculation. Summing up: in relation to other religions, "... bezeichnet das solus Christus ... das Moment der Wirklichkeit gegenüber dem bloßen Gedanken und dem
erdachten Heilande". (CW, 142)

Althaus carries on this line of reasoning: such "thoughts" of salvation within
the religions are not only empty, they are also sinful, for they have *no right to
exist and to be asserted*! With an attitude which very much resembles the precon-
ciliar Catholic position towards the "rights" and liberties of "false" religions,
Althaus argues that since the truth of salvation is found only in Christ, all
other doctrines of salvation have no right to exist. "Man (in the religions)
nimmt sich das, was kein Mensch angesichts seiner wirklichen Lage vor Gott
sich nehmen dürfte: den Gedanken der erbarmenden Liebe Gottes als in
sich einleuchtende und gültige Wahrheit." (CW, 146) "Das lebendige Gewissen
darf den Gedanken der dem Sünder vergebenden Liebe Gottes nicht denken."
(MR, 203) Such thoughts therefore are "unsittlich". (ibid.) Thus, Althaus repeats
his general verdict: no matter how "true" such ideas may be, without Christ they

---

38 "Das Christentum – Religion unter Religionen?", p. 1135.
39 "Natürliche Theologie", p. 39; WE 2, 280; GD/II, 25; CW, 103–104.
40 *Die Kraft Christi*. Predigten (Gütersloh, 1958), p. 35, (Sermon, February 3, 1957).

have lost all their rights and are meaningless. "Erlösungsgedanken ohne Christus sind Lüge, so wahr die Richtung sein mag, in die sie zeigen. Es gibt *nicht einmal* einen "Rechtfertigungsgedanken", der ohne Christus *recht hätte* und abgesehen von ihm etwas bedeutete." (WE 2, 290)

Althaus' final "no", as demanded by the physical-objective necessity of the "solus Christus", therefore seems to *negate* the real content of his positive evaluation of the religions which we presented in Chapter IV. This negation can be summed up as follows: "Der 'Wahrheitsgehalt' ihrer (the religions') Heilslehren ist Lüge, *weil* er nicht auf *Wirklichkeit* ruht, auf der Wirklichkeit der geschichtlich handelnden Liebe Gottes. Die Wahrheit des Evangeliums gegenüber allen Religionen und *wider* sie ist die echt geschichtliche Wirklichkeit Jesus Christus." (GD/I, 102, emphasis mine) Because the religions do not have this historical-physical reality of Christ, they have nothing that can be considered true and positive in the economy of salvation.

3. The understanding of the Reformers' "solus Christus" as a physical-objective necessity for the presence of salvation means, we feel, that the criterion according to which Althaus voiced his ultimate verdict on the religions was a very strict and a very "physical" interpretation of: *Extra Christum nulla salus*, (much akin to the rigorous Catholic application of the "Extra Ecclesiam nulla salus" in past centuries.)[41] This was the criterion he was setting up and applying when he insisted that the "Rechtfertigungslehre" or "Christus der Geschichtliche" or "das Kreuz" is the "Maßstab" according to which the theologian must "order and understand" the religions. (ER, 16–17; WE, 11) "Alles vor Christus, alles außer ihm ist eben 'Adam', verloren ohne ihn." (BR, 58; cf, also 53) For Althaus this rigorous understanding of the particle "solus" was part of the logic of divine redemption. Simply: because God has worked salvation in Christ, he works it nowhere else: "Wenn es überhaupt wahr sein soll, daß Gott in Christus mit den Menschen als Richter und Heiland handelt, dann gibt es keine andere heilvolle Begegnung mit Gott außer und neben dieser." (GD/I, 98) If we allow this salvation to be mediated, even remotely or imperfectly, through the religions, "... dann ist das Evangelium offenbar nicht beim Worte zu nehmen. Müssen wir glauben, daß auch im Brahmanismus und Buddhismus Gott sich gleich ernst und gleich erlösend Menschen zuwendet, dann ist offenbar das Wort der Vergebung in Jesus Christus und der Glaube daran nicht ... die *einzige* Weise, mit Gott zu verkehren ..." (CW, 136)

But is not this a *form of Christomonism*? Althaus accused Barth of a Christomonistic doctrine of revelation: because God revealed himself in Chirst, there can be no revelation outside of the physical reality of Christ, even if this revelation be subordinated and directed to Christ. But was not he proposing a *Christomonistic doctrine of justification*: because God justifies in Christ, there can be no justifi-

41 Cf. Ch. IV, ann. 119. – The Reformers also held to this narrow understanding of "Extra ecclesiam nulla salus": "Fides ex auditu: Der Glaube ist angewiesen auf die leiblichen Zeichen von Wort und Sakrament, die durch das Amt in der Kirche vermittelt werden. Von daher gilt auch für Luther und die CA (Confessio Augustana): Außer der Kirche kein Heil." V. Pfnür, *Einig in der Rechtfertigungslehre?* (Wiesbaden, 1970), p. 96; for extensive corroborative references to WA and CA, cf. op. cit., pp. 107–108. K. Haendler shows that Melanchthon also proposed the same view of the "Extra Ecclesiam", *Wort und Glaube bei Melanchthon* (Gütersloh, 1968), pp. 176–178.

cation outside of the physical reality of Christ, even though this justification be subordinated and directed to Him?

Is this the true — or the only — interpretation of the Reformational "solus"?

That Althaus' interpretation of this "solus" leads not only to a Christomonistic view of justification but also to what we may call a severe Christomonistic limitation of revelation in the religions is evident when, in the next paragraph, we consider his understanding of the "psychological-subjective" necessity of the "solus Christus".

§ 60. Necessity of the "Solus Christus" — Psychologically-Subjectively

Physically-objectively, the grace of the "sola fide" is *granted* only through the instrumentality of Christ; we shall now see that psychologically-subjectively, this grace can be *received* only through the same instrumentality. We shall try to show this in two steps: only in Christ can man *know* what justification through "sola fide" is, and only in Christ can he *accept* it.

1. *Only in Christ can the "sola fide" be known.*

a) We have seen above that man must approach God "sola fide" because of the otherwise unbridgeable natural (i.e. theocentric) and sinful (hamartic) distance between him and God. In his interpretation of the "solus Christus" Althaus now adds that man can fully and sufficiently know this *distance* only in Christ. All other knowledge or experience of the rift between God and man is only a partial knowledge and therefore *insufficient for salvation*. Althaus argues, firstly, that although a knowledge of the chasm between the human and the divine can come "mehr oder weniger zum Bewußtsein" (BR, 41), only in Christ and his cross can man understand its true depths. Only from the cross, in other words, can man realize that this dividing line cannot be crossed, that man left to himself is totally separated from God. "... die Bedeutung des Kreuzes (ist), daß es *die wahre Stellung* des Menschentums zu Gott rücksichtslos enthüllt ... So tut sich am Kreuze Christi der Riß in seiner ganzen Tiefe auf, von dem jeder Beter ein weniges fühlt: der Riß zwischen dem Heiligen und dem Menschenwesen." Without the cross, this rift remains "das Menschheitsgeheimnis".[42] Before Christ, "das Menschenwesen in seiner tiefsten Gottlosigkeit" cannot be grasped. (LD, 177) Only in him is the separation revealed as an "Abgrund".[43]

Further, without the "solus Christus", Althaus maintains that this abyss cannot be properly understood as the result of God's personal *Gericht*. We have already seen that on the basis of Uroffenbarung Althaus could allow an experiencing and knowledge of God's personal judgment within the contradictions of life.[44] But within his doctrine of "solus Christus" he seems to take this back, or at least to qualify it radically, for he states that Christ's revelation concerning God's "Zornesverhängnis" as his personal condemnation of man is something "schlechthin Neues".[45] Without Christ, God's "Zorneswalten" which is "überall wirksam" is "nirgends als solches (i.e. as God's judgment) verstanden". (GD/I, 32) "Wie ist das

42 "Das Kreuz Christi als Maßstab", pp. 70—71, emphasis mine.
43 *Die Kraft Christi*, p. 35.
44 Cf. § 38.
45 "Das Kreuz Christi", pp. 120—121.

möglich, wie kann es in der Menschheit zur vollen Erfahrung des Gerichtes kommen? Offenbar *nur so, daß der Vergebende zugleich der Leidende ist*".[46] And that is only in Christ. "Dem Menschen vor der Begegnung mit dem Evangelium ist vielfach die eigene Sünde und damit das Gericht Gottes noch verhüllt." (CW, 409) Again, this implies that the "experience" and "partial knowledge" of God's judgment against man which is possible before Christ is never such a knowledge as is required by the act of "sola fide". – Now we can more fully understand why Althaus could not allow the "form of faith", i.e. the "existentieller Glaube" of Uroffenbarung to become salvific faith: because it does not arrive at a sufficient understanding of the abyss of sin between God and man. Therefore it is a faith which in the end fails. "Die Christus-Offenbarung wiederum begrenzt das existentielle Erkennen der Vernunft (i.e. through Uroffenbarung), denn sie enthüllt, wie die Sinn-Gebungen des existentiellen Erkennen zerbrechen gegenüber der in ihrer echten Wirklichkeit erkannten Welt der Sünde und des Todes." (GD/I, 91; cf. also 92)

b) It is also only in Christ that man can experience and grasp the *necessary* "*Spannung*" between God's wrath and love within the act of "sola fide", and therefore, only in Christ does he see justification as a "*Durchbrechung*". Outside of Christ it is impossible to comprehend the necessary "unity" between God's love and wrath, i.e. that God, in asserting his wrath, allows his love to break through, " ... daß er im Gerichte Gemeinschaft begründet und in der Gemeinschaft Gericht hält ... daß er 'rechtfertigt'".[47] "Christus heißt: der Akt Gottes, daß Gott den ewigen Zorn, den wir zu erwarten haben, nicht walten läßt, sondern *wider das Erwarten unseres Gewissens* uns begnädigt, den ewigen Zorn zum heilsamen Gerichte wandelt. *Allein in Christus* ist uns die Einheit von Zorn und Gnade gegeben, die Durchbrechung des ewigen Zornes ... *Nur in Christus*, auf dem Boden der Gottestat, die er bedeutet, können wir Gottes Gerechtigkeit und Liebe ... in eins sehen ..." (CW, 288, emphasis mine) That God can thus affirm the validity of his law and judgment and at the same time assert his love – "das ist, vom Gesetz her gesehen, unerhört und unmöglich". (CW, 599) This, according to Luther, is the special knowledge of God which is so different from the "general knowledge" of Uroffenbarung and which can come *only* in Christ: "quid deus nobis cogitet, quid dare et facere velit, ut a peccatis et morte liberemur et salvi fiamus, quae propria et vera est cognitio Dei."[48] This, Althaus affirms, is what distinguishes Christ's work from that of all other religious leaders and religions: his revelation of a "Vergebung" which unifies God's love and wrath. Without Christ, no other religion can attain to such a knowledge. (GD/II, 104–106)

2. *Only in Christ can the "sola fide" be accepted.*

a) Althaus holds that only in Christ is man enabled to renounce his own works and accept the grace of "sola fide". The constantly recurring impediment to man's approach to God is that because of his "Grundhaltung" and because of his sinfulness, he ever tries to work his own justification; he never allows the "sola" to be totally "sola". He never remains entirely passive under the divine workmanship.

---

46 Ibid., pp. 129–130.
47 Review of K. Barth's *Das Wort Gottes und die Theologie. Gesammelte Vorträge* (1924), in *Theologischer Literaturbericht*, 48 (1925) 5.
48 Quoted in CW, 139, from WA, 44, 87, 15.

The only avenue of escape from this constant return-to-self, Althaus insists, is when the "sola fide" is founded on and arises out of the "solus Christus". Only when man consciously knows that Christ has done all and, in his act of faith, is doing all — only then can his faith be "sola" enough to be salvific. " ... 'rechtfertigender Glaube' oder fides salvifica ... als solcher ist ... keine Möglichkeit des natürlichen Menschen. Der Verzicht auf die selbstherrliche Grundhaltung des Menschen ist das Wunder des Geistes Gottes in ihm. Er gewinnt sie ihm *durch das Evangelium* selbst ab", i.e. only through Christ. (CW, 600—601, emphasis mine) " ... der Glaubens-Akt ist *allein* auf die Wirklichkeit der Gnade Gottes in Christus gerichtet." (GD/II, 146, emphasis mine) Only where the "sola fide" is explicitly known to be "propter Christum" is such a faith possible. (CW, 604) If Christ is not known, as in the religions, man cannot passively accept God's gift. (GD/II, 147)

b) Also, Althaus fells that only in Christ does man receive the *surity* that the acceptance of the "sola fide" is possible. Such a surity, he specifies, must be *historical*. The only way man can be certain that God does the impossible and lets his love win over his wrath, the only way he can be certain that this love is something he can depend on and accept in the "sola fide" is when he sees this victory of love in an *historical event*. "Diese Begründung der Gemeinschaft kann nur als ein *geschichtliches Konkretum* vollzogen werden ... Gemeinschaft mit Gott als Gericht und Vergebung kann nur in einer Religion der geschichtlichen Gottesoffenbarung wirklich werden ... Die Vergebung muß als das Konkretum einer *unzweideutigen Tatsache*, in der Härte einer Handlung geschichtlich werden."[49] Althaus implies that man's consciousness of his sin and separation from God is so penetrating that he can feel safe that God's love is stronger than his wrath and justice only if this is illustrated in a concrete historical event.[50] Only in Christ can man *dare* to produce an act of faith which is truly salvific: "Glauben heißt: nicht erfahren, nicht sehen, sondern wider Erfahrung und wider das Sichtbare es auf Gottes in Jesus Christus ergangene Zusage wagen." (CW, 601) "Die Liebe Gottes ist Wahrheit, auf der wir ruhen können, nur in Jesus Christus."[51] Althaus, then, implies that without knowledge of this historical assurance in Christ, the "sola fide" is irrational — simply a blind leap in the dark.

3. In the light of Althaus' understanding of the psychological necessity of the "solus Christus", we have another reason why he had to "take back" so many of his "allowances" that the religions might be "viae salutis". He had to, for instance, restrict his assertions about the "universal Christ". Although Christ has an "übergeschichtliche Gegenwärtigkeit ... eine Unmittelbarkeit zu jeder Zeit, jedem Geschlechte",[52] this universal, immediate presence must be "mediated" through knowledge of and preaching of the historical Christ — for only in the historical Christ can man *know* and *accept* the mystery of justification. It remains possible for the universal Christ to effect salvation without knowledge of the historical Christ, but this calls for "außerordentliche Wege" which are always "Ausnah-

---

49 "Das Kreuz Christi", p. 122, emphasis mine; cf. also GD/II, 33.
50 Even though, as we have just seen, he also held that man can never fully experience the radicalness of his separation from the divine. Cf. § 60/1, a; CW, 288.
51 "Natürliche Theologie", p. 40.
52 Cf. § 46.

162

men". (In other words, it is an exception that the "immediate presence" of the universal Christ is really immediate!) "In der Regel begegnet Jesus dem Glauben allein durch das Zeugnis von seinem irdischen Leben." (CW, 492) " ... man kann die Tat Gottes in Christus ... nur konkret-tathaft in der Verkündigung und in den Sakramenten empfangen ..."[53]

Here we can also provide an even more certain answer to our question raised in Chapter IV as to whether the Spirit can work salvation outside the historical event of Christ.[54] He *cannot* because the "sola fide" can be grasped and accepted only through knowledge of this event. Even though the illumination of the Spirit always exercises the decisive role in the act of faith, Althaus had to restrict this role to one historical mediation. Even though the historical event of Christ labors under much the same "Verhüllung" as all history, it remains the sole avenue of the Spirit.

Also, because of this bond of psychological necessity between the "sola fide" and the "solus Christus", Althaus implicitly makes it impossible for the universal salvific will[55] to be realized within history. When he so brightly speaks about community with God and forgiveness within the religions he is speaking about "effects" for which he can offer no psychological cause. Without Christ, man cannot subjectively know or accept such "effects". Althaus can assert a possible "relative salvation" within the religions, but he cannot say how it got there!

Furthermore, Althaus' concept of the psychological necessity of the "solus Christus" refocuses the delicate query concerning the ultimate *causality* of man's fundamental, inescapable sinfulness. We have seen that this sinfulness consists in a "Grundhaltung" by which man cannot allow God to be God or to be Judge — and thus cannot elicit an act of "sola fide". We noted Althaus' unclarity as to the *why* and *whence* of this "Grundhaltung".[56] — Here we may venture the response: it is there and it is inescapable *because man does not have Christ*. Only "in Christo" can man realize and accept what he himself is and thus allow God to be Creator and Judge. (Cf. esp. GD/II, 145—147; CW, 600—601; 603—604) Therefore, without Christ man must fall into this "Grundhaltung". Of course, we cannot call Christ the cause of human sinfulness. Yet his absence brings it about that man has no other choice but to rebel against God. Such an understanding of the "causality" of original sin may imply an intimate bond between the order of creation and of redemption: i.e. man's nature is such that without contact with the God-man, it cannot be what it is and must turn against itself by turning against God. On the other hand, because this view calls for an explicit encounter with Christ — with the historical event of Christ — it bears somber consequences for the religions: the religions, because they do not know the "solus Christus", are locked within the causality of sin. They may know God, but they can never have him and experience his love in justification.

---

53 "Natürliche Theologie", pp. 39—40.
54 Cf. § 45/5.
55 Cf. § 43.
56 Cf. § 56/2, 3.

§ 61. The Final "No" to the Religions — Psychologically-Subjectively

1. Under the demands of the psychological-subjective necessity of the "solus Christus", Althaus once again had to pronounce a final and decisive "no" to the religions.

It led, first of all, to what we have called a "Christomonistic restriction" of revelation in the religions. If it is impossible without Christ to understand the nature of justification — especially the theocentric and hamartic distance between God and man — revelation in the religions can never contain a true understanding of the nature of God and man. This is why, as we saw in Chapter V, Althaus had to admit to a drastic "Entstellung" of Uroffenbarung in the religions.[57] This is why, in the last analysis, all the "analogies", "Vorbilder" and "Gleichnisse" within the religions turn out to be not "Analogien" but *Paralogien*; they really have only non-essentials in common, for there is an unbridgeable difference between these "Bilder" and the reality of justification as understood in Christ. (GD/II, 106) Without Christ, revelation in the religions *cannot* understand man's needs, his sinfulness, his need of grace — all of which are essential elements in any anthropology. "Sie verkennt die Teife und den Grund der Not." (GD/I, 100) Neither can this revelation come to a true knowledge of God — his love, his justice, his personalism, his way of dealing with man. (CW, 141; GD/I, 100)[58] Because of the absence of Christ, the "Erkenntnis Gottes" which Althaus spoke of within Uroffenbarung turns out to be not so true and reliable after all, " ... denn nur der Gott des Kruzes ist der ganze und der lebendige Gott."[59]

Because of the psychological necessity of the "solus Christus", much of what Althaus presents in his phenomenology of Uroffenbarung in the religions does *not* seem *possible without Christ*. This is why he constantly had to be throwing in his own "Rückversicherung" of the *von Christus her*. This is why the "von Christus her" turns out to be necessary not only to perfect and fulfill Uroffenbarung but to deliver Uroffenbarung's own message concerning man and God; this is why, in the end, Althaus cannot allow Uroffenbarung to carry out as "independent" a role as he originally proclaimed.[60]

Also, by reason of the psychological necessity of the "solus Christus", Althaus could not allow the religions to have the *historical surity* which is necessary for venturing an act of "sola fide". This is why no religion can find the "Gewißheit" that God's love is stronger than his wrath; no religion can produce an understanding of salvation which will satisfy the needs of the human heart.[61] "Das Wesen des Heidentums wird durch die Grenze bezeichnet, daß keine außerchristliche Religion die Gewißheit der heiligen Liebe Gottes erreicht oder festhalten kann." (MR, 194; cf. also GD/I, 101)

2. With even more devastating consequences for the religions, Althaus must conclude that because they do not have Christ, anytime that they do accept or assert salvation, it will end up as a way of *self-redemption*, as a way of sin.

---

57 Cf. § 49/4.
58 *Grundriß der Ethik* (Gütersloh, 1953[2]), pp. 35–36.
59 "Das Kreuz Christi als Maßstab", p. 74.
60 Cf. § 48/1.
61 "Natürliche Theologie", p. 39; GD/I, 100.

Without Christ, he decrees, "geht er (man) den Weg der Selbsterlösung, die *alle* natürliche Religion kennzeichnet."[62] Because they do not understand man's sinfulness nor God's wrath, all their doctrines or "thoughts" of salvation represent " ... Flucht vor der Wirklichkeit des wahren Gottes und somit die Ursünde der Religion ... Wo er (man) Gottes Liebe denkt (i.e. without Christ), da verleugnet er die Strenge Gottes. Wo er Gott als Liebe bestimmt, da macht er sich einen Abgott nach seinem Bedürfnis." (WE 2, 288–289) – Also, because the religions are seeking salvation without Christ, they will always, somehow, be proposing their own *works* as means by which to effect justification. This is true, even when certain religions, apparently, propose a doctrine of justification through faith alone. Such faith is always a work, for as we have seen, total passivity, complete "sola fide" is possible only through and on the basis of the "solus Christus". "Wie verschieden die Religionen auch sind, in dem einen kommen sie überein, daß der Mensch etwas vor Gott bringen zu müssen meint, daß er nicht an die bedingungslose Versöhnung glaubt."[63] Indeed, without Christ, the "truer" such doctrines of justification are, i.e. the more clearly they might understand the nature of the "sola fide" – the more they become "die Lüge der natürlichen Theologie gerade in ihrer höchsten Gestalt" and the more "todfeind" they are to the Gospel.[64]

Here, within the psychological necessity of the "solus Christus", we have the final reason why Althaus had to classify all religions, as we have seen,[65] within the sinful boundaries of either *mysticism* or *moralism*. "Die beiden großen Hauptmöglichkeiten der Religion sind Gesetzesreligion und Mystik." (WE 2, 285; cf. also WE, 12; CW, 141–142; GD/I, 100–101) Because both of them do not have Christ, because they therefore do not understand the true nature of justification and, in the words of Paul, "eifern um Gott, aber mit Unverstand" (Rom. 10, 2–3) (WE 2, 286) – " ... beide sind Gestalten der Selbstverwirklichung des Menschen, beide tragen das Zeichen der Flucht vor dem wahren Gott." (WE 2, 287) Mysticism does not grasp either the reality and tragedy of man's sinfulness – or the true personalism of the Divine, and therefore, through a false form of "sola fide", too hastily and "unjustly" seeks union with the Transcendent. Moralism, respecting the distance and the personalism of God, seeks however to span the separation through works of the Law – man's own activity. (MR, 196; WE, 13) – No matter how much good a religion may contain, no matter how much of an insight into the doctrine of "sola fide", without Christ it cannot burst the borders of self-redemption, i.e. " ... die tatsächliche Unfruchtbarkeit der Religionen, über jene Alternative von Mystik und Moralismus wirklich hinauszukommen. Aller Fortschritt der Religionsgeschichte verläuft innerhalb dieser Grenze." (MR, 203–204)

---

62 "Natürliche Theologie", p. 40, emphasis mine.
63 "Gottes Gottheit als Sinn der Rechtfertigungslehre Luthers", p. 23
64 "Natürliche Theologie", pp. 39–40.
65 Cf. § 49/4.

§ 62. The Final "No": Sine Christo = Contra Christum

This final "no" to the religions, which we have traced within the preceding pages, was, according to Althaus, Luther's final verdict — and the only verdict which Reformational theology can draw if it applies the "Rechtfertigungslehre" to the religions: "Der scharfe Gegensatz zwischen den Religionen und dem Evangelium besteht ihm (Luther) darin, daß allein das Evangelium Rechtfertigung des Sünders um Christi willen verkündet. Der Glaube an die Versöhnung und Rechtfertigung ist Standort und Maßstab seiner Kritik der Religion." (MR, 205) — What this "Maßstab" boils down to was expressed succinctly by Luther, and forms the concluding sentence to Althaus' first extensive study of the religions: *"Necesse est enim, ut contra Christum doceant, qui non Christum docent"*. (MR, 205)[66]

Here, we feel, we have the final key to the tensions and contradictions within Althaus' theology of the religions: "Sine Christo = Contra Christum". On the basis of his doctrine of Uroffenbarung he made a genuine attempt to afford the religions a positive place within the divine scheme of salvation; but because Uroffenbarung and the religions do not yet have Christ, all this had to be turned against Christ. And still, because the conclusions he drew from Uroffenbarung were, as we have seen, so positive, this "turning against" frequently seems arbitrary and contradictory. This, still more clearly, reveals the tensions within Althaus' view of the religions as a clash between his doctrine of Uroffenbarung and justification, between his anthropology and soteriology. The former's "yes" cannot be reconciled with the latter's "no".

To conclude our study of Althaus' doctrine of justification and the religions, we can illustrate this clash within his analysis of two concrete non-Christian religions: Bhakti Hinduism and Amida Buddhism.

III. An Example of Uroffenbarung's "Yes" and Justification's "No": The Religions of Grace

§ 63. A Verification of the Clash

In all of his major studies of the non-Christian religions, Althaus always has a word — usually a closing word — for the so-called "Religions of Grace": Bhakti-Hinduism and Mahayana — Amida — Buddhism. (CW, 142–146; MR, 199–202; WE, 9–10, 14–15; WE 2, 287–292; WC, 1–20) His evaluation of these forms of Hinduism and Buddhism offer, as it were, a phenomenological summing up of his entire theology of the religions. It shows to what lofty and lucid heights he could

---

66 Althaus offers no reference for this quotation; it can be found in Luther's *Operationes in psalmos* (1519–1521) in the Erlanger Ausgabe, XIV, 22. — Althaus founds his understanding of Luther's evaluation of the religions on: H. Voßberg, *Luthers Kritik aller Religionen* (Leipzig, 1922) — cf. esp. pp. 31–41; W. Holsten, *Christentum und nichtchristliche Religion nach der Auffassung Luthers* (Gütersloh, 1932). Cf. also: K. Holl, "Was verstand Luther unter Religion?", *Gesammelte Aufsätze zur Kirchengeschichte*, Bd. I (Tübingen, 1923³), pp. 1 ff.; E. Wolf, *Martin Luther, das Evangelium und die Religionen* (ThEx, Heft 6, München, 1934).

allow Uroffenbarung to bring the religions. Yet it also makes clear the totality and the rigor with which he felt he had to apply the "sola fide" and the "solus Christus" to these doctrines. Within Althaus' views of the Religions of Grace we hear "phenomenologically" the clash between his ideas on Uroffenbarung and those on "Heilsoffenbarung" — between his hearty "yes" and his resolute "no" to the religions. Here, too, we see that the last word is definitely that of the "no". — In these examples it also becomes clear that his "Maßstab" of "solus Christus" rules over not only the theological "facts" of Uroffenbarung but also the phenomenological facts of the history of religions. Whatever positive contents there may be in the findings of phenomenologists and historians of religions, they, too, must be subjected to the demands of justification only in Christ.

In order to properly weigh Althaus' final evaluation of these religions, we shall, for the most part, limit ourselves to his own description of them.[67] He forms his picture of the Bhakti tradition within Hinduism chiefly from Rudolf Otto's *Die Gnadenreligionen Indiens und das Christentum*[68] While he admits that this Bhakti piety "runs throughout the history of India", he refers mainly to its widely-known and enduring presentation in the 2nd (or 3rd?)Century B.C. epic-hymn, the Bhagavadgita[69] and to one of its clearest and most influential theological formulations under Ramanuja (1055–1137). (CW, 143; MR, 199)[70] For his description of Mahayana Buddhism, Althaus refers primarily to Hans Haas, *Amida Buddha*

---

67 For the necessary background to understanding Althaus' presentation of Bhakti and Amida Buddhism, the following works may be consulted: For *Bhakti*: F. Heiler, *Die Religionen der Menschheit* (Stuttgart, 1963), pp. 382–397, 399–400;Klaus Klostermaier, *Hinduismus* (Köln, 1966), esp. pp. 306–319; Joseph Neuner, ed., *Hinduismus und Christentum, Eine Einführung* (Wien, 1962), pp. 138–149, 160–169, 182–188; T. Ohm, *Die Liebe zu Gott in den nichtchristlichen Religionen* (München, 1950), pp. 200–267, esp. pp. 200–208, 230–233; C. Regamey, "Die Religionen Indiens", *Christus und die Religionen der Erde*, Bd. III, hrsg. von F. König (Wien, 1961²), pp. 73–227, esp. 146–151; R. C. Zaehner, *Hinduism* (London, 1962). pp. 164–193. *Amitabha–Amida–Buddhism*: Anesaki, *History of Japanese Religion* (Tokyo, 1963), pp. 170–187; E. Conze, *Buddhism: Its Essence and Development* (New York, 1952²), pp. 119–160, 205–207; F. Heiler, op. cit., pp. 318–321, 346–349; H. de Lubac, *Amida* (Paris, 1955); J. Kitagawa, *Religion in Japanese History* (New York, 1966), pp. 86–118; G. Mensching, *Buddhistische Geisteswelt* (Darmstadt, 1955), pp. 243–294; F. K. Numazawa, "Die Religionen Japans", *Christus und die Religionen der Erde*, op. cit., pp. 416–436, esp. pp. 428–432; T. Ohm, op. cit., pp. 276–287, esp. 282, 284–86; Y. Okura, *Principal Teachings of the Sect of Pure Land* (Tokyo, 1925); E. Okusa, *Die Hauptlehren von Shinshu, dem wahren Lehrsystem* (Kyoto, 1915).

68 Gotha, 1930. Althaus' final verdict on Bhakti draws heavily from Otto, often without giving any explicit or clear reference.

69 Althaus uses R. Garbe's translation, *Die Bhagavadgita* (Leipzig, 1905, 1921²) and refers to Bertholet-Lehmann, *Lehrbuch der Religionsgeschichte* (Tübingen 1925), II, p. 150 ff.; cf. MR, 199. – Specialists differ as to the dating of the Gita. Garbe argues that it took form between 300 and 250 B.C. and during the 2nd Century B.C. was reworked and edited into our present form. (Cf. Ohm, p. 210, Neuner, pp. 139–140) As for the origins of the Bhakti movement itself, it is commonly believed to have taken shape between 600–400 B.C.; some trace it back as far as 1000 B. C. (Cf. Conze, p. 145; Ohm, p. 207)

70 One can say that Ramanuja brought Bhakti "back to life", after Sankara, at the beginning of the 8th Century, reasserted the monism of the ancient Vedas; cf. Heiler, pp. 397–399; Neuner, pp. 170–181.

unsere Zuflucht,[71] and to R. L. Reichelt, *Der chinesische Buddhismus.*[72] Mahayana, which Althaus feels transformed Buddhism from an atheistic to a theistic religion (CW, 144), began already in India under the influence of Bhakti.[73] Yet he focuses his study of Mahayana on the Chinese "School of the Pure Land", founded by Hui-yuan (333–416) and especially on the Japanese 12th and 13th Century schools of Genku (or, with his priestly title, Honen) (1133–1212) and Shinran (1173–1262) – the so-called Jodo or Amida schools of Japanese Buddhism.

What is evident – and what must be stressed – throughout Althaus' treatment of these Religions of Grace is that his acquaintance with them is not only *secondary* but *limited.* This is true of his knowledge of the religions in general. Althaus was definitely not a historian of religions, not even on a subordinated or "part time" basis. Although one of his dominating interests was to come to a more balanced theology of the religions, he did not make any special efforts to get to know them – or any one of them – at first hand and at greater depth. This, perhaps, will help us understand the ease and astounding self-surity with which he could frequently apply – we might say "impose" – his theological principles on phenomenological facts.

§ 64. Uroffenbarung's "Yes" to the Religions of Grace

1. The "Gnadenreligionen" are, in Althaus' estimation, one of the high points in the entire history of religions – instances, that is, where the religions seem to break out of the limits of either mysticism or moralism. (WC, 5)[74] They come to an amazingly clear insight into what is and must be the relationship between God and man: the reality of man's total inability to do anything for his salvation, and the reality of divine, saving love – ready to make up for man's inability. This insight is contained in Bhakti's abandoning of the "Karma-marga", the way of works, and of the "Inana-Marga" or "Samkhya-marga", the way of knowledge, as means by which man may find salvation. Man is too weak and too sinful to be able to make use of these means. Thus, his only hope is God's personal love for him. What is being taught here, Althaus comments, is clearly the doctrine of "sola gratia". And he adds: "Diesem 'sola gratia' entspricht ein 'sola fide'". (CW, 143) Redemption comes through bhakti – i.e. "liebende Hingabe an die personale Gottheit" (ibid.), "hingebendes Vertrauen auf Gottes Liebe". (MR, 199) Man is being called upon to accept salvation through an act of "sola fide" in the love of a personal Deity. This insight was clarified even more sharply under Ramanuja who taught that man, laboring under the effects of an "Urfall", cannot of himself even elicit this loving abondonment to God. His faith, therefore, cannot be considered

---

71 *Urkunden zum Verständnis des japanischen Sukhavati-Buddhismus* (Leipzig, 1910).

72 (Basel–Stuttgart) 1926, tr. by. W. Ohler. Althaus also makes reference to Bertholet-Lehmann, op. cit., I, pp. 229 ff., 348 ff.; cf. WC, 5.

73 The Maha-yana, or Great Vehicle, as opposed to the Hinayana, or Little Vehicle, developed from the split between the Sthaviravadins and the Mahasanghikas around 240 B.C. But it was chiefly around the time of the Christian era that Bhakti made its decisive invasions into Buddhism. Cf. Conze, pp. 119–125; 144–146.

74 Within his analysis of these religions, Althaus does not explicitly state that their achievements and their "content of truth" are the product of Uroffenbarung. Yet considering his general understanding of religious truth and Uroffenbarung, there can be no doubt that this was presupposed. Thus, Althaus could approve R. L. Reichelt's argument that definite traces of the "Logos spermatikos" can be found in Amida Buddhism. WC, 19.

a "work" or a "condition" by which he earns or fashions his salvation. It, too, must be given him by the Deity. Thus, all he can do is stand before the Divine in total passivity, in humble acknowledgement that all depends on His gift and election. (CW, 143)

A similar "preview" of the Christian doctrine of "sola fide" and "sola gratia" is contained in devotion to the "Amitabha" as proposed by Hui-yuan's "School of the Pure Land".[75] One can find access to paradise, i.e. to "the Pure Land in the West", not through works of self-redemption but through faith and trust in Amitabha, the Lord of the Pure Land, who made a vow that he would become Buddha by aiding all creatures to overcome their weakness, thus bringing them to redemption. This Amitabha, Althaus observes, is the tenuous incorporation of the "historical account" of Buddha's vow not to enter Nirvana before making known to all men his path to liberation. (WC, 6–7) Althaus feels that the development of this Chinese devotion to Amitabha was influenced by Christian Nestorian missionaries who preached in China in the 7th Century. (loc. cit.)[76] – "Die schönste Entwicklung" of this doctrine of salvation through "sola fide" came, Althaus feels, in the Japanese schools of Genku and Shinran. Both of them rebelled against the empty ritualism and the proliferation of religious works within Japanese Buddhism during the Middle Ages and sweepingly rejected salvation through "ji-riki", i.e. rebirth through self-redemption. They proposed the way of "ta-riki": faith and complete trust in Amida, whose love and mercy were expressed in his vow to aid even the most helpless and miserable sinner. No one will be lost, if he only believes. Althaus can only marvel at such faith: "Dieser Glaube ist Heilsgewißheit."[77]

Within both Bhakti piety and Amida Buddhism Althaus traces "reformational" developments, very similar to those within Christianity, by which the concepts of "sola fide" and "sola gratia" were purified and made even more exclusive. Within Bhakti, the teachings of Ramanuja gave rise to the controversies between the "North and the South Schools". The former taught salvation according to "the way of the monkey" (Markatanyaya) by which the young is saved by its mother but only if it supplies its own effort and hangs on; the latter proposed "the way of the cat" (Marjaranyaya) in which salvation is afforded only by "being carried" – in total passivity and lack of one's own performance. This latter school, then, disqualified good works totally from the efficacy of the "sola fide". Here we have, as R. Otto pointed out, the absolute supremacy of divine grace and the total subordination of man under the Transcendent. (CW, 144)

The same restressing of "sola fide and sola gratia" came in the disagreements between Genku's "Pure Land School" (Jodo-Shu) and Shinran's "True Sect of the Pure Land" (Jodo-Shin-Shu). The former, which Althaus terms "buddhistic Catholicism", indeed seeks salvation from Amida's mercy but urges the faithful to constantly call upon his name, especially at the

---

75 The devotion to Amitabha originated in the Northwest of India, in the borderland between India and Iran, and shows strong Iranian influence. It was brought to China by missionaries around 150 A. D. Hui-yuan based his devotion to Amitabha on the Sukhavati Sutra. At first, other Buddhas or Bodhisattvas received the main cult; Amitabha became popular around 650 A. D. Amitabha is the Buddha of Infinite (amita) Light (abha), and his kingdom is in the West. Cf. Conze, pp. 205 ff.; Heiler, pp. 318–321.

76 Heiler would agree; cf. p. 320. H. M. Enomiya-Lasalle, however, who speaks in the name of many Japanese authors, denies any real Christian influence. Cf. "Der Heilsweg des Buddhismus", *Die vielen Wege zum Heil*, hrsg. von W. Molinski (München, 1969), pp. 26–27.

77 "Natürliche Theologie", p. 38.

moment of death. (WC, 9–10) The Jodo-Shin-Shu, on the other hand, was already identified by Francis Xavier as "the Lutheran form of Buddhism"[78] because it discouraged personal works and placed salvation solely in Amida's grace. One should invoke his name, but only as an expression of gratitude for salvation already granted. Althaus comments: "Das Grundwort (in Jodo-Shin-Shu) ist geradezu sola fide ... Soweit wird der Gnadengedanke durchgeführt." (WC, 10–11; cf. also CW, 144; WE, 10) And he summarizes what this doctrine, which forms the epitome of the Religions of Grace, contains:

> Ein barmherziger Heiland; das Vertrauen auf ihn als Weg zum Heil; ein Leben aus dem Glauben an das stellvertretende Verdienst, Leben aus dem Danke für die Barmherzigkeit, nun selber als Barmherziger, vom Namen Amidas erfüllt und gewandelt; Freudigkeit, Lebens- und Todeszuversicht in diesem Glauben – haben wir es hier nicht mit einer offenkundigen Entsprechung zum Evangelium, zum evangelischen Christentum zu tun? (WC, 11–12)

2. Althaus' description of these two non-Christian religions shows the "theological content" which Uroffenbarung possesses and which it can bring forth within the religious world, *without Christ*. Here we seem to have all the requisites for a true knowledge of God (though still imperfect) and a true possibility of salvation (also, still imperfect): a) Althaus not only implies that the teachings and "Heilswege" of these religions are the result of a divine revelation insofar as they spring from Uroffenbarung; he also directly links up this revelation with the *activity of the divine Logos.* Approvingly, he quotes Reichelt's estimation of Mahayana Buddhism: "Wenn nirgend Justins des Märtyrers berühmtes Wort von dem 'Logos spermatikos' ... seine Anwendung fände, so fände es sie hier."[79] b) On the basis of this revelation, the followers of these religions can gain a genuine knowledge of the *personal* God. "Die Gottheit ist für sie nicht unpersönlich, sondern trägt persönliche Züge." (CW, 143) This is precisely why these religions of grace surpass the loftiest forms of mystical religion: " ... an die Stelle der mystischen Versenkung in Gott tritt der Grundbegriff geschichtlicher persönlicher Religion, der Glaube ..." (WC, 5) Hence, these religions grasp not only that God is personal ("quod Deus sit") but also that he is a God of mercy and love, willing to take the most despicable sinner to himself – ("quid Deus velit") (WC, 9) c) Althaus also notes that this revelation rests on a certain *historical basis*: "einen gewissen geschichtlichen Anhalt" – "Grundbegriff *geschichtlicher*, persönlicher Religion" (WC, 5–6) This is especially the case with the figures of the Chinese Amitabha and the Japanese Amida who have their origins in Buddha's "historical" vow. d) This revelation also contains a well-nigh complete *knowledge of man* and his *situation before God.* They realize that there is a separation between man and God which man, of himself, cannot cross. Ramanuja thus came to the concept of an "Urfall" (CW, 143), which would imply the idea of personal responsibility and guilt. e) And in their soteriologies, as we have shown, these religions do not, apparently, fall into the blunder of so many other religions; they do not seek "Selbsterlösung" but propose a "Weg der Fremderlösung" – from God alone. (WC, 6)

Can we not conclude, therefore, that at least in these Religions of Grace, the universal saving presence of Christ can make use of their historical forms and doctrines and bring men to salvation? Cannot the Spirit, who is always the deci-

---

78 Ibid.
79 Quoted from R. L. Reichelt, op. cit. p. 12, in WC, 19.

sive element in the act of faith, enable these doctrines of "sola fide" and "sola gratia" to achieve justification? If anywhere, could not the "form of faith" contained so lucidly in these religions become salvific faith? This faith and this salvation, naturally, would not have the clarity of Christ's revelation; yet why could they not bring about a "Gemeinschaft mit Gott" which, through the work of the missions, would be fully illuminated "in Christo"?

§ 65. Justification's "No" to the Religions of Grace

Such conclusions Althaus cannot draw — *because of the "solus Christus".* Using the doctrine of justification as his "Maßstab", he had to reject the Religions of Grace on three accounts:

1. *The Religions of Grace do not allow God to be God.* Even though Althaus could so enthusiastically praise these religions for giving top priority to God's grace and allowing God to do all, he turns around and states that, according to the standards of "sola fide" as known in the "solus Christus", such faith is *not theocentric* enough. In both Amida Buddhismus and Bhakti man, Althaus feels, does not throw himself into God's loving hands to give God the glory but mainly because he himself cannot do the job. (WC, 18) "Die Not des Menschen, nicht Gottes umfassende Herrschaft steht im Mittelpunkte." (WE, 14) Also, in the Bhagavadgita, Bhakti is proposed as one among other ways to salvation; man might further seek his salvation through works. Because Bhakti makes this allowance, Althaus draws the surprising conclusion. that its own doctrine of "sola fide" appears "als eine Art Werk". (MR, 200)[80] In other words, because these religions do not bow sufficiently to "Gottes Gottheit" as Luther understood it, (WE, 14) their "sola fide" is never "sola" enough.

Althaus also argues that the soteriology of the Religions of Grace is not theocentric enough insofar as the salvation they seek is not really union with God in his Kingdom but liberation from the law of rebirth — the law of Karma. (WE, 14; WC, 16—17) "Es geht in der Heilsfrage nicht eigentlich um Gott selber, um seine Liebe, um die Gemeinschaft mit ihm als das Eine, was Not ist — darum ist die Empfehlung der bhakti *etwas völlig anderes* als das *sola fide* des Evangeliums." (MR, 200, emphasis mine) Because of this, Althaus can also conclude that these religions are not really proposing and seeking after a *personal* God. " ... der in ihr (Bhakti) spürbare personalistische Zug wird immer wieder verschlungen vom Unpersönlichen." (MR, 200) Neither Bhakti or Amida Buddhism are able to overcome the monism which, he feels, is characteristic of the main and theoretical body of Hinduism and Buddhism. (ibid.)[81] — Althaus' rejection of these religions'

---

80 Althaus refers to the *Bhagavadgita*, XII, 8—12; V, 27—28.
81 In WE, 14, Althaus is more cautious and only "hints" that Bhakti is not able to truly overcome the influence of monism. In CW he seems to contradict himself when he admits: "So ist die Erlösung in der Bhakti-Religion nicht nur Lösung aus dem Schicksal der Vergänglichkeit und des Leidens des Lebens; sie ist auch Bekehrung zur liebenden Hingabe an die Gottheit, Erlösung zur Seligkeit in der Liebe Gottes." (CW, 145) Did Althaus change his estimation ot the personal God in Bhakti? Then why does he in CW refer to his previous articles on the religions without any indication of retractions or clarifications? Cf. CW, 130, 144.

concept of God seems to proceed as follows: although the Grace Religions propose and seek after a personal Deity, this personalism is not understood in the same way or with the same clarity as within the Christian doctrine of "sola fide"; therefore their God remains basically impersonal, shrouded in monism.

2. *The Religions of Grace do not allow God to be Judge.* Here the transformation of the "yes" into the "no" becomes even more radical. Althaus applies the psychological necessity of the "solus Christus". After admitting that in these religions there is a definite knowledge of the Fall, of personal sin, of the need of forgiveness (CW, 145), he reneges these statements by arguing that, in the light of the "solus Christus" such knowledge does not sufficiently comprehend the divine "Zorn und Gericht". Thus it turns out to be false knowledge. Using Otto's terminology, Althaus claims that the "axes" of the Gospel and these religions are different.[82] " ... zentral ist im Evangelium die Erlösung von der Schuld durch sühnende Verzeihung; zentral ist in der Bhakti-Religion die Erlösung vom furchtbaren Schicksal, vom Rade der Wiedergeburten, von der fesselnden Macht des Karman, von der Ohnmacht." (CW, 145) Althaus draws the conclusion (which from the viewpoint of the phenomenology of religions might well be challenged)[83] that these religions do not interpret man's general "Existenznot" as the result of sin and the outcome of the "Gericht der Gottheit". (ibid.) Thus, other conclusions which seem equally suspect follow: "Der furchtbare Ernst der Heiligkeit Gottes, die Schwere der Sünde wird nicht gewertet ... Das Vertrauen hat nicht den Untergrund der Furcht Gottes." (WE, 15) Indeed, he claims that "Der Glaube der Gnadenreligionen ist Verneinung der Furcht".[84] Missing in these religions, he feels, is "die hohe *Spannung* des Glaubens, der aus Furcht aufsteigt ..." (WC, 18) "Man kennt eben das eine Thema aller Gottesbeziehung nicht, die Frage nach der Gemeinschaft mitten in dem Widerspruch menschlicher Schuld und göttlichen Zornes." (MR, 200) "Wie harmlos wird von Gottes Liebe, vollends von der Vergebung geredet!" (MR, 202) God's love is conceived as "Mitleid" and not as "Zorn". (CW, 145) Which means that these religions are " ... nur Erlösungs- und nicht im Zentrum Versöhnungsreligionen."[85]

Therefore comes Althaus' rejection of these religions: their savior-figure must be abandoned, for he is "ein Mitleidiger, aber kein für seine Brüder unter Gott Leidender; er ist Asket, aber nicht der von Gott Geschlagene". (CW, 145) " ... der östliche Heilandsglaube bedeutet ein eigenmächtiges Fliehen vor der ganzen Wirklichkeit Gottes, ein Verkennen seiner Heiligkeit und seines Zornes." (CW, 146) Hence, the divine pity and forgiving love proclaimed by these religions " ... ist wahrlich nicht das Gleiche wie das Vergeben Gottes ... Es ist ein anderer Gott, der hier handelt, als der Gott der Bibel." (CW, 145)

---

82 Cf. *Gnadenreligionen*, pp. 46–47, 76–77; Althaus' general critique of the religions' limping concept of sin and guilt is, for the most part, a summary of Otto's, who also uses as his criterion an understanding of justification in which the "terror conscientiae Lutheri" must be a necessary element. Op. cit., pp. 64–85, cf. esp. pp. 65, 75.

83 Cf. § 66.

84 "Außerchristliche Gnadenreligionen und das Evangelium", *Korrespondenzblatt der evang.-luth. Geistlichen in Bayern*, 60 (1935) 253 (which is a summary of a lecture delivered on June 24, 1934).

85 Ibid.

3. *Without the historical fact of Christ, the Religions of Grace are products of phantasy.* While the first two steps in Althaus' rejection of these religions result from the psychological necessity of the "solus Christus", here he argues more from its physical-objective demands. As lofty and clear-visioned as these religious doctrines of "sola fide" and "sola gratia" may be, they are not based on the historical reality of Christ — and therefore they are *empty thoughts*, the products of *human phantasy and longing.* Although Althaus admitted a "historical Anknüpfung" (MR, 202) and a "geschichtlicher Anhalt" in Mahayana Buddhism's savior-figures, he now must turn around and state that the "historicity" is overshadowed by phantasy and meaninglessness. (MR, 202) "Gebilde der Phantasie, aus Sehnsucht geboren, nicht bezeugte Geschichte." (CW, 142) "Amida ist 'eine Schöpfung der spekulativen Phantasie des theistisch gewordenen Buddhismus', die mit dem echten geschichtlichen Buddha so gut wie nichts zu tun hat."[86] These religions are working only with ideas, which they clothe as myths; but the myths remain *empty.* In this sense, Althaus can brand these religions as a form of *idealism*: "Der Mahayana Buddhismus ist Idealismus insofern, als eine Erlösungsidee sich einen anschaulichen Mythus schafft." (WC, 15)

Because of the physical necessity of the "solus Christus" Althaus can also argue that *even if* (per absurdum) the religions could come to a perfect knowledge of the "sola fide" (i.e. overcome the psychological necessity of the "solus Christus"), such "thoughts" would still be empty of salvation, for only in the historical fact of Christ is salvation to be found; only in him are such thoughts allowed. (MR, 203) "Diese Liebe (God's love as understood by the religions) ist nicht die wirkliche Gnade des wirklichen Gottes. Sie haben wir *nur in dem Ereignis* der Vergebungsvollmacht Jesu Christi, mitten im Gerichte Gottes. Wer sie ohne Jesus zu haben meint, ergibt sich einer Lüge. Er bemächtigt sich in dem Gedanken der rettenden Liebe dessen, was nur Gottes Freiheit und was sie nur in Christus gibt." (CW, 146) Althaus can even conclude that because these religions are so close to Christianity in their doctrines of "sola fide" and yet because they propose these doctrines without Christ, they are even *more opposed* and "besonders fest verschlossen" to the Gospel than other, "lower" religions. "Die beiden (Grace Religions and Christianity) stehen in schärfstem Gegensatze, gerade in der scheinbaren Nähe und Verwandtschaft der Erlösungsgedanken hier und dort." (CW, 146; WC, 19)

Within Althaus' evaluation of the Religions of Grace, therefore, we see that his overall negation of the religions rests upon and receives its final force from his understanding of the "solus Christus". While the demands of the "sola fide" serve to negate the bulk of non-Christian religions as ways of self-redemption, this negation becomes *absolute* — even for the "higher religions" — through the "solus Christus". The following citation, meant for the Religions of Grace, sums up the application of Althaus' doctrine of justification to his theology of the religions:

> Das *sola gratia, sola fide,* mit dem das Evangelium die Religionen der offenkundigen Selbsterlösung richtet, gewinnt seine *volle Schärfe* erst in dem *solus Christus*: dieses bedeutet das Nein des Evangeliums zu den Religionen der mittelbaren, heimlichen Selbsterlösung, (the Religions of Grace). Die Losungen *sola gratia* und *sola fide* können nie für sich genommen werden, als ein "Prinzip" des Heils, das man auch ohne den

---

86 Quotation from H. Haas, "Amida", RGG² I, 302, in CW, 145.

Glauben an Christus haben könnte; sie gelten *nur an und mit dem "solus Christus".* *Solus Christus* – und daher *sola gratia, sola fide,* in diesem Dreiklang erst ist das Evangelium ausgesagt. (CW, 142, emphasis mine)

§ 66. A Question of Method: Theological Principles and Phenomenological Facts

This analysis of Althaus' evaluation of the Religions of Grace brings into focus some fundamental questions concerning his *method* of judging the religions – indeed, concerning the methodology in any Christian theology of the religions: did he have to "manipulate" or "force" the phenomenological data of these religions in order to fit his theological principles? Did his theological principles too hastily rule out other possible (even probable) interpretations of these data?[87] Even: do the phenomenological facts, which he himself admits, seem to sometimes contradict his theological principles?

Or, to formulate these questions concretely:

1. Can Althaus be so certain that these religions do not contain a sufficiently *theocentric understanding of divine transcendence*? They abandon themselves into the hands of the Deity; they await salvation entirely from him. Is not this sufficient? Even though the occasion or the motivation for this abandonment may be the experience of their own insufficiences (was not this also the case with Paul in Rom. 7?), the intent is to let God take over, to recognize his love and his omnipotence. Also, even though these religions may allow man, in other situations, to "do something" for his liberation, such efforts of themselves are not necessarily considered to produce salvation and in the last analysis can remain subordinated to the reality of the Absolute.[88] Here Althaus seems to brush over the fact that while Bhakti acknowledges the way of works, this way is never placed above that of love and devotion.[89] And Ramanuja brought full "evangelical" clarity when he rejected all other ways to salvation except that of Bhakti. "Die Wege der Erkenntnis und der Werke führen nur zur Liebe hin, bewirken aber nicht die Erlösung selber."[90] This same resolute insistence on the exclusivity of the way of faith for attaining salvation is found in Shinran's Jodo-Shin-Shu.[91]

---

87 For "other" possibilities of Christian dialogue with Hinduism and Buddhism, cf.: *Bhakti*: M. Dhavamony, "The Idea of God – a Hindu-Christian Dialogue", *Bulletin* – Secretariatus pro non Christianis (Vatican), 5 (1967) 80–86; P. Johanns, *La Pensée religieuse de l'Inde* (Louvain, 1952); id., *A Synopsis of the "To Christ through the Vedantas"* (Calcutta, 1930 ff.); P. de Letter, *The Christian and Hindu Concept of Grace, The Light of the East Series*, No. 52 (Calcutta, 1958); R. Panikkar, *The Hidden Christ of Hinduism* (London, 1964); C. P. Papali, "Exkurs zum Konzilstext über den Hinduismus", LThK[2], *Das 2. Vatikanische Konzil* II, pp. 478–482. *Amida-Buddhism*: E. Cornelis, *Christliche Grundgedanken in nicht-christlichen Religionen* (Paderborn, 1967); W. Corswant, "Le salut par la foi dans le Bouddhisme japonais du Grand Véhicle", RThPh, 1941, pp. 113–134; H. Dumoulin, "Exkurs zum Konzilstext über den Buddhismus", LThK[2], op. cit., pp. 482–485; H. M. Enomiya-Lasalle, "Der Heilsweg des Buddhismus und das Christentum", *Die vielen Wege zum Heil*, hrsg. von W. Molinski (München, 1969), pp. 15–40.

88 This is what Hinayana and Mahayana Buddhism have in common: salvation or liberation comes only through the extinction of human activity. "The Buddha's demand that, in order to be saved, one should learn to do nothing in particular, is fulfilled in this way (Amida Buddhism) as perfectly as in any other." Conze, p. 160; cf. also Heiler, p. 284.

89 Ohm, p. 205.

90 Ohm, p. 232.

91 "Shinran hat nicht nur die Möglichkeit der guten Werke verneint, sondern auch ihren Wert zur Erlangung der Erlösung abgelehnt." Numazawa, p. 431.

In general we might say (somewhat rhetorically) that if any religions have taken seriously what Althaus calls "the main theme" of 20th Century Protestant Theology[92] – i.e. "Let God be God" – it has been Hinduism and Buddhism. In fact, this determination to let God be God has been the reason for their falling into what Western Christians consider the error of monism. "Doch selbst in diesem fatalen Fehler muß man ein gewisses Verdienst anerkennen: Gezwungen, zwischen der Realität der Welt und der absoluten Vollkommenheit Gottes zu wählen, opferten die Alten (i.e. of the Upanishad) sozusagen die Welt, um Gott zu retten."[93] And to Althaus' accusations that these religions do not make clear enough statements on God's holiness, his wrath and demands for amendment, the faithful Buddhist or Hindu would respond that they avoid such "clarity" precisely to insure that the Absolute remains the Absolute. The Transcendent cannot be grasped, cannot be described anthropomorphically. No perfection given the Deity can determine it, for once determined, it is limited and no longer Absolute. All the Upanishads prefer to state about the Deity is: "neti, neti" ("not so, not so").[94] – The Christian theologian may and must discuss with these religions such doctrines on the knowledge of God; but to accuse them of not being "theocentric" would be, we feel, to miss their true content and intent – and to argue too much from one's own premises.

2. Althaus' conclusions that Bhakti and Amida Buddhism are not really seeking after a *personal God* appear even more suspect of pre-judgments and over-simplification. He readily accepted Otto's opinion that Amida Buddhism does not burst the bounds of Buddhistic monism and that its personal Paradise is only a forecourt to the final impersonal Nirvana. (WE, 14) Yet he passed over Otto's equally clear statement, in the very same context, that this is *not* the case with Bhakti: "Ganz anders in der Bhakti-religion ... hier lebt und gilt fest und bestimmt 'Isvara', der 'Herr', der einige und ewige Gott, der der Gott personalen Heilbesitzes ist für seine Gläubigen, und der sie nicht zu einem unpersönlichen 'Nirvana' leitet ..."[95] Other historians of religions agree that although a perfect resolution with monism may not be achieved, we can speak of a personal God and personal salvation within Bhakti and Ramanuja's theology.[96] Concerning Amida Buddhism, Althaus might also have pointed out that while it is true that according to its official doctrine, final salvation is found in Nirvana, the vast majority of its faithful believe in salvation as personal union with the personal Amida. As a living faith, Amida Buddhism is the same as Bhakti.[97] This must be noted in general of Bhakti religion and Mahayana Buddhism: although one can always find traces of monism within their teachings, they represent genuine and lasting efforts to present their faithful with a personal Deity with whom they can carry out personal relations – and on the level of living faith, we can say, they succeed![98]

But even when dealing with the original Hindu or Sankara's understanding of Brahman or with Hinayana's concept of Nirvana, the Christian theologian must be extremely careful of

92 "Wo steht die evangelische Theologie heute?", p. 1296.
93 Papali, p. 479; cf. also Neuner, pp. 17–25.
94 Kena Up. 9; 11–13; cf. Dhavamony, pp. 81, 84.
95 *Gnadenreligionen*, pp. 9–10, cf. also pp. 15–16.
96 Ohm, p. 201; cf. K. Hutten, *Die Bhakti-Religion in Indien und der christliche Glaube im Neuen Testament* (Veröffentl. des Orientl. Inst. der Univ. Tübingen, Heft 1, Stuttgart, 1930), p. 7; Heiler, p. 383; Neuner, p. 167. Concerning Ramanuja, with whom "der Riß zwischen impersonalem und personalem Vedanta endgültig geworden (ist)", cf. Otto, op. cit., p. 11, 21–28; Heiler, pp. 399–400; Ohm, 231–233; Neuner, pp. 182–188.
97 Cf. Numazawa, pp. 429, 432; Mensching, p. 341; Ohm, pp. 276–277.
98 Cf. Papali p. 481. K. Goldammer offers a practical and logical rule of thumb when he concludes that the phenomenologist of religions (and the theologian!) can consider "den heilsvermittelnden Erlösungstyp als personbezogene Religiosität..." K. Goldammer, *Die Formenwelt des Religiösen* (Stuttgart, 1961), p. 50. Where salvation is *granted* to man, belief in a personal God is somehow involved.

too facilely applying his preconceived notion of personhood and concluding that these doctrines are totally impersonal, nihilistic or even, especially in the case of Buddhism, atheistic.[99] As we have pointed out, the Hindu or Buddhist will refrain from calling the Absolute personal, precisely to make sure that it remains Absolute; it cannot be described. This does not mean that the Hindu Deity is a blind, abstract, ruthless Being; it is a spiritual Reality. Though it is not called personal, it is real, eternal, infinite, present. As the innermost self of all beings and all men, it is part of all selfhood and personhood.[100] And as historians of religions warn us, we cannot look on Nirvana as a state of pure nothingness, "als ein Nichts an Gehalt und Existenz", "als das völlige Nichts", "as a mere nought or a blank".[101] "'Nirvana' ... meint ... trotz der negativen Sprachform[102] sein (Buddhism's) höchstes Positivum, das alle menschlichen Begriffe und alles Menschenwort übersteigt."[103]

> ... we are told that Nirvana is permanent, stable, imperishable, immovable, ageless, deathless, unborn, and unbecome, that it is power, bliss and happiness, the secure refuge, the shelter, and the place of unassailable safety; that it is the real Truth and the supreme Reality; that it is the *Good*, the supreme goal and the one and only consummation of our life, the eternal, hidden and incomprehensible Peace.[104]

Is not this the same God – the Good, the True, the "ens per se et a se" whom the Christians seek and whom they believe to be personal?[105] Cannot the Christian theologian conclude that even within the Hindu Brahman and the Buddhist Nirvana, the one, true and personal God is revealing *and* communicating himself?[106] For Althaus, such conclusions are extremely cult, if not completely impossible. He cannot even accept the "personalistischen Züge", which he recognizes in Bhakti and Amida, as sufficient to bring man to an encounter with the true, personal God – for his personal God is exclusively defined and limited within the Christian "sola fide" and "solus Christus".

3. We can also ask whether Althaus was overruling the facts when he concluded that within these religions there is no really clear understanding of *human guilt* and especially of *divine wrath* and *judgment*. Within both Bhakti and Amida Buddhism there is the recurring

99 Cf. Enomiya-Lasalle, p. 32; Le Saux, *Sagesse Hindoue-Mystique Chrétienne* (Paris, 1965), p. 135; Goldammer, *Formenwelt*, pp. 51–52, 108. H. von Glasenapp argues that Buddhism is an atheistic religion: *Der Buddhismus – eine atheistische Religion* (München, 1966).

100 Cf. Dhavamony, p. 84.

101 Cornelis, pp. 146–147; Heiler, pp. 280–282; Conze, pp. 131–132.

102 Pāli: Nibbâna means, literally, "extinction".

103 Dumoulin, LThK, p. 484.

104 Conze, p. 40; cf. Heiler, p. 283 for an almost identical description.

105 "When we compare the attributes of the Godhead as they are understood by the more mystical tradition of Christian thought, with those of Nirvana, we find almost no difference at all." Conze, p. 39; Heiler, p. 283; cf. also C. Regamey who believes that Buddhism, from its very origins, was a theistic religion, pp. 229 ff.; Cornelis, pp. 138–139; Ohm, p. 274.

106 Thus the Second Vatican Council could offer a surprisingly positive interpretation of Hinduism and Buddhism, even in their so-called monistic or impersonal forms. Within Hinduism's penetration into the "mysterium divinum...inexhausta fecunditate mythorum et acutis conatibus philosophiae" and within Buddhism's search "animo devoto et confidente" after the "statum perfectae liberationis" and "summam illuminationem", the Council Fathers recognized the possibility of genuine knowledge of God – "aliquando agnitio Summi Numinis vel etiam Patris" – and of union and salvation with him. *Nostra Aetate*, no. 2; cf. J. Türk, *Was sagt das Konzil über nichtchristliche Religionen* (Mainz, 1967), pp. 35–36; K. Müller, *Die Kirche und die nichtchristlichen Religionen* (Aschaffenburg, 1968), pp. 92–95; Dumoulin, LThK^2, p. 484.

doctrine that man's "Existenznot" is the result of a rupture with the divine which constitutes man's sinfulness. Man is corrupt; he does not submit to the Absolute; therefore he is fettered within an imperfect existence. This is especially clear in Bhakti and Ramanuja's teachings which see "Karmen mit seiner bindenden Gewalt" as "auf einer ursprünglichen Abkehr von Isvara beruhend ..."[107] Mahayana Buddhism's general doctrine that suffering is the result of man's sin[108] received an even greater personal content in Shinran's teachings that only divine grace can save man from his total sinfulness – "daß wir böse, falsch und heuchlerisch sind."[109]

Thus these religions do contain definite insights into the fact that man is a sinner, that "something is wrong" between him and the Deity, that the Deity must set things aright through forgiveness and love. Indeed, these insights do not possess "Reformational clarity" – and in this sense we perhaps can speak of "different axes". Their picture and experience of man's guilt and God's anger – the "terrores conscientiae Luthers" – are not as intense. But must they be rejected simply because they are not as clear? And must the biblical elements of wrath and fear (which are not the only components in the New Testament doctrine of redemption) be explicitly present for a valid and salvific concept of sin and reparation?[110] For Althaus, who insisted on the psychological necessity of the "solus Christus", they must.

4. Finally, might Althaus have been pre-interpreting the facts – or excluding other possible interpretations – when he insisted that these religions' ideas of "sola fide" and their savior-figures, Krishna and Amida, are nothing but the product of *human phantasy and longing*? Does not this smack of Feuerbach's preconceived notions?[111] Indeed, Krishna and Amida were not factual, historical personages; and it is true that the Eastern religions in general have an astounding disregard for history. Yet even though the Hindu or Buddhist may well know that their "saviors" are not historical, they still firmly believe that they are *real*.[112] Can one affirm with certainty that this belief in something real is only empty phantasy? When faced with two religious doctrines which are practically the same (and Althaus admitted this in the case of the Religions of Grace and Christianity) can either the phenomenologist of religions *or* the theologian say with certainty that the one is the product of God's revelation and the other of man's musing? This question is especially applicable to a theologian who, like Althaus, admits that there is a divine revelation outside of Christ, even in the non-Christian "prophets"[113], that the illumination of the Spirit is not confined to the Christian order[114], and especially that the universal salvific presence of Christ is to be found within history.[115] – Yet because of the "physical-objective necessity" of the "solus Christus" he sould not allow this revelation, this Spirit, this cosmic Christ to be salvifically present through Krishna or Amida.

5. All these questins point out, we feel, the necessity of the theologian first schooling himself soundly in the history of religions (or at least in one of them) before he works out his absolutely certain theological principles and before he applies them to these religions. This

---

107 Otto, *Gnadenreligionen*, p. 75.

108 Cf. Lasalle, p. 34.

109 Numazawa, p. 431.

110 Such questions become particularly urgent in the light of present-day Lutheran admissions that the doctrine of justification can no longer be understood only from the starting point of "How do I find a merciful God?". Cf. *Rechtfertigung heute*, Studien und Berichte (from the 4th Meeting of the Lutheran World Assembly in Helsinki, 1963), (Beiheft zur *Lutherischen Rundschau*, Stuttgart, 1965), pp. 7–8, 24–25.

111 Cf. "Der himmlische Vater", *Evangelium und Leben*, pp. 46–48; GD/I, 22–23.

112 Conze, p. 150.

113 Cf. § 20/4.

114 Cf. § 34/3.

115 Cf. § 46.

does not mean that his final criteria are to be drawn from the science of religions. He remains a theologian, bound to his faith's "first principles". And yet, if the clear data of the history of religions seem to contradict these principles, he must at least ask himself whether he has understood them properly.

In conclusion to this section, we venture the hypothetical but nonetheless meaningful speculation: Had Althaus acquainted himself more thoroughly with the non-Christian religions, in a deeper and more personal encounter, might he – like Paul Tillich after he came to know the religions personally[116] – have wanted to recast much of his theology?

IV. Justification: The "Articulus Cadentis Religionis"

§ 67. A Necessary and Decisive Clash

The preceding pages have indicated, we hope, that Althaus' understanding of the Reformational "Rechtfertigungslehre" brought about both a *necessary* and a *decisive* clash with his doctrine of Uroffenbarung and with his attempt at a positive evaluation of the non-Christian religions. In the various steps of this chapter we have pointed out that his understanding of the demands and the effects of the "sola fide" and especially of the "solus Christus" lead to the following general conclusions concerning the religious world before or without Christ: 1) the religions are basically *sinful* – a sinfulness which pervades their entire doctrine and morality (because they do not observe the "sola fide" and allow God to be God – cf. § 56); 2) they are *condemned* and under God's *wrath* (because they do not observe the "sola fide", God must be Judge – cf. § 57); 3) they in no way can come into *possession of salvation* and in no way can receive or become instruments of the salvific causality of Christ (the physical-objective necessity of the "solus Christus" – cf. § 68–59); 4) they in no way can really *understand* what *justification* is (the psychological-subjective necessity of the "solus Christus" – cf. § 60–61).

Therefore, if Althaus took the doctrine of justification (as he understood it) seriously – and he had to, for it is the "center of gravity" for Reformational theology – he had to "take back" much of what he stated, or implied, or allowed within his doctrine of Uroffenbarung and its positive presence in the religions. Or, to look at it from the opposite direction, much of what is contained in his presentation (especially his phenomenology) of Uroffenbarung stands in an uncomfortable contradiction to what he states about justification or "Heilsoffenbarung". And to solve the contradiction, there can be no doubt as to which side holds the final word: the "articulus justificationis" is the final court of appeals; it stands firm, even if all else must fall.

To recapitulate the meaning of this chapter, we can place it in the middle (as the "center of gravity") between Chapter IV and V as the *reason* for the tensions and contradictions between the two (which we summed up in § 54/1) and as an *indication* of which Chapter wins out.

116 Cf. M. Eliade, "Paul Tillich and the History of Religions", P. Tillich, *The Future of Religions* (New York, 1966), p. 31; also, P. Tillich, "The Significance of the History of Religions for the Systematic Theologian", op. cit., p. 91.

Because of Uroffenbarung (CH.IV)	*But because of Justification (CH.VI)*	*Therefore (CH.V)*
Uroffenbarung can shine within the religions and be effective with its *"eigenes Licht"*.	Only in Christ can the religions *understand* justification: therefore only in Christ do they understand the relationship between *God and man.*	Only *"von Christus her"* is the light of Uroffenbarung meaningful and "valid".
The religions are used by God as a *"Vorgeschichte"* in the plan of salvation.	Only in Christ is the "sola fide" possible; therefore only in Christ does *salvation history* really begin.	The religions are confined in an unsalvific *"Diesseitigkeit"*; salvation for them is something entirely new.
There can be a real *"Erkenntnis Gottes"* within the religions.	Only in Christ can man receive the "sola fide" and know *God as God and Judge.*	The knowledge of God in the religions is really a "Nicht-Wissen um Gott", i.e. of the real God.
The religions can experience God as a "Du" and his personal offer of love.	Only in the "historical surity" of Christ does God allow and show that his *love breaks through his wrath.*	The religions must experience more wrath than love; they cannot escape *despair.*
The religions contain a genuine *"content of truth"*.	Only in Christ can man understand the demands of human *sinfulness* and of divine *wrath*; only in Him can man use "truth" to elicit an act of "sola fide".	The religions use their truth as ways of self-redemption and thus turn truth into *"Lüge"* and *"Trug"*.
The religions contain *"Anknüpfungspunkte"* and there is a *"positive relation"* between them and Christianity.	Only in Christ does God work salvation; it is something *entirely* new. Outside of Christ nothing has positive meaning for salvation.	Salvifically, the religions have nothing; what they have, they misuse. Therefore, *nothing to relate to:* "ganze Antithese", "totaler Bruch".
Within their dialogue, Christianity must allow itself to *"be measured"* by the contents of the religions.	Only in Christ is the *sola fide understood*; only in him is the nature of God and the nature of man understood.	There can be *no other criterion* outside of Christ to understand the relation between God and man.
There is the possibility of a *"relative salvation"* within the religions, especially through following one's conscience.	Only in Christ, in his "Vollmacht", in his *"geschichtlichen Tatsächlichkeit"*, in his "Einzigartigkeit", does God grant salvation.	The religions remain in and cannot escape from the realm of *"Heillosigkeit"*.
God can grant his *"Vergebung"* and bring about *"Gemeinschaft"* in religious communities outside of Christianity.	Only in Christ is "Vergebung" understood for what it is; only in him is God's wrath broken through; outside of Christ God's wrath "holds back" his love.	The religions and all they contain are overshadowed by God's *wrath* and his *"Gericht"*.
There is a *universal presence* of Christ which effects "community" with God within history.	Only through an *explicit contact* with the physical-historical "Tatsächlichkeit" of Christ (through Word and Sacrament) is salvation possible.	For those who have not known Christ this contact with him is postponed *beyond history.*

At the end of this chapter, then, we can raise the same question which resulted from Chapter V: did Althaus succeed in tracing a "middle way" between Troeltsch and Barth? In Chapter V, we concluded that because of the tensions and contradictions between his positive and negative pictures of the religions, his "middle way" became *unclear*, and therefore *unviable* (§ 54/2). Here, after having studied the cause of these contradictions and their final resolution, we might conclude that Althaus' "way" seems *so close to that of Barth*, that it loses its quality of "middle". After Althaus applies the full content of his doctrine of justification to Uroffenbarung and the religions, what, we must ask, is left of the non-Christian world? He does not, like Barth, simply sweep away the religions as meaningless and as theologically irrelevant. But what is left of their positive content — what is left of a positive theology of the religions — if they are totally sinful, confined under God's wrath, and if they in no way can play a positive role in bringing man to a salvific encounter with God, if all they have is constantly used as a means of "self redemption" and therefore opposed to Christ?

Yet Althaus does not simply fall back to Barth's position. The difference between them makes up what we feel is the only possible "positive" attitude towards the religions which Althaus' understanding of justification will allow:

§ 68. Althaus' Final Attitude towards the Religions:
They are a "Praeparatio Negativa" for the Gospel

1. The religions serve as a negative preparation for the encounter with Christ and the Gospel. This, we feel, is the basic and, really, the *only* positive content in Althaus' theology of the religions in the light of his doctrine of justification. His survey of Uroffenbarung in the religions certainly seemed to contain — and *did* contain — more than this; and yet, after he resolutely applied the "Maßstab" of the "sola fide" and the "solus Christus", this, it seems, is all that is left: the religions' role is to prepare the way of the Lord, to make men ready for and susceptible to his coming by revealing to them their *deep and painful need* of Christ and his redemption. This is the final purpose of the "positive" content of truth within the religious world: what the non-Christian *has* is meant to show him, even more existentially, what he *doesn't* have. His encounter with God in Uroffenbarung ends up in laying bare his separation from God. His experience of the divine offer of love draws back the veil on his sinfulness and his absolute impotence in responding to and truly experiencing this love. His knowledge of God and of himself turns out to be a knowledge which frustrates because of its incompleteness.

The "positive" content of Uroffenbarung and the religions are not able, in any way, to satisfy man's personal and religious needs — even in an imperfect manner. Satisfaction, response to these needs, comes only in Christ — only in the "sola fide" realized within the "solus Christus". All the religions can do — no matter how glowingly one may speak about them — is to reveal these needs. And in doing so, they render man ready and ripe for Christ's Word in the Gospel. According to Althaus' doctrine of justification, then, the "positive" in the religions stands in exclusive service of the "negative". Their positive content or role is to carry out a negative preparation.

2. Althaus' final positive evaluation of the religions as a "praeparatio negativa" for the encounter with Christ is, we feel, an expression and application of the traditional Reformational understanding of the *Law and the Gospel.* As we have seen, Althaus presented his teaching on Uroffenbarung within the structures of the Law; and in doing so, he tried to go beyond a purely negative understanding of the content and function of the Law. The Law, for him, was to contain and make known God's offer of love; it provides the religions with positive elements which are not to be covered over with sin and which therefore offer a positive point of contact with the Gospel.[117] And yet, when all is said and done — i.e. after we have placed the religions under the verdict of the doctrine of justification — this positive function is no longer really effective. The religions are left with not much more than the primary and negative purpose of the Law as understood in Reformational tradition:[118] to constitute him a sinner *and* to enable him to experience this sin — and thus to prepare him, negatively, for the Gospel. The Law indeed has a function of its own, a supernatural, necessary function; it, too, contains "truth"; it, too, provides a necessary "Anknüpfungspunkt" for the Gospel — but all in the negative sense of revealing the truth of man's sinfulness and the frustrating depths of his needs.

Althaus' understanding of the "sola fide" and the "solus Christus" left him with no other alternative, we feel, than to interpret the religions within this negative functionality of the Law. According to his presentation of the "traditional" Reformational doctrine of justification this was *the most* he could offer as a positive theology of the religions.

* * * * * *

Our case study of Althaus, then, poses two central questions: have contemporary Protestant theologians, who also wish to remain faithful to the "Articulus stantis et cadentis Ecclesiae", said more about the religions than Althaus' "most"? And *can* they say more?

117 Cf. § 37/3.
118 Cf. Pöhlmann, *Rechtfertigung*, pp. 50–57.

Chapter VII

The Verification of this Case Study: Protestant Theology
and the Non-Christian Religions

§ 69. A Case Study for Contemporary Protestant Attitudes

The basic findings and conclusions of our case study are, we hope, clear. Summing them up: Althaus made a concerned and significant attempt to elaborate a theology of the non-Christian religious world which would avoid the extremes represented by both Troeltsch and Barth. (Chapter I and II) Proceeding chiefly on the basis of his understanding of Uroffenbarung (Chapter III), he arrived at a view of the religions which saw them as products and bearers of a divine (supernatural) revelation, which enabled a truly positive encounter and dialogue between the Gospel and the religions, and which, at least implicitly or potentially, seemed to allow the religions to be, in given instances, ways of salvation. And all this, without denying the essential differences between the religions and the Gospel and the need of purification and perfection in Christ. (Chapter IV) And yet in describing the limitations of the religions and the nature of their purification and perfection in Christ, he confusedly and sometimes plainly contradicted many of the elements within his positive view. (Chapter V) We traced the source of this tension and contradiction to Althaus' doctrine of justification, as expressed in the soteriological principles of "sola fide" and "solus Christus". Because of his understanding of salvation only in Christ, Althaus had to, as it were, "take back" much of Uroffenbarung's positive implications for the religions. Salvation through the religions turns out to be an absolute impossibility. His final "positive" evaluation is that the religions provide a negative preparation for Christ: in them man can experience his state of sinfulness and his need of redemption; he raises questions but finds no real answers. (Chapter VI)

We call all this "A Case Study for a *Protestant* Theology of the Religions" — because, as much as Althaus sought after a more positive understanding of the religions, — he was determined to base his efforts on his "Protestant heritage", especially on the "articulus stantis et cadentis ecclesiae": the doctrine of justification. As a "case study", he would seem to imply that *any theologian who adheres to this traditional understanding of justification cannot really judge the non-Christian religious world as anything more than a negative preparation for Christ*. The religions can never be ways of salvation; they can only voice "questions"; never can they provide real answers.

Is this true? Does our case study really "apply"? This is the question we would like to take up in this final chapter. As a verification of our case study, we would like to take an *overall and schematic view of contemporary Protestant efforts to understand the non-Christian religions*, and ask whether the conclusions we drew from our study of Althaus also apply to them. Since it would be impossible to present even a schematic picture of world Protestantism, we shall limit ourselves to contemporary *German* Protestant theologians.[1] Has present-day German Protestant theology of the religions gone beyond Althaus?

1 More than practical reasons prompt this limitation to German Protestant theology. As the

§ 70. Present State of German-Protestant Theology of Religions

1. The *lack of a formed and integrated Theology of the Non-Christian Religions* among Protestant thinkers is painfully evident, still today. This is admitted as a "nostra culpa" by numerous Protestant theologians.

> Die Forderung einer "Theologie der Religion" ... (i.e. wie das Verhältnis Christentum und Religionen grundsätzlich theologisch bestimmt werden kann und muß) ... ist in den letzten 20 Jahren immer wieder erhoben worden. Aber es ist auch in der Gegenwart eigentlich erstaunlich wenig getan, um diese Dinge zu klären.[2]

> There have been very few attempts (within present-day Protestant Theology) to synthesize insights from contemporary theology, the study of other religions, and the history of missions, in order to reflect upon the problem of the encounter between Christianity and the religions.[3]

> Im Gegensatz zu der allein quantitativ imponierenden Aufnahme dieser Herausforderung durch die katholische Theologie seit Karl Rahner mit ihrer beachtlichen inneren Geschlossenheit erscheint − von rühmlichen Ausnahmen abgesehen − die Reaktion der protestantischen Theologie zögernd und uneinheitlich, gedanklich oft vage oder spekulativ.[4]

It is also commonly admitted that one of the most weighty reasons for this lack of concern for the religions is the inescapable influence of Karl Barth. As we mentioned above[5], his critique of religion as being basically opposed to revelation − coupled with Bonhoeffer's widely accepted insistence on a "religionsloses Christentum" − casts a very suspicious shadow over all religious phenomena. One may rightly point out that this condemnation of religion is greatly mellowed and clarified when we remember that it was intended also − or better, primarily − for the Christian religion.[6] Yet the fact remains: when such a concept is part of a study of the "other religions" it obstructs any real encounter with them and colors them as, essentially, irrelevant for theology. "Sobald aber dieser spezifisch

---

site of the Reformation, the German milieu can be expected to be in closer and more consciously-faithful contact with the traditions of the Reformers. If it is true that our case study of Althaus *does* apply to this milieu, this, we feel, is a significant finding for both German and non-German theology, Protestant and Catholic. Also, it will enable us to ask whether there are essential differences between this milieu's attitudes towards the religions and other non-German Protestant approaches, especially within the World Council of Churches. We shall touch on this question in our Conclusion. (Cf. § 86/4, esp. ann. 52.)

2 C. H. Ratschow, "Die Religionen und das Christentum", *Der christliche Glaube und die Religionen* (Hauptvorträge des Evangelischen Theologen-Kongresses, Wien, 26.−30. September 1966), hrsg. von C. H. Ratschow (Berlin, 1967), pp. 97−98.

3 J. A. Veitch, "The Case for a Theology of Religions", SJTh, 24 (1971) 418−419.

4 P. Beyerhaus, "Zur Theologie der Religionen im Protestantismus", KuD, 15 (1969) 100. Cf. also H. W. Gensichen "Die Herausforderung der protestantischen Mission durch das zweite Vatikanische Konzil", MdKI, 17 (1966) 86; cf. also id., "Die christliche Mission in der Begegnung mit den Religionen", *Kirche in der außerchristlichen Welt* (Regensburg, 1967), p. 74; K. Nürnberger, *Glaube und Religion bei Karl Barth* (Diss. Marburg, 1967), pp. 11−12, 134; P. Rossano, "Le Religioni Non Christiane nella Storia della Salvezza. Rassegna delle Posizioni teologiche attuali", *La Scuola Cattolica*, 1965, supplemento 2, p. 11.

5 Cf. § 19/1, also § 10/3.

6 For such a reminder, cf. Hans Strauss, "Krisis der Religion oder Kritik der Religionen? !? ", *Parrhesia*, Karl Barth zum 80. Geburtstag (Zürich, 1966), pp. 305−320.

gebrauchte Begriff Religion zu verallgemeinernden Urteilen verwendet wird, blockiert er das Verständnis der Religionen."[7] To those who argue that this is a misuse of Barth's and Bonhoeffer's concept of religion, we may answer that the *de facto* situation of Protestant theology of the religions proves that this *has* been its effects.[8]

2. And yet we must also point out that attitudes of German Protestant theology towards the religions have developed and changed since Barth unleashed his apocalyptic "No" to religion and since it took on added resonance — mainly through the works of Hendrik Kraemer — in the third World Missionary Conference in Tambaram in 1938. Even though the majority of theologians still do not give the religions sufficient attention or significance, there are a number of thinkers (and their ranks seem to be happily increasing) who show a growing awareness that the non-Christian religious world cannot be ignored, and that it does have a meaning for Christian theology.

The question which concerns us is: how these new, more positive attitudes towards the religions compare with Althaus'? Many contemporary German Protestant theologians share his concern and efforts to go beyond Barth and understand the religions more positively. But within these efforts, do they avoid the unclarities and certain contradictions which we noted in Althaus' thinking? Or more precisely: what role and effect does the doctrine of justification exercise in these new positions? If these contemporary theologians allow revelation within the religions, how do they relate it to and reconcile it with redemption in Christ? Does their understanding of the "sola fide" and "solus Christus" allow or enable them to confront the problem of salvation through the religions and to offer this problem any clearer or more integrated answers?

To give our general survey of the answers to these questions better orientation and more precision, we shall first outline the views of three systematic theologians — Hans Georg Fritzsche, Carl Heinz Ratschow, and Wolfhart Pannenberg — who, we feel, have dealt with the religions more extensively and who represent the general tendencies within German Protestant Theology. Under these theologians we will then give examples of what seems to be the "opinio communis" of systematic theologians and then of mission theologians.

---

7 W. Kohler, "Theologie und Religion", *Glaube, Geist, Geschichte*. Festschrift für Ernst Benz zum 60. Geburtstag, hrsg. von G. Müller und W. Zeller (Leiden, 1967), p. 461.

8 For Barth's negative influence on Protestant attitudes towards the religions, cf.: Ratschow, "Die Religionen", p. 100; G. Rosenkranz, *Der christliche Glaube angesichts der Weltreligionen* (Bern, 1967), p. 218; Nürnberger, p. 134; W. Bühlmann, "Die Theologie der nichtchristlichen Religionen als ökumenisches Problem", *Freiheit in der Begegnung*. Zwischenbilanz des ökumenischen Dialogs, hrsg. von J.-L. Leuba und H. Stirnimann (Frankfurt, 1969), p. 456; O. Wolff, *Anders an Gott glauben*. Die Weltreligionen als Partner des Christentums (Stuttgart, 1969), p. 55; C. F. Hallencreutz, *New Approaches to Men of Other Faiths*. 1938–1968. A theological discussion (Geneva, 1970), p. 27; W. H. van de Pol, *Die Zukunft von Kirche und Christentum* (Wien, 1970), pp. 104–108; P. Knitter, "Paul Althaus: An Attempt at a Protestant Theology of the Non-Christian Religions", *Verbum SVD*, 11 (1970) 214–215.

184

§ 71. H. G. Fritzsche[9] — Example of Reformed Tendency

1. As one picks up Fritzsche's treatment of the non-Christian religions in his "Lehrbuch der Dogmatik"[10] one's first impressions are that he is reading a re-phrasing of Althaus' basic views. Reviewing modern history of Protestant thought, Fritzsche distinguishes three different attitudes towards the religions: a) the *dogmatic*, which boils down to a rejection of the non-Christian religious world, as seen especially in Barth's works; b) the *historical*, which ends up denying any real difference between Christianity and the religions, as represented by Troeltsch; and c) the *practical*, which tries to recognize the positive values of the religions and thus establish a true encounter with them. Fritzsche declares that his own way is that of the practical approach, seeking "einen mittleren Standpunkt zwischen Troeltsch und Barth" and using the "dogmatic" and the "historical" positions as "correctives"; he implies that he will be following at least part of Althaus' lead: "Dieser praktischen oder missionstheologischen Konzeption steht auch Paul Althaus sehr nahe ..."[11]

Similar to Althaus, he urges his fellow theologians to distinguish the "good from the bad" in the religions. Even though there may be much that is rooted in sin, one must be able to separate the plant from the roots — and make use of it. The "Vielfalt des empirischen Erscheinungsbildes" of the religions contains many valuable elements which provide the basis for a positive encounter with them.[12] "In den Religionen ist ein echtes und ernst zu nehmendes Fragen nach Gott und Erlösung lebendig, an das die christliche Verkündigung anknüpfen kann und muß."[13] And, like Althaus, when he goes into an empirical or phenomenological description of these positive elements, he seems to imply even more than "questions". He sums up what the religions and Christianity have in common under three general headings: a) *"Gemeinsame Themen"*, i.e. "Gottheit, Erlösung, sitt-liche Kraft, Weltanschauungsfragen". b) *"Gemeinsame Fragestellungen bzw. Vor-aussetzungen"*; by this he means the experience of the contradictions and distor-tions of human existence which point man in a direction outside himself for solutions. c) *"Gemeinsame Antworten* (!) *bzw. Einzelaussagen"*, and here, again with Althaus, he has some particularly positive words for Mahayana Buddhism's insights and "answers" concerning faith based on "sola gratia et sola fide".[14]

2. And yet after (and even within) this quite positive commentary on the world of religions, Fritzsche sets up an interpretation of the "solus Christus" which empties them of any real value in themselves, i.e. before their meeting with Christ. Although he tries to find a middle way between Troeltsch and Barth, he ends up much closer to Barth — even, we feel, still within Barth's position. For God has touched the world only in Christ; this means that only on this christologic mathe-matical point are both revelation and salvation to be found. The positive content of the religions can never be termed a revelation; it does not make God known to

---

9 Professor of Systematic Theology at Humboldt University, Berlin.
10 § 5 "Christlicher Glaube und 'Religion'", *Lehrbuch der Dogmatik*, Teil I (Göttin-gen, 1964) pp. 207–278.
11 Ibid., pp. 208–209, 223.
12 Ibid., pp. 222–223.
13 Ibid., p. 209.
14 Ibid., pp. 226–227.

the non-Christians. This is what, Fritzsche feels, "belastet" Althaus' middle way: his assertion of a revelation in the religions.[15] Theologically, the most that the religions can contain is a "resonance" for Christian revelation — *but* a resonance which can be heard "nur *von der Bibel her;* ursprünglich aus Natur und Geschichte heraus gibt es keine Offenbarung Gottes".[16] What the religions contain is "nur die Möglichkeit von Offenbarung" — a possibility which can be realized only in the "Christusereignis".[17] "Gott ist durchaus *in* der Natur erfahrbar, aber nicht *aus* ihr heraus."[18]

On the basis of this even more exclusive understanding of the "solus Christus", Fritzsche's *back-tracking* on the positive phenomenological values of the religions becomes even more drastic and confusing than Althaus'. All the "common elements" between Christianity and the religions turn out to be more opposed than similar.

Fritzsche lists these differences, again under three headings: a) the *Verständnis Gottes,* which consists of a twofold opposition: "Entweder wird 'Gott' als leeres Prinzip und damit als unpersönliches Es verstanden, oder sein Personsein ist mit ganz anderen Zügen ausgestattet als denjenigen des in Jesus Christus offenbarten einen Gottes." And here, too, he feels that even Bhakti's concept of the divinity is not personal enough; b) in the *Streben nach Erlösung,* in which Fritzsche argues that the religions do not really understand the nature of justification and corrupt it by seeking redemption "vom Ich" or "von der Existenz als solcher" instead of accepting from God a liberation from sin which enables them to find their responsible selves; c) in *ethischen und praktischen Fragen,* where Fritzsche's verdict seems even more "preordained". He states categorically that while "Das Evangelium befreit zu echter Sachlichkeit und macht die Kräfte frei für die eigentliche Arbeit des Tages", the religions waste their efforts ("leerlaufen und heißlaufen"!) "in sinnlosen kultischen Anstrengungen sowie in der Sicherungshysterie der Opfermentalität".[19]

"Der entscheidende Gegensatz" which is contained in all these differences and which is illustrated especially in "den ostasiatischen *Erlösungs*-religionen" (in Althaus' terminology: the Religions of Grace) is that because the religions do not have Christ they are *works of the Law.* Man is trying to fashion his salvation by himself; he is dealing only with himself. Fritzsche expresses this by calling these religions "psychologische Religionen". While Christianity, "die Religion der Wahrheit", accepts its redemption as an *historical,* divine fact and as an "objektive Realität", the religions search for a man-made psychological redemption; a doctrine is true if it works psychologically. Fritzsche therefore ennunciates the final and separating difference between Christianity and the religions as: "Theozentrismus and Anthropozentrismus ... Erlösung und Selbsterlösung".[20] These differences are clearly demanded by his understanding of justification as limited to the historical reality of Christ. The religions remain, as Barth proclaimed, works of sin.[21]

The final relation, therefore, between Christianity and the religions, is overpowerly negative: "Zusammenfassend kann man sagen, daß es die Losung, 'Chri-

15 Ibid., p. 224.
16 Ibid., p. 296.
17 Ibid., p. 297.
18 Ibid., p. 301. On p. 307 he says the very same thing about history; cf. pp. 307–313.
19 Ibid., pp. 247–253.
20 Ibid., pp. 255–257.
21 Ibid., p. 222.

stus des Gesetzes Ende' (Röm. 10,4) ist, womit in einem Aufhebung der Sünde, Aufhebung der Religion und Aufhebung des Aberglaubens gegeben sind."[22]

3. What is left of Fritzsche's "practical and more positive middle way" is even less than what we found in Althaus after he applied his "solus Christus". Whatever positive content might be in the religions is really and effectively not there until confronted with Christ's revelation; Fritzsche's "von Christus her", like Barth's, is absolute. And then, when the actual confrontation takes place, all that the religions seem to be able to offer are distorted and sinfully-misused longings; this, apparently, is the essence of their "Anliegen" and "Anknüpfungspunkte" upon which Fritzsche seeks to establish an encounter and dialogue.[23] In the end, the religions offer questions and only questions; they constitute only a *negative preparation* for Christ — and much more negative than in Althaus' views.

§ 72. C. H. Ratschow — Example of Lutheran Tendency[24]

1. Few present-day German Protestant theologians can rival C. H. Ratschow in the open-mindedness and freshness of his approach to the non-Christian religions. He sees the long-neglected problem of the religions and resolutely attempts the necessary and perhaps unexplored steps in trying to solve it. His efforts have been called "bei weitem die leistungsfähigste" in arriving at a theology of the religions.[25] What really seems to give these efforts their originality and their boldness is Ratschow's extensive *knowledge of the religions* themselves. He remains a systematic theologian and insists that a theology of the religions must be based on the first premises of the Gospel.[26] — But with equal resoluteness he insists that the theologian must know not only his faith but also the religions before he can pass judgment! Theologians have produced too much abstract musing about "religion", forgetting: "Die Religion gibt es nur in den Religionen."[27]

2. Arguing as both theologian and historian of religions, then, Ratschow concludes to a real and active *presence of God* within the religions. In varying terminology, he describes this presence as the "zentrale Geschehen in den Religionen: Das ist der Gott! Sein Hervortreten, Seine Präsenz, Sein Heil und Seine Versöhnung sind das Subjekt und der Kern allen religiösen Tuns. Das erste Bewegende in aller Religion ist die Unwiderstehlichkeit des Gottes!"[28] The terms which Ratschow seems to prefer are "das Hervortreten Gottes" or his "Eindrücklichkeit" in

---

22 Loc. cit.
23 Ibid., p. 258, cf. pp. 259–267.
24 Others have referred to Ratschow as a representative of the Lutheran attitude towards the religious world. Cf. Beyerhaus, "Zur Theologie", pp. 98–99; K. Lüthi, "Ist Christentum Religion?", *Wort und Wahrheit*, 24 (1969) 105–106. For a concise characterization of Ratschow's theological method, cf. K. Nürnberger, "Systematisch-theologische Lösungsversuche zum Problem der anderen Religionen und ihre missionsmethodischen Konsequenzen", NZSTh, 12 (1970) 30–37.
25 Nürnberger, "Systematisch", p. 37; Nürnberger here is comparing Ratschow especially with Barth's and Bultmann's views of the religions.
26 Ratschow, "Die Religionen", pp. 89, 95.
27 Ibid., p. 94.
28 Ibid., p. 105.

the religions. "Religion ist in den Religionen ja geradezu dadurch zu definieren, daß der Mensch eines Wesens inne wird, dessen Hervortreten ihm als der letzte Grund wie als die letzte Grenze seines und seiner Welt Daseins unabweisbar wird."[29]

Although Ratschow is adverse to calling this "Hervortreten Gottes" an "Offenbarung" or "revelatio generalis" or "bloßer notitia dei", he remains in full agreement, we feel, with the substance of Althaus' Uroffenbarung.[30] The reason why he shuns such terminology both in theology and in comparative religions is that it is "irreführend" and "nichtssagend": it does not bring out the real and special experience of God within this process and implies that man takes cognitional possession of God instead of encountering him.[31] Ratschow, like Althaus, insists that man's encounter with God in the religions is God's work — in Catholic terminology, a supernatural occurance. It cannot be deduced "aus einer gemeinsamen anthropologischen Grundlage"[32] or from the "religiösen ... a priori's seines (man's) 'natürlichen' menschlichen Daseins".[33] Ratschow feels that this is "religionswissenschaftlich unbestreitbar";[34] it is attested to in the beliefs of the religions themselves and especially in the phenomenological facts of the "Kontingenz und überschaubaren Spontaneität im Hervortreten der Gottheit"[35] and the "eminent großen Verschiedenheit der Götter". All this points out a unique, individual divine action.[36]

3. Ratschow holds not only that all religions are alive with the divine (not man-made) presence of God, but "... daß alle Religionen als Religionen *Erlösungs-Religionen* sind".[37]

The basis for this assertion is what Ratschow calls "die Ausgangssituation von Religion" — for the non-Christian *and* Christian religion: man's "Angefochtenheit". Man experiences God but cannot reconcile this experience with the contradictoriness and apparent meaninglessness of himself and the world. Thus he clashes with the "undurchschaubaren Ambivalenz" of God and the world, which Ratschow describes in various contexts as the clash between "Zorn und Liebe", "Ordnungsmacht und Verderbenseinbruch", "Liebe–Barmherzigkeit und Unheil–Ungerechtigkeit".[38] Within the "ambivalence of God" the non-Christians experience and come to a knowledge of the realities of sin and guilt: "Es geht in den Religionen wie im Christentum um die Erlösung des Menschen und um die Erlösung der Welt aus der Gefangenschaft des

29 Ratschow, "Die Möglichkeit des Dialogs angesichts des Anspruchs der Religionen", *Evangelisches Missions-Jahrbuch*, 1970, p. 111; cf. also, id., "Glaube und Erkenntnis", *Anstöße*. Berichte aus der Arbeit der Evangelischen Akademie Hofgeismar (1968, Nr. 5/6), pp. 153–156.

30 Beyerhaus also feels that Ratschow here is following his "Lehrer" Althaus. Cf. "Zur Theologie", p. 98.

31 "In den ganzen sogen. Offenbarungen wird nunmal nichts offenbar gemacht, was verborgen wäre...", "Die Religionen", p. 107.

32 "Die Möglichkeit", p. 112.

33 "Die Religionen", p. 126, cf. also pp. 114–115.

34 Ibid., p. 126.

35 "Die Möglichkeit", p. 112.

36 "Die Religionen", pp. 115–116; cf. also Nürnberger, "Systematisch", p. 34.

37 "Die Möglichkeit", p. 113, emphasis mine; cf. also Ratschow, *Magie und Religion* (Gütersloh, 1955) p. 97.

38 Ratschow, *Der angefochtene Glaube* (Gütersloh, 1957), p. 279; "Die Religionen", pp. 118–120, 123–124.

Todes und der hinter ihm stehenden *Grundschuld* des Menschen ... Die Anthropologie der nichtchristlichen Religionen *weiß* um die mit dem Menschen gesetzte Unausweichlichkeit von *Schuld* ... Die Erlösungsbedürftigkeit des Menschen wie der Welt ist das Thema aller Religionen."[39] The "homo religiosus" experiences a "Preisgegebenheit als Gottes Zorn zum Todesschrecken".[40] And again, Ratschow feels that this is not merely a theological assertion; it is born out by the science of religions as seen in Rudolf Otto's categories of the Holy and in Gerardus van der Leeuw's objective phenomenology.[41]

Here Ratschow expressly admits that "das Phänomen, um das es bei der Anfechtung geht", is included in Althaus' concept of Uroffenbarung which also attests to "die Ambivalenz des Lebendigen, die sich in der Ambivalenz der Gottheiten widerspiegelt". Thus we see that although Ratschow does not adopt Althaus' terminology he does accept "den gleichen Grundbestand".[42]

This experience of ambivalence, however, is not the essence of the religions' insight into redemption. "Die Grundeinsicht der Religionen als Erlösungsreligionen besteht in der Erkenntnis: *'Nur durch das Sterben bleibt das Leben wach'*."[43] Ratschow is convinced that the "common denominator" of all religions, expressed in a multitude of forms, is the realization that "vivificatio" can come only through "mortificatio".[44] Man in his religions declares that he must give way to God; in practicing his religion, he tries to do just this! "Die Lösungen des Weges der Religions-Übung zeigen überall den Charakter, daß der Mensch sich aufzugeben hat, um dem Gotte und seinem Willen Raum zu geben. In der Religion-Übung geht es um ein Sterben. Dieses Sterben bringt das wahre Leben! Das ist die einheitliche Struktur des Vorganges, den wir in den Religionen sehen."[45]

4. On the basis of his theological-phenomenological understanding of the religions, Ratschow concludes to what has been called "eine frappante und lückenlose Parallelität" between Christian and non-Christian faiths.[46] The same God gives himself to man's experience and knowledge — always in different forms and processes. And there is the same "theme" of redemption: the experiencing of unredemption and the seeking after life through death. In all this there is a "von Gott stammende Wahrheit ... die 'nicht fern vom Reiche Gottes' ist".[47] And therefore Ratschow points out the foundation for and necessity of a *positive dialogue* between Christianity and the religions. One of the clearest examples of such a dialogue — and one of the soundest supports for a "theology of the religions" — he finds, like Althaus, in the historical dialogue with the religions which took place in both the Old and the New Testaments — "die Tatsache der religionsgeschichtlichen Parallele im Alten wie im Neuen Testament wie im Tun

---

39 "Die Möglichkeit", p. 113.
40 *Der angefochtene Glaube*, p. 260.
41 Loc. cit.
42 *Der angefochtene Glaube*, pp. 281–82; "Wenn wir uns den Inhalt von der Uroffenbarung bei Althaus so klarmachen, so liegt die Analogie zu dem, was wir von der Anfechtung aus aufzeigten, ja auf der Hand." Ibid., p. 284.
43 "Die Möglichkeit", p. 115, emphasis mine.
44 "Die Religionen", pp. 127–128, 124.
45 Ibid., pp. 123–124, cf. also p. 120.
46 Nürnberger, "Systematisch", p. 33.
47 "Die Möglichkeit", p. 116.

und Glauben der Kirche seither."[48] The full content of such parallels have not fully been seen or evaluated by Christian theology.

5. Ratschow's vision of the religions, then, sharing much the same starting point with Althaus, seems to "go further" and be more open-ended. And yet, when he "draws the line" and points out the differences between the religions and Christianity – as every theologian must – certain perplexing questions arise. Ratschow stresses that despite and within "dieser weitreichenden Gemeinsamkeit der Religion und des Christentums" there is "eine ganz zentrale Trennung",[49] "ein tiefer und sehr grundsätzlicher Unterschied",[50] elements which are "kontradiktorisch verschieden"[51] and which bring about a "schlechthinnige Antithese".[52] These contradictory differences are contained within the *doctrine of justification*: "Die Selbstaufgabe des Menschen ist im Christentum dem Heile konsekutiv, in den Religionen aber konstitutiv."[53] "... daß den Religionen die mortificatio konstitutiv ist für die vivificatio, daß im Christentum aber die mortificatio der vivificatio konsekutiv folgt."[54] Simply: in the religions man tries to achieve salvation through his own works; in Christianity, he accepts it as a gift, "sola fide, sola gratia". What Althaus stated explicitly, Ratschow implies: the religions of themselves cannot attain to a proper understanding of justification. That the reason for this position is rooted in the "solus Christus" is clear in one of his closing statements: "Der zureichende Grund für die Unterschiedenheit dieses Verhältnisses ist in der christologischen Überlegung zu finden."[55]

The basic difference between religions and Christianity would therefore seem to be that between *Law and Gospel*. In his *Der angefochtene Glaube* Ratschow asserts this quite clearly: since the religions try to appease the wrath of God through observance of the Law, "... tragen *alle* Religionen den Charakter der Gesetzlichkeit ... Über diese Situation hinaus geht der homo religiosus den Weg, Gott durch Gesetzeswerke und Opfer zu versöhnen, sich also vor Gott gerecht zu machen ... In den Religionen geht es um Selbstrechtfertigung durch Gesetzeserfüllung. Im Glauben geht es um Selbstaufgabe in Gesetzesnot."[56] Even the so-called Religions of Grace remain within the precincts of the Law; even they show a difference from Christianity which is "wie von Himmel und Erde".[57]

In his later treatments of the religions, Ratschow modifies this category of Law-Gospel insofar as he adds that the "consecutive-constitutive-difference" does not allow "einen einfachen Gegensatz von Religion und Christentum als Gegensatz von Gesetz und Evangelium;"[58] the opposition is not "ausschließend". But this is only because also in "der kirchlichen Erscheinungsform des Christentums" there is the constant tendency to make saving use

48 Loc. cit.
49 "Die Religionen", p. 128.
50 Ibid., p. 125.
51 *Der angefochtene Glaube*, p. 261.
52 Ibid., p. 280.
53 "Die Religionen", p. 126.
54 Ibid., p. 128.
55 Loc. cit. Within his studies of the religions, however, Ratschow does not unfold this christological foundation.
56 *Der angefochtene Glaube*, pp. 260–261.
57 Ibid., p. 280.
58 "Die Religionen", p. 126.

of the Law; also in Christianity there is the same experience of the Law. But Christianity has the means to overcome this tendency and find the true resolution of this experience; the religions don't. Thus, even in his later works, Ratschow holds: "Daß sehr grundsätzlich die nichtchristlichen Religionen im Modus des Gesetzes dem Christentum als Modus des Evangeliums gegenüberstehen, ist zwar grundsätzlich richtig ..."[59] And he still accepts the substance of Luther's definition of the religions as "Law".[60]

That the religions do not and cannot understand the "sola fide", that they cannot break out of the borders of the "Law", is the reason, we feel, why Ratschow, like Althaus, has to severely restrict the clarity of God's "Hervortreten" in the religions and has to impose his own "von Christus her". In *Der angefochtene Glaube* Ratschow implies that in the pre-Christian realm, man cannot really understand his situation as an "Anfechtung" or his own sinfulness. We can speak of "Anfechtung" only from "einem Glaubensgeschehen", only "unter Voraussetzung der Gottestaten im Alten und Neuen Testament ..."[61] "Es ist so, wie das Alte und das Neue Testament es bezeugen, daß ohne das Wort Gottes und das Gekommensein Jesu das peccatum gar nicht sichtbar wird."[62]

Therefore the religions cannot be considered as a "vor- oder außerchristlicher Bereich, der möglicherweise als Vorstufe oder Vorverständnis angesehen werden könnte". That the process of "Anfechtung" is "in eminenter Weise erhellt" in the religions is something we can see only from the viewpoint of the Gospel.[63] — This leads one to ask just how much of a "Gotteserfahrung" or of a "Grundeinsicht von Erlösung"[64] can the religions really attain on their own, i.e. without the "von Christus her?"

6. Ratschow does not conclude from the "schlechthinnigen Antithese" and from the religion's character as Law that they are therefore works of sin and completely "heillos", as Althaus did. He does not condemn the religions. And yet if such a conclusion is not stated nor even implied, is it not contained within Ratschow's position that all religions seek salvation "constitutively" and therefore remain within the Law? Within the order of the Law, one cannot yet find salvation, even though one is being, negatively, prepared for it. Also, as soon as one tries to achieve salvation through his own works, i.e. "constitutively", isn't he excluded from justification? Doesn't he fall into sin? Such questions, we feel, are not answered or sufficiently considered within Ratschow's position.

Also, Ratschow does not explicitly say that the religions contain only questions. Yet if they can never understand justification "sola fide", if they remain within the order of the Law, then, it seems, all they possess are questions and searchings. Salvation — the answers — come only in the Gospel. The religions seem to be left with only a preparatory role — a negative preparatory role: to express questions and needs.

It seems, then, that also in Ratschow's very bright picture of the religions, the doctrine of justification introduces contrasting, negative lines. Within the religions, despite all their positive content, an understanding of the "sola fide" (and

---

59 "Die Möglichkeit", p. 114.
60 "Die Religionen", p. 125.
61 *Der angefochtene Glaube*, p. 286.
62 Ibid., p. 280.
63 Ibid., pp. 286–287.
64 "Die Möglichkeit", p. 116.

therefore justification itself) is not possible because of the "solus Christus", i.e. because of "der christologischen Überlegung" which Ratschow doesn't go into. With Nürnberger, one can suggest: "Daß der wesentliche Unterschied zwischen christlichem Glauben und anderer Religion – jeder anderen Religion! – gerade an dieser Stelle liegt (i.e. justification "constitutively or consecutively") bedarf einer sorgfältigen theologischen und religionswissenschaftlichen Begründung."[65] But is such a "Begründung" possible?

§ 73. W. Pannenberg[66] – Example of Historical Nonconfessional Approach

1. Pannenberg,[67] just as resolutely as Ratschow and Althaus, admits the *presence of God* within the history of religions. The following citation sums up his understanding of this divine presence:

> Aus solchen Erwägungen ergibt sich, daß die Religionsgeschichte nicht zureichend verstanden ist, wo sie nur als Geschichte der Vorstellungen und des Verhaltens bestimmter Menschen und Gruppen gilt, die ihrerseits durch rein profane Kategorien beschrieben werden. Sachgemäßer ist die Religionsgeschichte als Geschichte des *Erscheinens des in der Struktur des menschlichen Daseins vorausgesetzten göttlichen Geheimnisses* zu verstehen, dessen Wirklichkeit und Eigenart aber im *Prozeß dieser Geschichte* selbst auf dem Spiele stehen.[68]

This passage pinpoints the two basic principles of Pannenberg's theology which support his ability to discover God's presence (we can say, God's revelation) within the religions: his *anthropology* and his *concept of history*.[69]

Pannenberg's anthropology sees "the structure of human existence" as forcing man to step beyond himself, to be dissatisfied with what he is and can see and therefore to constantly search beyond his own existence and his own particular point in history. Man is essentially *Fraglichkeit*. He uses his freedom "über alle vorfindliche Regelung seines Daseins hinauszufragen und hinwegzuschreiten"; he experiences a "chronische Bedürftigkeit" and an "unendliche

65 Nürnberger, op. cit., p. 34.
66 Presently Professor of Systematic Theology at the University of München.
67 The main elements of Pannenberg's approach to the religions can be found in: "Erwägungen zu einer Theologie der Religionsgeschichte", *Grundfragen systematischer Theologie* (Göttingen, 1967), pp. 252–295; *Offenbarung als Geschichte*, in Verbindung mit R. Rendtorff, U. Wilckens, T. Rendtorff (Beiheft zu KuD, Göttingen, 1965³); "Die Frage nach Gott", *Grundfragen*, pp. 361–386; "Weltgeschichte und Heilsgeschichte", *Probleme biblischer Theologie*. Gerhard von Rad zum 70. Geburtstag, hrsg. von H. W. Wolff (München, 1971), pp. 349–366; "Wie wahr ist das Reden von Gott?" *Evang. Kommentare*, Nov. 1971, pp. 629–633.
68 "Erwägungen", p. 290, emphasis mine.
69 For an overall picture of Pannenberg's thought, cf.: *Theologie als Geschichte* (Neuland in der Theologie, Bd. III), hrsg. von J. M. Robinson und J. B. Cobb, Jr. (Zürich-Stuttgart, 1967); esp. J. M. Robinson "Offenbarung als Wort und als Geschichte", pp. 11–134 (for a clear presentation of Pannenberg's theology). C. E. Braaten, *History and Hermeneutics* (Philadelphia, 1966); F. Konrad, *Der Offenbarungsbegriff in der evangelischen Theologie* (München, 1971), pp. 277–425; I. Berten, *Geschichte, Offenbarung, Glaube*. Eine Einführung in die Theologie Wolfhart Pannenbergs (München, 1970). Berten gives an exceptionally lucid presentation of Pannenberg's concept of history without going into details concerning his anthropology. On pp. 69–124 he offers a generally positive critique.

Angewiesenheit" to a "Gegenüber jenseits aller Welterfahrung".[70] The resemblances to Althaus' Uroffenbarung of the "Ur-Macht" in man's existence are striking. Yet what distinguishes Pannenberg's anthropological understanding of man as question from other theological anthropologies is that he situates this questioning not so much in the individual's experience of himself as in his experience of and relation to the *totality of the world and universe*. This is seen in the varigated terminology with which Pannenberg expresses man's "Fraglichkeit". He describes man as *Weltoffenheit*. Man searches not only for himself but for a world in which he can find and be himself.[71] — Pannenberg also sees man searching after *Wirklichkeit*. He is seeking a reality which is not only himself but beyond and more than himself. "Das allgemeine Wirklichkeitsverständnis ist der Ort, wo die Gottesfrage wie die Frage nach dem Menschen auszutragen sind."[72] — Man's "Weltoffenheit" and his quest for reality are summed up and can be realized only in an *Einheit* or *Ganzheit*. Man must feel himself part of a unified totality. He "(kann) der Ganzheit seines eigenen Lebens nur in Verbindung mit der Ganzheit der Wirklichkeit überhaupt gewiß werden ..."[73] "Nur in einer Welt, die eine Einheit ist, kann unser Leben als Ganzes gelingen, kann es heil bleiben oder werden."[74]

Pannenberg's anthropology, by its very nature, is related to – is the expression of – his concept of *history*. Man's "Fraglichkeit" can be expressed, experienced – and for the scientist, known – *only* within history. The phrase, "Der Mensch als Geschichte" illustrates the close connection between anthropology and historicity.[75] Man can find the reality he seeks – and the unity and totality of this reality – only within history. "Geschichte ist die Wirklichkeit in ihrer Totalität."[76] For history itself is a totality; it is "Universalgeschichte", its parts, which include both human and physical nature, form – or are forming – a unity. The fullness of this unity, however, will take shape and be revealed only at the end of history. In the meantime there is a proleptic movement of history towards this final unity, a movement in which the parts are related to each other and progressively clarify each other.[77]

2. This limited sketch of Pannenberg's anthropology and concept of history becomes clearer and more meaningful when seen as the foundation stone for his theology of religions and for his understanding of God's presence within them: for it is precisely within the religions that man's "Fraglichkeit" and "Weltoffenheit" are expressed and his search for "Wirklichkeit" and "Ganzheit" takes place in an historical process; and it is precisely within the religions that this quest and this historical process shows itself to be inspired by and directed to "the divine mystery" or the "divine reality".

"Denn wenn irgendwo, so haben es die Menschen in ihrer religiösen Erfahrung, in ihren Religionen mit dem Ganzen ihres Daseins zu tun, mit dem Universum, ... das in den endlichen Inhalten der Erfahrung angeschaut wird als darin sich bekundend."[78] "... die Religionen haben es mit dem Gesamtverständnis der Wirklichkeit zu tun."[79] This unified and unifying reality is God. "Die in der jeweiligen Erfah-

---

70 *Was ist der Mensch?* Die Anthropologie der Gegenwart im Lichte der Theologie (Göttingen, 1962), p. 6, 11; cf. Konrad, pp. 287–288; Berten, pp. 14–17.
71 *Was ist der Mensch?*, p. 10; H. Obayashi, "Pannenberg and Troeltsch: History and Religion", JAAR, 38 (1970) 405; Konrad, p. 298.
72 "Wirkungen biblischer Gotteserkenntnis auf das abendländische Menschenbild", *Stud. Gen.*, 15 (1962) 587.
73 "Hermeneutik und Universalgeschichte", *Grundfragen*, p. 109.
74 *Was ist der Mensch?*, p. 44.
75 Title of Chapter 11 in *Was ist der Mensch?*, cf. p. 95.
76 "Heilsgeschehen und Geschichte", *Grundfragen*, p. 27.
77 Cf. Konrad, pp. 328–330; Berten, pp. 19–26; Obayashi, p. 403.
78 "Wie wahr ist das Reden von Gott?", p. 632.
79 "Erwägungen", p. 270.

rung der Wirklichkeit im Hinblick auf ihre Ganzheit — als Welt — begegnende Macht, die als die einende Einheit jenes Ganzen in Erscheinung tritt, ist die Wirklichkeit, mit der es die Religionen zu tun haben und die — wenn sie sich personhaft manifestiert — allein 'Gott' heißen darf."[80] The divine reality is the central force and manifesting "Macht" behind all religions. Thus Pannenberg can speak of the "Einheit" of the history of religions, which is nothing else than the "Einheit der göttlichen Wirklichkeit selbst".[81]

But Pannenberg insists that he is not asserting this divine reality and man's search for it as a theological or philosophical principle or a "religious apriori" which he applies to the religions. Rather, he finds this reality and search within the *history* of the various religions and *therefore* asserts it. "In solchem tatsächlichen *Umgang* der Menschen mit dem Geheimnis des Seins (i.e. in the religions), auf das die Struktur ihres Daseins sie verweist, muß sich dessen *Wirklichkeit* erweisen. In diesem Sinne kann die Wirklichkeit Gottes oder göttlicher Mächte sich nur durch ihr *Widerfahrnis* erweisen ..."[82]

We can conclude that this presence of God within the religions, founded in man's existential structure and realized only in an historical process, is a form of *universal, divine (supernatural) revelation.* With Althaus, Pannenberg holds to a revelation behind the religions: He states "... daß die Offenbarung Gottes nicht nur irgendwo in der Menschheitsgeschichte als supranaturales Ereignis senkrecht von oben einbreche, sondern das Thema dieser Geschichte selbst ist, die sie im Tiefsten bewegende Macht".[83] "Es ist nicht so, daß die Offenbarung, die Selbstenthüllung Gottes, fertig vom Himmel fällt und am Anfang aller Gotteserkenntnis stehen müßte, weil man sonst gar nichts von Gott wissen könnte."[84]

3. And with Althaus, Pannenberg can insist on the necessity of a *positive relation* — a dialogue — between Christianity and the religions. His reasoning is basically the same as that of Althaus', yet because it is founded on the universal meaning of the historical process he concludes to an even more absolute necessity of relating to the religions. For Jesus Christ "ist ... die endgültige Offenbarung Gottes nur im Zusammenhang mit der ganzen Geschichte ..."[85] This is clear in the New Testament: the "Vollmachtsanspruch Jesu (war) nicht isoliert für sich zum Grunde des Glaubens an die Offenbarung Gottes in Jesus Christus geworden". Rather it "presupposed" a 'Wissen von Gott" both among the Jews and the Gentiles, without which it would have been ineffective,

---

80 Ibid., pp. 285—286.
81 Ibid., pp. 276—277.
82 Ibid., pp. 284, cf. also 283, 270. This, he feels, is the error of K. Rahner's theology of the religions: Rahner asserts man's transcendental relationship instead of tracing it and concluding to it within the historical process. Loc. cit., cf. also p. 255. — Therefore it is unjust to accuse Pannenberg, as Hamilton does, of arguing from a religious apriori. (Cf. "Die Eigenart der Theologie Pannenbergs", *Theologie als Geschichte*, pp. 227—231) As Pannenberg himself answers: he is not arguing aprioristically "aus der Struktur der Fraglichkeit" but "aus dem Widerfahrnis der Wirklichkeit", i.e. from history; cf. op. cit., p. 289, footnote 2.
83 *Grundfragen*, Vorwort, p. 5.
84 "Die Offenbarung Gottes in Jesus von Nazareth", *Theologie und Geschichte*, p. 152.
85 Ibid., p. 160.

meaningless, "unbegründet".[86] Which means for our present situation: "Das ist bis heute *das einzige Kriterium* (!) für die Wahrheit der Offenbarung Gottes in Jesus von Nazareth, daß sie sich nachträglich immer wieder bewahrheitet an der Erfahrung der Wirklichkeit, in der wir leben."[87] From this, Pannenberg draws the explicit and the bold conclusion for the religions: Christianity must prove itself within the history of religions! "Eine Überprüfung theologischer Aussagen wird sich daher an die Religionen und an die Geschichte ihrer Veränderungen zu halten haben. Denn in den Religionen ist jene Sinntotalität der Wirklichkeit immer schon thematisch, an der die Wahrheit theologischer Aussagen geprüft werden soll." Through "eine kritische Untersuchung der Religionsgeschichte" in which the theologian as it were suspends his own conviction concerning "die Besonderheit des Christentums und seines Wahrheitsbewußtseins", the theologian is able "die Besonderheit der eigenen religiösen Überlieferung im Zusammenhang der übrigen Religionen zu begründen". The result will never be a final, conclusive proof; this comes only at the end of history. But "eine vorläufige Bewährung" is possible.[88]

Pannenberg finds, again like Althaus, the practical example for such a dialogue with the religions in the relation between the Old and New Testaments with their religious worlds. Here he notes *not only* a "Bewährung" but a relationship and exchange which was necessary *for the formation* of Old and New Testament revelation itself. Israel did not merely assimilate other religious traditions in the light of her own supernatural revelation; she and her revelation *grew out of* the history of religions. Thus the "Werden der religiösen Traditionen Israels" is not to be imagined without this exchange with the religions; and the same applies to the "Auftreten Jesu".[89] This same process of exchange and formation is found in the New Testaments's use of the Greek understanding of reality.[90]

4. But within this dialogue with the religions, Pannenberg clearly holds to both the *finality* and the *superiority* of Christ and his revelation. Christ brings an "endgültige Offenbarung" insofar as he proleptically contains the end of all history which is the source, motivating force and goal of all religions. "Im Auftreten und Geschick Jesu, also in seiner Person, ist die endgültige Offenbarung der Gottheit Gottes am Ende aller Zeiten schon im voraus Ereignis.[91] Pannenberg explains the two elements which incorporate this prolepsis: "Jesus von Nazareth ist die endgültige Offenbarung Gottes, sofern in ihm das Ende der Geschichte erschienen ist, in seiner *eschatologischen Botschaft*, wie durch seine *Auferweckung von den Toten.*"[92] In his message Christ turned men's minds towards the future and assured them that the end of all history is *God's* and *is* coming; and by rising from the dead he proved that this message was true and that it already contained the end. Such an understanding of Christ's finality places him both *within* and *beyond* the history of religions and seems to offer a valuable insight into the conflict of

---

86 Ibid., p. 143, 141; *Offenbarung als Geschichte*, p. 136.
87 "Die Offenbarung Gottes", p. 169, emphasis mine.
88 "Wie wahr ist das Reden von Gott?", pp. 632–633.
89 "Die Offenbarung Gottes", pp. 139–140; *Offenbarung als Geschichte*, p. 97.
90 *Offenbarung als Geschichte*, p.98; cf. also "Die Aufnahme des philosophischen Gottesbegriffs als dogmatisches Problem der frühchristlichen Theologie", *Grundfragen*, pp. 296–346.
91 "Die Offenbarung Gottes", p. 159. "Gerade in der Gestalt einer bloßen Vorwegnahme ist die Geschichte Jesu die endgültige Offenbarung Gottes." Ibid., p. 167.
92 Ibid., p. 160, emphasis mine.

Christianity's absoluteness and the positive role of the religions. "Als der Macher der Zukunft ist der von Jesus verkündete Gott der kommenden Gottesherrschaft allen späteren Epochen der Geschichte der Kirche und der außerchristlichen Religionen schon voraus. Von daher stellt sich die Religionsgeschichte auch über die Zeit des Auftretens Jesus hinaus als Erscheinungsgeschichte des Gottes dar, der sich durch Jesus offenbart hat."[93]

5. We might conclude that Pannenberg's "theology of the religions", both in its positive verdict and in its balance and clarity, seems to go beyond Althaus. — Yet in much of what Pannenberg states about the religions — and much more so, in what he does *not* state — many of the same questions, unclarities and even contradictions which we noted in Althaus remain. Questions which, we feel, are essential for an integrated theology of religions and especially for a fruitful dialogue with them are left unresolved: Can the non-Christians find salvation in and through their religions — i.e. does the God of Jesus Christ reveal himself through the religions as the God who saves and satisfies man's heart? Or, phrased differently: do the religions express only "Fraglichkeit"? Can they also find answers which, though not the final answer, are still saving answers?

It seems that Pannenberg does not (or cannot?) explicitly state that the religions can be "ways of salvation"; he does not directly confront this question. True, he does explicitly say that "Heilsgeschichte" extends throughout "Weltgeschichte". And he criticizes Oscar Cullmann for restricting salvation history to a "ganz schmale Linie" within general history, i.e. to the Old and New Testaments.[94] And while approving Karl Rahner's understanding of the universality of salvation history, he calls him to task for arguing from a supernatural viewpoint and limiting the "Ausdrücklichkeit" of salvation to the Christian order.[95] — But within these statements and these critiques, what Pannenberg seems to be asserting is only that salvation is the *theme* of all history, that within the historical expression of man's "Fraglichkeit", salvation is being *sought*. In his article on "Weltgeschichte und Heilsgeschichte" he understands salvation as the realization of "Ganzheit" — the goal towards which man and his religions are tending and searching. But he does not state that this "Ganzheit" or salvation can be *achieved* within history. Against Cullmann, he counters that God is working "in den übrigen Ereignissen der Geschichte" and that this activity is "auf die eine oder andere Weise auf das Heil der Menschen bezogen".[96] But does this activity actually bring forth salvation? Against Rahner he states: "Die Ausdrücklichkeit der Heils*thematik* (or "Heilssinns") ist vielmehr spezifisch für die Religionen überhaupt und für die Geschichte religiöser Veränderungen."[97] Salvation becomes an express theme or intent in the religions; but can it also become a reality? Pannenberg therefore expressly states that salvation is the object, the theme, the purpose of the religions — as Rahner does. But he does not expressly state that salvation can also be realized in and through the religions — as Rahner does. Perhaps within his historical methodology he meant to imply that salvation can become a reality in the religions. If so, we feel that the implication is not clear enough.

And from other aspects of Pannenberg's approach to the religions, such a possible implication seems difficult to support. In the end, one has the impression that the religions cannot break out of their *Fraglichkeit*, that all they have are

93 "Erwägungen", pp. 291–292; cf. also Obayashi, p. 418.

94 "Weltgeschichte und Heilsgeschichte", pp. 358–359; cf. O. Cullmann, *Heil als Geschichte* (Tübingen, 1965), p. 146.

95 "Weltgeschichte und Heilsgeschichte", pp. 361–363; cf. K. Rahner, "Weltgeschichte und Heilsgeschichte", *Schriften* V, pp. 115–135, esp. pp. 119–129.

96 "Weltgeschichte", p. 359.

97 Ibid., p. 363.

questions, that they *cannot really know God* sufficiently to receive the salvation he effected in Christ. This impression rests on three overlapping considerations:

a) Pannenberg's understanding of history as receiving its meaning *only at the end of history* implies that the presence of God — his revelation — although felt and experienced throughout history can be understood and seen as what it is only at the end, or, only in the "prolepsis" or anticipation of this end in Jesus Christ.[98] Thus, when Pannenberg speaks of the revelation of God as the theme and "im Tiefsten bewegende Macht" of all history, he immediately adds that we can speak "sinnvoll von einer Offenbarung Gottes ... nur im Hinblick auf das *Ganze* der Wirklichkeit" and this "Ganze" is seen only "von einem Ende alles Geschehens her". The "end" therefore has "konstitutive Bedeutung ... für die Frage der Gotteserkenntnis".[99] This means, apparently, that there is no real "Gotteserkenntnis" before the end, or before the anticipation of the end in Jesus Christ.[100] And since Pannenberg identifies revelation and salvation, this means that salvation is truly possible only at the end, i.e. only in Christ's revelation. [101] For the religions this seems to imply that while they experience God, they do not really know him or come into possession of him. God as the "Einheit" of all religions can be seen only in Christ and Christianity. "... erst daraufhin läßt sich von einer allgemeinen Religionsgeschichte der Menschheit sprechen. Die Einheit der Religionsgeschichte ist also nicht an ihren Anfängen, sondern eher an ihrem Ende zu suchen."[102]

b) If we can speak of true revelation only at the end, in Jesus Christ, then the religions apparently *are* confined within the bonds of their *Fraglichkeit*. And it seems that, of themselves, they cannot even understand their own searching or the contents of their own questions. Pannenberg confronts this question explicitly:

> Das Problem liegt nur darin, ob die Fraglichkeit des Daseins sich erst von der Antwort in der Offenbarung Gottes her enthüllt, oder ob sie allgmein zugänglich ist. Nicht nur Bultmann, auch Tillich und Ebeling möchten an dem für Barth entscheidenden Gesichtspunkt festhalten, daß die Fraglichkeit des menschlichen Daseins und aller endlichen Wirklichkeit überhaupt erst von der göttlichen Antwort her in ihrem wahren Sinn zu verstehen ist.[103]

Pannenberg agrees basically with this position, although, with Tillich and against Barth, he holds that the "Fraglichkeit" in its unclarity still has an apologetic meaning (i.e. as an "Anknüpfungspunkt").[104] Yet if man in his religions has only questions — which are not really understood — can we say he really knows God? This problem becomes all the more pressing when we see that Pannenberg qualifies the "Wissen von Gott" in the religions by adding that its "eigentliche

98 Cf. Berten, pp. 24—25; 35—37.
99 *Grundfragen*, pp. 5—6.
100 *Offenbarung als Geschichte*, p. 103; cf. also, Mann, *Theogonische Tage*, p. 695, footnote 18.
101 "Die Selbstenthüllung Gottes aber ist das Heil für die Menschen, weil nur in der Nähe Gottes, in Gemeinschaft mit Gott, das Dasein der Menschen Erfüllung findet." "Die Offenbarung Gottes", p. 153. The term "Selbstenthüllung" is applied here to the final revelation, i.e. in Christ.
102 "Erwägungen", p. 275, cf. also p. 264; Obayashi, p. 414.
103 "Die Frage nach Gott", p. 371.
104 Ibid., p. 386.

Wirklichkeit (wird) erst durch Jesus enthüllt". "Am Anfang steht ... — bildlich gesprochen — die Verhüllung (velatio) Gottes, und erst am Ende wird die Hülle beseitigt, erfolgt die revelatio." In this "Verhüllung" God is indeed "erfahren", but only in Christ is God's "Selbstenthüllung" given; only in Christ is he known.[105]

Franz Konrad's critique, therefore, would seem to be correct: according to Pannenberg, man before Christ can have only a questioning experience of God; answers cannot be achieved. The first relation of Christ's revelation to the non-Christian therefore is a negative one.[106]

c) Further, in a terminology reminiscent of Althaus and even of Barth, Pannenberg states that the religions *corrupt their experience and knowledge of God*, "... daß in ihnen das Widerfahrnis (of God), auf dem sie beruhen, zugleich verkehrt worden ist dadurch, daß die Mächte, die hier als Wirklichkeit gelten, in Wahrheit noch zum Bereich des Endlichen gehören".[107] The "Selbstbekundungen des wahren Gottes" in them is "wie Paulus sagt, 'in Ungerechtigkeit niedergehalten'..."[108] The knowledge of God in the religions is "durch mancherlei Verkehrung verdunkelt. Sie verwechseln die Gestalt des Schöpfers mit der der Geschöpfe". (Röm. 1, 18 ff.)[109] The religions, therefore, not only cannot fully grasp the mystery of God, they also *misuse* it. "Freilich lassen die Religionen in der Tat ein eigentümliches Widerstreben der Menschen gegen die Unendlichkeit (Nichtendlichkeit) des göttlichen Geheimnisses beobachten ... Die außerchristlichen Religionen nahmen das Erscheinen des göttlichen Geheimnisses nur in gebrochener Weise wahr, weil sie sich ihren eigenen Wandlungen, ihrer eigenen Geschichte verschlossen."[110] — Any theologian would admit that in many religions this corruption of the knowledge of God is a fact. But Pannenberg here seems to assert that this corruption *must* take place, that it is *unavoidable*.

6. It is clear that what we may call the *"negative side"* to Pannenberg's theology of the religions is *by no means as harsh* as that of Althaus'; he does not brand the religions as "works" or the Law or as man's attempts to save himself. The reservations and unclarities within his position *do not stem*, explicitly, from the traditional doctrine of *justification*, i.e. that God leads men to the "sola fide" (which means to true revelation) only "solo Christo" — as in the case with Althaus and, indirectly, with Ratschow. And yet, these reservations are founded on Pannenberg's Christology — on his understanding of Christ as the *sole or historically limited "prolepsis"* in which God reveals the "end" — and that means, in which God brings men to salvation. Therefore, despite Pannenberg's positive anthropological approach to the religions, despite his new historical-phenomenological method, we still can confront him with the same questions that resulted from our study of Althaus: Can the religions as religions bring their followers to a salvific

---

105 "Die Offenbarung Gottes", pp. 152–153; cf. also p. 160.
106 Konrad, p. 327, also p. 368; cf. Obayashi, p. 417.
107 "Die Frage nach Gott", pp. 380–381.
108 Ibid., p. 386.
109 "Die Offenbarung Gottes", p. 144.
110 "Erwägungen", p. 293. Pannenberg adds that this is a theological statement which should not be used as a dogmatic rule in researching the religions. But he feels that it is a rule which will prove itself to be true; ibid., p. 294.

encounter with God? Do they contain more than just questions and searching? Can we "dialogue" with them as something more than a "negative preparation" for the Gospel? Pannenberg seems to neglect clear answers to these questions. And in many instances, he seems to give much the same answers as Althaus.

§ 74. "Opinio Communis" within Systematic Theology

1. Fritzsche, Ratschow and Pannenberg reflect what we feel is the "opinio communis" concerning the non-Christian religions as found within present-day German Protestant theology. The general consensus of other theologians does not go beyond these three examples (certainly not beyond Pannenberg, most of them remaining close to either Fritzsche or Ratschow) — which means it does not seem to go beyond Althaus' final verdict on the religions. We shall outline now a few *examples* of this "opinio communis".[111] In so doing we shall try to avoid the danger of brevity becoming over-simplification.

2. *Peter Brunner*[112] — His understanding of the religions is determined, even more radically and negatively than Althaus', by the doctrine of the Law. The religions contain a form of revelation in that, through creation, they receive a "Strahl seiner gottheitlichen Glorie". Yet they cannot come to a true knowledge of God's will and law: the real God is not revealed to them. In the religions we find a "Urverweigerung gegenüber der suchenden, liebenden Hand Gottes". The religions remain shackled in "der Kreatürlichkeit der Kreatur". Why? The reason appears to be "solus Christus": only in Christ is the real God revealed; only in him can we understand and properly use the Law. Only in Christ do we realize that mankind outside of him is captured in an absolute "Verlorenheit".[113]

3. *Wolfgang Trillhaas*[114] — Admitting that "eine theologische Lehre von der Religion ... kaum je innerhalb der protestantischen Dogmatik versucht worden ist", he also insists that such a teaching on the religions can be established "nur von einer Lehre vom Gesetz aus". Yet his application of the "Law" to the religions is not as negative as P. Brunner's. Trillhaas is in basic agreement with Althaus when he argues that the religions spring from the experience of the mystery behind the world and from the attempt to establish a relation of security with this mystery. Yet he does not allow this effort to succeed (just as the Law can never of itself lead to the Gospel). The religions contain only "Fragen", "Erwarten", "Vorverständnis". He explicitly states that they cannot be a "Weg des Heiles". Rather,

---

111 Within this survey we shall not be considering the views of P. Tillich, which definitely do go beyond those of Althaus and the "opinio communis" of contemporary German theology. The reasons for this exclusion are not only Tillich's death in 1965 but also the fact that he was, for the most part, "removed" from the German theological scene. Cf. § 19.

112 Professor Emeritus of Systematic Theology at the University of Heidelberg.

113 *Pro Ecclesia* I (Berlin, 1962), pp. 100–105. — In their christomonistic understanding of revelation, *Otto Weber* and *Albrecht Peters* offer this same sharply negative verdict on the religions. Peters, "Die Frage nach Gott", *Fuldaer Hefte* 17 (Berlin, 1967), pp. 80, 92, 95–100.

114 Professor of Systematic Theology, University of Göttingen.

they are meant for the "Erhaltung" of fallen man. At the most, they can be considered "ein Pädagoge auf Christus hin".[115]

4. *August Kimme*[116] — He attempts a theology of the religions based on the doctrine of the Trinity. Through "appropriation" we can admit an activity of God the Creator "unter Mitwirkung seines ewigen Sohnes" in the hearts of the non-Christians which prepares them for an encounter with Christ.[117] And yet, Kimme's outlook remains basically negative. Revelation in creation is "infralapsarisch".[118] It cannot escape the infection of sin; man in his religions must misuse this revelation, for the saving Logos and the saving Spirit are to be found *only in Christ.* "Denn die Heilsbotschaft von dem dreieinigen Gott und dem einzig rettenden Namen Jesus Christus schließt eine positive Darstellung und Wertung anderer Heilswege und Glaubensweisen radikal aus."[119] Kimme can even distinguish the "außerchristologische Regiment Gottes des Schöpfers" in the religions and the "trinitarische Regnum Christi" in the Gospel. Salvation is found only in the "Regnum Christi".[120] He explicitly states that this means "Extra ecclesiam nulla salus".[121] — The religions, therefore, under God the Creator but without Christ the Savior, are, at the most, a negative preparation for Christianity.

5. *Willy Böld*[122] — In a Protestant-Catholic Conference concerning the religions (1966)[123] Böld stresses the necessity of dialoguing with the religions. But he adds that this dialogue must be built on the principle of Christianity's "Absolutheit"[124] which in turn is determined by Böld's interpretation of the "solus Christus": because God's truth was expressed in the person of Christ and thus becomes personal truth, this truth becomes not only "letztgültig" and "allgemeingültig" but also "alleingültig".[125] To preserve this understanding of Christianity's "Alleingültigkeit" is the role of the Reformational "dreifachen Solus ... Solus Christus ... Sola Scriptura ... Sola Fide". It means that truth can be found only in the person of Christ and in the "personalen Akt" of faith in the "Christuswahr-

115 W. Trillhaas, *Dogmatik* (Berlin, 1962), pp. 226–231; cf. also id., *Religionsphilosophie* (Berlin, 1972), which appeared too late to be evaluated in this context.
116 As Director of the "Leipziger Mission", Kimme's views might well be listed also among the mission-theologians below. But because his evaluation of the religions is built predominantly on a systematic-trinitarian foundation, we have deemed it more logical to present it here.
117 A. Kimme, "Universalität und Exklusivität der christlichen Heilsbotschaft. Ein dogmatischer Versuch zum Thema 'Theologie der Religionen'", *Fuldaer Hefte* 16 (Berlin, 1966, Paper given at the "Tagung des Theologischen Konvents Augsburgischen Bekenntnisses", Fall, 1963), p. 180.
118 Ibid., pp. 169–171.
119 Ibid., p. 166; cf. also pp. 146–152, 155, 160–161.
120 Ibid., p. 172.
121 Ibid., p. 176.
122 Professor at the "Pädagogische Hochschule des Saarlandes", Saarbrücken.
123 Held in April, 1966 in the "Evangelische Akademie, Tutzing". The four papers read at the conference (others by J. Ratzinger, H. W. Gensichen and H. Waldenfels) were published in *Kirche in der außerchristlichen Welt* (Regensburg, 1967). Cf. W. Böld, "Das Problem der Absolutheit des christlichen Heilsweges", op. cit., pp. 31–63. pp. 31–63.
124 Ibid., pp. 32–35.
125 Ibid., pp. 37–40.

heit".[126] Böld warns against relativizing Christ by setting him up as the expression or summing-up of truth in other philosophical systems or religions.[127] This means that the role of the religions is only to point out "die noch ungelöste und im Grunde unlösbar scheinende Schicksalsproblematik der Menschheitsgeschichte",[128] — i.e. a negative role.

6. *Wilhelm Dantine*[129] — Describing the formula "sola fide" as the "wesentlichen Beitrag" which Protestantism must make in the ecumenical dialogue with the religions, Dantine seems to offer a much more positive interpretation of this formula. He not only recognizes God's presence in all religions in the form of an "ontological thirst"[130] but also admits that many religions have come to a clear understanding of the "sola fide", even clearer than many "äffische" and synergistic brands of Christianity. He singles out Amida Buddhism and Bhakti mysticism.[131] But an essential difference remains — because of the "solus Christus", i.e. because of the "christologische Fundierung des 'sola fide'", which the religions do *not* have. He interprets this christological foundation as "die forensische Dimension der christlichen Sola-Fide-Lehre".[132] "Der Glaube wird nie davon ablassen, zu bezeugen, daß solche Freiheit und Gewißheit an den Namen Jesus Christus gebunden ist. Denn das 'sola fide' hat seine eigentümliche Fundierung im Kreuzweg Christi, d.h. darin, daß Jesus von Nazareth ... sich dem Gericht unterwarf, in die forensische Situation eintrat, in der der Mensch stets coram deo existiert, und sich ihr auslieferte."[133] This would imply that the religions cannot understand the "sola fide", that they cannot attain the salvation built on Christ's resolution of the forensic situation. The most Dantine can say of such doctrines is that they are "not far from the kingdom of God".[134] The religions remain within the unredeemed realm of the Law.[135]

7. *Ulrich Mann*[136] (his position before 1970) — Just as clearly as Althaus, Ratschow and Pannenberg, Mann affirms a genuine revelation within the religions. He even favors Hegel's understanding of religious history "als Entwicklung der

126 Ibid., pp. 44—47.
127 Ibid., pp. 47, 43.
128 Ibid., p. 32.
129 Professor of Systematic Theology at the University of Vienna. Dantine's assessment of the religions was delivered as a main lecture at the "Evangelischen Theologen-Kongreß" (September, 1966); thus, *as an Austrian* he can be listed here as reflecting attitudes among German-speaking theologians. Cf. "Die christologische Fundierung des SOLA FIDE. Dogmatische Überlegungen im Horizont von Religionskritik", *Der christliche Glaube und die Religionen* hrsg. von C. H. Ratschow (Berlin, 1967), pp. 28—41.
130 Here Dantine draws from M. Eliade, *Das Heilige und das Profane. Vom Wesen des Religiösen* (1957), pp. 8, 34—35, cf. op. cit., pp. 30—33.
131 Ibid., pp. 37, 39.
132 Ibid., p. 38.
133 Loc. cit.
134 Ibid., p. 39. Therefore Dantine calls Schlette's understanding of the religions as "ways of salvation" a "völlige Fehlanzeige" concerning christology and the doctrine of justification. Ibid., p.32; cf. H. R. Schlette, *Die Religionen als Thema der Theologie* (Freiburg, 1963), p. 109.
135 Dantine, pp. 36—37.
136 Professor of Systematic Theology and Philosophy of Religion at the University of Saarbrücken.

absoluten Religion" in which "Gott sich in der Geschichtlichkeit seiner selbst bewußt wird und sich eben darin bewußt macht".[137] "Die Geschichte der Religion ist die Geschichte der Gottesoffenbarung."[138] Yet he also insists that for a Lutheran theology the doctrine of the *Law* is "eine Schlüsselstelle ... für das theologische Verständnis der Religion" — which means: "Das Gesetz führt nicht zum Heil, denn unter dem Gesetz versucht der Mensch sich der Offenbarung Gottes zu bemächtigen." This implies that while revelation remains in the religions "diese Offenbarung ist immer auch durch Menschenwerk und Menschenbeiwerk verfälscht". The most Mann can conclude is that "wo also das Gesetz zum Tode führt, da ist zugleich eine dialektisch zu verstehende äußerste Nähe zum Heil in Christus gegeben. Eine Nähe, wenngleich keine Identität! Es gibt wirklich ein 'Nichtfernsein vom Reiche Gottes' (Mk 12,34)".[139] But the religions can never attain any "real answers" and are left with only questions.

Interestingly and somewhat enigmatically, Mann, in his recent works, *Theogonische Tage* (1970) und *Das Christentum als absolute Religion* (1970) makes a radical shift in the method and conclusions of his theology of the religions. Drawing heavily on the depth psychology of C. G. Jung and interpreting the history of religions as the development of divinely-instilled "archetypes", he expressly admits not only revelation but also salvation — not only the Law but the Gospel — within the religions! It would take a special study to weigh and sift out theology and psychology in Mann's new approach;[140] yet it remains one of the most challeng-

137 "Theologie und Religionsgeschichte", *Luth. Monatshefte*, 1964, p. 252, cf. also p. 259.
138 "Religion als theologisches Problem", *Christentum und Religion* (Regensburg, 1966), pp. 88–89.
139 "Theologie und Religionsgeschichte", p. 255. cf. also p. 261.
140 Mann states that because of his studies in the history of religions (especially through personal contact in his travels) and because of his involvement with C. G. Jung's depth psychology he came to the realization that we must seek "neue Wege des theologischen Denkens" concerning the religions (cf. *Tage*, pp. 15, 21–22, 652 footnote 9), i.e. "neu...nur gegenüber der heutzutage gängigen protestantischen Theologie". (p. 21) Tracing these new ways, Mann maintains that God is revealing himself in man's psyche and that this revelation is expressed in the religions. God undergoes, therefore, a "Werdeprozeß" and the religions are "beteiligt an Gottes geschichtlichem Werden". (ibid., p. 183, cf. also pp. 16–18, 168, 178; *Das Christentum*, p. 214.) "Gott hat also eine Geschichte, die sich in der Religion offenbart, sein Sein ist ins menschliche Werden eingegangen. ...Die Geschichte der Psyche ist die Religionsgeschichte, und die Religionsgeschichte ist die Geschichte Gottes selbst..." (*Tage*, p. 21; *Das Christentum* pp. 215–216.)
We must admit not only the possibility of revelation but also of salvation in the religions. (cf. *Tage*, pp. 146, 151, 156, 182, 186–187) Here Mann point-blankly contradicts his earlier position: "Es kann nicht unser Ziel sein, die Religion von der theologischen Kategorien des Gesetzes überhaupt zu lösen. Wir wollen also nicht bestreiten, daß Religion Gesetz ist; wir bestreiten nur, daß sie nur Gesetz ist, Gesetz und nichts anderes... Religion ist Gesetz und Evangelium." (ibid., pp. 153–154) In a footnote he admits that he is reversing his early position — but that he had already forecast this reversal in *Vorspiel des Heils* (Stuttgart, 1962, pp. 401 f., footnote 46).
And still Mann feels that he can be faithful to his "Lutheran obligations" (*Tage*, p. 22) and hold to "die Absolutheit des Christentums". (ibid., 132, 140–141; *Das Christentum*, pp. 58–67, 202–209) But his understanding of Christianity's and Christ's absoluteness, couched in Jungian categories, seems to be substantially that of Hegel or the early Troeltsch. Christ's revelation is expressed as the "letzte, eschatologische und das heißt absolute Bedeutung". (*Tage*, p. 16, cf. also p. 187) The history of religions therefore is in

ing attempts at a theology of the religions among present-day German Protestant theologians.[141]

8. What seems to be the "opinio communis" of these systematic theologians was reflected quite clearly in the discussions and reports of the 18th and 19th Meetings of the "Theologischen Konvent Augsburgischen Bekenntnisses" (1962–1963).[142] Although the participants openly called for a more positive encounter with the religions and rejected a rigid Christomonism[143] they also resolutely opposed the "cosmic Christology" of New Delhi,[144] unanimously rejected the teaching of the "logos spermatikos" in the religions, and asked: "Kann wirklich vom Wirken Christi und vom Wirken des Heiligen Geistes in den Religionen gesprochen werden? Ist hierbei nicht die Trinitätslehre in einer entschei-

process of evolution; "eine gewisse Tendenz zu immer höheren Formen, alles Erstarren setzt neue, tiefere und reichere Religionen frei..." Christianity's place is understood "vom Gedanken der Achsenzeit her", the point "in welchem der Geist endgültig zur Fülle und Eigentlichkeit gekommen ist". (ibid., pp. 17–18, also p. 20; *Das Christentum*, pp. 104–119) Thus he interprets the Incarnation as the historization of an archtype which is already found ontologically throughout the history of religions. Christ is "ein Archetyp, der geschichtlich geworden ist!... der zugleich schon im Ontologischen angelegt war... Christus ist ein Archetyp, er muß als solcher von Anfang an in der Psyche angelegt gewesen sein." (*Tage*, p. 561, cf. also pp. 570, 585, 23, 199; *Das Christentum*, p. 214, 180–188. For a critique of Mann's approach cf. C. H. Ratschow's review of *Theogonische Tage* in ThLZ, 98 (1971) 452–455.

141 One other contemporary German-speaking theologian whose views on the non-Christian religious world certainly go far beyond any of the theologians we have presented is *Fritz Buri*. We have not considered Buri's position since he stands quite distinctly on the sidelines of continental Protestant theology and since, in our estimation, his approach to the religions is totally relativistic. Within his program of "Entkerygmatisierung" and under the influence of his teacher, Karl Jaspers, Buri explains both revelation and salvation philosophically and detaches them from any kind of influence or causality originating from Christ. "Entgegen der Berufung auf ein sogenanntes Heilsfaktum, das sich ein für allemal in der Geschichte ereignet haben soll, halten wir dafür, daß das wahre und wirkliche Heil sich je in unserem Selbstverständnis ereigne, und zwar dann und dort, wo der Mensch in seinem Selbstverständnis zu seiner Eigentlichkeit gelangt." ("Theologie und Philosophie", ThZ, 8 (1952) 131; cf. also "Entmythologisierung oder Entkerygmatisierung der Theologie?", *Kerygma und Mythos* II (1952), p. 99) Christ is but one of the many symbols or myths to express this mystery of salvation which takes place outside of him and without him. (Cf. "Entmythologisierung oder Entkerygmatisierung", p. 97; *Dogmatik als Selbstverständnis des christlichen Glaubens*, II. *Der Mensch und die Gnade* (Bern–Tübingen, 1962) pp. 39, 50; *Denkender Glaube. Schritte auf dem Weg zu einer philosophischen Theologie* (Bern–Stuttgart, 1966), p. 100; *Dogmatik als Selbstverständnis des christlichen Glaubens* I. Vernunft und Offenbarung (Bern–Tübingen, 1956), pp. 41, 135 ff., 315.) Thus: "Weder als Selbstverständnis noch als Tranzendenz noch in seinem Anspruch auf Wahrheitsgeltung unterscheidet sich christlicher Glaube von anderem Glauben". *Dogmatik* I, p. 146; For Buri's sketchy and not entirely coherent treatment of the religions, cf. *Dogmatik* I, pp. 229–231, 242–245.

142 Cf. Reports by P. Reinhardt, *Fuldaer Hefte* 16, op. cit., pp. 181–186; E. Rose, op. cit., pp. 187–198.

143 Rose, p. 194.

144 Especially as in J. Sittler's paper, "Zur Einheit berufen", in *Neu-Dehli*, 1961, hrsg. von W. A. Visser't Hooft (Stuttgart, 1962), pp. 512–523.

denden Weise verfälscht?"[145] The religions must be interpreted in a twofold (and essentially negative) dialectic as "Ausdruck der frommen Selbstbehauptung des Menschen gegenüber Gott" and as ways in which God "die Menschen in diesen Religionen auf(bewahrt) für die Begegnung mit Christus".[146] Any final verdict on the religions must bear in mind the insistence of the "Reformatoren": "Errettung vor Gott im Jüngsten Gericht gibt es nur durch den Glauben an Christus, und dieser Glaube kommt aus dem Wort ... der Fluch des Gesetzes gilt allen Menschen, die Gnadenzusage aber nur den Christusgläubigen."[147] – Again, any positive contents in the religions are overshadowed by the "sola fide" and "solus Christus".

§ 75. "Opinio Communis" within Mission-Theology

1. Examples drawn from the views of present-day German Protestant mission-theologians concerning the religions present pretty much the same picture as those of the systematic theologians. The missiologists, as might be expected, show more of a determined effort to "encounter" the religions and in general they work with more of a factual knowledge of non-Christian faiths. But their final evaluation follows, for the most part, that of Hendrik Kraemer,[148] the Dutch missiologist who, perhaps more than any other thinker, molded Protestant mission theology during the first half of this century: they reject the extreme tones of Barth's "No" to the religions, seek to communicate with them, but do not really arrive at a counter-position to Barth; the religions remain "man's works" – within the precincts of the Law – a negative preparation for Christianity.

2. *Gerhard Rosenkranz*[149] – Here again we hear a sincere plea for dialogue with the religions,[150] and for a thorough, phenomenological knowledge of them.[151] Rosenkranz also clearly recognizes a presence of God within the reli-

145 Reinhardt, pp. 184–185.
146 Ibid., p. 182.
147 Rose, p. 197.
148 Kraemer's position – which exercised a minor influence on Althaus (CW, pp. 138, 144; GD/I, p. 103) – was basically Barthian, especially as expressed in his classical and highly influential work written for the Tambaram Conference, *The Christian Message in a Non-Christian World* (London, 1938). In his *Religion and the Christian Faith* (London, 1956) he admits that his earlier work saw the religions too exclusively as human achievements and did not allow for true dialogue. (cf. Preface) Yet in his post-War studies on the religions he does not arrive at a "fully consistent alternative" and in fact asserts a "reinforced emphasis on discontinuity, which, it seems, is more radical than his earlier view of controversy". (Hallencreutz, *New Approaches*, pp. 48, 52–53). For Kraemer's final reassertion of discontinuity cf. *The Communication of the Christian Faith* (London, 1957), pp. 71–79; *World Cultures and World Religions* (London, 1960), pp. 96–97; *Why Christianity of All Religions?* Foundations of the Christian Mission (London, 1962).
149 Professor Emeritus of Missiology and Ecumenical Theology at the University of Tübingen.
150 Rosenkranz, *Der christliche Glaube angesichts der Weltreligionen* (Bern, 1967), pp. 47–54, 214, 283–291.
151 "Wege und Grenzen des religionswissenschaftlichen Erkennens", *Religionswissenschaft und Theologie*, Aufsätze zur evangelischen Religionskunde (München, 1964), pp. 28, 35.

gions and is against considering them only as "Entartung".[152] Yet with equal
vigor he is opposed to speaking about a real revelation within the religious world.
Such a doctrine, based on the concept of the "logos spermatikos", is "ein lebens-
gefährliches Symptom" for a theology of religions,[153] and is stoutly contradicted
by the "facts" of the history of religions; the religions' concept of God and their
religious terminology in general are opposed to that of Christianity.[154] Rosenkranz therefore accepts "die Kritik Feuerbachs": the religions are a purely human
affair in which man seeks self-redemption and self-glorification.[155] The
foundation for such a verdict is clearly Rosenkranz' understanding of Christ and
justification. Only here do we find revelation and salvation.[156] Because Christ
proclaimed the "Word" of "sola fide" it is "ein Wort radikal anderer Art"[157]
which leaves the world of religions under "der Decke der Selbsterlösung", in
"grenzenloser Verlorenheit und Verlassenheit".[158] This means: "Der Schau der
Religionen im Namen Christi bleibt versagt, in ihnen Anknüpfungspunkte, logoi
spermatikoi, auch nur 'Petites traces' oder ein 'dunkel Fünklein' zu finden."[159]
The only possible ground of dialogue is to be found in the "Existenzerfahrung" –
i.e. the religions' failing attempts to answer the questions of "des Leidens, der
Not, der Schuld, des Todes ...".[160]

3. *Walter Holsten*[161] – In his efforts to establish comparative religions as a
theological discipline[162] Holsten renders even clearer the central place which the
doctrine of justification is to hold in a theological understanding of the religions.
Presupposing that every science needs a point of reference, he proposes "als
gemeinsame Voraussetzung der Religionswissenschaft" the Christian Kerygma, i.e.
"das Kerygma nach reformatorischem Verständnis" – man's lost state and salvation only through faith and grace in Christ. The religions are therefore seen as
various expressions of the same human condition: man's need of God's intervention in "sola fide" and "solus Christus".[163] This "presuppostion", which excludes any possibility of revelation or salvation in the religions and which provides
"eine prinzipielle Erledigung" for "das viel verhandelte Problem der Anknüpfung",[164] is the basis on which Holsten also seeks to carry on a dialogue with the
religions – a dialogue, we feel, in which the religions have nothing more than a
negative contribution to make.

---

152 *Der christliche Glaube*, p. 215; id., "Was müssen wir heute unter Absolutheit des Christentums verstehen?", ZThK, 51 (1954) 111–113.
153 "Wege und Grenzen", p. 21; "Absolutheit", pp. 114–115.
154 Ibid., p. 116. cf. also *Der christliche Glaube*, p. 243.
155 Ibid., p. 116; "Wege und Grenzen", pp. 35–36.
156 "Absolutheit", p. 119; "Wege und Grenzen", p. 34–35.
157 *Der christliche Glaube*, p. 278, cf. also p. 296.
158 Ibid., pp. 301–302.
159 "Wege und Grenzen", p. 36.
160 *Der christliche Glaube*, p. 291.
161 Professor of Missiology at the University of Mainz.
162 *Das Kerygma und der Mensch*. Einführung in die Religions- und Missionswissenschaft
   (München, 1953), pp. 9–10, 34–38, 85.
163 Ibid., pp. 43–55.
164 Ibid., pp. 86–89.

4. *Peter Beyerhaus*[165] — Seeking after a theology of the religions which balances the traditional approaches of continuity or discontinuity, Beyerhaus affirms that it is necessary "das sola fide und solus Christus im reformatorischen Sinne neu zu bezeugen".[166] This demands a "tripolares Religionsverständnis" in which the religions show a "Bezogenheit auf Gott", "das Bemühen Gottes" and "den Einflußbereich der dämonischen Mächte".[167] The practical consequences of such an understanding: the religions can never be "ways of salvation"; they are caught up in a "sündige Abwandlung der religiösen Aufgabe"; they are "gezwungen aus Gott gegen Gott zu leben ... immer weiter von Gott weg und damit in den Streit wider Gott"; they never can fully lose their quality as "Gegner" to the Gospel. [168] — Their role, so it seems, turns out to be basically negative.[169]

5. *Georg F. Vicedom*[170] — In Vicedom we find a much clearer and more personal plea to understand the religions, to take them seriously and to avoid all hasty condemnations deriving from "einer maßlosen Überheblichkeit der Christen".[171] He acknowledges a revelation within and as the origin of the religions and finds in them "die volle Würde der Gottesebenbildlichkeit".[172] And yet, because of his understanding of true revelation and salvation only in Christ, he places the religions within the "Erhaltungsordnung Gottes" as opposed to the order of salvation.[173] "... dürfen wir mindestens so viel sagen, daß er (God) durch die Religionen die Erlösungssehnsucht in den Menschen wachgehalten hat ..."[174] The religions, however, have "das Gottesverhältnis so umgekehrt, daß sie anderen Mächten und nicht mehr Gott die Ehre geben".[175] What they do not have and cannot understand and what Christianity brings as "etwas radikal Neues" is "die Erlösung aus Gnaden".[176] Christianity must therefore also be "Kritik und Ende des falschen Glaubens" in the religions and bring them "eine *neue* Gottesgemeinschaft" which is given in faith in Christ.[177]

---

165 Professor of Missiology and Ecumenical Theology at the University of Tübingen.
166 "Christliche Theologie verdient ihren Namen nur insoweit, wie sie entschlossen ihren Stand in der christologischen und soteriologischen Mitte der biblischen Botschaft nimmt." "Zur Theologie der Religionen im Protestantismus", KuD, 15 (1969) 101.
167 Ibid., p. 103.
168 "Religionen und Evangelium", pp. 131–132.
169 Cf. also P. Beyerhaus, *Die Grundlagenkrise der Mission* (Wuppertal, 1970), in which he defends this same basic position against modern sociological-political interpretations of missionary work.
170 Professor of Missiology at the Augustana-Hochschule, Neuendettelsau.
171 *Jesus Christus und die Religionen der Welt* (Wuppertal, 1966). p. 86.
172 Ibid., pp. 64–72, 86, 141, 150; cf. also, id., "Die Religionen in der Sicht von Neu-Delhi", in *Fuldaer Hefte* 16, p. 22.
173 *Jesus Christus und die Religionen*, p. 150.
174 Ibid., p. 141.
175 Ibid., p. 150.
176 Ibid., p. 151; "Die Religionen in der Sicht von Neu-Delhi", p. 21.
177 *Jesus Christus und die Religionen*, p. 152. Yet Vicedom, in his Christian concern, feels that on the basis of 1. Tim. 4,10 we cannot exclude salvation within the religions. But neither can we say just how it takes place. Here he states that salvation is possible for the individual, without implying that the religions themselves exercise any kind of an instrumentality (i.e. as "Heilswege") in the gift of justification; cf. ibid., p. 142.

6. *Hans-Werner Gensichen*[178] — Even more resolutely than Vicedom, he calls for a new, more positive approach to the religions, abandonment of the old discontinuity-continuity pattern and a dialogue in which the religions are respected and thoroughly known.[179] Yet, his own theological position within this dialogue is not always perfectly clear. He urges direct encounter, especially in the missions, through simple witnessing, without asking what is the salvific state of the non-Christians or whether they offer "Anknüpfungspunkte".[180] And still, when he does touch on a theological judgment of the religions, he seems to prefer Dantine's approach from justification "sola fide" and Ratschow's dialectic of Law and Gospel.[181] He himself can remark that "die guten Werke" of the religions are always "ambivalent und vermögen den rechtfertigenden Glauben nicht zu ersetzen",[182] that the Gospel is not only "Herausforderung" but also "Krisis aller Religionen",[183] "daß für die Menschheit in keinem änderen Heil ist als in Jesus Christus, und daß nur im Kraftfeld dieses Heils die Solidarität der Sünde von der Solidarität des Glaubens überboten wird".[184] But just how far does this "Kraftfeld" extend? Can the religions find salvation? Or do they remain within the realm of the Law? — Such questions, we feel, are not necessarily answered negatively but neither are they answered clearly.

7. *Horst Bürkle*[185] — He represents one of the boldest calls for dialogue and one of the most positive theological approaches to the religions which we find among contemporary Protestant mission-theologians in Germany. To an extent he stands as an *exception* to the "opinio communis". This is seen especially in his general approval of the "cosmic Christology" as proposed by the young mission Church, mainly in India,[186] and in his argument that "Jesus Christus ... als Herr der Geschichte" participates in the movement of all history and makes all history and all religions theologically relevant.[187] Yet, in our opinion, Bürkle does not fully respond to the objections he himself lists against a "cosmic Christology"; i.e. that it does not do justice to the traditional doctrine of justification and the reality of sin in the religions.[188] Further, one has the impression that he interprets God's and Jesus Christ's presence in the religious world only insofar as God is bringing about "die Voraussetzungen für sein (the non-Christian's) Christwerden",[189] or,

178 Professor of Missiology and Comparative Religions, University of Heidelberg.
179 "Wirklichkeit und Wahrheit", pp. 41–43; "Die christliche Mission", pp. 66–72.
180 "Die christliche Mission", pp. 72–79.
181 "Wirklichkeit und Wahrheit", pp. 96–97.
182 "Der Synkretismus als Frage an die Christenheit heute", EMZ, 23 (1966) 61.
183 Ibid., p. 64; cf. also p. 65 where he refers to the new religions as "theologisch beurteilt, Werke des Gesetzes".
184 "Herausforderung", p. 86.
185 Professor of Missiology and Comparative Religions at the University of München.
186 "Die Frage nach dem 'kosmischen Christus' als Beispiel einer ökumenisch orientierten Theologie", KuD, 11 (1965) 103–115, esp. 110–113.
187 "Zum Problem des Dialogs", *Jahrbuch Evangelischer Mission*, 1968, pp, 42–43.
188 "Die Frage", p. 107; cf. W. Andersen, "Jesus Christus und der Kosmos", *Christus und die Welt*, Heft 13 (Bad Salzuflen, 1963), also in EvTh, 23 (1963) 471–493; G. Rosenkranz, "Die Rede vom kosmischen Christus angesichts der indischen Geisteswelt", EMZ, 20 (1963) 145–160.
189 Bürkle, "Zum Problem", p. 42.

in the terminology frequently employed by Bürkle, only insofar as God is providing "Auslegungsmittel" for the Gospel.[190] How positive is this "Auslegungsmittel"? Can the religions, before they encounter Christ, overcome sin and find salvation through it? Is God's presence in them only "preparatory" or can it also be salvific? Again, we feel that such questions are not clearly confronted.[191]

8. *Der Deutsche Evangelische Missions-Tag* together with "Die Arbeitsgemeinschaft Evangelischer Missionen", in their Meeting in September 1966, offer a particularly sharp formulation of the "opinio communis" of mission theologians. It was expressed as part of their *commentary on "Nostra Aetate"*, Vatican II's Declaration on the Non-Christian Religions.[192] They flatly state that they cannot accept Vatican II's positive evaluation of the religions because it is not consistent with the *Evangelium von der Rechtfertigung des Sünders*.[193] The Council, they feel, bypassed the Gospel and based their views on a "Verständnis der natürlichen Offenbarung". Loyal to the doctrine of justification, they counter: "So finden wir auch nirgends in den nachchristlichen Religionen eine besondere Offenheit für das Evangelium." There can be no "Anknüpfung an die Religiosität" of the religions. Rather there must be a clear "Bruch".[194] – A similar attitude was voiced in the "Frankfurter Erklärung zur Grundlagenkrise der Mission": "(Wir) verwerfen ... die Irrlehre, als ob die Religionen und Weltanschauungen auch Heilswege neben dem Christusglauben seien." The statement insists on the necessity of conversion and sees dialogue with the religions as "allein eine gute Form missionarischer Anknüpfung".[195] – Therefore: absolutely no salvation in the religions; at the most, a negative preparation for the Gospel.

190 "Die Frage", p. 112; "Synkretismus", p. 150; "Zum Problem", pp. 42–43, where he speaks of "Auslegungsprinzip". And in this context he proposes dialogue in the sense of H. Kraemer! cf. "Synkretismus", p. 149.

191 Even in Bürkle's statement that the cosmic Christ is "das 'punctum mathematicum' der Rechtfertigung in seiner Projektion auf die Welt als Ganzes" it is not celar whether this projection means only a preparation for or also a realization of justification in the non--Christian world. "Die Frage", p. 114.
   Holding more or less the same "progressive" position as Bürkle is Werner Kohler. He states that the very nature of theology and Christianity demand a more informed study of the religions. "Towards a Theology of Religions", *Japanese Religions*, 4.3.1966, pp. 33–34; "Theologie und Religion", op. cit., pp. 462–463. And in a rather general way, he states that a "good theology" will recognize God's presence and activity in the religions ("Theologie und Religion", p. 465–467) and that missioners should not simply seek to "convert" the religions. "Kirche und Mission im Umdenken", EvTh, 30 (1970) 390–391. Yet here, too, the vital questions as to what kind of divine activity we can find in the religions and whether in the light of the "solus Christus" they can serve as ways of salvation, are not, we feel, sufficiently confronted.

192 As published in "Unser Verhältnis zur römisch-katholischen Mission", EMZ, 24 (1967) 33–38.

193 Ibid., p. 36.

194 Ibid., p. 37.

195 Released by the "Theologische Konvent", March 4, 1970, Thesis 6, as quoted in epd Dokumentation 35/70, p. 5. Cf. M. Mildenberger, "Dialogfähige Theologie", ÖR, 21 (1972) 47.

§ 76. Conclusion: Althaus Still a Valid Case Study

Our brief analysis of three representative contemporary Protestant theologians — Fritzsche, Ratschow and Pannenberg — and our survey of what seems to be the "opinio communis" of present-day systematic and mission theologians indicates that our presentation and critique of Althaus as a Case Study for a Protestant Theology of the Religions still is valid for contemporary Protestant thinking in Germany. Summing up our survey, we can draw basically the *same conclusions* and raise the *same questions* as we did after our study of Althaus:

Conclusions:

a) All of the theologians we studied show the clear resolve to abandon or avoid the *extreme negativsm of Barth's early position,* and at the same time not to fall into a *relativistic watering down of the Gospel,* as exemplified in Troeltsch.

b) They all call for a new and serious confrontation with the religions, a *dialogue* with them. Most of the theologians also emphasize the need for a sound, factual study and *knowledge of the science of religions.*

c) In their attempts to come to a theology of the religions, they all hold to what we may call *some form of revelation* within them, even though many rule out or avoid such terminology (Fritzsche, Ratschow). For all of them, God is somehow present in the religions — in a God-inspired "Fragen nach Gott" (Fritzsche) in his "Hervortreten" (Ratschow), in the divine "Wirklichkeit" (Pannenberg), in a "Strahl gottheitlicher Glorie" (P. Brunner), in the activity of the "Schöpfer" (Kimme), as an "ontological thirst" (Dantine), as a "Bezogenheit auf Gott" (Beyerhaus). And this divine presence or revelation must have a definite meaning within a theology of the religions.

d) Yet in all these cases, in explicit or implicit reference to the *doctrine of justification* or to the unique *salvific role of Christ* there is a *negative attitude* concerning the *possibility of salvation* in or through the religions:

— either salvation is expressly ruled out and the religions are considered to be works of sin and attempts at self-redemption (Fritzsche, P. Brunner, Kimme, Rosenkranz, Holsten, Beyerhaus);

— or without expressly condemning the religions, it is implied that they cannot find salvation insofar as they do not understand the "sola fide" or cannot find satisfying answers (Ratschow, Pannenberg, Trillhaas, Böld, Dantine, Mann [in early stage] Vicedom);

— or the question of possible salvation through the religions is passed over or not given a clear answer. (Gensichen, Bürkle)

e) The result of this express or indirect denial of the possibility of salvation within the religions is that the revelation or presence of God within the religions is either

— *practically denied*: the possibility of knowing God never becomes an actuality, or the "true" God is never known.

— *severly limited*: the non-Christian always misuses this revelation and thus renders it ineffective; or its true contents can be known only "von Christus her"; or it remains in the realm of searching and questioning and can never find any satisfying answers.

Questions — Does not all this mean:

a) The religions are to be interpreted within the categories of the *Law*: they can prepare the non-Christians for Christ but they can never be instruments in bringing them Christ and his salvation?

b) Their positive elements or their "truth" amount to only a *searching* and *questioning* but never to a finding of God (i.e. salvation)?

c) Their *role of preparing* for Christ is therefore basically a *negative* one: they reveal man's need, his searching, and his sinfulness?

d) In our dialogue with the religions we must insist that *only we* who have Christ have the *real answers* — i.e. answers which bring salvation? [196]

196 Agreeing with our evaluation of the "opinio communis" within present-day Protestant thinking on the religions is *Owen C. Thomas* who also feels: "The interpretation of other religions most widely held among contemporary Protestant theologians is based on the ideas of a general or universal divine revelation and of human sin." — i.e. in which "this divine self-disclosure is distorted and corrupted by sin" and man "always turns away from the true God and worships an idol". (*Attitudes toward Other Religions*. Some Christian Interpretations (London, 1969), pp. 24—25) — English-speaking Protestant theologians who propose much the same evaluation and approach to the religions as that contained in the German "opinio communis" are: S. Neill, *Christian Faith and Other Faiths*: The Christian Dialogue with Other Religions (London, 1961); id., *Creative Tension* (London, 1959); N. Smart, *A Dialogue of Religions* (London, 1960); L. Newbigin, *The Finality of Christ* (London, 1969); id., *A Faith for this one World* (London, 1965).

210

Conclusion

Agenda for a Protestant-Catholic Dialogue Concerning the Religions

The purpose of this study was not merely to point out and clarify the achievements and problematic of a Protestant Theology of the Religions as illustrated in Althaus and verified in our survey of contemporary German Protestant theologians. We also want to make a small contribution to "setting the stage", as it were, and to determining the "Anknüpfungspunkte" for a dialogue between Protestant and Catholic thinking on the religions — and thus to arrive at a more balanced *Christian* theology of the religions. *Only through such dialogue*, we feel, can this balance — which today seems to be missing on both sides — be achieved.

In a sense, the foregoing pages in themselves have been a form of critical dialogue by the very fact that they have been written by a Catholic, from his Catholic standpoint. From this same standpoint — which, to be more precise, is that of the *"new view"* of the religions as proposed by the school of Karl Rahner and fostered by Vatican II[1] — we would now like to suggest the *guidelines*

---

1 The following works represent this new, more positive attitude towards the religions within present-day Catholic theology: K. Rahner, "Christentum und die nichtchristlichen Religionen", *Schriften zur Theologie* V, pp. 136–158; id., "Weltgeschichte und Heilsgeschichte", *Schriften* V, pp. 115–135; id., "Die anonymen Christen", *Schriften* VI, pp. 545–554; id., "Anonymes Christentum und Missionsauftrag der Kirche", *Schriften* IX, pp. 498–515; id., "Kirche, Kirchen und Religionen", *Schriften* VIII, pp. 355–373; id., "Der Mensch von heute und die Religion", *Schriften* VI, pp. 13–33; id., "Atheismus und implizites Christentum", *Schriften* VIII, pp. 187–212. – K. Rahner and H. Vorgrimler, "Offenbarung", *Kleines Theologisches Wörterbuch* (Freiburg, 1961) pp. 265–269; op. cit., "Uroffenbarung", pp. 372–373; op. cit., "Nichtchristliche Religionen", pp. 261–263. – H. R. Schlette, *Die Religionen als Thema der Theologie* (Freiburg, 1963); id., *Colloquium salutis – Christen und Nichtchristen heute* (Köln, 1965); id., *Die Konfrontation mit den Religionen* (Köln, 1964); id., "Religionen", *Handbuch Theologischer Grundbegriffe*, Vol. II (München, 1963) pp. 441–450; id., "Einige Thesen zum Selbstverständnis der Theologie angesichts der Religionen", *Gott in Welt*, Vol. II (Freiburg, 1964), pp. 306–316. – O. Karrer, *Das Religiöse in der Menschheit und das Christentum* (Freiburg, 1934); J. Masson, "Face aux religions non-chrétiennes", *Spiritus*, 25 (1965) 416–425. – J. Heislbetz, *Theologische Gründe der nicht-christlichen Religionen* (Freiburg, 1967); G. Thils, *Propos et Problèmes de la Théologie des Religions Non Chrétiennes*, 1966; id., "La Valeur Salvifique des Religions Non-Chrétiennes", *Repenser la Mission* (35ème Semaine de Missiologie de Louvain, 1965), Louvain, 1965; – E. Schillebeeckx, "The Church and Mankind", *Concilium* 1 (1965) 34–50, J. Feiner, "Kirche und Heilsgeschichte", *Gott in Welt*, Vol. II (Freiburg, 1964), pp. 317–345; J. Neuner, ed., *Christian Revelation and World Religions* (London, 1967); H. Nys, *Le Salut sans l'Evangile* (Paris, 1966); P. Schoonenberg, *Gottes werdende Welt* (Limburg, 1963).
Concise summaries of the new Catholic position are offered by: H. Waldenfels, "Das Verständnis der Religionen und seine Bedeutung für die Mission in katholischer Sicht", *EMZ*, 27 (1970) 125–159; id., "Christentum und Weltreligionen in katholischer Sicht", *Kirche in der Zeit*, 22 (1967) 347–358; id., "Die Heilsbedeutung der nichtchristlichen Religionen in katholischer Sicht", *Die vielen Wege zum Heil*, hrsg. von W. Molinski (München, 1969), pp. 93–125. – E. Fahlbusch, "Theologie der Religionen. Überblick zu einem Thema römisch-katholischer Theologie", *KuD*, 15 (1969) 73–86; J. Finsterhölzl, "Zur Theologie der Religionen", *Kairos* 7 (1965) 308–318; P. Schreiner, "Roman Catholic Theology and Non-

according to which such a dialogue might be continued. Confronting the main conclusions of our study with the essential elements of this new Catholic Theology of the Religions, we will point out, as *concisely* as possible, the issues which must be clarified if dialogue is to be fruitful and a more balanced view of the religions is to be achieved. Our intent is not to *begin* the dialogue but to indicate its *contents*.

Since we are speaking from "the Catholic side" we will show first where the Catholic theologian must *listen to* and then where he must *question* his Protestant partner.

I. Listening

Our emphasis, in these last chapters, on the "tensions, unclarities and contradictions" within our case study might have given the impression that therefore Althaus' "attempt" at a Protestant theology of the religions is to be rejected, or that only his "bright picture" of the religions is to be accepted and used in the dialogue with Catholic attitudes. On the contrary! There may be much within Althaus' negative view of the religions which we cannot accept or which we feel must be clarified. But at the same time, and this must be emphasized, it contains truths which *must* be part of any theological interpretation of the religions — truths which are not always so evident in many "progressive" Catholic theologians as they plot *their* way between Troeltsch and Barth.[2] A dialogue with Althaus and

Christian Religions", JES, 6 (1969) 376–399; E. Verastegui, *Les Religions non-chrétiennes dans l'histoire du salut* (Diss., Gregoriana, Rome, 1968) (manuscript); W. Bühlmann, "Die Theologie der nichtchristlichen Religionen als ökumenisches Problem", *Freiheit in der Begegnung* (Frankfurt, 1969), pp. 456–462; A. Darlapp, "Religionstheologie", *Sacramentum Mundi*, IV, pp. 263–271; D. Wiederkehr, "Die Aussage der heutigen katholischen Theologie über die nichtchristlichen Religionen", *Kath. Missionsjahrbuch der Schweiz* (Freiburg, 1966), pp. 6–28; J. Neuner, "The Place of World Religions in Theology", *The Clergy Monthly*, 32 (1968) 102–115.

For the "support" which Vatican II has provided this positive outlook on the religions, cf. Rahner, *Schriften* VIII, p. 357; K. Müller, *Die Kirche und die nichtchristlichen Religionen*, (Der Christ in der Welt 8, Aschaffenburg, 1968), esp. pp. 78–99; J. Masson, "La Déclaration sur les Religions non-chrétiennes", NRTh, 97 (1965) 1066–1083. — But that this support evinces a certain reservation and unclarity, cf. Waldenfels, "Das Verständnis", pp. 128–135; P. Hacker, "The Christian Attitude towards non-Christian Religions", ZMR (Münster), 55 (1971) 90–95.

2 That there is much within the "new Catholic views" of the religious world which seems to blur over many elements of Christian doctrine has also been argued by other Catholic theologians. In fact, a tendency within present-day Catholic theology shows a striking affinity to Althaus. It emphasizes that while there is a revelation in the religions, we must be extremely careful about calling the religions ways of salvation. Rather, they are imperfect (negative) ways of preparing for Christ. Such attitudes are reflected especially among French theologians, under the lead of J. Daniélou. J. Daniélou, *Le mystère du salut des nations* (Paris, 1948); id., "Histoire des religions et histoire du salut", *Essai sur le Mystère de l'Histoire* (Paris, 1953); id., *Dieu et nous* (Paris, 1956), cf. esp. Chapter II: "Le Dieu des religions"; id., *Holy Pagans of the Old Testament*, trans. by Felix Faber (London, 1957); id., *Prayer as a Political Problem*, trans. by J. R. Kirwan (New York, 1967), cf. Chapter VI:

contemporary Protestant thought will help them re-clarify (or relearn?) such truths. Such a "listening dialogue" would be directed to four main topics.

§ 77. The Reality of Sin and Rebellion against God

1. There is a certain danger within the new Catholic approach to the religions that the reality of sin in human nature and in the religions is not sufficiently recognized or is thrown unduly into the background.

a) In emphasizing the *universal possibility of grace* as not just a theoretical but an actual possibility which confronts every non-Christian in such a way that he cannot avoid it,[3] the impression is easily given that the possibility of salvation becomes a probability and even a certainty. As if salvation were necessarily the rule and sinfulness the exception!

b) Also, in stressing the universality and the potency of God's *salvific will*[4] a possible conclusion is that this will overcomes or nullifies the reality of man's rebellion against it. It is forgotten that while the universality of this will is certain, the universality of its realization is not. God's universal will to save does not destroy the possibility of the individual's — or religion's — will to sin and to turn from God.

"Religion and Revelation"; id., "Christianisme et religions non-chrétiennes", *Etudes*, 321 (1964) 323–336; J. Dournes, *Dieu aime les paiens*. Une mission de l'Eglise sur les plateaux du Vietnam (Paris, 1965); id., *Le Père m'a envoyé* (Paris, 1965); H. Maurier, *Theologie des Heidentums*, trans. by J. Bettray (Köln, 1967), cf. esp. "Fünfter Teil: Theologie des Heidentums und missionarische Pastoral", pp. 205–242; E. Cornelis, *Valeurs chrétiennes des religions non-chrétiennes*. Histoire du salut et Histoire des religions. Christianisme et Bouddhisme (Paris, 1965); H. de Lubac, *Paradoxe et mystère de l'Eglise* (Paris, 1967), cf. esp. Chapter IV, "Les religions humaines d'après les Pères", pp. 120–167; id., *Catholicism*. Les aspects sociaux du dogme (Paris, 1952⁵), cf. esp. Chapter VII: "Le salut par l'Eglise"; R. Girault, *Evangile et Religions aujourd'hui* (Paris, 1969); J. Ratzinger, "Kein Heil außerhalb der Kirche?", *Das neue Volk Gottes*. Entwürfe zur Ekklesiologie (Düsseldorf, 1967), pp. 339–361, esp. pp. 353–355, 360; id., "Das Problem der Absolutheit des christlichen Heilsweges", op. cit., pp. 362–375, esp. pp. 365–370; also in *Kirche in der außerchristlichen Welt* (Regensburg, 1967), pp. 7–63, esp. pp. 12–20; M. Seckler, "Sind Religionen Heilswege?", StZ, 9 (1970) 187–194; P. de Letter, "Non-Christian Religions", *The Clergy Monthly*, 29 (1965) 12–21; B. Stoeckle, "Die außerbiblische Menschheit und die Weltreligionen", *Mysterium Salutis* II, pp. 1049–1074, esp. pp. 1065, 1072–1074; H. Fries, *Wir und die anderen* (Stuttgart, 1966), pp. 240–272; L. Elders, "Die Taufe der Weltreligionen. Bemerkungen zu einer Theorie Karl Rahners", ThGl, 5 (1965)124–131; H. van Straelen, "Our Attitude Towards Other Religions", *Worldmission*, 16 (1965) 71–98; id., *The Catholic Encounter with World Religions* (London, 1966); Verastegui, pp. 58–135.

3 Rahner and his school can speak about a "universalen Heilsoptimismus" (*Schriften* VIII, pp. 196, 194), of a "Heilsuniversalismus" (Heislbetz, p. 39, cf. pp. 38–47) and can maintain that a "Heils-... und Glaubensgeschichte...der allgemeinen profanen Geschichte koexistent ist". (Rahner, *Schriften* V, p. 123) Cf. also: Rahner, *Schriften* V, pp. 145–147, 153–157; VI, pp. 549–550; VIII, pp. 207–208. Verastegui, pp. 186–190; P. Fransen, "How Can non–Christians Find Salvation in Their Own Religions?", *Christian Revelation and World Religions*, J. Neuner, ed. (London, 1967), pp. 67–122.

4 Cf. Chapter IV, ann. 119. Also: Rahner, *Schriften* V, pp. 144–145; VIII, pp. 193–196, pp. 357–362.

c) Catholic theologians speak so strongly of the religions being taken up in a *"supernatural existential"*[5] that it is easily forgotten that they are also infected by what we may call the "infralapsaric existential". It is not sufficiently pointed out that as closely as nature may be wed to grace, nature still retains the scars of its fallen state. Such theologians seem to forget that the radicality of sin and evil in man is also part of traditional and sound Catholic doctrine.[6] And while we must emphasize that in the religions "where sin did abound, grace did more abound" (Rom. 5,20), the fact remains that sin still can abound!

d) When the reality of sin and *evil* in the religions is acknowledged, it is sometimes *"played down"* by adding that there was also corruption in the Old Testament which did not prevent it from being a "valid religion"; or that there is a difference between doctrinal evil in the religions and ecistential evil in the individual;[7] or that there is evil on "both sides", in Christianity and in the religions, and God can allow and "get along" with such evil.[8] All this is true, but it must not blur the fact that evil remains in the religions, and it *can* corrupt both doctrine and individuals.

2. Therefore in their dialogue with Protestant Theology of the Religions, as outlined in our case study, Catholic theologians will have to listen carefully to the Reformational insistence on the reality of the *Law* and of God's *wrath*. (cf. § 51/1–2; § 56–57) Although they may feel that the order of the Law should not be separated from the order of the Gospel, they must concede that the two are *distinct* and that where Christ is not yet known, the quality of the Law, with the ensuing divine wrath, can easily predominate.[9] This does not lead to the automatic condemnation of the religions but to the *readiness*, when confronting them, to recognize their possible evil. It will help theologians not to close their eyes to the very real *opposition* to the Gospel which, as missionaries insist, is frequently to be found in the non-Christian religious world.[10]

§ 78. Christocentrism — Christ the Cause and Source of Salvation

1. There can be no doubt that Catholic theology of the religions seeks to evaluate the religions from a Christocentric standpoint; yet although the *figure* of Christ is strongly emphasized, the *centric* aspect of his redemptive role is not

---

5 Cf. § 30. Cf. Rahner and J. Ratzinger, *Offenbarung und Überlieferung* (Freiburg, 1964), pp. 14–19; Rahner, "Existential, übernatürliches", LThK[2] III, p. 1301; *Schriften*, VI, p. 549; VIII, p. 361; id., *Kleines theologisches Wörterbuch*, pp. 266–267; K. Riesenhuber, "Der Anonyme Christ, nach Karl Rahner", ZKTh, 86 (1964) 290–295; Heislbetz, pp. 56–66.

6 Cf. H. G. Pöhlmann's description of Catholic teaching on this point, *Rechtfertigung* (Göttingen, 1971), pp. 95–135, esp. pp. 133–135; also Rahner, "Gerecht und Sünder zugleich", *Schriften* VI, pp. 262–276.

7 Rahner, *Schriften* V, pp. 148–150, 128–129; VIII, p. 370; Heislbetz, pp. 169–175.

8 Schlette, *Die Religionen*, pp. 121–122; Feiner, pp. 337–338.

9 Cf. Pöhlmann's argumentation that the reality of the order of the Law was clearly admitted by the Councils of Trent and Arausicanum; op. cit., pp. 82–85, 63–71.

10 Cf. for instance, van Straelen, *The Catholic Encounter with World Religions*, pp. 29–41.

always clearly presented. The Christology of these new views forms one of their most controversial aspects.[11]

a) In the understanding of the "absoluteness" of Christ as the "rendering conscious", the "explicitation", the "reflex consciousness", the "concrete visibility", the "Gewußte" flowing from the "Bewußte", the final appearance of the revelation-salvation which was *already* (possibly) there in the religions,[12] there is a danger that this Christocentrism be reduced to the *intellectual realm of consciousness*. Christ then seems to have only an "akzidentelle Bedeutung" of rendering something consciously clear.[13] He comes as a "grundlegende und unüberholbare Deutung" of what the religions already are; but one must ask "... ändert sich die Welt im Kommen Christi?"[14] Some have even asked whether this clarifying-centric role even makes the "christologische Vermittlung" appear "überflüssig".[15] This danger is especially evident in the much-discussed theory of *"anonymous Christianity"*: did Christ come merely to give a name to a reality which, before him, was nameless? [16]

b) This leads to possible misunderstandings concerning Christ as the *final cause* or the *sacramental sign* of salvation within the religions.[17] The danger is that Christ is presented too much as a "finis" or a "signum" and not enough as a "*causa*" or as a "signum *efficax*" (which a sacrament, in Catholic doctrine, always is). He is not seen sufficiently as the real *source* of the salvation which the

---

11 Cf. P. Hacker, "The Christian Attitude", pp. 81–97, esp. pp. 88–89; A. Gerken, *Offenbarung und Transzendenzerfahrung*. Kritische Thesen zu einer künftigen dialogischen Theologie (Düsseldorf, 1969), pp. 56–62, 72–75... The bulk of criticism against Rahner's theory of "anonymous Christians" is aimed at his Christology. Cf. below, ann. 16.

12 Rahner, *Schriften* V, pp. 125–127; VIII, pp. 362–363; VI, pp. 548–549; IX, p. 175; id., *Kleines Theologisches Wörterbuch*, p. 267; id., *Offenbarung und Überlieferung*, pp. 15–16; Feiner, p. 325; Schlette, *Die Religionen*, p. 90.

13 M. Vereno, "Von der All-Wirklichkeit der Kirche", ThQ, 138 (1958) 398.

14 H. Waldenfels, "Das Verständnis", p. 147.

15 Gerken, p. 74, cf. also pp. 72–75, 56–62.

16 Rahner describes and defends his position in:"Die anonymen Christen", VI, pp. 545–554; "Atheismus und implizites Christentum", VIII, pp. 213–217; "Anonymes Christentum und Missionsauftrag der Kirche", IX, pp. 498–515. An excellent summary of his views is offered by K. Riesenhuber, op. cit.; Anita Röper "expands" on Rahner's theory in *Die anonymen Christen* (Mainz, 1963); cf. also L. Roberts, *The Achievement of Karl Rahner* (New York, 1967), pp. 275–288. Rahner's understanding of Anonymous Christianity is criticized and/or rejected by: H. Kruse, "Die Anonymen Christen exegetisch gesehen", MThZ, 18 (1967) 2–30; H. Schlier, "Der Christ und die Welt", GuL, 38 (1965) 416–428; H. de Lubac, *Geheimnis aus dem wir leben* (Einsiedeln, 1967), pp. 149–154; H. U. von Balthasar, *Wer ist ein Christ?* (Einsiedeln, 1967); id., *Cordula oder der Ernstfall* (Einsiedeln, 1966); id., *Rechenschaft* (Einsiedeln, 1965), p. 92.

17 Cf. ann. 12; also Rahner, *Schriften* IX, p. 510. The understanding of Christ as a "sign" or "final cause" is contained in the Catholic view of the Church as the "Signum universale salutis"; cf. P. Knitter, "The Church before the Non-Christian Religions", *Verbum*, 10 (1968) 359–365; K. Rahner, *Christian of the Future* (London, 1967), pp. 82–83; id., *Schriften* VI, p. 483; H. Küng, "The World Religions in God's Plan of Salvation", *Christian Revelation and World Religions*, pp. 58–66; Thils, *Propos et Problèmes*, pp. 191, 65; Schillebeeckx, "The Church and Mankind", pp. 46–47; Feiner, p. 325; for the teaching of Vatican II, cf. "Lumen Gentium", § 1, § 16, § 48; Ad Gentes, § 1.

religions might attain — the *reason* why such salvation is at all possible. He becomes too easily merely the end-product or the final realization of a supernatural movement which was already there without him.

c) And this exposes the new Catholic theology of the religions to the danger of *explaining Christ in the light of the religions* instead of the religions in the light of Christ. (Barth would call it the danger of "Religionism")[18] Or: the religions seem to be in a process of bringing themselves to Him rather than He, as the sole and universal Mediator, bringing the religions to Himself.

2. Therefore Catholic theologians will do well to lend an attentive ear to the Protestant insistence, typified so clearly in Althaus, on the "solus Christus" (cf. § 58–61) — i.e. on the necessary role of Christ in the mystery of redemption.

a) This will render Catholic thinkers more mindful that although they can discuss whether Christ brings salvation more as a "causa finalis" or as a "causa efficiens", he always remains the *cause* and source of salvation. This is also "Catholic doctrine".[19] He alone is mediator between God and man. (1. Tim. 2,5) In no other name is there salvation. (Acts, 4,12) Thus even though other religions may, in God's disposition, share in Christ's causality, they remain subordinate causes and cannot function without him.

b) In their dialogue Catholic theologians will have to ask themselves what it means to come into *direct contact* with this cause, i.e. what it means for a non-Christian religion to be "fulfilled" in Christ. Since such contact is with not only a "sign" but a "cause" and "source", it will have to bring something more than greater "clarity" or "consciousness".[20]

c) Conversely, Catholic theologians will also have to ask themselves: where this *direct contact* with Christ through Word and Sacraments is *not* had in a religion, will not this lack necessarily be evident in their systems and doctrines? Will not their revelation and their understanding of salvation *necessarily* be incomplete? And does not this lack imply a *warning* against too facile statements that the religions can already have everything the Christian Faith has, except the name? What is missing will frequently be something more than "full consciousness" or clarity.

d) Althaus' reformational insistence that salvation can be found only in the historical "*Tatsache*" and the "*Wirklichkeit*" of Christ (cf. § 58/2, § 59) can also serve Catholic theology as a reminder against too readily and assuredly concluding that since *grace* is a universal reality, it *must receive an historical visible expression*

---

18 Cf. § 10/3.

19 Denzinger-Schönmetzer, *Enchiridion Symbolorum*, 1523, 1560; cf. Bühlmann, p. 472; Rahner, *Schriften* VI, pp. 545–546; VIII, pp. 355–356; Thomas Aquinas: "Sed gratia non derivatur a Christo in nos mediante natura humana, sed per solam personalem actionem ipsius Christi." ST III, q.8, a.5, ad 1.

20 Just what this "something more" is, has to be determined through further dialogue and study. We feel that it does not simply mean that we as Christians have "more salvation" or that we are more "secure" or more easily saved. Perhaps it can be said that, *objectively*, knowing Christ we are granted access to God in a way "preferred" by God before all other ways. God's plan is realized fully. *Subjectively*, being in direct contact with Christ through Word and Sacrament, we can more fully *enjoy* God's revelation and the glory of being his children. We do not possess more of God's grace and love, but our capacity to participate in this grace and love is rendered greater in Christ.

and mediation in the religions. This is one of the key arguments in the new Catholic interpretation of the religions: grace must take on historical — social forms.[21] This is true in itself. But it is frequently forgotten that the only historical-social form which grace, as it were, *had* to assume (according to God's plan) was Jesus Christ. All other forms — and this includes the religions — can or cannot be made use of; and all other forms, once adopted as "means of grace", remain ambivalent: they can help or they can hinder.

§ 79. Proper Relation between General and Special Economies of Salvation

1. While unanimously admitting that there is a twofold economy of salvation, contemporary Catholic theologians sometimes offer misleading explanations as to how the two economies unfold and how they are related to each other. Such unclarities or dangers are closely tied together with those we noted concerning Christ as the cause and source of salvation. They can be summed up under two concentric considerations:[22]

a) In many Catholic proposals for a theology of the religions the *basic unity of salvation history* — i.e. God's one plan for mankind — seems to suffer. These theologians attest to the unity of the divine economy in Christ, and yet the general and special orders of salvation are often presented in such a way that they seem to run entirely *parallel*[23] or *independently* of each other — as if they were two totally different orders, as if they could and were meant to function on their own. It is stated: "daß die Religionen Heilswege sind, ist von Gott gewollt, — *unabhängig* von dem speziellen Heilsweg Israels und der Kirche."[24] The general order of salvation is said to *suffice* of itself, without the special order.[25] Further, it is suggested that God does not intend any "innergeschichtliches" coming together of the two orders,[26] that it be God's will that they run parallel until the "eschata" and only then will a relation and unity between them be established.[27]

b) Missing the prevading and divinely-intended unity in the history of salvation, Catholic theologians also incur the danger of obfuscating the *subordination* of the general order of salvation to the special. If the two orders can run parallel to each other, can it still be argued (as every Christian theologian must argue) that the special order of the Gospel and Christianity is really *necessary* — or that the

---

21 Rahner, *Schriften* V, pp. 150–152, 154, 124; VIII, pp. 370; Heislbetz, pp. 70–101; Feiner, p. 337; Schlette, *Die Religionen*, p. 82.

22 For an excellent and widely-praised summary of the two stages within God's History of Salvation, cf. A. Darlapp, "Fundamentale Theologie der Heilsgeschichte", *Mysterium Salutis*, I, pp. 1–156.

23 Schlette, *Die Religionen*, p. 122.

24 Ibid., pp. 84–85.

25 Feiner, pp. 325–326; Schlette, *Die Religionen*, p. 90.

26 Schlette, *Die Religionen*, p. 106.

27 Feiner, pp. 329–332; Schlette, *Die Religionen*, pp. 119–120; id., "Einige Thesen", pp. 312–313; cf. also Rahner, *Schriften* V, p.129; VIII, p. 364. — This danger of splitting the unity of salvation history is less evident in Rahner's and Schillebeeckx's views — although their highly optimistic descriptions of the availability of revelation and salvation in the general orders might give the impression that this order can and should be left to operate on its own. Cf. eg. Schillebeeckx, "The Church and Mankind", p. 40.

general order is of itself imperfect until it is incorporated into the special — or that the general order contains a dynamic orientation towards this completion in the special order of Christ? Such arguments become dangerously difficult especially in the Catholic proposal that the religions be considered the *ordinary* way of salvation and Christianity the *extraordinary*.[28] What is "extraordinary" would seem to be only an addition to or embellishment of the ordinary. This is also the danger in speaking of the Christian or special order as merely the "Epiphany" or full expression of the general order in the religions: we end up explaining the Christian order as the result or end effect of the general order; Christ and the Gospel, as we noted above, lose their role as the cause of salvation and as the dynamic force within the general order.[29]

2. So once again, Catholic theologians will have to listen carefully — this time to Althaus' insistence, in the name of his Reformational heritage, that "Uroffenbarung" or the general phase of God's plan, is *different* from "Heilsoffenbarung", or his special stage in Christ — a difference which will set the two in a relationship of subordination within the *one* history of salvation. Such dialogue will remind Catholic thought that God's "general" activity within the religions is not yet his "special" working in Christ and that therefore this general order must be imperfect and insufficient and cannot be left or thought to operate on its own. Although Catholic theologians may argue about the degree of these imperfections, they will have to agree with their Protestant partners that this order is imperfect, that it needs Christ, that it cannot come to itself until it has come to Him — until the full unity of God's plan is achieved. Catholic thought on the religions, therefore, will have to take seriously the Protestant repetition of the *"von Christus her"* which we have heard throughout these pages. It will insure that in their efforts to interpret the general order of the religions more positively and to grant them a role as "ways of salvation" they will also bear in mind and try to understand more fully that the religions, in God's one plan, remain only a *temporary* way, a way of *preparation* (negative and positive!) for God's special intervention in the Incarnation of his Son.

§ 80. The Abiding Meaning of Mission

1. One of the most virulent criticisms against recent Catholic evaluations of the religions has been that they undermine the meaning, the élan and the practical carrying-out of the Church's *"missio"* to the nations. Much in these criticisms, in our estimation, is emotionally overloaded and oversimplified.[30] Yet they do point

28 Schlette, *Die Religionen*, pp. 85–86.
29 Schlette can even claim that "der erste Sinn" and "das wesentliche Motiv" of the special order in Christ is not salvation but the "Epiphanie Gottes" — the clarification of salvation. But does not this imply that salvation can be offered without Christ's mission? *Die Religionen*, pp. 90, 92, 79.
30 This is the case, for instance, when it is argued that the preacher of the Word cannot burn with a sense of mission unless he feels he is bringing salvation to the otherwise lost. Cf. the lamentations of F. Legrand, editor of the apostolic review, *Christ to the World*. Cf. op. cit., "Is it the Purpose of the Mission to Bring Salvation?", 10 (1965) 221–231, cf. also 288–290; also van Straelen, "Our Attitudes towards Other Religions", *Worldmission* 19 (1965) 76; id., *The Catholic Encounter*, pp. 71–91. — For the general problematic,

out an uncomfortable obscurity as to the "why" and "what" of missionary endeavors.

a) If Christ is not really the cause or the bringer of salvation might we not be content to let the religions abide with their own God-given expressions of revelation and salvation?

b) If the general order of the religions is really a parallel, independent way of revelation and salvation, why must we try to urge them to "change their ways"? Or, if they constitute the "ordinary" path to God, is it really so imperative that we add on what is "extraordinary"?

c) If the purpose of heralding the Word is not so much to change the religions themselves or to bring them anything which essentially they did not already have, but only to change their "reflex consciousness" and offer them a "new name", is this task really so pressing? [31]

2. Therefore in their dialogue with Protestant proposals for a theology of religions, Catholic theologians will have to take seriously what was Althaus' *motivation* in confronting the religions: to *defend* and *clarify* the abiding purpose of Christianity's *mission* to all nations. (cf. § 16/1) A deeper understanding of the religions, if it is a truly Christian understanding, will lead to a deeper grasp of the Kerygma and its urgency.

a) Catholic attitudes will also have to weigh carefully Althaus' and the Protestant conviction that if we take Jesus Christ seriously we will have something *new* to offer the religions, something which they do not yet have and which they *need*. If Catholic thought insists that this "something" is not simply "salvation for the heathen", Protestant views add that neither is it merely an "illumination" or "identification" of the salvation which was already there.

b) Further, Catholic theologians will have to try to integrate into their own views Althaus' insistence that missionary dialogue and confrontation with the religions will always include some form of "Kampf" and dialogical intolerance (WE,6; CW, 135—136; ER, 17), and that it will always lead to some form of "Bruch" and of "conversio". (cf. § 50) Here is a healthy warning against an imbalanced stress on missionary work as a process of simply fulfilling or bringing the religions to themselves. Catholic theology of the religions, in dialoguing with our case study, will have to ask itself whether it has neglected the element of "metanoia" which is always included in the acceptance of the Gospel.

cf.: J. Schütte, *Mission nach dem Konzil* (Mainz, 1967); J. Masson, "Salvation Outside the Visible Church and the Necessity of the Mission", *Christian Revelation and World Religions*, J. Neuner, ed. (London, 1967), pp. 123—142; Schlette, "Mission — Ende oder Anfang?", *Hochland*, 55 (1962) 74—79; M. J. Le Guillon, "Die Mission als ekklesiologische Problematik", *Concilium* 2 (1966) 194—218; E. Hillman, "Die Hauptaufgabe der Mission", *Concilium*, 2 (1966) 159—162; P. Knitter, "Anonymous Christianity and the Missions", *Verbum*, 10 (1968) 402—405; Verastegui, pp. 314—320.

31 As an indication that such questions are not unfounded cf.: Rahner, *Schriften* V, p. 155; VI, p. 487; IX, pp. 512—514; E. Hillman, "Anonymous Christianity and the Missions", *Downside Review* 85 (1966) 361—380; id., "Ecumenism and Grace", *African Ecclesiastical Review*, 8 (1966) 16 ff.; Schlette, *Die Religionen*, p. 19; Heislbetz, pp. 214—218. — This entire question becomes all the more consequent when it is argued that missionary work should have "keine andere Sorge...als daß der Hindu ein besserer Hindu, der Buddhist ein besserer Buddhist, der Moslem ein besserer Moslem werde". H. Halbfas, *Fundamentalkatechetik* (Düsseldorf, 1968) p. 241.

II. Questioning

We will now try to formulate the *questions* which, as a Catholic theologian, we would like to propose for consideration by our Protestant colleagues. This is but a summing up of the questions we have already confronted and partially articulated throughout this study. They are questions which, we feel, pinpoint the *central unclarities* and *weaknesses* in many of the Protestant views we have studied — questions which, hopefully, *can* be clarified through Protestant-Catholic dialogue and which *must* be clarified in order to reach a unified, balanced Christian theology of the religions.[32]

Our questionings can be broken down into *two practical* and *four dogmatic* areas.

Practical Questions

§ 81. Concerning Dialogue

1. Is it *possible* to carry on a practical, effective dialogue with the religions if they know that before meeting them we aprioristically and categorically *deny* them the *possibility of finding salvation* through their doctrines and practices? We have witnessed Althaus' and contemporary theologians' fervent desire for true encounter with the religions. But is such an encounter with the religions as religions — not just with the non-Christian individual and his "good will" — possible when they know that because of our "Christian premises" we cannot allow them a true encounter with God? Can we expect them to seek dialogue with us if they know they are looked upon only as a "negative preparation for Christ", as an expression of "Bedürftigkeit" and unsuccessful seeking after union with God, as "Auslegungsmaterial" for the Gospel? Can the religions feel themselves to be true partners in dialogue if, from the Christian standpoint, all they can have are *questions* which at the most "point in the right direction", while only we can have true answers — i.e. answers which include God's gift of redemption?

2. Does not effective and true religious dialogue require that *both* partners have the grace-given capacity to be children of God, not only "in potentia" but "in actu" — and that this capacity be acknowledged and respected on both sides? This does not mean that to dialogue we must concede, apriori, that the religions *are* ways of salvation — but only that they *can* be. Whether we can judge the capacity to be a reality will be the fruit of dialogue.

§ 82. Concerning the Relation between Theology and Comparative Religions

1. Can a theology of the religions be elaborated and take on final form without a thorough, personal knowledge of the religions? Can a theologian attempt to be a "theologian of the religions" without being a "Religionswissenschaftler"? We have

32 We should add that although these questions have flowed from our case study of Althaus and are directed to Protestant thinking, they can also frequently be well applied to many aspects of present-day Catholic interpretations of the religions.

220

heard Althaus' argument that theology is possible only in constant dialogue with the immediate situation; (cf. § 18/2) and applying this to the religious world, he could even speak, somewhat vaguely, about a necessary verification of Christian assertions through study of the religions. (cf. § 16/1) Such methodological principles were clarified and emphasized even more strongly by contemporary theologians, especially by Ratschow and Pannenberg.

2. And yet our study of Althaus' and contemporary theologians' "conclusions" concerning the religions prompts the question whether they have sufficiently given ear to the "facts" of the science of religions? Frequently they pronounced categorical statements about the religions which are difficult to verify in the concrete study of comparative religions − eg. concerning the religions' faulty concept of a personal God or of guilt, or their false understanding of salvation as a divine gift. Historians and phenomenologists of religions warn especially against too blithely judging the religions according to "das reformatorische Rechtfertigungs- und Gnadenprinzip" and concluding that all religions seek salvation through their own works. Such an "interpretation of the facts" is "geschichtlich und religionsphänomenologisch eine unzulässige Vereinfachung",[33] "einfach nicht wahr".[34] Indeed, recent Protestant theology of the religions seems to have "developed from the logical implications of the doctrine of revelation and sin ... *apart from direct knowledge* of or contact with other religions. That is, it often tends to become an abstract theological exercise rather than a real attempt to interpret *the reality* of the other religions from the point of view of Christ".[35]

3. Will not a more thorough, concrete knowledge of the religions prevent theologians from rashly drawing either too negative *or* (and here we turn to Catholic theologians) too positive judgments concerning the religious world outside of Christ?

Dogmatic Questions

§ 83. Concerning God's Salvific Will

1. Can theologians assert *the reality* of God's universal salvific will *without acknowledging and trying to trace* the *effects* of this reality *in the extra-Christian order?* We have seen that Althaus held firmly to the "Heilswillen Gottes" in Christ and that he attested to the universality of this will and its radiance beyond the forms of the Christian community. (cf. § 43) Yet we also noted his reluctance to

---

33 K. Goldammer, "Die Bibel und die Religionen", *Fuldaer Hefte* 16 (Berlin, 1966), p. 122.
34 U. Mann, *Theogonische Tage* (Stuttgart, 1971), pp. 145; cf. also Kohler, "Theologie und Religion", *Glaube, Geist, Geschichte* (Leiden, 1967), pp. 462−463. Examples of historians of religions who argue for a genuine understanding of the "sola fide" in certain religions are: G. Mensching, *Söhne Gottes* (Wien, 1958), pp. 407 ff. and 359; F. Heiler, *Erscheinungsformen und Wesen der Religion*, 1961, pp. 509−514, 564; Joachim Wach, *Religionssoziologie* (Tübingen, 1951), p. 430; P. O. Ingram, "Shinran Shōnin and Martin Luther: A Soteriological Comparison", JAAR, 39 (1971) 430−447, esp. 442−446.
35 O. Thomas, ed., *Attitudes toward Other Religions*. Some Christian Interpretations (London, 1969), Forward, p. 25. emphasis mine.

admit the effects of this will in any historical or social form outside of Christ. He preferred to call its workings a mystery forbidden to theological examination. More often he preferred to transfer the concrete effects of this will to some point beyond time and history. (cf. § 51/4) We also noted this same reluctance among some of the contemporary theologians we surveyed: while admitting the force of God's will to save all men, they neglected or forbad any conclusions concerning "Heilsmöglichkeiten" outside of Christ. (cf. eg. § 75/5—6) — Is this not curtailing the task of the theologian, who, always beginning with the truths of revelation (in this case, the "voluntas salvifica"), is to seek after the meaning and effects of these truths in the concrete order? And is there not a certain contradiction in asserting that God's salvific will is universal, and at the same time maintaining that the effects of this will cannot be experienced or certified within the concrete order? Would not this imply that God carries out his salvific will in a certain docetistic manner — beyond the body and beyond human history?

2. More concretely, can a theologian assert God's universal will to save all men and at the same time insist that it is absolutely impossible for the religions ever to be ways of salvation — i.e. that this divine will can never have any effects within or make use of these religions? No doubt, God's ways are multifarious and his salvific will can take many forms in confronting the individual. Yet it is an existential fact that for the majority of men the questions of God, of good and evil, of dedication to something beyond one's self are mediated through their religions. Can we be so certain that God's salvific will, as expressed in Jesus Christ, will never make use of such pre-Christian forms of mediation? And if we do deny this, are we not only denying what, humanly speaking, seems to be a "logical" expression of this will but also the freedom and omnipotence of God? — To avoid a misunderstanding: by this we are not arguing that the religions *must be* or *always are* "ways of salvation" but only that we cannot exclude the possibility — or the probability — of them being instruments of God's salvific will.

§ 84. Concerning Revelation

1. Can we *separate* the reality of *revelation* from that of *salvation*? — We have seen how Althaus, throughout his doctrine of Uroffenbarung, sought to distinguish between revelation in the religions and revelation in Jesus Christ. The two, though related and though forming one salvific plan of God, are *not* the same. Such a distinction can never be neglected, for otherwise we run the risk of falling into the "Catholic error" of placing the "general" and the "special" orders of salvation history on the same level and letting them run parallel and totally independently of each other. We need differences in order to preserve unity through subordination — differences in the nature, forms and efficiency of revelation in Christ and revelation in the religions. But our question is: can — or may — these differences be expressed in the basic distinction "Uroffenbarung" in the religions and "*Heils*offenbarung" in Jesus Christ? In other words: on the one side — divine revelation *without* salvation, and on the other — divine revelation *with* salvation? This leads us to the very fundamental question concerning the theological concept of revelation.

2. Does not the *nature of all revelation*, as defined by Althaus and as traditionally understood by both Protestant and Catholic theologians, include the *possibili-*

ty of salvation? Where genuine, divine revelation is acknowledged, there is also the offer of saving grace and the possibility of man being opened to this offer. True revelation cannot take place without illuminating grace and the gift of the Spirit – and it is this grace and Spirit which enable man to respond to the gift of divine love.[36] Where true revelation is present, salvation must be possible. We pointed out such an apparent possibility in Althaus' understanding of Uroffenbarung. He spoke about Uroffenbarung as always being accompanied by an interior illumination which makes known not the God of reason but the personal God and his offer of love. (cf. § 35/3, § 44) And yet even though Althaus could posit these essential divine ingredients for an act of faith, he could not posit the possibility of their product. Is there not a contradiction here? If Althaus can speak of such a richly equipped revelation "extra Christum sed propter Christum", why should he not allow the possibility of salvation outside of but because of Christ?

3. Therefore, if Protestant theologians, as we have noted, can speak of a truly divine revelation outside of Christ – i.e. not just a "natural revelation" or man's natural seeking after meaning and happiness but an active presence of God, a real "Hervortreten" of the divine – then should they not be able to speak also of the possibility of divine salvation outside of Christ? Not to do so seems to introduce a caesura in the normal progression of divine activity and communication. Can God truly reveal himself without truly offering himself? – Here we would prefer the hard logic of Barth: if one insists on the impossibility of salvation outside the historical point of Christ, then one must also include the impossibility of revelation outside of Christ.

§ 85. Concerning Justification

1. If we adhere to the *"traditional" Reformational doctrine* of justification, as "faithfully" preserved and applied by Althaus, is it at all *possible* to come to a *positive evaluation of the religions*? Our study has indicated that it does *not* seem to be possible. As much as Althaus, and so many contemporary German Protestant theologians, seek a more open confrontation with the religions, their final verdict, because of the "sola fide" and "solus Christus", cannot allow the religions to be "Heilswege" and must evaluate them basically as an expression of man's needs and questions – a negative preparation for Christ. – This conclusion prompts the further and more fundamental question:

2. Does the *substance* of the doctrine of justification as contained in the New Testament and reaffirmed by the Reformers *allow for further (not different!) interpretations* which in turn would render possible a more positive verdict on the non-Christian religious world? In the light of recent Protestant-Catholic dialogue concerning justification we feel that it *does*. Indeed, if it is today generally conceded, from both sides, that "justification" is no longer a dividing line and that Protestant and Catholic theologians can agree as to the substance of this doctrine,

---

36 Rahner, *Offenbarung und Überlieferung*, pp. 18–23; *Schriften* VIII, p. 210; H. Waldenfels, *Offenbarung*. Das Zweite Vatikanische Konzil auf dem Hintergrund der neueren Theologie (München, 1969), pp. 83–84, 121–122, esp. 282–293; R. Latourelle, *Théologie de la Révélation* (Desclée, 1963), pp. 403–415; J. Alfaro, *Adnotationes in tractatum de Virtutibus* (Roma, 1959), pp. 157–163; Heislbetz, pp. 47–56.

then can they not agree as to the possibility of justification within the religions? In other words, if this deeper, common understanding of justification allows Catholic theologians to formulate a new, more positive judgment on the religions, cannot Protestant theology seek a similar judgment? The following questions indicate how this deeper or "further" interpretation of the "Rechtfertigungslehre" in relation to the religions might be made.[37]

3. Must justification, as a personal experience and as a doctrine, *necessarily contain* an *explicit experiencing* or *formulation* of *sin* as sin, of *guilt*, of *divine wrath*, of *God as Judge*? Must it require an explicit searching after a "gnädigen Gott"? As the Lutheran World Assembly in Helsinki (1963) admitted, it is "das Charakteristikum des modernen Menschen ... keine Not zu kennen" for which the traditional doctrine of justification provides an answer.[38] Man today seems to experience his perennial state of sin and guilt differently — in the frustrations of modern life, in alienation from self and others, in neglected responsibility to others and to society. If this is admitted for modern Western society, must not the theologian also be extremely careful in judging that the religions do not have a sufficient grasp of sin or guilt or judgment? Might not this necessary experience of sinfulness be sufficiently contained in what Althaus noted to be the religions' universal seeking after redemption or in what Ratschow termed their insight into "mortificatio-vivificatio"? Man can experience his sin without calling himself a sinner — and, if at the same time he turns to a supreme Being for an answer, is not this enough to open him to the gift of God's saving grace?

4. Must the "*works*" of the religions — their efforts to appease God or attain union with him through cult and ascetical practices — necessarily be considered *means of "self-redemption"* and thus inimical to the attitude of "sola fide"? Today it is admitted that according to Reformational teaching: "Die Rechtfertigung ereignet sich nicht *et* gratia *et* homine, aber auch nicht *sola* gratia sine homine, sondern paradoxerweise *sola* gratia *non sine* homine."[39] Therefore, as Althaus himself emphasizes: "Sola fide nunquam sola".[40] "Alles kommt aus dem Glauben, aber zugleich: alles liegt am Werk." (BR, 24) Works are not merely consecutive but also constitutive to the act of faith.[41] Faith can live only in works; they

---

37 Cf. esp.: Pöhlmann, *Rechtfertigung*, pp. 378–388, 17–18; V. Pfnür, *Einig in der Rechtfertigungslehre?* Die Rechfertigungslehre der Confessio Augustana (1530) und die Stellungnahme der katholischen Kontroverstheologie zwischen 1530 und 1535 (Wiesbaden, 1970), esp. pp. 385–399; H. Küng, *Rechtfertigung*. Die Lehre Karl Barths und eine katholische Besinnung (Paderborn, 1957⁴), esp. pp. 267–276; O. Pesch, *Theologie der Rechtfertigung bei Martin Luther und Thomas von Aquin* (Mainz, 1967), esp. pp. 949–956; A. Peters, "Reformatorische Rechtfertigungsbotschaft zwischen tridentinischer Rechtfertigungslehre und gegenwärtigen evangelischen Verständnis", LuJ, 41 (1964) 77–128, esp. p. 77; M. Bogdahn, *Die Rechtfertigungslehre Luthers im Urteil der neueren katholischen Theologie* (Göttingen, 1971), pp. 262–271.

38 *Offizieller Bericht* der 4. Vollversammlung des Lutherischen Weltbundes, Helsinki, 1963 (Berlin, 1965), p. 514; cf. also Ch. VI, ann. 129. Althaus makes a similar admission in *Die lutherische Rechtfertigungslehre und ihre heutigen Kritiker* (Berlin, 1951), pp. 5–7.

39 Pöhlmann, *Rechtfertigung* p. 153.

40 P. Althaus, "Sola fide numquam sola — Glaube und Werk in ihrer Bedeutung für das Heil bei M. Luther", *Una Sancta*, 16 (1961) 227–235.

41 Therefore the "überlieferten Formeln, der Glaube wirkt die Werke, die Werke folgen dem Glauben, sind unzulänglich. Er lebt in den Werken, in der konkreten Haltung und nicht

224

are a necessary, constitutive sign of the "sola fide".[42] "Glaube und Werke sind nicht *zwei Wirklichkeiten*, sondern *zwei Seiten* einer *einzigen Wirklichkeit* und so zwar *unter*scheidbar, aber *un*scheidbar."[43] — If all this is Protestant doctrine, can we exclude the possibility that the "works" of the religions might be expressions of a genuine submission to the majesty of God and the primacy of his grace? Can they not be a "signum constitutivum" of an attitude of "sola fide"? And can we be so certain that these works might not be the fruit of God's saving grace, which because of the salvific will, we know is universal? For the Christian, where there is genuine faith, there are works; for the religions, where we see works, might there not also be faith — two sides of the same reality?

5. Does the category of the *Law and the Gospel* allow for a *further interpretation* which would not necessarily brand the religions as Law and only Law? What cannot be re-interpreted or changed in this category is the existential *process* which it represents and which must always be present in every act of justification: man must experience his insufficiency, his sinfulness, and must suffer under the pain of the Law before he can experience and respond to the gift of the Gospel. Yet Reformational theology has also given this existential process a stringent historical or *epochal* meaning: it signifies not only two different "phases" within the mystery of justification but also *two different* phases or *stages within salvation history*. No doubt the epochal interpretation has its foundations in Scripture, as seen in Rom. 1,18—3,20; but its existential significance is just as essential — perhaps even more so — as indicated in Rom. 7. Therefore can we be certain that the epochal application is so clearly definable, i.e. that it divides history into two stages, one unredeemed and the other redeemed? While certain areas or phenomena within history, after investigation, can be called "Law" and others "Gospel", can we be certain that the Law corresponds neatly to the non-Christian order and the Gospel to the Christian? Could we not say, rather, that the vital process represented by the Law and the Gospel can be found in *both* orders of the economy of salvation? Just as the Law can and must continue to carry out its function in the special order of Christianity, so the Gospel, because of God's universal salvific will and the universal workings of the Incarnation, could anticipate its effects in the general order of religions. Thus, the Law would not be confused with the Gospel; it would continue to carry out its primary function as the "lex accusans, non-justificans, mortificans";[44] but this function would stand

---

ohne sie und außer ihr". (Althaus, "Gebot und Gesetz. Zum Thema 'Gesetz und Evangelium'", *Gesetz und Evangelium*, hrsg. von E. Kinder und K. Haendler (Darmstadt, 1968), p. 226, cf. pp. 227—234). "Die Liebe ist nicht nur konsekutivum, sondern konstitutivum des Glaubens, sosehr sie ihn nicht bedingt, sondern durch ihn bedingt ist." Pöhlmann, *Rechtfertigung*, pp. 264—265.

42 Althaus, "Sola fide numquam sola", pp. 232—234; CW, 643.

43 Pöhlmann, *Rechtfertigung*, p. 282. Pöhlmann shows that this is the traditional understanding of justification within the Lutheran Confessions (op. cit., pp. 256—265) and according to contemporary German Protestant theologians (pp. 265—268); cf. Althaus, *Die lutherische Rechtfertigungslehre und ihre heutige Kritiker*, pp. 21—28.

44 Pöhlmann, *Rechtfertigung*, pp. 50—57. It is this "existential" understanding of the Law which is endorsed by Catholic ecumenical theologians; cf. G. Söhngen, "Gesetz und Evangelium", *Catholica*, 14 (1960) 81—105; cf. also Bogdahn, pp. 218—236.

for a necessary element in *every* act of justification and not for a clearly-demarcated section of religious history.[45]

6. All these questions and considerations lead up to the broader query: is the *concept of* δικαιοσύνη — with its heavily negative content of "sin", "guilt", "wrath", "Law" — the only and the *best theological yardstick* to measure the question of salvation within the religions? Protestant theology today admits that in the New Testament the wonder of God's self-communication to man is expressed in other, quite different categories.[46] In the Synoptics man finds redemption in the *Kingdom of God* or of Heaven; John expresses the gift of salvation under the terms "ζωή", "φῶς", "δόξα".[47] While these other concepts by no means stand in contradiction to the contents of "justificatio", neither are they identical with or subordinated to it. Rather, all these concepts are but various aspects of the central mystery and work of Jesus Christ.[48] Therefore we can ask whether such other concepts might provide a more positive approach to the possibility of the religions being "ways of salvation". Althaus and Protestant theology in general can more easily speak of God's "light" or "life" or "glory" already shining partially within the religions; God's kingdom is already taking shape. Might these concepts and realities already contain a presence of salvation? This "life" or "light" would not yet shine with the radiance of Christ; this salvation therefore would not yet contain his "fullness of grace and truth". (John 1, 16—17) Yet, though in an imperfect stage, it would already be there. The non-Christians could therefore already be God's children not just "in potentia" but "in actu", although they would still have to grow into the fullness of age in Christ. (cf. Eph. 4,13)

7. The final answer to all these questions concerning the possibility of a further interpretation of the doctrine of justification hinges on the central and determinative question: *can the gift of justification and redemption be granted outside of* — but certainly not independently of — *the historical reality of Jesus Christ*? Or: is the "solus Christus" physically-objectively and psychologically-subjectively necessary for faith so that if a man is not in contact with or does not know of the "Tatsache" of Christ through Word or Sacrament he cannot attain salvation? Whether the religions might attain a sufficient understanding of sin and guilt in other categories, whether their works might be a sign of "sola fide" and "sola

---

45 Thus a failure to distinguish the Gospel and the Law would not lead to a "Gnadenmonismus" as Pöhlmann maintains (op. cit., pp. 71—72, 85, 381—382) but to an illogical, meaningless bestowal of grace to someone who doesn't realize why he needs it.

46 "Die Reformatoren glaubten, daß die Rechtfertigung das Thema sei, das das gesamte Neue Testament beherrsche. Jetzt erkennen wir, daß die Rechtfertigung zwar ein Bild ist, das in der frühesten christlichen Überlieferung erscheint, aber nur ein Bild unter den vielen, die herangezogen werden, um die Bedeutung der Tat Gottes in Jesus Christus zu entfalten...Können wir weiterhin behaupten, daß der Artikel von der Rechtfertigung der articulus stantis et cadentis ecclesiae sei, wenn sogar in der frühesten Periode des Lebens der Kirche die Möglichkeit bestand, das Evangelium ohne Bezugnahme auf ihn zu verkündigen?" *Über die Rechtfertigung.* Dokument Nr. 3, p. 7, 1963 (Prepared for Lutheran World Assembly, Helsinki, 1963), quoted in Pöhlmann, p. 31.

47 Pöhlmann, *Rechtfertigung*, pp. 34, 39—49. H. Conzelmann, *Grundriß der Theologie des Neuen Testaments* (München 1967), pp. 359—360; G. Klein, "Rechtfertigung", RGG[3] V, 827—828; also K. Kertelge, *"Rechtfertigung" bei Paulus* (Münster, 1967), pp. 286—304.

48 Pöhlmann, *Rechtfertigung*, p. 35.

gratia", whether the Law *and* the Gospel might be found in the religions, whether the Kingdom of God or his Light and Life might already be realized within them − all this will depend on whether the saving effects of the Incarnation extend beyond the historical visibility of Jesus Christ. Thus, our final and most essential question concerns Christology.

§ 86. Concerning Christology

1. Must the reformational *"solus Christus"* be understood as the *historically-limited fact of Christ* and as the historically-limited proclamation of this fact? Is the salvific activity of Christ to be limited to contact with him through the Word or Church? Our study has shown that Althaus and contemporary German Protestant attitudes towards the religions adhere to such a limitation. And they do so, in gereral, in the name of a sound Christocentrism. Yet, is not such a Christocentrism, when directed to the religions, only half effective? Is it not even more *intellectual* than *real*? By this we mean: from Christ as the center of all, Protestant theology seeks to *understand* the reality of the religions; it *interprets* their state of insufficiency and at most it detects a certain directedness of religious phenomena towards Christ. But *the reality* of the religions remains unaffected; they remain, basically, in their fallen state, confined in sin, able to seek but not to find. From Christ, the religions *are understood* but they are *not really changed* in the real order. The Incarnate Word makes them intelligible, perhaps directs them, but does not really change them and save them. Does not such a Christocentrism lead to what we have called a "christomonistic doctrine of justification"? (cf. § 68/3) Just as Barth, from his Christocentrism, proposed a christomonistic understanding of revelation and limited revelation only to the historical dimensions of Christ, has not Althaus, in the name of the Reformational heritage, done the same with justification?

2. Is not this a *too hasty* and *exegetically questionable limitation of the effects of the Incarnation*? Present-day Protestant theology stresses that the Incarnate Word fashions not only the "Erlösungsordnung" but also the "Schöpfungsordnung", that the two orders, while remaining different, are intertwined. In Jesus Christ, the order of creation is already part of the order of redemption − and vice versa.[49] Althaus himself clearly acknowledged this when he spoke of the universal presence of Christ or of the essential relationship or even unity between "Christusoffenbarung" and Uroffenbarung, or when he detected the presence of the Logos within the religions. (cf. § 46, § 22/2, § 40/1, § 34/4) If Jesus Christ is already present within the order of creation − the order of religions − and if this presence permits the theologian to speak of a divine revelation in the religions, why cannot this presence also bring about the possibility of justification and salvation? Why cannot the Universal Christ be truly universal in that he works not only revelation

---

49 Barth, KD III/1, § 41 "Schöpfung und Bund", pp. 44–377, esp. 46, 63–64, 262ff.; R. Prenter, "Die Einheit von Schöpfung und Erlösung", ThZ, 2 (1946) 161–182; G. von Rad, *Theologie des Alten Testaments*, Bd. 1 (München, 1961), pp. 140–144; C. H. Ratschow, "Das Heilshandeln und das Welthandeln Gottes", NZSTh, 1 (1959) 25–80; G. Wingren, *Schöpfung und Gesetz* (Göttingen, 1960); Küng, *Rechtfertigung*, pp. 138–150.

but salvation? This, we feel, would bring about a true Christocentrism and a complete "von Christus her": we would not be interpreting Christ from creation or from the religions, but "von Christus her" we would be able to speak about the possibility of both revelation and salvation throughout the universe.

3. Is not such an understanding of the universal Christ effecting a universal possibility of salvation not only possible but, in a sense, "*easier*" for Protestant theology — a theology, which, as illustrated in Althaus, holds that although salvation is mediated through the Word, it is essentially something internal; it is essentially the work of the "Spiritus Christi" bringing about personal illumination and encounter; without this Spirit — Word, historicity, witness, community and Church are meaningless. (cf. § 45)

> ... dann sollte es eigentlich einer sich. so verstehenden Kirche leichter sein als der katholischen, die so sehr ihren sichtbaren, inkarnatorischen Charakter betont, anzunehmen, daß der Mensch nicht nur ohne physischen Kontakt mit dem Sakrament, sondern auch ohne physischen Kontakt mit dem Wort, durch das verborgene Heilshandeln Gottes, durch den Geist (we can add: through the universal Christ), der letztlich keine Zeugen und keine Gemeinde 'braucht', gerettet werden und irgendwie der Geist-Kirche angehören kann, und zwar durch die mit der Schöpfung gegebenen Strukturen des persönlichen Gewissens und der geschichtlich gewordenen Religionen hindurch, deren sich der erlösende Gott (the universal Christ) als dem Menschen kongruente Medien bedient.[50]

This does not mean that Protestantism would be giving up its hallmark as "Worttheologie". Rather, the question is raised whether this theology has perhaps neglected other and broader dimensions of the "Word" — whether (similar to Catholic theology) it has too much limited the efficacy of this Word to a determined human mediation. Cannot Christ's saving Word make use of other and less perfect forms of mediation outside the Word of the Church to work salvation outside the Christian community?

4. A final, summarizing question: In their dialogue with recent Catholic theology of the religions and with the religions themselves, could not German Protestant theologians examine more carefully the contents and implications of the new attitude towards the religions proposed in recent years by various organs of the World Council of Churches and summed up, quite loosely, under the term *cosmic Christology*? We have not directly considered this new approach in our study since it is for the most part an "extra-continental" phenomenon and has not been absorbed into German Protestant thinking on the religions — and since it seems to be still in a process of self-clarification. While its terminology is highly controversial and perhaps not the best, it does represent, in its basic content and especially in the way it has been applied, an approach which, we feel, must be explored further. Proposed by Protestant theologians as consistent with their Reformational heritage,[51] it seeks to understand and encounter the religions not so

50 Bühlmann, op. cit., p. 476.
51 J. Sittler argues: "Mitten in einem gewaltigen Wandel in der Beziehung des Menschen zur Natur wurde wohl in der Tat die Souveränität und der Wirkungsbereich der Gnade durch die Reformatoren bezeugt und freigelegt. Aber nachreformatorische Verhärtungen ihrer Lehre führten dazu, daß die Wiedergewinnung der Christusbezogenheit der ganzen Natur als eines Bereiches der Gnade wieder zu einem untergeordneten Thema herabsank." "Zur Einheit berufen", *Neu Delhi 1961*. Dokumentarbericht über die Dritte Vollversammlung des Ökumenischen Rates der Kirchen, hrsg. von W. A. Visser't Hooft (Stuttgart, 1962), p. 516.

228

much from the doctrine of justification, not even from the doctrine of revelation – but from Christology and the mystery of the Incarnation. With this christological method they argue for a true Christocentrism which propels the reality of the Incarnation, its revealing and saving dynamism, into the "$\tau\grave{\alpha}\ \pi\acute{\alpha}\nu\tau\alpha$" – into the entirety of creation. (Col. 1, 15–20)[52]

52 The term "cosmic Christology" was introduced into World Council of Churches vocabulary by Joseph Sittler in his now famous address at the Third General Assembly of the WCC in New Delhi, 1961. (*New Delhi 1961*, pp. 512–523). Yet it reflects and intensifies the positive attitude which had begun to develop in the WCC already in 1952 at the Conference of the International Missionary Council in Willingen when the religions were seen to be part of the relationship between creation and redemption. This new approach gained momentum during the following years as the WCC abandoned the controversial category of continuity-discontinuity and sought to encounter and study the *concrete* religions. By 1958 the new attitude had established itself, as is evident in the Consultations in Bossey in which the relation between creation-providence and the reality of Christ was proposed as the pattern for judging the religions. Increasingly and with ever more positive results, the universal effects of the Christ-event (expressed frequently in the universal activity of the Spirit) were recognized in the religions: at the General Assembly in New Dehlhi, 1961 (*New Delhi 1961*, pp. 85–100); the World Mission Conference in Mexico City, 1963 (*In sechs Kontinenten*. Dokumente der Weltmissionskonferenz, Mexico, 1963, hrsg. von Th. Müller–Krüger, Stuttgart, 1964, pp. 147–157); at the Ecumenical Consultations in Kandy-Ceylon ("Christians in Dialogue with Men of Other Faiths", *Study Encounter* 3 (1967) 52–56; the inter-religious Consultations at Ajaltoun, Lebanon in March, 1970, and the "Zürich Aide–Mémoire" of European theologians in May, 1970 to the Ajaltoun sessions (in *Living Faiths and the Ecumenical Movement*, S. J. Samartha, ed., Geneva, 1971, pp. 15–45) and the Consultations in Addis Abeba 1971 (op. cit.., pp. 47–54). Some of the most stimulating incentives to this more positive approach to the religions have come from Indian theologians, in particular: Paul Devanadan, M. M. Thomas, A. J. Appasamy, P. Chenchiah, V. Chakkarai, and S. J. Samartha. (Cf. H. Wagner, *Erstgestalten einer einheimischen Theologie in Südindien*, München, 1963. S. J. Samartha, *Hindus vor dem universalen Christus*. Beiträge zu einer indischen Christologie, Stuttgart, 1970). – For an excellent presentation of the development in the WCC attitudes towards the religions, cf. the Münster Dissertation of Gérard Vallée, *Eine ökumenische Diskussion über die inter-religiöse Begegnung – von Tambaram nach Uppsala 1938–1968* (soon to appear in German and French) as well as his article "Die Zukunft des ökumenischen Dialogs mit Nicht-Christen", *Una Sancta* 26 (1971) 166–173; and, "The Word of God and the Living Faiths of Men: Chronology and Bibliography of a Study Process", *Living Faiths*, pp. 165–182.
For a presentation and analysis of the new "cosmic Christology" cf.: J. W. Winterhager, "Das Bekenntnis zum Christus Pantokrator und die Anfänge einer ökumenischen Theologie", (Ökumenischer Vorspruch) in: *Christus Pantokrator*, O. A. Dilschneider (Berlin, 1962), pp. 77–13; id., "Neu Delhi und die Anfänge einer ökumenischen Theologie", *Theologia Viatorum* VIII, Jahrbuch der Kirchlichen Hochschule Berlin, 1961–62 (Berlin, 1962), pp. 299–311; T. Ahrens, *Die ökumenische Diskussion kosmischer Christologie, seit 1961 – Darstellung und Kritik* (Promotionsarbeit, Hamburg, 1969); H. Bürkle, "Die Frage nach dem 'kosmischen Christus' als Beispiel einer ökumenisch orientierten Theologie", KuD, 11 (1965) 103–115; R. Scheffbuch, "Die Herausforderung von Neu-Delhi", *Lutherische Monatshefte*, 1 (1962) 2–13; W. Andersen, "Jesus Christus und der Kosmos", EvTh, 23 (1963) 471–493; G. Rosenkranz, "Die Rede vom kosmischen Christus angesichts der indischen Geisteswelt", EMZ, 20 (1963) 145–160; Hallencreutz, *New Approaches*, pp. 56–62.

Critically reviewing his own theology, Althaus could write:

> Es scheint mir, daß wir ... in der Christologie und Versöhnungslehre zu einer viel größeren Freiheit von der dogmatischen Tradition und ihren Begriffen und zu einem viel entschlosseneren Neubau verpflichtet sind, als das bisher im allgemeinen verwirklicht wurde. Ich habe das für meine Person vor allem an den beiden genannten Punkten versucht, vielleicht noch nicht radikal genug, noch nicht einfach genug, noch nicht lebensbezogen genug, ich weiß es nicht.[53]

Here, perhaps, is the fundamental neglect in Althaus' and many contemporary theologians' attempts to interpret the religions: they have not examined "Christologie", the mystery of Christ (and only then the "Versöhnungslehre") radically, simply and universally enough. Yet here, too, is the starting point and the roadsign which not only Protestant theology but Christian thought in general must adopt in their efforts for a theology of the religions: Jesus Christ and his work of redemption — Christology before all other dogmatic doctrines. For after all, this is the acknowledged central truth and common ground for all Christian confessions — not the "Rechtfertigungslehre", not ecclesiology, not the doctrine of revelation but the reality and mystery of Jesus Christ.[54] The more we understand him and what his coming meant for the entire world, the more we will understand, together, the religions.

III. A Final Word: The Hermeneutics of a Theology of the Religions

§ 87. Theological Principles Not Sufficient

Throughout this study we have been dealing with theological principles. We have pointed out what we considered to be the merits of our case study's principles for judging the religions, especially as contained in its allowance for divine revelation and a genuine content of truth in the religious world. We have also enunciated what seemed to be the weaknesses and unclarities in these principles, stemming from an all too stringent understanding and application of the doctrine of justification: "sola fide et solo Christo". And then, especially in this last section, we presented in question-form other "principles" by which these weaknesses might be removed and the positive content clarified.

But in all this, we *do not wish to imply* that once our theological principles have been clarified and perhaps even accepted by both Protestant and Catholic theologians, we will have thus arrived at a theology of the religions. This, precisely, is what can be called the "hermeneutical failing" in both Protestant and Catholic attempts to interpret the religions: they have worked exclusively or excessively — with principles; they have tried to come to final understanding — to judgments —

---

53 Quoted in W. Lohff, "Paul Althaus", *Theologen unserer Zeit*, hrsg. von L. Reinisch (München, 1960), p. 69. Cf. also *Tendenzen*, p. 301.

54 "Der articulus stantis et cadentis ecclesiae ist nicht die Rechtfertigungslehre als solche, sondern ihr Grund und ihre Spitze: das Bekenntnis zu *Jesus Christus*", Barth, KD IV/1, p. 588. "Die Rechtfertigungslehre ist *nicht* das Zentraldogma des Christentums...das *Zentraldogma* des Christentums ist das *Christus*geheimnis." Hans Küng, *Rechtfertigung*, p. 128. Pöhlmann, *Rechtfertigung*, pp. 23–49, esp. 30, 47–49.

primarily on the basis of their theoretical theological criteria. Working with what they felt were certain theological doctrines, they have judged and decided what a certain portion of reality *must* be, before they actually confronted this reality. And in this process, as we have frequently indicated throughout this study, they have seemed not only to misinterpret this reality of the religions but they have also misinterpreted, or exaggerated, or brought into contradiction their own theological principles.

Therefore we must emphasize: theological principles, or theological "clarity" is *not* enough to establish a theology of the religions which is deserving of this name. A theological understanding of the facts of the religious world can come only when our principles are confronted with these facts — i.e. only when our criteria are applied to, tested on and, even, understood within the phenomenological and existential data of the religions' creeds and practices. And this means that the theologian of the religions, before he can start "producing" or drawing conclusions, must study the religions and get to know them as personally as possible. These are what we feel to be the *three essential elements in the hermeneutics of a theology of the religions*: a) Well pondered and definite theological *principles* — from personal faith and reflection; b) A sound, *extensive knowledge* of the *contents* and *doctrines* of the religions — from the science of religions; c) A *personal knowledge* of the *living faith* of the religions — through dialogue with them. All three elements are essential. Naturally, the theological principles must hold the first place, otherwise we no longer are dealing with a *theology* of the religions. But if the other two elements are missing, the hermeneutic process is incomplete and proper understanding is not possible. .

§ 88. A Truly Dialectical Attitude Required

What our case study of Althaus and of contemporary Protestant approaches to the religions has sought to do is clarify theological principles *in order that* the hermeneutical process might more smoothly and efficiently unfold — in order that the theologian might more effectively and profitably study and encounter the religions and *thus* come to a theological understanding of them. The preservation of the positive elements in Althaus' Protestant approach to the religions and a correction of what we felt were its weaknesses (both indicated in the "Listening" and "Questioning" sections of this chapter) will lead to what we can call a *truly dialectical attitude* towards the world of religions which will make possible the necessary *openness* for confronting them and which will prevent undue pre-judgment or violation of the phenomenological facts.

By a "truly dialectical attitude" we mean: before approaching the religions or any one religion, we do not say from our theological principles that they cannot attain salvation, that they are confined in sin or that they contain only questions and searching; yet neither do we say that they are definitely ways of salvation, instruments of grace and in possession of a true knowledge of God. Rather, we are "open" to both these alternatives. For we know that sin and guilt and the "lex accusans" and God's wrath are realities — realities which can lock an individual or a religion in the state of "unfaith", of rebellion against God, of separation from Him — realities which have been overcome only in the incarnation, life, death and resurrection of the God-man, Jesus Christ. And yet precisely because God has entered the world in Jesus Christ, because he has been incarnated in and into the world, we also know that the effects of his coming — his revelation and his redemption — have been injected into the whole of creation. Therefore there is the possibility (not the necessity!) of true encounter with God, of salvation, throughout the world, also outside the visible dimensions of Christ, but not without Him. Wherever this possibility of salvation outside the visible Christ is realized, it is *genuine* salvation and communion with God, yet at the same time it is a salvation which, in God's one plan of redemption, must be completed in Christ, for here is the "final sign" and the "one cause" of God's gift of himself to man.

Therefore, our theological principles should place us in a truly dialectical attitude towards the religions, an attitude which opens us to alternatives in our judgments on the religions and which impels us to search for these judgments.

§ 89. Final Judgment through Confrontation

We can seek to formulate these judgments only through confrontation with the religions, in study and dialogue. In this concrete, personal encounter with them we will try to apply, test and better understand our theological principles. In examining the religions and especially in speaking with them, we will try to ascertain which of the dialectical alternatives seems to show itself or to predominate: — falsification of or rebellion against the one living God, or true knowledge of and devotion to him. By immersing our theological principles in this dialogical process, we will allow the truth to show itself. And we will not be afraid of whatever this truth may be: the discovery of hardened opposition to the Gospel, of irremovable differences and thus the necessity of our Christian "No" — or the discovery of the Kingdom of God, of genuine faith and thus the necessity of a brotherly "Yes". — In judging such truths we shall remain humble, knowing that our judgments remain human and are therefore open to correction — and especially that we are judging religious systems and doctrines, not individuals. Whether we pronounce a "Yes" or a "No" to a religion, we have not yet said anything about the state of the individual non-Christian in his conscience before God.

This process therefore will lead us to judgment on the religions. But it will also lead us to judgments on our own theological principles and doctrines. We will be examining not only the religions but ourselves. We will be "exposing" the contents and formulation of our own faith. This means that we will be open to the possibility that in this confrontation and dialogue with the religions we will see that we have perhaps not formulated our theological principles correctly, that we have not yet grasped the full contents and implications of our faith, that we have perhaps presented the alternatives between sin and salvation outside of Christ too sharply. Our encounter with the religions may lead us to an even clearer perception of the reality of sin and rebellion in the world — *or* to the reality and extent of the world's redemption in Jesus Christ.

******

To understand the religions, as we have said, we must try to grasp the heighth and breadth and depth of the mystery of Christ; and yet, by confronting the religions, by dialoguing with them and trying to understand them we will at the same time be led to an ever deeper penetration into this mystery which is the center of the Gospel and the center of all creation.

Zusammenfassung

Gegenstand und Ziel dieser Arbeit ist Paul Althaus' Theologie als ein "case study". Althaus' Werk soll uns eine Hilfe sein bei der Beantwortung der Frage: Was kann eine dem reformatorischen Erbe verpflichtete Theologie über die nicht-christlichen Religionen heute aussagen? Außerdem soll dieses "case study" ein kritischer Beitrag sein zur gegenwärtigen Besinnung der protestantischen Theologie auf die Welt der Religionen und zur ökumenischen Diskussion zwischen Katholiken und Protestanten über die Probleme der Begegnung mit den nicht-christlichen Religionen. Wir wählen Althaus' Theologie als Gegenstand unseres "case study", weil Althaus in seinem Versuch, die Religionen zu würdigen, 1) einen "Mittelweg" zwischen dem Relativismus Troeltschs und dem Exklusivismus Barths zu gehen versuchte und zugleich 2) der reformatorischen Tradition treu bleiben wollte (§§ 1–2).

Kap. I: *Between Troeltsch and Barth (Zwischen Troeltsch und Barth)*

I. In seinem Versuch eines neuen und "revolutionären" Verständnisses des Verhältnisses zwischen Christentum und anderen Religionen war *Ernst Troeltsch* ein gewaltiger Anreger nicht allein für Althaus, sondern auch für die gesamte protestantische Theologie (§ 3). Sein neuer Weg bestand in folgenden drei hermeneutischen Prinzipien: 1) Wissenschaftlicher Historismus, 2) Individualismus, 3) Evolutionismus. In der Aufstellung und Anwendung dieser Prinzipien zeigte sich Troeltsch als *der* "systematische Theologe" der "religionsgeschichtlichen Schule" (§ 4).

Aufgrund dieser drei Prinzipien kam Troeltsch zu einer *universalen, relativierten Offenbarungs*anschauung. Sie basierte auf einer Metaphysik der immanenten Transzendenz und einer Psychologie des religiösen apriori (§ 5). Dies führt Troeltsch zu einem Verständnis *der Religionen* als individueller Lebensformen oder Ausdrücke der universalen Offenbarung und als Elemente einer historischen Entwicklung. Jede Religion ist eine gültige, aber immer relative Bewegung auf ein absolutes Ziel hin, das jedoch erst am Ende der Zeiten offenbar wird. Dennoch konnte Troeltsch gewisse wissenschaftlich fundierte Werturteile über die Religionen fällen (§ 6). Deshalb unterscheidet sich nach Troeltsch das Christentum nicht wesentlich von den anderen Religionen und darf nicht als absolute Religion verstanden werden. Alle Theologie ist daher zweitrangig; den ersten Platz nimmt die Religionswissenschaft ein. Während Troeltsch früher von Christentum oder Christus als dem "Konvergenzpunkt" der Religionsgeschichte sprechen konnte, stellte er später eine Theorie der polymorphen, kulturellen Wahrheit auf, die alle Religionen total relativierte (§ 7).

II. Mit seinem Weg "von oben", d.h. der Transzendenz Gottes und seines Wortes, stand *Karl Barth* im diametralen Gegensatz zu Troeltsch (§ 8). Aus der Tatsache, daß Gott sich in Jesus Christus offenbart hat, zog Barth die christomonistische Schlußfolgerung: "Extra Christum nulla *revelatio*". Diese These hatte er schon im *Römerbrief* (2. Aufl., 1922) aufgestellt, noch deutlicher wurde sie in der *KD § 17* (1938) (§ 9). Barth kommt darüber hinaus *(KD 17)* zu dem Schluß: "Extra

Christum nulla *religio*". In den Religionen versucht der Mensch das zu erlangen, was ihm eigentlich nur in Christus begegnen kann: Offenbarung und Heil. Deshalb brandmarkte Barth alle Religionen als "Unglaube" und "Sünde" (§ 10). Wenngleich Barth der Religion zubilligte, eine gültige, untergeordnete Rolle zu spielen, und er nicht nur eine "destructio" der falschen Religion, sondern auch eine "elevatio" der echten Religion wollte, so war das für ihn jedoch nur in Christus, d.h. im Christentum möglich. Deshalb: "In Christo *una religio*". Das ereignet sich in einer Weise, in der Christus nichts von der Religion annimmt; Christentum ist "die eine wahre Religion", nicht in ihrem "Aktinhalt", sondern einzig und allein in ihrem göttlichen "Subjekt": Christus (§ 11).

Kap. II: *A Middle Way – A Protestant Way*
           (Ein Mittelweg: Ein protestantischer Weg)

I. Troeltsch und Barth bildeten die "Scylla und Charybdis" von Althaus' (und einer jeden) Theologie der Religionen und machten ihre Motivation,, Ziele und Grenzen deutlich (§ 13). In der Frage der *Offenbarung* lehnte Althaus Troeltschs relativistische Sicht als eine extreme Form des Idealismus ab. Andererseits konnte er auch nicht Barths christomonistischem Konzept folgen, das seiner Meinung nach eher in der zeitgenössischen Philosophie als in der Offenbarung und Heiligen Schrift seinen Grund hatte. Auf der Suche nach einem "Mittelweg" blieb Althaus Troeltschs Position näher als derjenigen Barths, indem er eine allgemeine Offenbarung lehrte und mit Troeltschs metaphysischer Grundlage vieles gemeinsam hatte (§ 14).

Althaus lehnte auch Troeltschs *Religions*lehre ab, die er sich in vielen jüngeren und zeitgenössischen Religionstheorien widerspiegeln sah. Auf der anderen Seite nahm er aber auch Stellung gegen Barths "rein anthropologische Religionstheorie". Sein "Mittelweg" zwischen beiden war wieder Troeltsch näher, insofern er den Religionen eine positive Funktion im Heilsplan Gottes zugestehen wollte (§ 15).

Althaus vermochte Troeltschs *Verständnis* des Verhältnisses zwischen *Christentum* und nicht-christlichen *Religionen* nicht zu folgen, weil es offenbar Sinn und Ziel der Mission zu untergraben schien. Diese Sicht verhinderte obendrein eine echte Theologie der Religionen, indem sie der Religionswissenschaft das erste und letzte Wort zubilligte. Aber Barths Auffassung der Absolutheit des Christentums gefährdete ebenso die Mission dadurch, daß sie jegliche "Anknüpfung" ausschloß. Gleichzeitig verhinderte sie die für eine Theologie der Religionen notwendige Beziehung zwischen Theologie und Religionswissenschaft. Auf diesem schwierigen "Mittelweg" war Althaus diesmal Barth näher als Troeltsch: Die Offenbarung und Religion Jesu Christi ist von jeder anderen fundamental unterschieden (§ 16).

II. Die Basis für Althaus' "Mittelweg" war eine theologische Methode, die man als *"protestantisch"* und *"inkarnatorisch"* charakterisieren kann. Althaus' Treue zum reformatorischen Erbe wurde ihm eingeprägt durch seine Familie, sein Göttinger und Tübinger Studium, seine Zugehörigkeit zur "Erlanger Tradition" und vor allem durch sein Lutherstudium und seine persönliche Zuneigung zu dem Reformator (§ 17).

Seine inkarnatorische oder anthropologische Methode war wiederum das Ergebnis der "Erlanger Tradition" und ihrer Betonung des Persönlichen, aber noch mehr ging sie auf A. Schlatters und M. Kählers Einfluß zurück. Schließlich verlangte auch Althaus' Verständnis der Natur Gottes und des Glaubensvollzuges, daß die Theologie sich in der gegenwärtigen Situation inkarniert. So kann man Althaus im guten Sinne des Wortes einen "Vermittlungstheologen" nennen (§ 18).

Althaus ist nicht nur *ein*, sondern ein *einzigartiges* "case study" für eine protestantische Theologie der nicht-christlichen Religionen, denn nach der Barthschen "Revolution" war er einer der ersten, der eine positivere Würdigung der Religionen versuchte, und zwar eine andere als jene, die Emil Brunner und Paul Tillich damals wagten (§ 19).

Kap. III: *The Religions: Echo of Uroffenbarung*
          (Die Religionen – ein Echo auf die Uroffenbarung)

I. Die Uroffenbarungslehre ist der *Ausgangspunkt* und das *Mittel*, mit denen Althaus seine Theologie der Religionen als einen "Mittelweg" zwischen Troeltsch und Barth ausgearbeitet hat. In seiner Definition der Religion sieht Althaus die Uroffenbarung als Ursprung der Religion und die Religion als Ausdruck der Uroffenbarung, was besonders in der religiösen Prophetie deutlich wird (§ 20). So kann man sagen, daß Althaus' Theologie der Religionen in seiner Theologie der Uroffenbarung enthalten ist. Er betonte, daß beide – Religionen und Uroffenbarung – nur in ihrem gegenseitigen Verhältnis zueinander voll verstanden werden können (§ 21).

II. Die *Realität* der *Uroffenbarung*, die ein besonderes Kennzeichen der Althausschen Theologie ist, wird definiert als eine wirklich göttliche Offenbarung, als unterschieden von, aber auch wesentlich bezogen auf Christi Offenbarung, und als eine immer gegenwärtige, dynamische Realität. Althaus konnte diese Realität in mannigfaltigen Termini beschreiben, aber im allgemeinen bevorzugte er den Ausdruck "Uroffenbarung", den er seit den frühen 30er Jahren gebrauchte (§ 22).

Althaus glaubte, daß die Existenz einer Uroffenbarung klar im Neuen Testament bezeugt ist: in *Röm. 1, 18*ff lehrt Paulus eine göttliche Offenbarung, die sich von der Offenbarung in Christus unterscheidet; ob der Mensch auf Grund dieser Offenbarung zu einer echten Erkenntnis Gottes gelangen kann, ist jedoch unklar (§ 23/2). In *Röm. 2, 14*ff und *7, 14*ff wird Uroffenbarung als das "in des Menschen Herz geschriebene Gesetz" bezeichnet, und ihr wirklich positiver Gehalt wird klar. Hier ist deutlich, daß Uroffenbarung wesenhaft mit dem Gesetz Israels wie mit der protestantischen Kategorie des "Gesetzes" verbunden ist, jedoch nicht identifiziert (§ 23/3–4). Uroffenbarung findet sich weiterhin in *Apg. 14, 15–17* (§ 23/5) und vor allem in *Joh. 1, 1*ff, wo sie als das Werk des ewigen, universalen Logos gesehen ist. Im Johannesprolog wird die wesenhafte Beziehung zwischen Uroffenbarung und Christusoffenbarung noch deutlicher (§ 23/6).

Althaus' biblisches Argument ist oft kritisiert worden, weil der Uroffenbarung dadurch eine zu unabhängige Rolle zugebilligt wurde und weil es den negativen Aspekt des "Gesetzes" und der Zornoffenbarung Gottes vergaß. Aber Althaus' Kritiker scheinen nicht weniger "Vor-urteile" als er gehabt zu haben (§ 23/8).

Althaus berief sich auch auf die *protestantische Tradition*, um seine Uroffenbarungslehre zu stützen, speziell auf Luther und die Theologen der lutherischen Orthodoxie (§ 24).

III. Obwohl beide, Althaus wie seine Kritiker, verschiedene Möglichkeiten kannten, die *Phänomenologie* der Uroffenbarung zu beschreiben (§ 25), kann man sie am besten unter den folgenden vier Kategorien darstellen: a) Gott offenbart sich selbst als die *Ur-Macht* im menschlichen Dasein. Das setzt eine Metaphysik der menschlichen Existenz als einer transzendenten Beziehung voraus. Der Mensch erfährt sein Sein als gegeben, aber nicht als voll gegeben (§ 26). b) Gott offenbart sich als das *Ur-Ich* — als der Grund und als das letzte Ziel jeder zwischenmenschlichen Beziehung (§ 27). c) Der *Ur-Wille* offenbart sich selbst in dem Gewissen und besonders im Gang, in der Verantwortung und im Ruf der Geschichte. Hier erfährt der Mensch einen persönlichen Gott und kann eine "Gewißheit Gottes" erlangen (§ 28). d) Die Uroffenbarung im *Ur-Geist* gründet sich auf die ontologische Beziehung zwischen Geist und Welt oder Denken und Sein; sie wird erfahren in des Menschen natürlichem Suchen nach Wahrheit und in seiner Fähigkeit, eine Ordnung und einen Plan hinter der Natur zu entdecken (§ 29).

Mit seiner Lehre und Phänomenologie der Uroffenbarung hat Althaus im wesentlichen denselben *Ausgangspunkt* wie die neuere *katholische Theologie* in bezug auf die Religionen. Moderne katholische Theologen basieren ihre Würdigung der Religionen auf der Realität einer göttlichen, allgemeinen Offenbarung (§ 30).

Kap. IV: *Althaus' Positive Evaluation of the Religions*
(Althaus' positive Würdigung der Religionen)

I. Wendet man die Althaussche Uroffenbarungslehre auf die Religionen an (§ 31), so kann man schließen, erstens, daß die Religionen eine *Rolle in der Heilsökonomie spielen.* Diese Rolle ist nicht nur von derjenigen des Evangeliums und des Christentums unterschieden, sondern sie kann sogar aus sich selbst heraus wirken: "Durch sich selbst und in ihrem eigenen Licht" (§ 32). Deshalb wurde Althaus' Uroffenbarungslehre und seine Religionsanschauung so oft als "natürliche Theologie" gebrandmarkt (§ 33). Solche Beschuldigungen waren jedoch unbegründet, denn nach Althaus' Ansicht war die Rolle der Religionen, um es mit einem katholischen Terminus zu sagen, *übernatürlich.* Sie waren nicht nur Menschenwerk, sondern Werk Gottes, seines Heiligen Geistes, des Logos (§ 34). Deshalb waren die Religionen tatsächlich ein Teil der *Heilsgeschichte*, d.h. der "Stationen und Epochen" innerhalb dieser Geschichte. Das entspricht Althaus' Theologie der Geschichte. Die Religionen bilden die Vorgeschichte zum Evangelium. Sie sind Gottes Werkzeuge und sogar Teil einer gewissen Entwicklung auf Christus hin (§ 35).

II. Es gehört zur Natur dieser Rolle der Religionen, den Nicht-Christen einen *Wahrheitsgehalt* anzubieten. Zunächst ermöglichen sie die Erkenntnis des einen, wahren Gottes. In seiner Phänomenologie der Uroffenbarung innerhalb der Religionen versichert Althaus, daß eine Gewißheit Gottes oder Erkenntnis Gottes nicht nur möglich, sondern sogar wirklich ist (§ 36). Gegenstand dieser Erkenntnis ist der *persönliche* Gott und sein *Liebesgebot.* Das alles gehört zur Personhaftigkeit jeder Offenbarung, sei sie besonders oder allgemein, und gehört zur Tatsache, daß die Uroffenbarung nicht eine "demonstratio", sondern eine "confessio" und eine "appellatio" beinhaltet, eine "Anrede" des göttlichen Du. Diese Erkenntnis wird noch deutlicher in Althaus' Gesetzesverständnis, wonach Gesetz nicht nur die "lex mortificans", sondern das persönliche Gebot der göttlichen Liebe ist (§ 37).

Außerdem kann die Wahrheit der Uroffenbarung und der Religionen auch ein Wissen um die menschliche *Schuld* und *Sündhaftigkeit* ermöglichen und die Notwendigkeit der Wiedergeburt und *Erlösung* durch eine außermenschliche Macht (§ 38). Alles in allem können wir sagen, daß die Religionen nicht nur eine negative Wahrheit enthalten, die sich immer in Lüge verkehrt (wie F. Konrad meint), sondern auch eine *positive* reale greifbare *Wahrheit*. Mit anderen Worten: Die Religionen haben nicht nur echte Fragen, sondern echte *Antworten* (§ 39).

III. In der Bestimmung des *Verhältnisses* zwischen *Christentum* und nichtchristlichen Religionen hielt Althaus zunächst die Möglichkeit einer positiven (und nicht nur negativen, wie Konrad meint) *Anknüpfung* und *Erfüllung* für gegeben. Althaus begründete diese Möglichkeit mit dem Beispiel des Dialoges zwischen Neuem Testament und den Religionen. Dies basiert auch auf der Lehre von der Gottesebenbildlichkeit des Menschen, die ihre Erfüllung in Christus findet, auf der Lehre vom Erlösungswirken des Heiligen Geistes, der das Schöpfungswirken Gottes zur Vollendung bringt, und schließlich auf der Lehre des Gesetzes, das im Evangelium zu seinem Ziel kommt (§ 40).

Dieses positive Verhältnis ist nicht allein eine Möglichkeit, sondern eine *Notwendigkeit*. Es wird gefordert durch die Natur der Heilsoffenbarung, die ganz und gar auf die Wahrheit der Uroffenbarung bezogen ist. Althaus kann sogar so argumentieren, daß die Offenbarung Christi, obgleich sie der einzige Maßstab ist, gemessen werden muß an der Uroffenbarung in den Religionen (§ 41).

IV. Obwohl Althaus nicht expressis verbis die typisch katholische Frage behandelt, ob die Religionen "*viae salutis*" sein können, ist er gezwungen, diese Frage implizit zu bedenken, und oft scheint es so, als gäbe er eine positive Antwort darauf (§ 42). Die erste Prämisse für solch eine positive Antwort ist klar: Gottes *universaler Heilswille*. Jene, die Christus nicht kennen, sind nicht automatisch verloren. Gottes Heilswerk ist nicht an die Gnadenmittel des Christentums gebunden (§ 43).

Daß Althaus zugestehen konnte, daß ein solcher Heilswille Gottes in den Religionen zum Ausdruck kommt, ist begründet in den folgenden drei Überlegungen: a) Er erlaubte eine *Art Glauben* innerhalb der Uroffenbarung und der Religionen, einen Glauben der noch nicht rettender Glaube ist, aber ihm doch schon angehört, einen Glauben, der von einem innerlichen "Reden Gottes" hervorgerufen wird (§ 44). b) Obwohl Althaus an der Notwendigkeit des historischen Jesus für die Offenbarung und den rettenden Glauben festhielt, maß er der *inneren Erleuchtung* durch den Heiligen Geist eine größere und entscheidende Bedeutung bei. Ja, er glaubte sogar, daß alle Geschichte, auch die Geschichte Jesu Christi, eine verhüllende Rolle im Akt des Glaubens spielt. Das würde bedeuten, daß der Heilige Geist nicht an die historische Mittlerrolle Jesu gebunden ist, sondern auch die Vermittlung durch die Religionen gebrauchen kann (§ 45). c) In seiner Lehre über den *universalen Christus* behauptet er sogar, daß die Erlösung auch durch andere historische Formen außerhalb des historischen Jesus und des Evangeliums möglich ist. Er stellt fest, daß die Religionen "vielleicht" diese historischen Formen vermitteln und daß sie ihren Gläubigen "relatives Heil", "Gnade" und "Vergebung" gewähren können (§ 46).

Kap. V: *Althaus' "No" to the Religions: Dialectical or Contradictory?*
           (Althaus' "Nein" zu den Religionen: dialektisch oder widersprüchlich?)

I. Aufgrund seiner Uroffenbarungslehre mußte Althaus auch ein "Nein" zu den Religionen sagen, das er als einen dialektischen Teil seines "Ja" verstanden wissen wollte. Aber es erhebt sich die Frage, ob dies wirklich in einer Dialektik und nicht vielmehr in einem einfachen, ungelösten Widerspruch endete (§ 47). Viele in diesem Zusammenhang stehenden Äußerungen Althaus' scheinen zunächst einmal jede reale "Gültigkeit" einer bestimmten Rolle der Religionen in der Heilsgeschichte zu leugnen, und oft bestand er in einer Weise auf dem "von Christus her", die der Uroffenbarung selbst auf ihrem ureigensten Felde keine echte Wirkungsmöglichkeit mehr einräumte (§ 48).

Ebenso leugnete Althaus jeden praktischen Wert des *Wahrheitsgehaltes* der Religionen. Des Menschen Wissen um den persönlichen Gott endet in Verzweiflung und im "Nicht-Wissen um Gott". Der Mißbrauch und Irrtum in den Religionen scheint so stark zu sein, daß er die Wahrheit untergräbt (§ 49).

Während Althaus einerseits das Problem von *Anknüpfung und Erfüllung* in den nicht-christlichen Religionen positiv beurteilen konnte, betonte er aber andererseits immer wieder, daß das Evangelium keinen Vergleich mit irgendetwas anderem zuläßt, sich mit nichts anderem messen läßt; die Begegnung mit ihm verlangt schließlich einen "totalen Bruch", "ein ganzes, nichts ausnehmendes Nein" gegenüber jeder Religion (§ 50).

Althaus' Ablehnung der Ansicht, die Religionen könnten *"viae salutis"* sein, ist noch entschiedener und härter. Der Mensch kann aufgrund der Uroffenbarung nicht zum Heil finden. Der vornehmliche Zweck der Uroffenbarung scheint es zu sein, dem Menschen sein sündiges Unerlöstsein klar zu machen. So widerstrebte es Althaus, Gottes Heilswissen zuzugestehen, daß er auch jede historische Vermittlung außerhalb Christi benutzen kann, um zu seinem Ziel zu gelangen. Althaus verlegte die Entscheidung über das Heil der Nicht-Christen lieber in einen außergeschichtlichen Bereich und unterstützte auf diese Weise die Apokatastasis-Lehre (§ 51). Dieses "Nein" zu den Religionen als möglichen Heilswegen muß als Ursache und der Hintergrund aller anderen Arten seines "Nein" verstanden werden (§ 52).

II. Zweifellos ist dieses "Nein" zu den Religionen Teil von Althaus' allgemeiner dialektischer Methode seines theologischen Denkens (§ 53). Es ist jedoch so extrem, daß es zu einem grundsätzlichen und verwirrenden Widerspruch zu fast jeder Art seines "Ja" wird, das in Kap. IV dargestellt wurde. Aufgrund dieser Verwirrung und Unklarheit kann sein "Mittelweg" letztlich nicht so erfolgreich sein, wie es wünschenswert wäre. In der Tat scheint Althaus in seiner Uroffenbarungslehre und in seiner positiven Behandlung der nicht-christlichen Religionen mehr gesagt zu haben, als er von seinen Prämissen her konnte. Er legte also ein Fundament, auf dem er seine Theologie der Religionen beim besten Willen nicht erfolgreich aufbauen konnte. Die Quelle dieses Widerspruchs und Unvermögens ist Althaus' Behandlung der Frage nach dem "Heil". Um dieses Problem klarer zu sehen, müssen wir seine Rechtfertigungslehre genauer untersuchen (§ 54).

Kap. VI: *Justification – The "Articulus Stantis et Cadentis Religionis"*
(Rechtfertigung als "Articulus Stantis et Cadentis Religionis")

I. Befähigt uns die Uroffenbarungslehre, die Religionen zu *verstehen*, so befähigt uns die Rechtfertigungslehre, die im Zentrum der Althausschen Theologie steht, sie zu *beurteilen*. Hier haben wir Althaus' endgültiges Verdikt der Religionen (§ 55).

Da der Mensch in seiner Religion niemals die Forderung des *"sola fide"* antreffen und Gott Gott sein lassen kann, befindet er sich in dem *unausweichlichen Bereich der Sünde*. Diese Unfähigkeit und diese Sündhaftigkeit gehören – um es in Althaus' Terminus zu sagen – zu des Menschen "Grundhaltung". Althaus versuchte, die Herkunft dieser Grundhaltung in seiner "Urstandslehre" zu erklären (§ 56).

Wegen dieser Sündhaftigkeit des Menschen mußte Gott zum *Richter* werden und die Menschen und ihre Religionen unter seinen Zorn und sein Gericht beugen. Deshalb muß jeder Akt des "sola fide", um heilswirksam zu sein, zunächst den Zorn dieses Richters und die notwendige Spannung zwischen seiner Liebe und seinem Gericht erfahren (§ 57).

II. Stehen aufgrund des "sola fide"-Prinzips die Religionen im Bereich der Sünde, so verhindert das "solus Christus"-Prinzip jeden Ausweg aus diesem Bereich. Das hängt mit dem zusammen, was wir die *physisch-objektive Notwendigkeit* des "solus Christus" nennen können, denn nur in Christi Leiden sind Gottes Zorn und Gericht ganz und gar angenommen und auf wunderbare Weise durchbrochen und überwunden. In diesem Sinne wirkt Christus als eine "causa efficiens" des Heils, und nur dort, wo jemand in direktem, physischen Kontakt mit dieser causa steht (durch Wort und Sakrament), ist Heil möglich. Jetzt verstehen wir, warum Althaus nicht zugestehen konnte, daß es noch eine andere historische Form von Heilsvermittlung gibt (§ 58). Die physisch-objektive Notwendigkeit erfordert ein *endgültiges "Nein"* zu den Religionen. Weil die Religionen keinen Kontakt mit dem historisch-physischen Faktum Jesus haben, gibt es kein Heil in ihnen, unterscheiden sie sich völlig vom Christentum; ihre Heilslehren sind leere Gedanken, die nicht einmal Existenzrecht haben. So hält Althaus an einer *christomonistischen* Rechtfertigungslehre fest: Weil Gott die Menschen in der physischen Realität Jesu rettet, rettet er sie nirgendwoanders (§ 59).

Althaus behauptet ebenso eine *psychologisch-subjektive Notwendigkeit* des "solus Christus": Nur in Christus kann man die Natur des "sola fide" *verstehen*, d.h. die unendliche Kluft zwischen Gott und Mensch und die notwendige "Spannung" zwischen seiner Liebe und seinem Zorn. Nur in Christus haben wir die Gewähr dafür, daß die Heilswirkung des "sola fide" zum Zuge kommt. Nur in Christus können wir *wissen* und *annehmen*, daß das "sola fide" Heil wirkt. Nun verstehen wir, warum Althaus soviel von dem zurücknahm, was er vorher über die Wahrheit und Heilsmöglichkeit in den Religionen gesagt hatte: Der Mensch kann die echte Wahrheit über Gott und sich selbst nur in Christus wissen und annehmen (§ 60). Die psychologisch-subjektive Notwendigkeit wird so zu einem *anderen endgültigen "Nein"* gegenüber den Religionen. Das ist der Grund, warum Althaus schließlich alle Religionen als sündige Versuche der Selbsterlösung verurteilt (§ 61).

Dieses durch die reformatorische Rechtfertigungslehre verursachte endgültige "Nein" kann in der Formel zusammengefaßt werden: *Sine Christo = Contra*

Christum. Weil sie außerhalb Christi sind, verkehren sich "das Gute und die Wahrheit" in den Religionen schließlich gegen ihn (§ 62).

III. Althaus' Analyse der *Gnadenreligionen* – Bhakti-Hinduismus und Amida Buddhismus – enthält eine phänomenologische Zusammenfassung seiner Theologie der Religionen (§ 63). Aufgrund der Uroffenbarungstheorie kann er einen überraschend positiven Gehalt der Religionen feststellen, sogar wesentliche Momente der reformatorischen Lehre über das "sola fide et sola gratia" (§ 64). Aber seine Rechtfertigungslehre zwingt ihn dazu, seine Position wieder zurückzunehmen und diese Religionen als sündiges Menschenwerk zu verurteilen (§ 65). Hier können wir die methodische Frage stellen, ob Althaus' theologische Prinzipien die phänomenologischen Fakten mißachten (§ 66).

IV. So wird die Rechtfertigungslehre zum *"articulus cadentis religionis"* und zur Ursache der Spannungen und Widersprüche in Althaus' Theologie der Religionen. Stellt man das Ergebnis von Kap. VI zwischen die Zusammenfassung von Kap. IV und V (vgl. Tabelle, S. 179), so werden die in Kap. IV und V aufgezeigten Widersprüche völlig klar (§ 67). Althaus' Würdigung der Religionen nimmt sich dann in ihrer Position näher bei Barth als bei Troeltsch stehend aus. Das einzig positive Element in Althaus' abschließendem Urteil über die Religionen ist, daß die Religionen eine "praeparatio negativa" für das Evangelium sind. Sie offenbaren des Menschen Nöte und artikulieren seine Fragen, ohne jedoch irgendeine genuine, heilsame Antwort zu geben. Mit anderen Worten: die Religionen bleiben innerhalb der Grenzen des Gesetzes. Ist das aber das einzig mögliche Urteil über sie, das man aufgrund der reformatorischen Rechtfertigungslehre fällen kann? (§ 68).

Kap. VII: *Verification of this Case Study: Protestant Theology and the Non-Christian Religions*
(Bestätigung dieses "Case Study": Die protestantische Theologie und die nicht-christlichen Religionen)

Wir wollen in einem Überblick über die Positionen, die die zeitgenössische deutschsprachige protestantische Theologie den Religionen gegenüber eingenommen hat, fragen, ob die Ergebnisse unserer Untersuchung über Althaus auch noch auf die gegenwärtige evangelische Theologie zutreffen (§§ 69–70).

I. Wir beginnen mit drei für diese Frage *repräsentativen Theologen*: a) *H. G. Fritzsche* (Beispiel für die reformierte Richtung) bemüht sich, die Werte der Religionen praktisch anzuerkennen, gelangt aber zu einer Verurteilung der nichtchristlichen Religionen, da er mit den Barthianern an dem "solus Christus"-Prinzip festhält (§ 71). b) *C. H. Ratschow* (Beispiel für die lutherische Richtung) bietet ein genuin positives Bild der Religionen. In allen Religionen gibt es ein "Hervortreten Gottes", und so können sie alle als "Erlösungsreligionen" bezeichnet werden. Jedoch scheint Ratschows christologisch begründete Behauptung, daß die Religionen Heil konstitutiv suchen, während das Evangelium es konsekutiv annimmt, die Religionen unter die Kategorie des Gesetzes zu subsumieren. Das wirft die ernste Frage auf, ob die Religionen Heil enthalten und mehr sein können als lediglich eine "praeparatio negativa" für das Evangelium (§ 72). c) *W. Pannenberg* (Beispiel einer mehr historisch ausgeprägten, konfessionell nicht gebundenen Richtung) interpretiert die Religionen nach seinem anthropologischen und historischen Konzept. Die

Religionen sind der notwendige, historische Ausdruck von des Menschen "Fraglichkeit" und seiner Suche nach Gott. So enthalten sie eine göttliche Offenbarung und können, ja müssen in positiver Beziehung zum Christentum verstanden werden. Jedoch fragt es sich, ob nach Pannenbergs Konzept der wahren Offenbarung, die erst am Ende der Geschichte und – nach seinem Christusverständnis – als Prolepsis des Endes erscheint, eine Heilsfindung in den Religionen möglich ist, bevor sie Christus begegnet sind, und ob sie lediglich als Fragen nach dem Heil verstanden werden müssen (§ 73).

II. Nach einer Prüfung solcher "Beispiele" wie P. Brunner, W. Trillhaas, A. Kimme, W. Böld, W. Dantine, U. Mann (vor 1970) und der Äußerungen des Theologischen Konvents Augsburgischen Bekenntnisses (1962–1963) können wir feststellen, daß die *"opinio communis"* innerhalb der deutschsprachigen protestantischen *systematischen Theologie* heute nicht über die obengenannten Repräsentanten hinausgeht, d.h. sie geht nicht über Althaus' Urteil über die nicht-christlichen Religionen hinaus (§ 74). Dasselbe kann man durchweg auch für die *"opinio communis"* innerhalb der *Missionstheologie* sagen: G. Rosenkranz, W. Holsten, P. Beyerhaus, G. F. Vicedom, H.-W. Gensichen, H. Bürkle und die Äußerungen des Deutschen Evangelischen Missionsrates über die "Erklärung über das Verhältnis der Kirche zu den nichtchristlichen Religionen" ("Nostra Aetate") des 2. Vatikanischen Konzils (§ 75).

Dieser allgemeine Überblick zeigt, daß die in unserem "case study" herausgearbeitete Position Althaus' auch heute noch in der deutschsprachigen protestantischen Theologie Gültigkeit besitzt: Man lehnt Barths extremen Negativismus ab, sucht einen Dialog mit den Religionen und gesteht die Möglichkeit einer Offenbarung in ihnen zu. Wegen der Rechtfertigungslehre bzw. der Erlösungslehre können diese Theologen jedoch eine Heilsmöglichkeit *in* den und *durch* die Religionen nicht anerkennen. Das führt aber praktisch zu einer Leugnung oder wesentlichen Begrenzung jeder Art von Offenbarung in den Religionen. Man billigt den Religionen nicht viel mehr als die Rolle einer "praeparatio negativa" für Christus zu (§ 76).

Kap. VIII: *Agenda for a Protestant-Catholic Dialogue concerning the Religions (Vorschläge für einen protestantisch-katholischen Dialog über die Religionen)*

Die Ergebnisse unseres "case study" über Althaus können eine Hilfe sein für einige Vorschläge zum protestantisch-katholischen Dialog über die Religionen. Der sogenannte "new approach" zu den Religionen innerhalb der katholischen Theologie (vor allem in der Schule K. Rahners) muß zuerst auf die protestantische · Position *hören* und ihr dann *Fragen stellen*.

I. Katholische Theologen müssen besonders auf jenen Gebieten das *Zuhören* lernen, wo sie Gefahr laufen, bestimmte grundlegende Wahrheiten des Evangeliums zu verwässern: a) In der Betonung der Universalität der Gnade neigen sie gerne dazu, die Realität der *Sünde und Rebellion gegen Gott* geringzuachten. Hier müssen sie das protestantische Insistieren auf dem Gesetz und göttlichen Zorn ernstnehmen (§ 77). b) In ihrem Verständnis Christi als der Manifestation des universalen Heils und des "anonymen Christentums" in den Religionen erliegen katholische Theologen oft der Gefahr, *Christus als die Quelle und Ursache der Erlösung* zu vergessen. Hier muß die mahnende Betonung des "solus Christus" in der protestantischen Theologie mit offenen Ohren gehört werden (§ 78). c) Die moderne katholische Sicht der Religionen neigt zuweilen zu einer Verschleierung der Einheit und notwendigen Unterordnung von *allgemeiner und spezieller Heilsökonomie*. Daher sollten die katholischen Theologen sorgfältiger auf die protestantische Wiederholung des "von Christus her" achten (§ 79). d) Der Dialog mit der protestantischen Theologie wird den katholischen Theologen auch dazu verhelfen, die Gefahr zu vermeiden, daß sie die grundlegende Bedeutung der Mission leichtfertig verkennen (§ 80).

II. Andererseits muß der katholische Theologe *praktische und dogmatische Fragen* an seinen protestantischen Partner stellen.

Praktisch: a) Die erste praktische Frage ist, ob ein *Dialog* mit den Religionen möglich ist, wenn man ihnen jede Heilsmöglichkeit abspricht und man sie lediglich als eine "praeparatio negativa" für Christus betrachtet (§ 81). b) Außerdem müssen wir fragen, ob *theologische Schlüsse* über die Religionen gezogen werden können, ohne zunächst die phänomenologischen Fakten der Religionswissenschaft berücksichtigt zu haben (§ 82).

Dogmatisch: a) In dogmatischer Hinsicht müssen wir fragen, ob ein Theologe *Gottes Heilswillen* behaupten kann, ohne die Wirkungen dieses Willens innerhalb der nichtchristlichen Welt zu suchen, speziell in den Religionen (§ 83). b) Können wir zugeben, daß es eine *Offenbarung* in den Religionen gibt, ohne eine Heilsmöglichkeit anzuerkennen? Beinhaltet eine genuine Offenbarung nicht immer auch die Möglichkeit zum Heil? (§ 84). c) Erlaubt die traditionelle protestantische *Rechtfertigungslehre* weitere Interpretationen, so daß man auch Heil in den Religionen annehmen könnte? Präziser: Muß der Nicht-Christ eine ausdrückliche Erfahrung von Gottes Zorn gemacht haben? Können die "Werke" der Religionen das Produkt des "sola gratia" sein? Schließt das Gesetz Heil notwendigerweise aus? Ist der Begriff der δικαιοσύνη die einzige und beste Kategorie, um das Problem der Erlösung außerhalb des Christentums zu prüfen? (§ 85). d) Die wichtigsten Fragen betreffen die Christologie: Kann das "solus Christus", d.h. die Erlösungsmacht Christi, beschränkt werden auf die historische Tatsache Jesus und auf ihre Kommunikation durch Wort und Sakrament? Ist das nicht eine fragwürdige Begrenzung der Wirkung der Inkarnation? Könnten wir nicht eine bessere Begegnung mit den Religionen auf der Basis einer "kosmischen Christologie" ermöglichen, wie sie in neueren Dokumenten des Weltkirchenrates vorgeschlagen wurde? (§ 86).

III. Wir schließen mit einem Vorschlag zu einer *Hermeneutik der Theologie der Religionen*: Obgleich unsere Studie hauptsächlich über die theologischen Prinzipien für eine Würdigung der Religionen handelte, reichen solche Prinzipien alleine nicht aus, um eine Theologie der Religionen zu entwerfen. Theologische Prinzipien können in ihrer ganzen Weite nur *verstanden werden*, wenn man die Religionen eingehend *studiert* und einen *Dialog* mit ihnen *führt* (§ 87). Unsere Prinzipien sollen uns befähigen zu der *echt dialektischen Haltung*, die für solch ein Studium und solch einen Dialog notwendig ist. Unsere Prinzipien machen uns deutlich, daß die Religionen *entweder* Werkzeuge von Gottes Offenbarung und Heil *oder* Hindernisse dazu sein können (§ 88). Welche Alternative die richtige ist, oder welche Prinzipien angewendet werden müssen, das wird einzig und allein entschieden durch das Studium und den Dialog der Religionen (§ 89).

Bibliography

I. Paul Althaus*

"Adolf Schlatters Gabe an die systematische Theologie", *Adolf Schlatter, Gedächtnisheft der Deutschen Theologie*, Stuttgart, 1938, pp. 28ff.; also in BFChTh, 40/1, Gütersloh, 1938, pp. 31–40; also in DTh, 5 (1938) 146–153.

"Adolf Schlatters Verhältnis zur Theologie Luthers", ZSTh, 22 (1953) 245–256; also in *Um die Wahrheit des Evangeliums*, pp. 145–157.

"Adolf Schlatters Wort an die heutige Theologie", ZSTh, 21 (1950/52) 95–109; also in *Um die Wahrheit des Evangeliums*, pp. 131–144.

"Das Alte Testament in der 'Naturgeschichte des Glaubens'", *Werke und Tage*. Festschrift für Rudolf Alexander Schröder zum 60. Geburtstag am 26. Januar 1938, Berlin, 1938, pp. 11–17.

"Althaus, Paul, evangelischer Theologe, geb. 1861, gest. 1925"..*Neue deutsche Biographie*, hrsg. von der Histor. Kommission bei der Bayerischen Akademie der Wissenschaften, Bd. I, Berlin, 1953, pp. 220–221.

Aus dem Leben von P. Althaus – Leipzig, Leipzig, 1928.

"Außerchristliche Gnadenreligionen und das Evangelium", *Korrespondenzblatt der evang.-luth. Geistlichen in Bayern*, 60 (1935) 253.

"Bedenken zur 'Theologischen Erklärung' der Barmer-Bekenntnis-Synode", *Korrespondenzblatt der evang.-luth. Geistlichen in Bayern*, 59 (1934) 318–320; also in *Lutherische Kirche*, 1934, pp. 117ff.

"Die Bedeutung der Theologie Luthers für die theologische Arbeit", LuJ, 28 (1961) 13–29.

"Die Bedeutung der Theologie Paul Tillichs". Vortrag, gehalten auf dem Generalkonvent des Sprengels Göttingen am 20. 5. 1964. Manuscript in the "Paul Tillich Archiv", Göttingen.

"Die Bedeutung des Kreuzes im Denken Luthers", *Evangelium und Leben*, pp. 51–62.

Der Brief an die Römer, übersetzt und erklärt, (NTD, 6), 10. Aufl., Göttingen, 1966 (1. Aufl., 1932).

"Christentum und Geistesleben", *Evangelium und Leben*, pp. 31–45.

"Das Christentum – Religion unter Religionen?" *Universitas*, 11 (1956) 1131–1135.

Die christliche Wahrheit, Lehrbuch der Dogmatik, 7. Aufl., Gütersloh, 1966 (1. Aufl., 1947).

"Christologie des Glaubens", *Festschrift für D. Ludwig Ihmels*, 1928, pp. 280ff.; also in *Theologische Aufsätze* I, pp. 206–222.

Die deutsche Stunde der Kirche, Göttingen, 1933 (2. Aufl., 1934).

"Durch das Gesetz kommt Erkenntnis der Sünde. Zur Auseinandersetzung mit der exklusiv christologischen Dogmatik", *So lange es heute heißt. Festschrift für Rud. Hermann*, Berlin, 1957; also in *Um die Wahrheit des Evangeliums*, pp. 168–180.

* A complete bibliography of Althaus' works can be found, for 1911–1957, in: *Dank an Paul Althaus*. Eine Festgabe zum 70. Geburtstag, hrsg. von W. Künneth und W. Joest (Gütersloh, 1958), pp. 246–272; and for 1958–1966 in: H. Graß, "Die Theologie von Paul Althaus", NZSTh, 8 (1966) 237–241. Here we list only those works which have been *expressly* mentioned in our study.

"Erfahrungstheologie", RGG[3] II, pp. 552–553.

"Die 'Erlanger Theologie'", *Die Erlanger Universität.* Beilage des Erlanger Tageblattes, 11 (1958) Nr. 2, 1–2.

"Das Evangelium und die Religionen", ELKZ, 13 (1959) 39ff.; also in *Um die Wahrheit des Evangeliums,* pp. 9–22.

Evangelium und Leben. Gesammelte Vorträge, Gütersloh, 1927.

Die Familie Althaus, Erlangen, s.d. (for private use of the Althaus family).

"Gebot und Gesetz. Zum Thema 'Gesetz und Evangelium'" (BFChTh, 46/2), Gütersloh, 1952; also in *Gesetz und Evangelium,* hrsg. von E. Kinder und K. Haendler, Darmstadt, 1968, pp. 201–238.

Der Gegenwärtige, Gütersloh, 1932 (Predigten).

Das Gesetz Christi (Der Herr der Kirche, Predigten, Bd. 8), Gütersloh, 1936.

"Die Gestalt dieser Welt und die Sünde. Ein Beitrag zur Theologie der Geschichte", ZSTh, 9 (1932) 319–338; also in *Theologische Aufsätze* II, pp. 45–64.

"Glaube und Mystik", *Zeitwende,* 3 (1927) 90–93.

"Gottes Gottheit als Sinn der Rechtfertigungslehre Luthers", *Jahrbuch der Luthergesellschaft,* 13 (1931) 1–28; also in *Theologische Aufsätze* II, pp. 1–30.

Gott ist gegenwärtig. Letzte Predigten, Gütersloh, 1968.

Grundriß der Dogmatik
1. Aufl.: I – Erlangen, 1929; II – Erlangen, 1932.
2. Aufl.: I – Erlangen, 1936; II – Erlangen, 1936.
3. Aufl.: I – Gütersloh, 1947; II – Gütersloh, 1949.
(4. und 5. Aufl.: Gütersloh, 1958, 1959)

Grundriß der Ethik, 1. Aufl., Erlangen, 1931; 2. Aufl., Gütersloh, 1953.

Der Heiland (Der Herr der Kirche, Predigten, Bd. 23), Gütersloh, 1940.

Das Heil Gottes, Gütersloh, 1926 (Predigten).

Der Heilige, Rostocker Predigten, Gütersloh, 1921.

"Heilsgeschichte und Eschatologie", ZSTh, 2 (1924/25) 605–676.

Die Herrlichkeit Gottes, Gütersloh, 1954 (Predigten).

"Der himmlische Vater", *Evangelium und Leben,* pp. 46–50.

"Der 'historische Jesus' und der biblische Christus. Zum Gedächtnis Martin Kählers", *Theologische Aufsätze* II, pp. 162–168.

"Höhen außerchristlicher Religion", *Die Weltreligionen und das Christentum.* Vom gegenwärtigen Stand ihrer Auseinandersetzung (mit H. W. Schomerus, K. Steck, W. Freytag), München, 1928, pp. 1–20.

"Die Inflation des Begriffs Offenbarung in der gegenwärtigen Theologie", ZSTh, 18 (1941) 134–149.

"Die Kirche", *Evangelium und Leben,* pp. 77–91.

"Kirche und Staat nach lutherischer Lehre", *Theologia Militans* 4, Leipzig, 1935; also in *Allgemeine evang.-luth. Kirchenzeitung,* 68 (1935) 746–754, 770–778.

Die Kraft Christi, Gütersloh, 1958 (Predigten).

"Das Kreuz Christi", ZSTh, 1 (1923) 107–152; also in *Theologische Aufsätze* I, pp. 1–50.

"Das Kreuz Christi als Maßstab aller Religionen", *Evangelium und Leben* pp. 63–76; originally in *Die Gewißheit der Christusbotschaft*. Drei Gegenüberstellungen mit der mystisch-idealistischen Zeitbewegung, hrsg. von H. Weber, 2. Aufl., Berlin, 1922.

Der Lebendige, Gütersloh, 1924 (Predigten).

Die letzten Dinge. Lehrbuch der Eschatologie, 9. Aufl., Gütersloh, 1964 (1. Aufl., 1922).

Die lutherische Rechtfertigungslehre und ihre heutigen Kritiker, Berlin, 1951.

"Mission und Religionsgeschichte", ZSTh, 5 (1927/28) 550–590, 722–736; also in *Theologische Aufsätze* I, pp. 153–205.

"Natürliche Theologie und Christusglaube", ZSTh 16 (1939) 417–425; also in *Um die Wahrheit des Evangeliums*, pp. 34–41.

"Das neue Verhältnis katholischer und evangelischer Theologie", *Evangelische Welt*, 5 (1951) 497–500.

"Niedergefahren zur Hölle", ZSTh, 19 (1942) 365–384.

"Offenbarung als Geschichte und Glaube. Bemerkungen zu Wolfhart Pannenbergs Begriff der Offenbarung", ThLZ, 87 (1962) 321–330.

Paulus und Luther über den Menschen, 4. Aufl., Gütersloh, 1963.

"Paulus und sein neuester Ausleger. Eine Beleuchtung von Karl Barths 'Auferstehung der Toten'", ChuW, 1 (1925) 20–30.

Politisches Christentum. Ein Wort über die Thüringer 'Deutschen Christen', (Theologia Militans 5), Leipzig, 1935.

Die Prinzipien der deutschen reformierten Dogmatik im Zeitalter der aristotelischen Scholastik. Eine Untersuchung zur altprotestantischen Theologie, Leipzig, 1914.

"Die Rechtfertigung allein aus dem Glauben in Thesen Martin Luthers", LuJ, 28 (1961) 30–51.

Religiöser Sozialismus. Grundfragen der christlichen Sozialethik. (Studien des Apologetischen Seminars in Wernigerode 5), Gütersloh, 1921.

Das sogenannte Kerygma und der historische Jesus. Zur Kritik der heutigen Kerygma-Theologie (BFChTh 48), Gütersloh, 1958.

"Sola fide numquam sola – Glaube und Werk in ihrer Bedeutung für das Heil bei M. Luther", *Una Sancta*, 16 (1961) 227–235.

"Die Theologie" – C. Schweitzer. *Das religiöse Deutschland der Gegenwart*, Bd. 2. Der Christliche Kreis, Berlin, 1930, pp. 121–150.

Die Theologie Martin Luthers, 2. Aufl., Gütersloh, 1963.

"Theologie und Geschichte. Zur Auseinandersetzung mit der dialektischen Theologie", ZSTh, 1 (1923) 741–786.

"Theologie des Glaubens", ZSTh, 2 (1924/25) 281–322; also in *Theologische Aufsätze* I, pp. 74–118.

Theologie der Ordnungen, Gütersloh, 1934 (2. Aufl., 1935).

Theologische Aufsätze I, Gütersloh, 1929.

Theologische Aufsätze II, Gütersloh, 1935.

"Die theologische Lage vor 50 Jahren", *Deutsches Pfarrerblatt*, 65 (1965) 742–745.

"Toleranz und Intoleranz des Glaubens", *Theologische Aufsätze* II, pp. 104–120.

Der Trost Gottes (Der Herr der Kirche, Predigten, Bd. 14), Gütersloh, 1937.

"Um die Reinheit der Mission", EMZ, 10 (1953) 97–104.

Um die Wahrheit des Evangeliums. Aufsätze und Vorträge, Stuttgart, 1962.

Una Sancta (Der Herr der Kirche, Predigten, Bd. 17), Gütersloh, 1938.

"Uroffenbarung", *Luthertum*, 46 (1935) 4–32.

"Vergeltung", RGG^2 V, 1540–1542.

"Zum Verständnis der Rechtfertigung", *Theologische Aufsätze* II, pp. 31–44.

Völker vor und nach Christus. Theologische Lehre vom Volke, (Theologia Militans 14), Leipzig, 1937.

"Vom Sinn der Theologie", *Evangelium und Leben*, pp. 15–30.

"Vom Sinn und Ziel der Weltgeschichte", *Um die Wahrheit des Evangeliums*, pp. 304–312.

Von der Kirche (Der Herr der Kirche, Predigten, Bd. 1), Gütersloh, 1934.

"Von der Präsenz Gottes im Menschsein des Menschen", *Mensch und Menschensohn.* Festschrift für Bischof D. Karl Witte, Hamburg, 1963, pp. 11–19.

Der Wahrheitsgehalt der nichtchristlichen Religionen und das Evangelium, Berlin, 1932; also in *Jahrbuch 1932* der vereinigten deutschen Missionskonferenz, pp. 3–16.

"Der Wahrheitsgehalt der Religionen und das Evangelium", NAMZ, 11 (1934) 277–292; also in *Theologische Aufsätze* II, pp. 65–82.

"Wiederbringung Aller", RGG^2 V, 1908–1910.

"Wiederbringung Aller, dogmatisch", RGG^3 VI, 1694–1695.

"Die Wirklichkeit Gottes", *Zeitwende*, 9 (1933) 81–92.

Die Wirklichkeit Gottes (Der Herr der Kirche, Predigten, Bd. 7), Gütersloh, 1935.

"Wo steht die evangelische Theologie heute?", *Universitas*, 5 (1950) 1291–1296.

"Zum Verständnis der Rechtfertigung", *Theologische Aufsätze* II, pp. 31–44.

Reviews

K. Barth: *Die Auferstehung der Toten*, 1924, Theol. Lit. Bericht, 49 (1926) 6–7.

–   *Dogmatik im Grundriß*, 1947 and *Die Christliche Lehre nach dem Heidelberger Katechismus*, 1949, ThLZ, 74 (1949) 610–612.

–   *Das Wort Gottes und die Theologie*, Gesammelte Vorträge, 1924, Theol. Lit. Bericht, 48 (1925) 3–5.

E. Brunner: *Der Mittler*, 1927, ThLZ, 54 (1929) 470–479; also in *Theologische Aufsätze* II, pp. 169–182.

R. Bultmann: *Der Begriff der Offenbarung im N.T.*, 1929, ThLZ, 45 (1929) 412–417.

G. Koch: *Die christliche Wahrheit der Barmer Theolog. Erklärung*, 1950, ThLZ, (1952) 433–434.

Recorded Interviews

With Pfarrer Gerhard Althaus in Traunstein, May 14, 1971.

With Frau Dorothea Althaus in Erlangen, May 16, 1971.

Correspondence: Althaus—Barth*

A. From Althaus to Barth
    7. 5. 1922 Letter from Rostock
    19.12. 1924 Post Card from Rostock
    13. 1. 1925 Letter from Rostock
    13. 6. 1925 Letter from Rostock
    29. 5. 1928 Letter from Erlangen
    4. 5. 1930 Letter from Erlangen
    Easter Sat.
        1930 Letter from Partenkirchen
    30. 7. 1933 Letter from Erlangen
    25.10. 1953 Letter from Erlangen
    15. 4. 1956 Post Card from Gößweinstein
    15.12. 1956 Letter from Erlangen

B. From Barth to Althaus
    19. 4. 1922 Letter from Göttingen
    20. 5. 1924 Post Card from Göttingen
    29.12. 1924 Post Card from Göttingen
    19. 9. 1927 Letter from Münster
    1. 2. 1928 Letter from Münster
    8. 1. 1930 Letter from Münster
    19. 4. 1930 Letter from Bonn
    3. 8. 1933 Letter from Bergli, Oberrieden (Kt.Zürich)
    17. 4. 1956 Letter from Basel

II. Background

Aagaard, J., "Revelation and Religion. The influences of dialectical theology on the understanding of the relationship between Christianity and other religions", StTh, 14 (1960) 148–185.

Adams, J. L., *Paul Tillich's Philosophy of Culture, Science and Religion*, New York, 1965.

Alberca, E. Escribano, *Die Gewinnung theologischer Normen aus der Geschichte der Religion bei Ernst Troeltsch* (Münchener Theolog. Studien II, 21), München 1961.

Alfaro, J., *Adnotationes in Tractatum de Virtutibus*, Roma, 1959.

—   , "Transcendencia e immanencia de lo sobrenatural", *Gregoriana*, 38 (1957) 5–50.

Anesaki, M., *History of Japanese Religion*, Tokyo, 1963.

Barth, K., "Der Christ in der Gesellschaft", *Anfänge der dialektischen Theologie* I, hrsg. von J. Moltmann, München, 1966, pp. 3–37.

—   , *Die christliche Dogmatik im Entwurf* Bd. I: Die Lehre vom Worte Gottes. Prolegomena zur christlichen Dogmatik, München, 1927.

—   , *Credo*. Die Hauptprobleme der Dogmatik dargestellt im Anschluß an das Apostolische Glaubensbekenntnis, München, 1935.

—   , *Dogmatik im Grundriß*, München, 1947.

* Originals are to be found in the archives of Gerhard Althaus, Traunstein and in the Karl-Barth-Archive, Basel.

–   , *Fides quaerens intellectum*. Anselms Beweis der Existenz Gottes, München, 1931.

–   , "Grundfragen der christlichen Sozialethik. Auseinandersetzung mit Paul Althaus", *Das neue Werk*, 14–15 (1922) 461ff.

–   , "Die Kirche und die Kultur", *Die Theologie und die Kirche*. Gesammelte Vorträge, Bd. II, München, 1928, pp. 264–291.

–   , *Kirchliche Dogmatik* I/1–IV/4, 1932–1967.

–   , *Die Menschlichkeit Gottes* (ThSt(B) 48), Zürich, 1956.

–   , *Nein! Antwort an Emil Brunner* (ThEx 14), München, 1937.

–   , "Parergon. Karl Barth über sich selbst", EvTh, 8 (1948–49) 268–275.

–   , *Der Römerbrief*, 1. Aufl., Bern, 1919; 2. Aufl., München, 1922 (10th Printing, Zürich, 1967)

–   , *Rudolf Bultmann. Ein Versuch, ihn zu verstehen* (ThSt(B) 34), 2. Aufl., Zollikon-Zürich, 1964.

Barth, P., *Das Problem der natürlichen Theologie bei Calvin* (ThEx 18), München, 1935.

Balthasar, H. U. von, *Karl Barth. Darstellung und Deutung seiner Theologie*, 2. Aufl., Köln, 1962.

Bandt, H., *Luthers Lehre vom verborgenen Gott*, Berlin, 1958.

Benckert, H., "Ohne Christus wäre ich Atheist. Zur Frage der natürlichen Gotteserkenntnis", EvTh 18 (1958) 445–460.

Benktson, B.E., *Christus und die Religion*. Der Religionsbegriff bei Barth, Bonhoeffer und Tillich (Arbeiten zur Theologie II/9), Stuttgart, 1967.

Bertholet-Lehmann, *Lehrbuch der Religionsgeschichte* Bd. I und II, Tübingen, 1925.

Beyer, A., *Offenbarung und Geschichte*. Zur Auseinandersetzung mit der Theologie von Paul Althaus, Schwerin, 1932.

Bietenhard, H., "Natürliche Gotteserkenntnis der Heiden? Eine Erwägung zum Röm. 1", *Festgabe für Karl Barth zum 70. Geburtstag*, ThZ, 12 (1956) 275–288.

Birkner, H.–J., "Beobachtungen und Erwägungen zum Religionsbegriff in der neueren protestantischen Theologie", *Fides et Communicatio*. Festschrift für Martin Doerne, hrsg. von D. Rössler, G. Voigt, und F. Wintzer, Göttingen, 1970, pp. 9–20.

–   , "Natürliche Theologie und Offenbarungstheologie. Ein theologiegeschichtlicher Überblick", NZSTh, 3 (1961) 279–295.

Bodenstein, W., *Neige des Historismus*. Ernst Troeltschs Entwicklungsgang, Gütersloh, 1959.

Bogdahn, M., *Die Rechtfertigungslehre Luthers im Urteil der neueren katholischen Theologie*, Göttingen, 1971.

Bornkamm, G., "Gesetz und Natur (Röm. 2, 14–16)", *Studien zu Antike und Urchristentum*, Ges. Aufs. II, 2. Aufl., München, 1959, pp. 93–118.

–   , "Die Offenbarung des Zornes Gottes (Röm. 1–3)", *Das Ende des Gesetzes*, Ges. Aufs. I, 5. Aufl., München, 1966, pp. 9–33.

Bouillard, H., "Karl Barth", LThK[2] II, 5–8.

Bousset, W., "Die Mission und die sogenannte religionsgeschichtliche Schule", ZMR, 22 (1907) 321–335; 353–362.

Brunner, E., *Christusbotschaft im Kampf mit den Religionen* (Basler Missionsstud., N.F. 8), Stuttgart, 1931.

   — , *Dogmatik* I, 2. Aufl., Zürich, 1960.

   — , *Natur und Gnade. Zum Gespräch mit Karl Barth*, Tübingen, 1934.

   — , *Offenbarung und Vernunft*, 2. Aufl., Darmstadt, 1961.

   — , *Religionsphilosophie evangelischer Theologie*, München, 1926.

Brunner, P., "Allgemeine und besondere Offenbarung in Calvins Institutio", EvTh, 1 (1934) 189–215.

Brunstäd, F., *Allgemeine Offenbarung. Zum Streit um die natürliche Theologie*, Halle a.S., 1935.

Bultmann, R., *Das Evangelium des Johannes* (Meyer K II), Göttingen, 1941.

Coffey, D., "Natural Knowledge of God, Reflections on Romans 1: 18–32", TS, 31 (1970) 674–691.

Conze, E., *Buddhism: Its Essence and Development*, 2. ed., New York, 1952.

Conzelmann, H., *Grundriß der Theologie des Neuen Testaments* (Einführung i. d. ev. Theologie II), München, 1967.

Cornehl, P., *Die Zukunft der Versöhnung*. Eschatologie und Emanzipation in der Aufklärung, bei Hegel und in der Hegelschen Schule, Göttingen, 1971.

Corswant, W., "Le salut par la foi dans le Bouddhisme japonais du Grand Véhicle", RThPh, (1941) 113–134.

Cullmann, O., *Heil als Geschichte*. Heilsgeschichtliche Existenz im Neuen Testament, Tübingen, 1965.

Delhougne, H., "Karl Barth et la critique feuerbachienne de l'idée de Dieu", MRS, 28 (1971) 121–163.

Dhavamony, M., "The Idea of God — a Hindu Christian Dialogue", *Bulletin* — Secretariatus pro non Christianis (Vatican), 5 (1967) 80–86.

Doerne, M., "Zur Dogmatik von Paul Althaus", ThLZ, 74 (1949) 449–458.

Dowey, A.E., *The Knowledge of God in Calvin's Theology*, New York, 1952.

Drescher, H.-G., *Glaube und Vernunft bei Ernst Troeltsch* (Diss. Marburg), Bochum, 1957.

Drey, J. S. von, "Die Urreligion durch die Uroffenbarung", ThQ, 8 (1826) 237–284.

Dumoulin, H., "Exkurs zum Konzilstext über den Buddhismus", LThK², Das 2. Vatikanische Konzil, II, 482–485.

   — , *Östliche Meditation und christliche Mystik*, Freiburg-München, 1966.

Elert, W., *Der christliche Glaube*. Grundlinien der lutherischen Dogmatik, hrsg. von E. Kinder, Hamburg, 1956.

Eliade, M., Das Heilige und das Profane. Vom Wesen des Religiösen (rde 31), Hamburg, 1957.

   — and Kitagawa, J. ed., *The History of Religions*. Essays in Methodology, Chicago, 1959.

Engelland, H., *Die Frage der Gotteserkenntnis bei Melanchthon*, Diss. Tübingen, 1930.

   — , *Melanchthon, Glauben und Handeln*, München, 1931.

Enomiya-Lasalle, H.M., "Der Heilsweg des Buddhismus", *Die vielen Wege zum Heil*, hrsg. von W. Molinski, München, 1969, pp. 15–40.

Flückiger, F., "Die Werke des Gesetzes bei den Heiden (nach Röm. 2, 14ff.)", ThZ, 8 (1952) 17–42.

–   , "Analogia entis und analogia fidei bei Karl Barth", *Studia Gen.*, 8 (1955) 678–688.

Frick, H., *Das Evangelium und die Religionen*, Basel, 1933.

–   , *Vergleichende Religionswissenschaft*, Berlin, 1928.

Fries, H., "Uroffenbarung", *Sacramentum Mundi* IV, 1124–1129.

Gärtner, B., *The Areopagus Speech and Natural Revelation* (ASNU 21), Uppsala, 1955.

Gebhardt, R., *Naturrecht und Schöpfungsordnung als Möglichkeit zur Erfassung der Wirklichkeit in der gegenwärtigen theologischen Ethik*, Diss. Marburg, 1955.

Gerhard, J., *Loci Theologici* I, hrsg. von E. Preuß, Berlin, 1863.

Gerken A., *Offenbarung und Transzendenzerfahrung*, Düsseldorf, 1969.

Gestrich, C., "Die unbewältigte natürliche Theologie", ZThK, 68 (1971) 82–120.

Glasenapp, H. von, *Der Buddhismus – eine atheistische Religion*, München, 1966.

Gloede, G., *Theologia naturalis bei Calvin*, Stuttgart, 1935.

Gloege, G., "Karl Barth", RGG[3] VI, 894–898.

–   , "Uroffenbarung", RGG[3] VI, 1199–1203.

Götz, J., "Theorie der Uroffenbarung", *Orientierung*, 21 (1957) 227ff.

Graß, H., "Erlanger Schule", RGG[3] II, 566–568.

–   , "Gedächtnisvorlesung für Paul Althaus", *Nachrichten der evangel.-luth. Kirche in Bayern*, August, 1966.

–   , "Die Theologie von Paul Althaus", NZSTh, 8 (1966) 213–241.

Grin, E., "Paul Althaus", RThPh, 17 (1967) 189–194.

Haas H., *Amida Buddha unsere Zuflucht.* Urkunden zum Verständnis des japanischen Sukhavatī-Buddhismus, Leipzig, 1910.

Haendler, K., *Wort und Glaube bei Melanchthon.* Eine Untersuchung über die Voraussetzung und Grundlagen des melanchthonischen Kirchenbegriffes, Gütersloh, 1968.

Heiler, F., *Die Bedeutung der Mystik für die Weltreligionen*, München, 1919.

–   , *Erscheinungsformen und Wesen der Religion*, Stuttgart, 1961.

–   , "Die Religionsgeschichte als Wegbereiterin für die Zusammenarbeit der Religionen", ThLZ, 78 (1953) 727–740.

Heinzelmann, G., *Glaube und Mystik*, Tübingen, 1927.

–   , *Ur-Offenbarung?* ThStKr, 106, N.F. 1 (1934–35) 415–431.

Heislbetz, J., "Uroffenbarung", LThK[2] X, 565–567.

Hempel, J., "Religionsgeschichtliche Schule", RGG[3] V, 991–994.

Heppe, H., Die Dogmatik der evangelisch-reformierten Kirche, neu durchges. u. hrsg. von E. Bizer, Neukirchen, 1958.

Hermann, R., *Fragen um den Begriff der natürlichen Theologie* (BFChTh 44), Gütersloh, 1950.

Hötzel, N., *Die Uroffenbarung im französischen Traditionalismus*, München, 1962.

Holl, K., "Was verstand Luther unter Religion?" *Gesammelte Aufsätze zur Kirchengeschichte*, Bd. I., 3. Aufl., Tübingen, 1923.

Holmström, F., *Das eschatologische Denken der Gegenwart.* Drei Etappen der theologischen Entwicklung des 20. Jahrhunderts, Gütersloh, 1936.

Holsten, W., *Christentum und nichtchristliche Religion nach der Auffassung Luthers* (Allgemeine Missionsstudien 13), Gütersloh, 1932.

Holte, R., "Logos Spermatikos", StTh, 12 (1958) 109–168.

Hübner, E., *Evangelische Theologie in unserer Zeit,* Bremen, 1966.

Hutten, K., *Die Bhakti-Religion in Indien und der christliche Glaube im Neuen Testament* (Veröffentl. des Orientl. Inst. der Univ. Tübingen 1), Stuttgart, 1930.

Ingram, P.O., "Shinran Shōnin and Martin Luther: A Soteriological Comparison", JAAR, 39 (1971) 430–447.

Jaspert, B. (Hrsg.), *Karl Barth – Rudolf Bultmann. Briefwechsel 1922–1966* (Karl Barth Gesamtausgabe V. Briefe, Bd. 1), Zürich, 1971.

– , "Zum Werk Paul Tillichs (1886–1965)", *Erbe und Auftrag,* 47 (1971) 325–328.

Johanns, P., *La Pensée religieuse de l'Inde,* Louvain, 1952.

– , *A Synopsis of the "To Christ through the Vedantas"* Calcutta, 1930ff.

Kähler, M., *Der sogenannte historische Jesus und der geschichtliche biblische Christus,* 2. Aufl., Leipzig, 1896.

Kantzenbach, F. W., *Orthodoxie und Pietismus* (Evangelische Enzyklopädie, Bd. 11/12), Gütersloh, 1966.

– , *Der Weg der evangelischen Kirche vom 19. zum 20. Jahrhundert* (Evangelische Enzyklopädie, Bd. 19/20), Gütersloh, 1968.

– , "Von Ludwig Ihmels bis zu Paul Althaus. Einheit und Wandlungen lutherischer Theologie im ersten Drittel des 20. Jahrhunderts", NZSTh, 11 (1969) 94–111.

Keller, C. A., "Versuch einer Deutung heidnischer Religion (im Anschluß an Karl Barths Lehre vom Menschen)", EMM, 100 (1956) 70–92.

Kertelge, K., *"Rechtfertigung" bei Paulus.* Studien zur Struktur und zum Bedeutungsgehalt der paulinischen Rechtfertigungslehre, Münster, 1967.

Kinder, E., "Das vernachlässigte Problem 'natürlicher Gotteserfahrung' in der Theologie", KuD, 9 (1963) 316–333.

Kitagawa, J., *Religion in Japanese History,* New York, 1966.

Klostermaier, K., *Hinduismus,* Köln, 1966.

Knitter, P., "Christomonism in Karl Barth's Evaluation of the Non-Christian Religions", NZSTh, 13 (1971) 99–121.

– , "Paul Althaus: An Attempt at a Protestant Theology of the Non-Christian Religions", Verbum SVD, 11 (1970) 214–235.

– , "Die Uroffenbarungslehre von Paul Althaus – Anknüpfungspunkt für den Nationalsozialismus? Eine Studie zum Verhältnis von Theologie und Ideologie", EvTh, 33 (1973) 138–164.

Koch, G., *Die christliche Wahrheit der Barmer theologischen Erklärung* (ThEx 22), München, 1950.

Köhler, W., *Ernst Troeltsch,* Tübingen, 1941.

Koepp, W., *Panagape.* Eine Metaphysik des Christentums, 1. Buch, Gütersloh, 1928.

252

Konrad, F., *Das Offenbarungsverständnis in der evangelischen Theologie* (Beiträge z. ökumen. Theologie 6), München, 1971.

Koppers, W., "Uroffenbarung im Lichte profaner Forschung", *Hochland*, 44 (1951) 69–72.

Krötke, W., *Das Problem "Gesetz und Evangelium" bei W. Elert und P. Althaus* (ThSt(B) 83), Zürich, 1965.

Küng, H., *Die Kirche* (ÖF I/1), Freiburg, 1967.

– *Rechtfertigung*, Die Lehre Karl Barths und eine katholische Besinnung, 4. Aufl., Paderborn, 1957.

Künneth, W. und Joest, W., (Hrsg.) *Dank an Paul Althaus*. Eine Festgabe zum 70. Geburtstag, Gütersloh, 1958.

Lackmann, M., *Vom Geheimnis der Schöpfung*. Die Geschichte der Exegese von Römer I, 18–23, II, 14–16 und Acta XIV, 15–17, VII, 22–29 vom 2. Jahrhundert bis zum Beginn der Orthodoxie, Stuttgart, 1952.

Langemeyer, L., *Gesetz und Evangelium*. Das Grundanliegen der Theologie Werner Elerts, Paderborn, 1970.

Latourelle, R., *Théologie de la Révélation* (Studia. Recherches de Philosophie et de Théologie publiées par les Facultés S.J. de Montréal. 15), Paris-Bruges, 1963.

Leese, K., *Recht und Grenzen der natürlichen Theologie*, Zürich, 1954.

Leeuw, G. van der, *Phänomenologie der Religion*, 2. Aufl., Tübingen, 1956.

Leipold, H., *Theorie der Verkündigung*. Der Streit um die Frage der "Anknüpfung" zwischen Emil Brunner und Karl Barth (Habilitationsschrift, Marburg), 1969, Manuscript.

Letter, P. de, *The Christian and Hindu Concept of Grace* (The Light of the East Series, No. 52), Calcutta, 1958.

Loewenich, W. von, "Paul Althaus als Lutherforscher", LuJ 35 (1968) 9–47.

Lohff, W., "Erfahrungstheologie", LThK² III, 981–982.

– , "Paul Althaus", *Tendenzen der Theologie im 20. Jahrhundert*, hrsg. von H.J. Schultz, Stuttgart, 1967, pp. 296–302.

– , "Wenzel Lohff über Paul Althaus", *Theologen unserer Zeit*, hrsg. von L. Reinisch, München, 1960, pp. 58–78.

– , "Zur Verständigung über das Problem der Ur-Offenbarung", *Dank an Paul Althaus*, pp. 151–170.

Lohse, B., "Martin Kähler", *Tendenzen der Theologie im 20. Jahrhundert*, hrsg. von H. J. Schultz, Stuttgart, 1967, pp. 19–23.

Lubac, H. de, *Amida*, Paris, 1955.

Lütgert, W., *Johanneische Christologie*, 2. Aufl., Gütersloh, 1916.

– , *Schöpfung und Offenbarung*, Gütersloh, 1934.

Luther, M., *Werke*. Kritische Gesamtausgabe, Weimar, 1883ff. (WA)

Lyonnet, S., "De naturali Dei cognitione (Rom 1, 18–23)", *Quest. in ep. Ad Rom. I*, Roma, 1955.

Maron, G., *Kirche und Rechtfertigung*. Eine kontroverstheologische Untersuchung, ausgehend von den Texten des Zweiten Vatikanischen Konzils, Göttingen, 1969.

Matczak, S. A., *Karl Barth on God*, New York, 1962.

Maurer, W., *Der junge Melanchthon zwischen Humanismus und Reformation,* Bd. I: Der Humanist, Göttingen, 1967; Bd. II: Der Theologe, 1969.

Mensching, G., *Buddhistische Geisteswelt.* Vom Historischen Buddha zum Lamaismus. Texte ausgewählt und eingeleitet von Gustav Mensching, Baden-Baden, 1955.

    —   , *Die Söhne Gottes.* Aus den heiligen Schriften der Menschheit ausgewählt und eingeleitet von Gustav Mensching, Wien, 1958.

Moltmann, J. (Hrsg.), *Anfänge der dialektischen Theologie,* (ThB 17), München, 1966.

    —   , "Gottesoffenbarung und Wahrheitsfrage", *Parrhesia,* Karl Barth zum 80. Geburtstag, Zürich, 1966, pp. 149–172.

Muck, O., *Die transzendentale Methode in der scholastischen Philosophie der Gegenwart,* Innsbruck, 1964.

Mußner, F., "Anknüpfung und Kerygma in der Areopagrede", TThZ, 67 (1958) 344–354.

Neuner, J. (Hrsg.), *Hinduismus und Christentum.* Eine Einführung, Wien, 1962.

Numazawa, F. K., "Die Religionen Japans", *Christus und die Religionen der Welt,* III, hrsg. von F. König, 2. Aufl., Wien, 1961, pp. 416–436.

Nürnberger, K., *Glaube und Religion bei Karl Barth.* Analyse und Kritik der Verhältnisbestimmung zwischen dem christlichen Glauben und den anderen Religionen in § 17 der 'Kirchlichen Dogmatik' Karl Barths (Diss. Marburg), 1967.

Offizieller Bericht der 4. Vollversammlung des Lutherischen Weltbundes, Helsinki, 1963, Berlin, 1965.

Ohm, T., *Die Liebe zu Gott in den nichtchristlichen Religionen,* München, 1950.

Okura, Y., *Principal Teachings of the Sect of Pure Land,* Tokyo, 1925.

Okusa, E., *Die Hauptlehren von Shinshu, dem wahren Lehrsystem,* Kyoto, 1915.

Oldenberg, H., *Buddha,* 13. Aufl., Stuttgart, 1959.

Ott, H., "Röm. 1, 19ff. als dogmatisches Problem", ThZ, 15 (1959) 40–50.

Otto, R., *Die Gnadenreligionen Indiens,* Gotha, 1930.

Pallas, "La Eschatologia de Paul Althaus", *Scriptorium Nitoriense,* 11 (1964) 7–17.

Pannenberg, W., "Zur Bedeutung des Analogiegedankens bei Karl Barth", ThLZ, 78 (1953) 17–24.

Papali, C.P., "Exkurs zum Konzilstext über den Hinduismus", LThK[2], Das 2. Vatikanische Konzil, II, 478–482.

Pesch, O.H., *Theologie der Rechtfertigung bei Martin Luther und Thomas von Aquin,* Mainz, 1967.

Peters, A., "Die Frage nach Gott", *Fuldaer Hefte* 17, Berlin, 1967, pp. 9–100.

    —   , "Reformatorische Rechtfertigungsbotschaft zwischen tridentinischer Rechtfertigungslehre und gegenwärtigem evangelischen Verständnis der Rechtfertigung", LuJ, 41 (1964) 77–128.

Peterson, E., "Über die Forderung einer Theologie des Glaubens. Eine Auseinandersetzung mit Paul Althaus", ZZ, 3 (1925) 281–302.

Pfnür, V., *Einig in der Rechtfertigungslehre?* Die Rechtfertigungslehre der Confessio Augustana (1530) und die Stellungnahme der katholischen Kontroverstheologie zwischen 1530 und 1535 (Veröffentlichungen des Inst. für Europ. Gesch. Mainz 60), Wiesbaden, 1970.

Pöhlmann, H., "Die Erlanger Theologie, ihre Geschichte und ihre Bedeutung", ThStKr, 80 (1907) 390–433, 535–563.

Pöhlmann, H. G., *Analogia entis oder Analogia fidei?* Die Frage der Analogie bei Karl Barth, Göttingen, 1965.

–   , "Das Problem der Uroffenbarung bei Paul Althaus", KuD, 16 (1970) 242–258.

–   , *Rechtfertigung.* Die gegenwärtige kontroverstheologische Problematik der Rechtfertigungslehre zwischen der evangelisch-lutherischen und der römisch-katholischen Kirche, Gütersloh, 1971.

Pol, W. H. van de, *Die Zukunft von Kirche und Christentum*, Wien, 1970.

Postema, G. J., "Calvin's Alleged Rejection of Natural Theology", SJTh, 24 (1971) 423f.

Prenter, R., "Die Einheit von Schöpfung und Erlösung", ThZ, 2 (1946) 161–182.

–   , "Das Problem der natürlichen Theologie bei Karl Barth", ThLZ 77 (1952) 607–612.

–   , *Schöpfung und Erlösung*, Dogmatik, I, Göttingen, 1960.

Preuß, H. D., *Verspottung fremder Religionen im Alten Testament.* Stuttgart, 1970.

Protokoll der Tagung des "Kreises ehem. Marburger Theologen" im Oktober 1931 in Marburg über "Die Frage der natürlichen Theologie", Marburg, 1932.

Prümm, K., "Offenbarung im Neuprotestantismus vom Aufkommen der Religionsgeschichtlichen Schule bis R. Bultmann", *Divinitas* 8 (1964) 417–523.

Rad, G. von, *Theologie des Alten Testaments* I, München, 1961.

Radhakrishnan, S., *Die Bhagavadgita*, Sanskrittext mit Einleitung und Kommentar, Baden-Baden, 1958.

Rechtfertigung heute. Studien und Berichte (Lutherischer Weltbund, Helsinki, 1963), Stuttgart, 1965 – (Beiheft zur "Lutherischen Rundschau")

Regamey, C., "Die Religionen Indiens", *Christus und die Religionen der Erde* III, hrsg. von F. König, 2. Aufl., Wien, 1961, pp. 73–227.

Reichelt, R. L., *Der chinesische Buddhismus,* Basel-Stuttgart, 1926.

Riedl, J., "Röm. 2, 14ff. und das Heil der Heiden bei Augustinus und Thomas", *Scholastik* 40 (1965) 189–213.

Ritschl, A., *Die christliche Lehre von der Rechtfertigung und Versöhnung* I, Bonn, 1903.

–   , *Unterricht in der christlichen Religion*, 6. Aufl., Bonn, 1903.

Robinson, J. M. und Cobb, J. B. Jr., (Hrsg.) *Theologie und Geschichte* (Neuland in der Theologie, Bd. 3), Zürich-Stuttgart, 1967.

Rückert, H., "Karl Holl", *Tendenzen der Theologie im 20. Jahrhundert*, hrsg. von H. J. Schultz, Stuttgart, 1967.

Sauter, G., *Zukunft und Verheißung.* Das Problem der Zukunft in der gegenwärtigen theologischen und philosophischen Diskussion, Zürich–Stuttgart, 1965.

Schempp, ᵔ., "Theologie der Geschichte. Kritische Bemerkungen zu H. W. Schmidts 'Zeit und Ewigkeit'", ZZ, 5 (1927) 497–513.

Schiffers, N., "Natürliche Gotteserkenntnis als ökumenisches Problem", *Catholica*, 21 (1967) 317–328.

Schlatter, A., *Das christliche Dogma*, Stuttgart, 1911.

Schleiermacher, F., *Der christliche Glaube* nach den Grundsätzen der evangelischen Kirche im Zusammenhange dargestellt, 2. Aufl., Berlin, 1830, neu hrsg. v. M. Redeker, 1960.

Schlier, H., "Über die Erkenntnis Gottes bei den Heiden", EvTh, 2 (1935) 9–26

–, "Von den Heiden. Röm. 1, 18–32", EvTh, 5 (1938) 113ff.; also in: *Die Zeit der Kirche*, Freiburg, 1956, pp. 29–37.

Schlink, E., "Die Offenbarung Gottes in seinen Werken und die Ablehnung der natürlichen Theologie", ThBl, 20 (1941) 1–13.

Schlippe, G. von, *Die Absolutheit des Christentums bei Ernst Troeltsch* auf dem Hintergrund der Denkfelder des 19. Jahrhunderts (Diss. Marburg) Neustadt a. d. Aisch, 1966.

Schmidt, H. W., *Zeit und Ewigkeit*. Die letzten Voraussetzungen der dialektischen Theologie, Gütersloh, 1927.

Schmidt, W., *Der Ursprung der Gottesidee* Bd. I., Münster, 1912; Bd. VI, 1926.

Scholz, H., *Religionsphilosophie*, Berlin, 1921.

Schott, E., "Systematische Theologie: Geschichte im deutschen Sprachgebiet im 19. und 20. Jh.", RGG^3 VI, 586–595.

–, "Vermittlungstheologie", RGG^3 VI, 1363.

Schreiner, H., ThLZ, 55 (1927) 404–406. (Review of H. W. Schmidt's *Zeit und Ewigkeit*)

Schröer, H., *Die Denkformen der Paradoxalität als theologisches Problem* (Diss. Göttingen), 1960.

Schwinn, W., "Paul Althaus", *Korrespondenzblatt der evang.-luther. Kirche in Bayern*, 81 (1966) 1–2.

–, "Dank an Paul Althaus", DtPfrBl, 63 (1963) 52–54.

Seeberg, R., "Die Lehre Luthers", *Lehrbuch der Dogmengeschichte* IV, 1, Leipzig-Erlangen, 1917.

Söderblom, N., *Der lebendige Gott im Zeugnis der Religionsgeschichte*. Nachgelassene Gifford-Vorlesungen, München, 1942.

Söhngen, G., "Gesetz und Evangelium", *Catholica*, 14 (1960) 81–105.

Song, C. S., *The Relation of Divine Revelation and Man's Religions in the Theologies of Karl Barth and Paul Tillich* (Diss. Union Theological Seminary, 1965), Manuscript.

Stephan, H. und Schmidt, M., *Geschichte der deutschen evangelischen Theologie* seit dem deutschen Idealismus, Berlin, 1960.

Strauss, H., "Krisis der Religion oder Kritik der Religionen? !?", *Parrhesia*. Karl Barth zum 80. Geburtstag, Zürich, 1966, pp. 305–320.

Szekeres, A., "Karl Barth und die natürliche Theologie", EvTh, 24 (1964) 229–242.

Tillich, P., "Natural and Revealed Religion", *Christendom*, 1 (1935), 158–170.

–, "Offenbarung", RGG^2 IV, 1227–1233; also in: *Gesammelte Werke* VIII, pp. 40–46.

–, "Rechtfertigung und Zweifel" *Vorträge der theologischen Konferenz zu Gießen*, F. 29 (Gießen, 1924), pp. 19–32; also in *Gesammelte Werke* VIII, pp. 85–100.

–, "What is Wrong with Dialectical Theology", JR, 15 (1935) 127–145.

Trendelenburg, A., *Logische Untersuchungen* II, 2. Aufl., Leipzig, 1862.

Trillhaas, W., "Paul Althaus", *Luther*, 38 (1968) 49–56.

–, "Die evangelische Theologie im 20. Jahrhundert", *Bilanz der Theologie im 20. Jahrhundert* II, hrsg. von H. Vorgrimler und R. van der Gucht, Freiburg, 1969, pp. 91–124.

Troeltsch, E., *Die Absolutheit des Christentums und die Religionsgeschichte*, 2. Aufl., Tübingen, 1912 (1. Aufl., 1902).

–, *Die Bedeutung der Geschichtlichkeit Jesu für den Glauben*, Tübingen, 1911.

–, *Gesammelte Werke*, Tübingen I (1912), II (1913), III (1922), IV (1925).

–, "Geschichte und Metaphysik", ZThK, 8 (1898) 1–69.

–, "Missionsmotiv, Missionsaufgabe und neuzeitliches Humanitätschristentum", ZMR, 22 (1907) 129–139; 161–166; also in *Gesammelte Werke* II, pp. 779–804.

–, "Protestantisches Christentum und Kirche in der Neuzeit", *Die christliche Religion mit Einschluß der israelitisch-jüdischen Religion* (Die Kulturen der Gegenwart, Teil I, Abt. IV, Bd. 1), Berlin-Leipzig, 1906, pp. 253–489.

–, *Psychologie und Erkenntnistheorie in der Religionswissenschaft*, Tübingen, 1905.

–, "Die Selbständigkeit der Religion", ZThK, 5 (1895) 361–436; and op. cit., 6 (1896) 71–110, 167–218.

Veitch, J. A., "Revelation and Religion in the Theology of Karl Barth", SJTh, 24 (1971) 1–22.

Voßberg, H., *Luthers Kritik aller Religionen*, Leipzig, 1922.

Wach, J., "Und die Religionsgeschichte? Eine Auseinandersetzung mit Paul Althaus", ZSTh, 6 (1929) 484–497.

–, *Religionssoziologie*, Tübingen, 1951.

Waldenfels, H., *Offenbarung*. Das Zweite Vatikanische Konzil auf dem Hintergrund der neueren Theologie (Beitr. z. ökumen. Theologie Bd. III), München, 1969.

Walker, R., *Zur Frage der Uroffenbarung*. Eine Auseinandersetzung mit Karl Barth und Paul Althaus, Bad Cannstatt, 1962.

Weber, O., *Karl Barths Kirchliche Dogmatik*. Ein einführender Bericht zu den Bänden I,1–IV,2, 2. Aufl., Neukirchen, 1957.

–, *Grundriß der Dogmatik* I, Neukirchen, 1966.

Wehrung, G., "Die Welt der Religionen in der Sicht des Neuen Testamentes", ZSTh 15 (1938) 194–226.

Wiedenmann, L., *Mission und Eschatologie*. Eine Analyse der neueren deutschen evangelischen Missionstheologie (Konfessionskundl. und kontroverstheol. Studien 15), Paderborn, 1965.

Wiesner, W., "Der Gott der 'Wirklichkeit' und der wirkliche Gott", VF (Theologischer Jahresbericht 1947–48), pp. 96–114.

Wingren, G., *Schöpfung und Gesetz*, Göttingen, 1960.

Witte, J., *Die Christusbotschaft und die Weltreligionen*, Göttingen, 1936.

Wolf, E., *Martin Luther, das Evangelium und die Religionen* (ThEx 6), München, 1934.

Wolff, H., *Der lebendige Gott*. Nathan Söderbloms Beitrag zur Offenbarungsfrage, 1938.

Zaehner, R. C., *Hinduism*, London, 1962.

Zahrnt, H., *Die Sache mit Gott*. Protestantische Theologie im 20. Jahrhundert, München, 1968.

Zasche, G., *Extra nos.* Untersuchungen zu dem umstrittenen Begriff des Übernatürlichen bei evangelischen Theologen der Gegenwart (Konfessionskundl. und kontroverstheol. Studien 26), Paderborn, 1970.

III. Contemporary Theology of the Religions

A. Protestant

Ahrens, T., *Die ökumenische Diskussion kosmischer Christologie seit 1961 – Darstellung und Kritik*, (Diss. Hamburg), 1969.

Amelung, E., "Die Funktion des Religionsbegriffes für die christliche Botschaft in der Gegenwart. Einige Bemerkungen zum Religionsbegriff Paul Tillichs", *Glaube, Geist, Geschichte. Festschrift für Ernst Benz zum 60. Geburtstage am 17. November 1967*, hrsg. von G. Müller und W. Zeller, Leiden, 1967, pp. 144–159.

Andersen, W., "Jesus Christus und der Kosmos", EvTh, 23 (1963) 471–493.

– , "Die theologische Sicht der Religionen auf den Weltmissionskonferenzen von Jerusalem (1928) und Madras (1938) und die Theologie der Religionen bei Karl Barth", *Fuldaer Hefte* 16, Berlin, 1966, pp. 23–54.

Beckmann, K.-M., "Theologie der Religion als ökumenisches Problem", *Kirche in der Zeit*, 22 (1967) 58–64.

Benz, E., "Ideas for a Theology of the History of Religions", *The Theology of the Christian Mission*, G. H. Anderson, ed., New York, 1961.

– , *Ideen zu einer Theologie der Religionsgeschichte* (AAMz, Abh. d. Geistes- u. Sozialwiss. Kl., Jg. 1960, Nr. 5), Mainz 1960.

– , "On Understanding Non-Christian Religions", *The History of Religions*, M. Eliade and J. Kitagawa ed., Chicago, 1959.

Berten, I., *Geschichte, Offenbarung, Glaube.* Eine Einführung in die Theologie Wolfhart Pannenbergs, München, 1970.

Beyerhaus, P., *Die Grundlagenkrise der Mission*, Wuppertal, 1970.

– , "Religionen und Evangelium. Kontinuität oder Diskontinuität", EMM, 111 (1967) 118–135.

– , "Zur Theologie der Religionen im Protestantismus", KuD, 15 (1969) 87–104; also in *Freiheit in der Begegnung.* Zwischenbilanz des ökumenischen Dialogs, hrsg. von J.-L. Leuba und H. Stirnimann, Frankfurt, 1969, pp. 433–452.

Blauw, J., "Gottes Offenbarung und die Religionen", EMZ, 11 (1954) 21–29.

Böld, W., "Das Problem der Absolutheit des christlichen Heilswegs", *Kirche in der außerchristlichen Welt*, Regensburg, 1967, pp. 31–63.

Bouquet, A. C., *The Christian Faith and Non-Christian Religions*, Digswell Place, 1958.

Brunner, P., *Pro Ecclesia I*, Berlin, 1962, pp. 96–107.

Bürkle, H., "Die Frage nach dem 'kosmischen Christus' als Beispiel einer ökumenisch orientierten Theologie", KuD 11 (1965) 103–115; also in *Indische Beiträge zur Theologie der Gegenwart*, hrsg. von H. Bürkle, Stuttgart, 1966, pp. 248–265 (with further annotations and literature).

– , "Synkretismus als missionstheologisches Problem", EvTh, 25 (1965) 142–154.

258

–   , "Zum Problem des Dialogs", *Jahrbuch Evangelischer Mission*, 1968, pp. 35–46.

Bultmann, R., "Anknüpfung und Widerspruch", GuV II, pp. 117–132.

–   , "Der Begriff der Offenbarung im Neuen Testament", GuV III, pp. 1–34.

–   , "Die Frage der natürlichen Offenbarung", GuV II, pp. 79–104.

–   , "Das Problem der 'Natürlichen Theologie'", GuV I, pp. 294–312.

Buri, F., *Denkender Glaube*. Schritte auf dem Weg zu einer philosophischen Theologie, Bern-Stuttgart, 1966.

–   , *Dogmatik als Selbstverständnis des christlichen Glaubens* I: Vernunft und Offenbarung, Bern-Tübingen, 1956; id., op. cit., II: Der Mensch und die Gnade, Bern-Tübingen, 1962.

–   , "Entmythologisierung oder Entkerygmatisierung der Theologie", *Kerygma und Mythos* II (1952), pp. 85–101.

–   , "Theologie und Philosophie", ThZ, 8 (1952) 116–134.

Conway, G. W., *An Exposition and Critical Analysis of the Theology of the Missions as Proposed by Dr. Hendrik Kraemer*, (Diss. Gregoriana) Winona, 1966.

Cooke, G., *As Christians Face Rival Religions*: An Interreligious Strategy for Community without Compromise, New York, 1962.

Cragg, K., "Encounter with Non-Christian Faiths", *Union Seminary Quarterly Review*, 19 (1964) 249–309.

Dantine, W., "Die christologische Fundierung des Sola Fide", *Der christliche Glaube und die Religionen*, hrsg. von C. H. Ratschow, Berlin, 1967, pp. 28–41.

–   , "Kirche und Sakrament", MdKI, 18 (1967) 41–47.

Devanadan, P., *The Gospel and Renascent Hinduism*, London, 1959.

Dewick, E. C., *The Christian Attitude to Other Religions*, Cambridge, 1953.

"Dialogue with Men of Other Faiths", *Study Encounter* (WCC), 3 (1967) 51–83.

Eliade, M., "Paul Tillich and the History of Religions", *The Future of Religions*, J. C. Brauer, ed., New York, 1966, pp. 31–36.

Fahlbusch, E., "Das Heil der Nichtchristen. Die Erklärung 'Nostra aetate' des II. Vatikanischen Konzils", MdKI, 19 (1968) 1–13.

–   , "Theologie der Religionen. Überblick zu einem Thema römisch-katholischer Theologie", KuD, 15 (1969) 73–86.

Fritzsche, H.-G., *Lehrbuch der Dogmatik*. Teil I: Prinzipienlehre. Grundlagen und Wesen des christlichen Glaubens, Göttingen, 1964.

Gensichen, H.-W., "Die christliche Mission in der Begegnung mit den Religionen", *Kirche in der außerchristlichen Welt*, Regensburg, 1967, pp. 65–93.

–   , "Die Herausforderung der protestantischen Mission durch das Zweite Vatikanische Konzil", MdKI, 17 (1966) 81–88.

–   , "Der Synkretismus als Frage an die Christenheit heute", EMZ, 23 (1966) 58–69.

–   , "Wirklichkeit und Wahrheit der Religionen – Bericht über ausgewählte Neuerscheinungen", *Luther. Monatshefte*, (1968), pp. 41–46. – id. op. cit., (1968), pp. 95–100.

Gerlitz, P., *Kommt die Welteinheitsreligion?* Das Christentum und die anderen Weltreligionen zwischen gestern und morgen (Stundenbücher 88), Hamburg, 1969.

–, "Der Λόγος Σπερματικός als Voraussetzung für eine ökumenische Theologie", ZRGG, 22 (1970) 1–18.

Goldammer, K., "Die Bibel und die Religionen", *Fuldaer Hefte* 16, Berlin, 1966, pp. 55–135.

–, *Die Formenwelt des Religiösen*, Stuttgart, 1961.

–, "Die Gedankenwelt der Religionswissenschaft und die Theologie der Religionen. Bemerkungen zu einigen Grundbegriffen und Hauptproblemen einer 'Theologie der Religionen' in religionswissenschaftlicher Sicht", KuD, 15 (1969) 105–135.

–, *Religionen, Religion und christliche Offenbarung*. Ein Forschungsbericht zur Religionswissenschaft, Stuttgart, 1965.

Hallencreutz, C. F., *Kraemer towards Tambaram*. A Study in Hendrik Kraemer's Missionary Approach, Uppsala, 1966.

–, *New Approaches to Men of Other Faiths, 1938–1968*. A theological discussion (Research Pamphlet no. 18, WCC), Geneva, 1970.

Holsten, W., "Begegnungen der Christenheit mit den Religionen und mit dem Judentum", ThR, 32 (1967) 61–87.

–, *Das Kerygma und der Mensch*. Einführung in die Religions- und Missionswissenschaft (ThB 1), München, 1953.

Kantzenbach, F. W., "Die ekklesiologische Begründung des Heils der Nichtchristen. Problematische und verheißungsvolle Wege und Tendenzen in der neuesten röm.-kath. Theologie", *Oecumenica* 2 (1967) 210–234.

Khodr, G., "Christianity in a Pluralistic World – The Economy of the Holy Spirit", ER, 23 (1971) 118–128; also in *Una Sancta*, 26 (1971) 186–194.

Kimme, A., "Universalität und Exklusivität der christlichen Heilsbotschaft. Ein dogmatischer Versuch zum Thema, 'Theologie der Religionen'", *Fuldaer Hefte*, 16, Berlin, 1966, pp. 136–180.

Kohler, W., "Kirche und Mission im Umdenken" EvTh, 30 (1970) 379–391.

–, "Theologie und Religion", *Glaube, Geist, Geschichte*, Festschrift für Ernst Benz zum 60. Geburtstage, hrsg. von G. Müller und W. Zeller, Leiden, 1967, pp. 459–468.

–, "Toward a Theology of Religions", *Japanese Religions*, (4. 3. 1966), pp. 12–34.

–, "Westliches Christentum in Begegnung mit den Völkern", *Der Auftrag der Kirche in der modernen Welt*. Festgabe für Emil Brunner, hrsg. von P. Vogelsanger, Zürich-Stuttgart, 1959, pp. 309–324.

Kraemer, H., *The Christian Message in a Non-Christian World*, London, 1938; (German: *Die christliche Botschaft in einer nichtchristlichen Welt*, Zürich, 1940).

–, *The Communication of the Christian Faith*, London, 1957.

–, *Religion and the Christian Faith*, London, 1956.

–, *Why Christianity of all Religions?* London, 1962.

–, *World Cultures and World Religions*, London, 1960.

Kühn, U., "Christentum außerhalb der Kirche? Zum interkonfessionellen Gespräch über das Verständnis der Welt", *Erneuerung der einen Kirche*, Festschrift für Heinrich Bornkamm, Göttingen, 1966, pp. 275–305.

Leeuwen, A. Th. van, *Christianity in World History*. The Meeting of the Faiths of East and West, London, 1964.

Lüthi, K., "Ist Christentum Religion?", *Wort und Wahrheit*, 24 (1969) 99–112.

Mann, U., *Das Christentum als absolute Religion*, Darmstadt, 1970.

–   , "Religion als theologisches Problem", *Christentum und Religion*, Regensburg, 1966, pp. 53–89.

–   , *Theogonische Tage*. Die Entwicklungsphasen des Gottesbewußtseins in der altorientalischen und biblischen Religion, Stuttgart, 1970.

–   , *Theologische Religionsphilosophie im Grundriß*, Hamburg, 1961.

–   , "Theologie und Religionsgeschichte", *Luth. Monatshefte* (1964), pp. 250–261.

–   , *Vorspiel des Heils*, Stuttgart, 1962.

Mildenberger, M., "Dialogfähige Theologie", ÖR, 21 (1972) 37–49.

Müller-Krüger, T., (Hrsg.), *In sechs Kontinenten*. Dokumente der Weltmissionskonferenz, Mexico, 1963, Stuttgart, 1964.

Neill, S., *Christian Faith and Other Faiths*, London, 1961.

–   , *Creative Tension*, London, 1959.

Newbigin, L., *A Faith for this One World*, London, 1965.

–   , *The Finality of Christ*, London, 1969.

Nürnberger, K., "Systematisch-theologische Lösungsversuche zum Problem der anderen Religionen und ihre missionsmethodischen Konsequenzen", NZSTh, 12 (1970) 13–43.

Obayashi, H., "Pannenberg und Troeltsch: History and Religion", JAAR, 38 (1970) 401–419.

Pannenberg, W., "Erwägungen zu einer Theologie der Religionsgeschichte", *Grundfragen Systematischer Theologie*, Göttingen, 1967, pp. 252–295.

–   , "Die Frage nach Gott", *Grundfragen*, pp. 361–386.

–   , "Heilsgeschehen und Geschichte", *Grundfragen*, pp. 22–78.

–   , "Hermeneutik und Universalgeschichte", *Grundfragen*, pp. 91–122.

–   , *Jesus God and Man*, London, 1968.

–   , *Offenbarung als Geschichte*, in Verbindung mit R. Rendtorff, U. Wilckens, T. Rendtorff (Beiheft zu KuD), 3. Aufl., Göttingen, 1965.

–   , "Die Offenbarung Gottes in Jesus von Nazareth", *Theologie als Geschichte*, hrsg. von J. M. Robinson und J. B. Cobb Jr., Zürich-Stuttgart, 1967, pp. 135–169.

–   , *Was ist der Mensch?* Die Anthropologie der Gegenwart im Lichte der Theologie, Göttingen, 1962.

–   , "Weltgeschichte und Heilsgeschichte", *Probleme biblischer Theologie*. Gerhard von Rad zum 70. Geburtstag, hrsg. von H. W. Wolff, München, 1971, pp. 349–366.

–   , "Wie wahr ist das Reden von Gott?", EvKom, 4 (1971) 629–633.

Ratschow, C. H., *Der angefochtene Glaube*, Gütersloh, 1957.

–   , "Glaube und Erkenntnis", *Anstöße*. Berichte aus der Arbeit der Evangelischen Akademie Hofgeismar (1968, Nr. 5/6), pp. 153–163.

–   , *Gott existiert*, Berlin, 1966.

–   , "Das Heilshandeln und das Welthandeln Gottes", NZSTh, 1 (1959) 25–80.

–   , *Magie und Religion*, Gütersloh, 1955.

   —, "Die Möglichkeit des Dialogs angesichts des Anspruchs der Religionen", *Evangelisches Missions-Jahrbuch* (1970), pp. 110–116.

   —, "Religion, theologisch", RGG^3 V, 976–984.

   —, "Die Religionen und das Christentum", *Der christliche Glaube und die Religionen*, hrsg. von C. H. Ratschow, Berlin, 1967, pp. 88–128.

Reinhardt, P., "Bericht über die 18. Tagung des Theologischen Konvents Augsburgischen Bekenntnisses vom 23. bis 26. Oktober 1962 in Berlin", *Fuldaer Hefte* 16, Berlin, 1966, pp. 181–186.

Rose, E., "Bericht über die 19. Tagung des Theologischen Konvents Augsburgischen Bekenntnisses vom 24. bis 26. September 1963 in Berlin", *Fuldaer Hefte* 16, Berlin, 1966, pp. 187–198.

Rosenkranz, G., *Der christliche Glaube angesichts der Weltreligionen*, Bern, 1967.

   —, *Evangelische Religionskunde*. Einführung in eine theologische Schau der Religionen, Tübingen, 1951.

   —, "Die Rede vom kosmischen Christus angesichts der indischen Geisteswelt", EMZ, 20 (1963) 145–160.

   —, "Was müssen wir heute unter Absolutheit des Christentums verstehen?", ZThK, 51 (1954) 105–123.

   —, "Wege und Grenzen des religionswissenschaftlichen Erkennens", *Religionswissenschaft und Theologie*. Aufsätze zur evangelischen Religionskunde, München, 1964, pp. 11–36.

Samartha, S. J., ed., *Dialogue with Men of Living Faiths*. Papers presented at a Consultation held at Ajaltoun, Lebanon, Geneva, 1971.

   —, *Hindus vor dem universalen Christus*. Beiträge zu einer indischen Christologie, Stuttgart, 1970.

   —, ed., *Living Faiths and the Ecumenical Movement*, Geneva, 1971.

Scheffbuch, R., "Die Herausforderung von Neu-Delhi", *Luther. Monatshefte* (1962), pp. 2–13.

Schlink, E., *Nach dem Konzil* (Siebenstern Taschenbuch 75), München-Hamburg, 1966.

Sittler, J., "Zur Einheit berufen", *Neu Delhi 1961*. Dokumentarbericht über die Dritte Vollversammlung des Ökumenischen Rates der Kirchen, hrsg. von W. A. Visser't Hooft, Stuttgart, 1962, pp. 512–523.

Smart, N., *A Dialogue of Religions*, London, 1960.

Smith, W. C., *The Meaning and End of Religion*, New York, 1963.

Taylor, J. V., *The Primal Vision: Christian Presence amid African Religions*, London, 1961.

Thomas, O. C., ed., *Attitudes toward Other Religions. Some Christian Interpretations*, London, 1969.

Tillich, P., *Biblical Religion and the Search for Ultimate Reality*, Chicago, 1955.

   —, *Christianity and the Encounter of the World Religions*, New York, 1963.

   —, "The Significance of the History of Religions for the Systematic Theologian", *The Future of Religions*, J. C. Brauer, ed., New York, 1966, pp. 80–94.

   —, *Systematic Theology* I, Digswell Place, 1953.

Trillhaas, W., *Dogmatik*, Berlin, 1962.

−   , *Religionsphilosophie*, Berlin, 1972.

"Unser Verhältnis zur römisch-katholischen Mission", EMZ, 24 (1967) 33−38 (Documentation of DEMR).

Vallée, G., *Eine ökumenische Diskussion über die interreligiöse Begegnung* − Von Tambaram nach Uppsala 1938−1968, (Diss. Münster), 1971.

−   , "The Word of God and the Living Faiths of Men: Chronology and Bibliography of a Study Process", *Living Faiths and the Ecumenical Movement*, S. J. Samartha, ed., Geneva, 1971, pp. 165−182.

−   , "Die Zukunft des ökumenischen Dialogs mit Nicht-Christen", *Una Sancta*, 26 (1971) 166−173.

Veitch, J. A., "The Case for a Theology of Religions", SJTh, 24 (1971) 407−422.

Vicedom, G. F., *Jesus Christus und die Religionen der Welt*, Wuppertal, 1966.

−   , *Die Mission der Weltreligionen*, München, 1959.

−   , "Die Religionen in der Sicht von Neu-Delhi", *Fuldaer Hefte*, 16, Berlin, 1966, pp. 9−22.

Visser't Hooft, W. A., (Hrsg.), *Neu Delhi 1961*. Dokumentarbericht über die Dritte Vollversammlung des Ökumenischen Rates der Kirchen, Stuttgart, 1962.

Wach, J., *Types of Religious Experience*, Chicago, 1951.

Wagner, H., *Erstgestalten einer einheimischen Theologie in Südindien*, München, 1963.

Warren, M., "Präsenz und Verkündigung", EMZ, 25 (1968) 158−171.

Winterhager, J. W., "Neu-Delhi und die Anfänge einer ökumenischen Theologie", ThViat, 8 (1961−62) 299−311.

−   , "Das Bekenntnis zum Christus Pantokrator und die Anfänge einer ökumenischen Theologie" − Ökumenischer Vorspruch in: O. A. Dilschneider, *Christus Pantokrator*, Berlin, 1962, pp. 7−13.

Wolff, O., *Anders an Gott glauben*. Die Weltreligionen als Partner des Christentums, Stuttgart, 1969.

B. Catholic

Balthasar, H. U. von, *Wer ist ein Christ?* Einsiedeln, 1965.

−   , *Cordula oder der Ernstfall*, Einsiedeln, 1966.

−   , *Rechenschaft*, Einsiedeln, 1965.

Baum, G., "Christianity and Other Religions. A Catholic Problem", *Cross Currents*, 16 (1966) 447−463.

Brooke, O., "Natural Religion in the Supernatural Existential", *The Downside Review*, 83 (1965) 201ff.

Bühlmann, W., "Die Theologie der nichtchristlichen Religionen als ökumenisches Problem", *Freiheit in der Begegnung*. Zwischenbilanz des ökumenischen Dialogs, hrsg. von J.-L. Leuba und H. Stirnimann, Frankfurt, 1969, pp. 453−478.

Capéran, L., *Le problème du salut des infidèles*. Tome I: Essai historique; Tome II: Essai théologique, 2ième éd., Toulouse, 1934.

Congar, Y., *Außer der Kirche kein Heil*, Essen, 1961.

—, *Heilige Kirche*. Ekklesiologische Studien und Annäherungen, Stuttgart, 1966.

—, "Salvation of the Non-Christians", *Blackfriars*, 38 (1957) 290–300.

Cornelis, E., *Christliche Grundgedanken in nichtchristlichen Religionen*, Paderborn, 1967; Original: *Valeurs chrétiennes des religions non-chrétiennes*, Paris, 1965.

Daniélou, J., "Christianisme et religions non-chrétiennes", *Etudes*, 321 (1964) 323–336.

—, *Dieu et nous*, Paris, 1956.

—, *Essai sur le Mystère de l'Histoire*, Paris, 1953.

—, *Holy Pagans of the Old Testament*, London, 1957.

—, *Le mystère du salut des nations*, Paris, 1948.

—, *Prayer as a Political Problem*, New York, 1967.

Darlapp, A., "Fundamentale Theologie der Heilsgeschichte", *Mysterium Salutis* I, pp. 1–156.

—, "Religionstheologie", *Sacramentum Mundi* IV, 263–271.

Dournes, J., *Dieu aime les paiens*. Une mission de l'Eglise sur les plateaux du Viet-Nam, Paris, 1965.

—, *Le Père m'a envoyé*, Paris, 1965.

Elders, L., "Die Taufe der Weltreligionen. Bemerkungen zu einer Theorie Karl Rahners", ThGl, 55 (1965) 124–131.

Eminyan, M., *The Theology of Salvation*, Boston, 1960.

Fahlbusch, E., "Theologie der Religionen. Überblick zu einem Thema römisch-katholischer Theologie", KuD, 15 (1969) 73–86.

Feiner, J., "Kirche und Heilsgeschichte", *Gott in Welt* II, Festgabe für Karl Rahner, hrsg. von J. B. Metz u.a., Freiburg, 1964, pp. 317–345.

Finsterhölzl, J., "Zur Theologie der Religionen", *Kairos*, 7 (1965) 308–318.

Fransen, P., "How can the Non-Christians Find Salvation in Their Own Religions?", *Christian Revelation and World Religions*, J. Neuner, ed., London, 1967, pp. 67–122.

Fries, H., *Wir und die andern*, Stuttgart, 1966.

Girault, R., *Evangile et religions aujourd'hui*, Paris, 1969.

Hacker, P., "The Christian Attitude toward Non-Christian Religions. Some critical an positive reflections", ZMR (Münster), 55 (1971) 81–97.

—, "The Religions of the Gentiles as Viewed by Fathers of the Church", ZMR (Münster), 54 (1970) 253–278.

—, "The Religions of the Nations in the Light of Holy Scripture", ZMR (Münster), 54 (1970) 161–185.

Heislbetz, J., *Theologische Gründe der nichtchristlichen Religionen* (Quaestiones Disputatae 22), Freiburg, 1967.

Hillman, E., "Anonymous Christianity and the Missions", *Downside Review*, 85 (1966), 361–380.

—, "Ecumenism and Grace", *African Ecclesiastical Review*, 8 (1966) 16ff.

—, "Die Hauptaufgabe der Mission", *Concilium*, 2 (1966) 159–162.

Karrer, O., *Das Religiöse in der Menschheit und das Christentum*, Freiburg, 1934.

Knitter, P., "Anonymous Christianity and the Missions", *Verbum*, 10 (1968) 402–405.

—, "The Church before the Non-Christian Religions", *Verbum*, 10 (1968) 359–365.

Kruse, H., "Die 'Anonymen Christen' exegetisch gesehen", MThZ, 18 (1967) 2–29.

Küng, H., "The World Religions in God's Plan of Salvation", *Christian Revelation and World Religions*, J. Neuner, ed., London, 1967, pp. 25–66.

Legrand, F., "Is it the Purpose of the Mission to Bring Salvation", *Christ to the World*, 10 (1965) 221–231.

Le Guillon, M. J., "Die Mission als ekklesiologische Problematik", *Concilium*, 2 (1966) 194–218.

Letter, P. de, "Non Christian Religions", *The Clergy Monthly*, 29 (1965) 12–21.

Liégé, P. A., "Le salut des 'autres'", *Lumière et Vie*, 18 (1954) 741–769.

Lohfink, N., "Die Religion der Patriarchen und die Konsequenzen für eine Theologie der nichtchristlichen Religionen", *Bibelauslegung im Wandel*. Ein Exeget ortet seine Wissenschaft, Frankfurt, 1967, pp. 107–128.

Lombardi, R., *La Salvezza di chi non ha fede*, Roma, 1948.

Lubac, H. de, *Catholicisme*. Les aspects sociaux du dogme, 5ième éd., Paris, 1952.

—, *Paradoxe et mystère de l'Eglise*, Paris, 1967; German: *Geheimnis aus dem wir leben*, Einsiedeln, 1967.

Maritain, J., "La dialectique immanente du premier act de liberté", *Nova et Vetera*, 20 (1945) 218–235.

Masson, J., "La Déclaration sur les Religions non-chrétiennes", NRTh, 97 (1965) 1066–1083.

—, "Face aux Religions non-chrétiennes", *Spiritus*, 25 (1965) 416–425.

—, "Salvation Outside the Visible Church and the Necessity of the Mission", *Christian Revelation and World Religions*, J. Neuner, ed., London, 1967, pp. 123–142.

Maurier, H., *Theologie des Heidentums*, Köln, 1967.

Müller, K., *Die Kirche und die nichtchristlichen Religionen* (Der Christ in der Welt 8), Aschaffenburg, 1968.

Neuner, J., ed., *Christian Revelation and World Religions*, London, 1967.

—, "The Place of World Religions in Theology", *The Clergy Monthly*, 32 (1968) 102–115.

Nys, H., *Le salut sans l'Evangile*, Paris, 1966.

Ohm, T., *Die Liebe zu Gott in den nicht-christlichen Religionen*, Krailling vor München, 1950.

Panikkar, R., *The Hidden Christ of Hinduism*, London, 1964.

Rahner, K., "Die anonymen Christen", *Schriften zur Theologie* VI, pp. 545–554.

—, "Anonymes Christentum und Missionsauftrag der Kirche", *Schriften* IX, pp. 498–515.

—, "Atheismus und implizites Christentum", *Schriften* VIII, pp. 213–217.

—, "Christentum und die nichtchristlichen Religionen", *Schriften* V, pp. 136–158.

—, *Christian of the Future*, London, 1967.

—, "Christologie im Rahmen des modernen Selbst- und Weltverständnisses", *Schriften* IX, pp. 227–241.

—, "Die Christologie innerhalb einer evolutiven Weltanschauung", *Schriften* V, pp. 183–221.

—   , "Erlösung", *Sacramentum Mundi* I, 1159–1176.

—   , "Existential, übernatürliches", LThK² III, 1301.

—   , *Geist in Welt*, Zur Metaphysik der endlichen Erkenntnis bei Thomas von Aquin, 3. Aufl., München, 1964.

—   , *Hörer des Wortes*. Zur Grundlegung einer Religionsphilosophie, neubearbeitet von J. B. Metz, München, 1963.

—   , "Kirche, Kirchen und Religionen", *Schriften* VIII, pp. 355–373.

—   , "Der Mensch von heute und die Religion", *Schriften* VI, pp. 13–33.

—   , u. H. Vorgrimler, "Nichtchristliche Religionen", *Kleines Theologisches Wörterbuch*, Freiburg, 1961, pp. 261–263.

—   , "Offenbarung", *Kl. Theol. Wörterbuch*, pp. 265–269.

—   , u. J. Ratzinger, *Offenbarung und Überlieferung* (Quaestiones Disputatae 25), Freiburg, 1964.

—   , "Über die Einheit von Nächsten- und Gottesliebe", *Schriften* VI, pp. 277–298.

—   , "Über das Verhältnis von Natur und Gnade", *Schriften* I, pp. 323–345.

—   , u. H. Vorgrimler, "Uroffenbarung", *Kl. Theol. Wörterbuch*, pp. 372–373.

—   , "Weltgeschichte und Heilsgeschichte", *Schriften* V, 115–135.

Ratzinger, J., "Kein Heil außerhalb der Kirche?", *Das neue Volk Gottes*. Entwürfe zur Ekklesiologie, Düsseldorf, 1967, pp. 339–361.

—   , "Das Problem der Absolutheit des christlichen Heilsweges", *Das neue Volk Gottes*, pp. 362–375; also in *Kirche in der außerchristlichen Welt*, Regensburg, 1967, pp. 7–63.

—   , u.a., *Kirche in der außerchristlichen Welt*, Regensburg, 1967.

Riedl, J., *Das Heil der Heiden nach Röm. 2, 14–16, 26, 27*, Mödling, 1965.

Riesenhuber, K., "Der anonyme Christ, nach Karl Rahner", ZKTh, 86 (1964) 286–303.

Roberts, L., *The Achievement of Karl Rahner*, New York, 1967.

Röper, A., *Die anonymen Christen*, Mainz, 1963.

Rossano, P., "The Bible and the Non-Christian Religions", *Bulletin*. Secretariatus pro non Christianis (Vatican), 4 (1967) 18–28.

—   , "Le Religioni non cristiane nella storia della salvezza. Rassegna delle posizioni teologiche attuali", *La Scuola Cattolica*, 1965, supplemento 2, pp. 3–12.

Schillebeeckx, E., "The Church and Mankind", *Concilium* 1, (1965) 34–50.

Schlette, H. R., *Colloquium salutis – Christen und Nichtchristen heute*, Köln, 1965.

—   , "Einige Thesen zum Selbstverständnis der Theologie angesichts der Religionen", *Gott in Welt* II, Festgabe für Karl Rahner, hrsg. von J. B. Metz, u.a., Freiburg, 1964, pp. 306–316.

—   , "Die Kirche und die Religionen", *Umkehr und Erneuerung*, hrsg. von T. Filthaut, Mainz, 1966, pp. 292–311.

—   , *Die Konfrontation mit den Religionen*, Köln, 1964.

—   , "Mission – Ende oder Anfang", *Hochland* 55 (1962–63) 24–79.

—   , "Religionen", *Handbuch theologischer Grundbegriffe* II, pp. 441–450.

   —   , *Die Religionen als Thema der Theologie* (Quaestiones Disputatae, 22), Freiburg, 1963.

Schlier, H., "Der Christ und die Welt", GuL, 38 (1965) 416–428.

Schoonenberg, P., *Gottes werdende Welt*, Limburg, 1963.

Schreiner, P., "Roman Catholic Theology and Non-Christian Religions", JES, 6 (1969) 376–399.

Schütte, J., (Hrsg.), *Mission nach dem Konzil*, Mainz, 1967.

Seckler, M., "Das Heil der Nichtevangelisierten in thomistischer Sicht", ThQ, 140 (1960) 38–69.

   —   , "Nichtchristen", *Handbuch theologischer Grundbegriffe* II, pp. 236–242.

   —   , "Sind Religionen Heilswege?", StZ, 9 (1970) 187–194.

Stoeckle, B., "Die außerbiblische Menschheit und die Weltreligionen", *Mysterium Salutis* II, pp. 1049–1073.

Straelen, H. van, *The Catholic Encounter with World Religions*, London, 1966.

   —   , "Our Attitude Towards Other Religions", *Worldmission*, 16 (1965) 71–98.

Thils, G., *Propos et problèmes de la théologie des religions non chrétiennes*, Paris, 1966.

   —   , "La Valeur Salvifique des Religions Non-Chrétiennes", *Repenser la Mission* (35iéme Semaine de Missiologie de Louvain, 1965), Louvain, 1965.

Türk, J., *Was sagt das Konzil über nichtchristliche Religionen*, Mainz, 1967.

Verastegui, E., *Les religions non-chrétiennes dans l'histoire du salut*, (Diss. Gregoriana), Rome, 1968, Manuscript.

Vereno, M., "Von der All-Wirklichkeit der Kirche", ThQ, 138 (1958) 385–427.

Waldenfels, H., "Christentum und Weltreligionen in katholischer Sicht", *Kirche in der Zeit*, 22 (1967) 347–358.

   —   , "Christentum unter Großreligionen", *Diakonia*, 2 (1971) 15–28.

   —   , "Die Heilsbedeutung der nicht-christlichen Religionen in katholischer Sicht", *Die vielen Wege zum Heil*, hrsg. von W. Molinski, München, 1969, pp. 93–125.

   —   , "Das Verständnis der Religionen und seine Bedeutung für die Mission in katholischer Sicht", EMZ, 27 (1970) 125–159.

Wiederkehr, D., "Die Aussage der heutigen katholischen Theologie über die nichtchristlichen Religionen", *Kath. Missionsjahrbuch der Schweiz*, 1966, pp. 6–28.

Index

The names of Paul Althaus and Jesus Christ are not mentioned